# Lecture Notes in Computer Science 1473

Edited by G. Goos, J. Hartmanis and J. van Leeuwen

**Springer**

*Berlin*
*Heidelberg*
*New York*
*Barcelona*
*Budapest*
*Hong Kong*
*London*
*Milan*
*Paris*
*Singapore*
*Tokyo*

Xavier Leroy   Atsushi Ohori  (Eds.)

# Types in Compilation

Second International Workshop, TIC '98
Kyoto, Japan, March 25-27, 1998
Proceedings

Springer

Series Editors

Gerhard Goos, Karlsruhe University, Germany
Juris Hartmanis, Cornell University, NY, USA
Jan van Leeuwen, Utrecht University, The Netherlands

Volume Editors

Xavier Leroy
INRIA Rocquencourt
Domaine de Voluceau, B.P. 105, F-78153 Le Chesnay, France
E-mail: Xavier.Leroy@inria.fr

Atsushi Ohori
Research Institute for Mathematical Sciences, Kyoto University
Kitashirakawa-Oiwakecho, Sakyo-ku, Kyoto 606-8502, Japan
E-mail: ohori@kurims.kyoto-u.ac.jp

Cataloging-in-Publication data applied for

Die Deutsche Bibliothek - CIP-Einheitsaufnahme

**Types in compilation** : second international workshop ; proceedings /
TIC '98, Kyoto, Japan, March 25 - 27, 1998. Xavier Leroy ; Atsushi
Ohori (ed.). - Berlin ; Heidelberg ; New York ; Barcelona ; Budapest
; Hong Kong ; London ; Milan ; Paris ; Singapore ; Tokyo : Springer,
1998
  (Lecture notes in computer science ; Vol. 1473)
  ISBN 3-540-64925-5

CR Subject Classification (1991): F.3, D.2, D.3, D.4

ISSN 0302-9743
ISBN 3-540-64925-5 Springer-Verlag Berlin Heidelberg New York

Typesetting: Camera-ready by author
SPIN 10638677    06/3142 – 5 4 3 2 1 0    Printed on acid-free paper

# Preface

This volume constitutes the proceedings of the second International Workshop on Types in Compilation (TIC'98), held at the Research Institute for Mathematical Sciences, Kyoto University, Japan, March 25–27, 1998.

Types (in the broadest sense of the word) play a central role in many of the advanced compilation techniques developed for modern programming languages. Standard or nonstandard type systems and type analyses have been found to be useful for optimizing dynamic method dispatch in object-oriented languages, for reducing run-time tests in dynamically typed languages, for guiding data representations and code generation, for program analysis and transformation, for compiler verification and debugging, and for establishing safety properties of distributed or mobile code. The Types in Compilation workshops bring together researchers to share new ideas and results in this area.

For TIC'98, the program committee received seventeen submissions in response to the call for papers, and selected thirteen papers among those. Each submission received at least four reviews, done by the program committee members or their subreferees (their names appear below). The program committee also invited five additional speakers to complement the presentations of the regular papers.

The 1998 Types in Compilation workshop was sponsored by the Research Institute for Mathematical Sciences, Kyoto University, and organized in cooperation with the Association of Computing Machinery Special Interest Group in Programming Languages (ACM SIGPLAN) and the Japan Society for Software Science and Technology Special Interest Group in Programming (JSSST SIG Programming). Their support is gratefully acknowledged.

June 1998

Xavier Leroy
Program Chair
TIC'98

# Organization

## Conference chair

Atsushi Ohori (Kyoto University)

## Organizing committee

Craig Chambers (University of Washington)
Robert Harper (Carnegie-Mellon University)
Xavier Leroy (INRIA Rocquencourt)
Robert Muller (Boston College)
Atsushi Ohori (Kyoto University)
Simon Peyton-Jones (Glasgow University)

## Program chair

Xavier Leroy (INRIA Rocquencourt)

## Program committee

Craig Chambers (University of Washington)
Urs Hölzle (University of California, Santa Barbara)
Satoshi Matsuoka (Tokyo Institute of Technology)
Yasuhiko Minamide (Kyoto University)
Simon Peyton-Jones (Glasgow University)
Zhong Shao (Yale University)
Andrew Wright (InterTrust STAR Lab)

## Local arrangements

Atsushi Ohori (Kyoto University)
Yoshikazu Sato (Oki Electric)

## Additional referees

Kenichi Asai
Haruo Hosoya
Atsushi Igarashi
Didier Rémy

Toshihiro Shimizu
Valery Trifonov
Steve Weeks

# Table of Contents

Introduction . . . . . . . . . . . . . . . . . . . . . . . . . . . . . . . . . . . . . . . . . . . . . . . . . . . . . . . .  1
   *Xavier Leroy*

## Typed intermediate languages

Compiling Java to a Typed Lambda-Calculus: A Preliminary Report . . . . .  9
   *Andrew Wright, Suresh Jagannathan, Cristian Ungureanu, Aaron Hertzmann*

Stack-Based Typed Assembly Language . . . . . . . . . . . . . . . . . . . . . . . . . . . . . 28
   *Greg Morrisett, Karl Crary, Neal Glew, David Walker*

How Generic is a Generic Back End? Using MLRISC as a Back End for
the TIL Compiler . . . . . . . . . . . . . . . . . . . . . . . . . . . . . . . . . . . . . . . . . . . . . . . . 53
   *Andrew Bernard, Robert Harper, Peter Lee*

## Program analyses

A Toolkit for Constructing Type- and Constraint-Based Program Analyses
(invited talk) . . . . . . . . . . . . . . . . . . . . . . . . . . . . . . . . . . . . . . . . . . . . . . . . . . . . 78
   *Alexander Aiken, Manuel Fähndrich, Jeffrey S. Foster, Zhendong Su*

Optimizing ML Using a Hierarchy of Monadic Types . . . . . . . . . . . . . . . . . . 97
   *Andrew Tolmach*

Type-Directed Continuation Allocation . . . . . . . . . . . . . . . . . . . . . . . . . . . . . 116
   *Zhong Shao, Valery Trifonov*

## Program transformations and code generation

Polymorphic Equality – No Tags Required . . . . . . . . . . . . . . . . . . . . . . . . . . . 136
   *Martin Elsman*

Optimal Type Lifting . . . . . . . . . . . . . . . . . . . . . . . . . . . . . . . . . . . . . . . . . . . . . 156
   *Bratin Saha, Zhong Shao*

Formalizing Resource Allocation in a Compiler . . . . . . . . . . . . . . . . . . . . . . . 178
   *Peter Thiemann*

## Memory management

An Approach to Improve Locality Using Sandwich Types . . . . . . . . . . . . . . . 194
   *Daniela Genius, Martin Trapp, Wolf Zimmermann*

Garbage Collection via Dynamic Type Inference — A Formal Treatment .. 215
*Haruo Hosoya, Akinori Yonezawa*

## Partial evaluation and run-time code generation

Strong Normalization by Type-Directed Partial Evaluation and Run-Time
Code Generation . . . . . . . . . . . . . . . . . . . . . . . . . . . . . . . . . . . . . . . . . . . . . . . . . . . 240
*Vincent Balat, Olivier Danvy*

Determination of Dynamic Method Dispatches Using Run-Time Code
Generation . . . . . . . . . . . . . . . . . . . . . . . . . . . . . . . . . . . . . . . . . . . . . . . . . . . . . . . . . 253
*Nobuhisa Fujinami*

## Distributed computing

Type-Based Analysis of Concurrent Programs (abstract of invited talk) . . . 272
*Naoki Kobayashi*

A Type-Based Semantics for User-Defined Marshalling in Polymorphic
Languages . . . . . . . . . . . . . . . . . . . . . . . . . . . . . . . . . . . . . . . . . . . . . . . . . . . . . . . . . . 273
*Dominic Duggan*

## Author Index . . . . . . . . . . . . . . . . . . . . . . . . . . . . . . . . . . . . . . . . . . . . . . . . . 299

# Introduction

Xavier Leroy

INRIA Rocquencourt
Domaine de Voluceau, 78153 Le Chesnay, France

## 1 Types in programming languages

Most programming languages are equipped with a type system that detects type errors in the program, such as using a variable or result of a given type in a context that expects data of a different, incompatible type. Such type checking can take place either statically (at compile-time) or dynamically (at run-time). Type checking has proved to be very effective in catching a wide class of programming errors, from the trivial (misspelled identifiers) to the fairly deep (violations of data structure invariants). It makes program considerably safer, ensuring integrity of data structures and type-correct interconnection of program components.

Safety is not the only motivation for equipping programming languages with type systems, however. Another motivation, which came first historically, is to facilitate the efficient compilation of programs. Static typing restricts the set of programs to be compiled, possibly eliminating programs containing constructs that are difficult to compile efficiently or even to compile correctly at all. Also, static typing guarantees certain properties and invariants on the data manipulated by the program; the compiler can take advantage of these semantic guarantees to generate better code. The "Types in Compilation" workshops are dedicated to the study of these interactions between type systems and the compilation process.

## 2 Exploiting type information for code generation and optimization

An early example of a type system directed towards efficient compilation is that of Fortran. The Fortran type system introduces a strict separation between integers numbers and floating-point numbers at compile-time. The main motivation for this separation, according to Fortran's designers, was to avoid the difficulties of handling mixed arithmetic at run-time [2, chapter 6]. Thanks to the type system, the compiler "knows" when to generate integer arithmetic operations, floating-point arithmetic operations, and conversions between integers and floats. Since then, this separation has permeated hardware design: most processor architectures provide separate register sets and arithmetic units for integers and for floats. In turn, this architectural bias makes it nearly impossible to generate efficient numerical code for a language whose type system does not statically distinguish floating-point numbers from integers.

Another area where compilers rely heavily on static typing is the handling of variable-sized data. Different data types have different natural memory sizes: for instance, double-precision floats usually occupy more space than integers; the size and memory layout of aggregate data structures such as records and arrays vary with the sizes and number of their elements. Precise knowledge of size information is required to generate correct code that allocates and operates over data structures. This knowledge is usually derived from the static typing information: the type of a data determines its memory size and layout. Languages without static typing cannot be compiled as efficiently: all data representations must fit a default size, if necessary by boxing (heap-allocating and handling through a pointer) data larger than the default size — an expensive operation. Statically-typed languages whose type system is too flexible to allow this determination of size information in all cases (e.g. because of polymorphism, type abstraction, or subtyping) make it more difficult, but not impossible, to exploit unboxed data representations: see [31, 21, 34, 16, 39, 22, 33, 28] for various approaches.

Guarantees provided by the type system can also enable powerful program optimizations. For instance, in a strongly-typed language (whose type system does not allow "casts" between incompatible types), two pointers that have incompatible types cannot alias, i.e. cannot point to the same memory block. This guarantees that load and store operations through those two pointers cannot interfere, thus allowing more aggressive code motion and instruction scheduling [13]. One can also envision different heap allocation strategies for objects of different types, as exemplified by the paper by Genius *et al.* in this proceeding.

Another area where type information is useful is the optimization of method dispatch in object-oriented languages. General method dispatch is an expensive operation, involving a run-time lookup of the code associated to the method in the object's method suite, followed by a costly indirect jump to that code. In a class-based language, if the actual class to which the object belongs is known at compile-time, a more efficient direct invocation of the method code can be generated instead. If the code of the method is small enough, it can even be expanded in-line at the point of call. Simple examination of the static type of the object and of the class hierarchy of the program uncovers many opportunities for this optimization. For instance, if the static type of the object is a class $C$ that has no subclasses, the compiler knows that the actual class of the object is $C$ and can generate direct invocations for all methods of the object [10, 15, 5].

## 3  Program analyses and optimizations based on non-standard type systems

There are many points of convergence between, on the one hand, algorithms for type checking and type inference, and on the other hand, static analyses of programs intended to support code optimization. This should not come as a surprise: both static analyses and type inference algorithms attempt to reconstruct semantic information that is implicit in the program source, and propagate that information through the program, recording it at each program point. A more formal evidence is that both static analyses and type inference problems can be recast in the common framework of abstract interpretation [9]. What is more remarkable is that essentially identical algorithms are used for type inference and for certain program analyses.

For instance, unification between first-order terms, as used for type inference in the Hindley-Milner type system of ML and Haskell, is also at the basis of several fast program analyses such as Steensgaard's aliasing analysis [37], and Henglein's tagging analysis [18]. Baker [6] reflects informally on this connection between Hindley-Milner type inference and several program analyses.

Another technique that has attracted considerable interest recently both from a type inference standpoint and a program analysis standpoint consists in setting up systems of set inclusion constraints (set inequations) and solving them iteratively. This technique has been used to perform type inference for type systems with subtyping [25, 3, 14]. The same technique is also at the basis of several flow analyses for functional and object-oriented languages [35, 36, 17, 1, 32, 19, 11]. These analyses approximate the flow of control and data in the presence of first-class functions and objects, and are very effective to optimize function applications and method invocations, and also to eliminate dynamic type tests in dynamically-typed languages. Palsberg and O'Keefe [29] draw a formal connection between those two areas, by proving the equivalence between a flow analysis (0-CFA) and a type inference algorithm (for the Amadio-Cardelli type system with subtyping and recursive types). The paper by Aiken *et al.* in these proceedings surveys the use of set inclusion constraints and equality (unification) constraints for program analyses.

Several non-standard type systems have been developed to capture more precisely the behavior of programs and support program transformations. The effect systems introduced by Lucassen and Gifford [23, 20] enrich function types with effects approximating the dynamic behavior of the functions, such as input-output or operations on the store. This information is useful for code motion and automatic parallelization. Jouvelot, Talpin and Tofte [38, 40] use region annotations on the types of data structures and functions to determine aliasing and lifetime information on data structures. The ML compiler developed by Tofte *et al.* [8] relies on these lifetime information for managing memory as a stack of regions with compiler-controlled explicit deallocation of regions instead of a conventional garbage collector. Tolmach's paper in these proceedings presents a reformulation of simple effect systems as monadic type systems. Shao and Trifonov's paper develop a type system to keep track of the use of first-class continuations in a program, thus allowing interoperability between languages that support `callcc` and languages that do not.

Finally, non-standard type systems can also be used to record and exploit the results of earlier program analyses. For instance, Dimock *et al.* [12] and Banerjee [7] develop rich type systems that capture and exploit the flow information produced by flow analyses. Another example is Thiemann's paper in these proceedings, which develops a type system that captures resource constraints that appear in compilers during register allocation.

## 4 Types at run-time

Many programming languages require compiled programs to manipulate some amount of type information at run-time. Interesting compilation issues arise when trying to make these run-time manipulations of types as efficient as possible. A prime example is the compilation of run-time type tests in dynamically-typed languages such as Scheme and Lisp: many clever tagging schemes have been developed to support fast run-time type tests. Another example is object-oriented languages such as Java, Modula-3, or C++ with run-time type inspection, where programs can dynamically test the actual class of an object. Again, clever encodings of the type hierarchy have been developed to perform those tests efficiently.

Even if the source language is fully statically typed, compilers and run-time systems may need to propagate type information to run-time in order to support certain operations. A typical example is the handling of non-parametric polymorphic operations such as polymorphic equality in ML and type classes in Haskell [41]. Another example is the handling of polymorphic records presented in [27]. There are several ways to precompile the required type information into an efficient form: one is to attach simple tags to data structures; another is to pass extra arguments (type representations or dictionaries of functions) to polymorphic functions. Elsman's paper in these proceedings compares the performances of these two approaches in the case of ML's polymorphic equality.

Passing run-time representations of type expressions as extra arguments to polymorphic function allows many type-directed compilation techniques to be applied to languages with polymorphic typing. The TIL compiler [39] and the Flint compiler [33] rely on run-time passing of type expressions (taken from extensions of the $F_\omega$ type system) to handle unboxed data structures in polymorphic functions and modules with abstract types. Constructing and passing these type expressions at run-time entail some execution overhead. The paper by Shao and Saha in these proceedings shows how to minimize this overhead by lifting those type-related computations out of loops and functions so that they all take place once at the beginning of program execution.

Non-conservative garbage collectors also require some amount of type information at run-time in order to distinguish pointers from non-pointers in memory roots and heap blocks. The traditional approach is to use tags on run-time values. Alternatively, Appel [4] suggested to attach source types to blocks of function code, and reconstruct type information for all reachable objects at run-time, using a variant of ML type reconstruction. The paper by Hosoya and Yonezawa in these proceedings is the first complete formalization of this approach.

Communicating static type information to the run-time system can be challenging, as it requires close cooperation from the compiler back-end. For instance, a type-directed garbage collector needs type information to be associated with registers and stack locations at garbage collection points; cooperation from the register allocator is needed to map the types of program variables onto the registers and stack slots. The paper by Bernard *et al.* in these proceedings discuss their experience with coercing a generic back-end into propagating type information.

Another operation that relies heavily on run-time type information is marshaling and un-marshaling between arbitrary data structures and streams of bytes – a crucial mechanism for persistence and distributed programming. In these proceedings, Duggan develops rich type systems to support marshaling in the presence of user-defined marshaling operations for some data types.

## 5 Typed intermediate languages

In traditional compiler technology, types are checked on the source language, but the intermediate representations used in the compilation process are essentially untyped. The intermediate representations maysometimes carry type annotations introduced by the front-end, but no provision is made for type-checking again these intermediate representations. Recently, several compilers have been developed that take the opposite approach: theirintermediate representations are equipped with typing rules and type-checking algorithms, and their various passes are presented as type-preserving transformations that, given a well-typed input, must produce a well-typed term of the target intermediate language.

The need for typed intermediate representations is obvious in compilers that require precise type information to be available till run-time, such as TIL and Flint [39, 33], or at least till late in the compilation process. Without requiring that each compiler pass be type-preserving and its output typable, it is nearly impossible to ensure the propagation of correct type information throughout the whole compiler.

Even in compilers that do not rely as crucially on types, typed intermediate languages can be extremely useful to facilitate the debugging of the compiler itself. During compiler development and testing, the type-checkers for the intermediate representations can be run on the outcome of every program transformation performed by the compiler. This catches a large majority of programming errors in the implementation of the transformations. In contrast with traditional compiler testing, which shows that the generated code is incorrect but does not indicate which pass is erroneous, type-checking the intermediate representations pinpoints precisely the culprit pass. The Glasgow Haskell compiler was one of the first to exploit systematically this technique [30].

So far, typed intermediate representations as described above have been applied almost exclusively to compiling functional languages. The paper by Wright *et al.* in these proceedings develop a typed intermediate language for compiling Java, and discuss the difficult issue of making explicit the "self" parameter to methods in a type-preserving way.

Typed intermediate languages usually do not go all the way down to code generation. For instance, Glasgow Haskell preserves types through its high-level program transformation, but the actual code generation is mostly untyped. The TIL compiler goes several steps further, in particular by performing the conversion of functions into closures in a type-preserving manner [24]. The paper by Morrisett *et al.* in these proceedings shows how to go all the way to assembly code: it proposes a type system for assembly code that can type-check reasonably optimized assembly code, including most uses of a stack.

## 6 Other applications of types

While the discussion above has concentrated on core compiler technology for functional and object-oriented languages, types have also found many exciting and sometimes unexpected applications in other areas of programming language implementation. For instance, type-directed partial evaluation is an interesting alternative to traditional partial evaluation based on source-level reductions. The paper by Balat and Danvy in these proceedings presents a type-directed partial evaluator that also uses run-time code generation. The paper by Fujinami presents a partial evaluator and run-time code generator for C++.

Languages for distributed programming based on process calculi are another area where the exploitation of type information is crucial to obtain good performances. Kobayashi's abstract in these proceedings surveys this topic.

Types have interesting applications in the area of language-based security for mobile code. Java applets have popularized the idea that foreign compiled code can be locally verified for type-correctness before execution. This local type-checking of compiled code then enables language-based security techniques that rely on typing invariants, such as the Java "sandbox". Advances in typed intermediate languages have an important impact in this area. For instance, while Java code verification is performed on unoptimized bytecode for an abstract machine, the paper by Morrisett *et al.* in these proceedings show that similar verifications can be carried on optimized machine code. Lee and Necula's work on proof-carrying code [26] show how to generalize this approach to the verification of arbitrary specifications.

In conclusion, there has been considerable cross-fertilization between type systems and compilers, and we hope to see more exciting new applications of types in the area of programming language implementations in the near future.

## References

1. Ole Agesen, Jens Palsberg, and Michael Schwartzback. Type inference of Self: analysis of objects with dynamic and multiple inheritance. In *Proc. European Conference on Object-Oriented Programming - ECOOP'93*, 1993.
2. Alfred V. Aho, Ravi Sethi, and Jeffrey D. Ullman. *Compilers: principles, techniques, and tools.* Addison-Wesley, 1986.
3. Alexander S. Aiken and Edward L. Wimmers. Type inclusion constraints and type inference. In *Functional Programming Languages and Computer Architecture 1993*, pages 31–41. ACM Press, 1993.

4. Andrew W. Appel. Run-time tags aren't necessary. *Lisp and Symbolic Computation*, 2(2), 1989.
5. David Bacon and Peter Sweeney. Fast static analysis of C++ virtual function calls. In *Object-Oriented Programming Systems, Languages and Applications '96*, pages 324–341. ACM Press, 1996.
6. Henry G. Baker. Unify and conquer (garbage, updating, aliasing, ...) in functional languages. In *Lisp and Functional Programming 1990*. ACM Press, 1990.
7. Anindya Banerjee. A modular, polyvariant, and type-based closure analysis. In *International Conference on Functional Programming 1997*, pages 1–10. ACM Press, 1997.
8. Lars Birkedal, Mads Tofte, and Magnus Vejlstrup. From region inference to von Neumann machines via region representation inference. In *23rd symposium Principles of Programming Languages*, pages 171–183. ACM Press, 1996.
9. Patrick Cousot. Types as abstract interpretations. In *24th symposium Principles of Programming Languages*, pages 316–331. ACM Press, 1997.
10. Jeffrey Dean, David Grove, and Craig Chambers. Optimization of object-oriented programs using static class hierarchy analysis. In *Proc. European Conference on Object-Oriented Programming – ECOOP'95*, pages 77–101. Springer-Verlag, 1995.
11. Greg DeFouw, David Grove, and Craig Chambers. Fast interprocedural class analysis. In *25th symposium Principles of Programming Languages*, pages 222–236. ACM Press, 1998.
12. Allyn Dimock, Robert Muller, Franklyn Turbak, and J. B. Wells. Strongly typed flow-directed representation transformations. In *International Conference on Functional Programming 1997*, pages 11–24. ACM Press, 1997.
13. Amer Diwan, Kathryn S. McKinley, and J. Eliot B. Moss. Type-based alias analysis. In *Programming Language Design and Implementation 1998*, pages 106–117. ACM Press, 1998.
14. Jonathan Eifrig, Scott Smith, and Valery Trifonov. Type inference for recursively constrained types and its application to OOP. In *Mathematical Foundations of Programming Semantics*, volume 1 of *Electronic Notes in Theoretical Computer Science*. Elsevier, 1995.
15. Mary F. Fernández. Simple and effective link-time optimization of Modula-3 programs. In *Programming Language Design and Implementation 1995*, pages 103–115. ACM Press, 1995.
16. Robert Harper and Greg Morriset. Compiling polymorphism using intensional type analysis. In *22nd symposium Principles of Programming Languages* ACM Press, 1995.
17. Nevin Heintze. Set-based analysis of ML programs. In *Lisp and Functional Programming '94*, pages 306–317. ACM Press, 1994.
18. Fritz Henglein. Global tagging optimization by type inference. In *Lisp and Functional Programming 1992*. ACM Press, 1992.
19. Suresh Jagannathan and Andrew Wright. Polymorphic splitting: An effective polyvariant flow analysis. *ACM Transactions on Programming Languages and Systems*, 20(1):166–207, 1998.
20. Pierre Jouvelot and David K. Gifford. Algebraic reconstruction of types and effects. In *18th symposium Principles of Programming Languages*, pages 303–310. ACM Press, 1991.
21. Xavier Leroy. Unboxed objects and polymorphic typing. In *19th symposium Principles of Programming Languages*, pages 177–188. ACM Press, 1992.

8

22. Xavier Leroy. The effectiveness of type-based unboxing. In *Workshop Types in Compilation '97*. Technical report BCCS-97-03, Boston College, Computer Science Department, June 1997.
23. John M. Lucassen and David K. Gifford. Polymorphic effect systems. In *15th symposium Principles of Programming Languages*, pages 47–57. ACM Press, 1988.
24. Yasuhiko Minamide, Greg Morrisett, and Robert Harper. Typed closure conversion. In *23rd symposium Principles of Programming Languages*, pages 271–283. ACM Press, 1996.
25. John C. Mitchell. Coercion and type inference. In *11th symposium Principles of Programming Languages*, pages 175–185. ACM Press, 1984.
26. George C. Necula. Proof-carrying code. In *24th symposium Principles of Programming Languages*, pages 106–119. ACM Press, 1997.
27. Atsushi Ohori. A polymorphic record calculus. *ACM Transactions on Programming Languages and Systems*, 17(6):844–895, 1995.
28. Atsushi Ohori and Tomonobu Takamizawa. An unboxed operational semantics for ML polymorphism. *Lisp and Symbolic Computation*, 10(1):61–91, 1997.
29. Jens Palsberg and Patrick O'Keefe. A type system equivalent to flow analysis. In *22nd symposium Principles of Programming Languages*, pages 367–378. ACM Press, 1995.
30. Simon L. Peyton-Jones. Compiling Haskell by program transformation: a report from the trenches. In *European Symposium on Programming 1996*, volume 1058 of *Lecture Notes in Computer Science*. Springer-Verlag, 1996.
31. Simon L. Peyton-Jones and John Launchbury. Unboxed values as first-class citizens in a non-strict functional language. In *Functional Programming Languages and Computer Architecture 1991*, volume 523 of *Lecture Notes in Computer Science*, pages 636–666, 1991.
32. John Plevyak and Andrew Chien. Precise concrete type inference for object-oriented languages. In *Object-Oriented Programming Systems, Languages and Applications '94*, pages 324–340. ACM Press, 1994.
33. Zhong Shao. Flexible representation analysis. In *International Conference on Functional Programming 1997*, pages 85–98. ACM Press, 1997.
34. Zhong Shao and Andrew Appel. A type-based compiler for Standard ML. In *Programming Language Design and Implementation 1995*, pages 116–129. ACM Press, 1995.
35. Olin Shivers. Control-flow analysis in Scheme. In *Programming Language Design and Implementation 1988*, pages 164–174. ACM Press, 1988.
36. Olin Shivers. *Control-Flow Analysis of Higher-Order Languages*. PhD thesis, Carnegie Mellon University, May 1991.
37. Bjarne Steensgaard. Points-to analysis in almost linear time. In *23rd symposium Principles of Programming Languages*, pages 32–41. ACM Press, 1996.
38. Jean-Pierre Talpin and Pierre Jouvelot. The type and effect discipline. *Information and Computation*, 111(2):245–296, 1994.
39. D. Tarditi, G. Morrisett, P. Cheng, C. Stone, R. Harper, and P. Lee. TIL: a type-directed optimizing compiler for ML. In *Programming Language Design and Implementation 1996*, pages 181–192. ACM Press, 1996.
40. Mads Tofte and Jean-Pierre Talpin. Region-based memory management. *Information and Computation*, 132(2):109–176, 1997.
41. Philip Wadler and Stephen Blott. How to make ad-hoc polymorphism less ad-hoc. In *16th symposium Principles of Programming Languages*, pages 60–76. ACM Press, 1989.

# Compiling Java to a Typed Lambda-Calculus: A Preliminary Report

Andrew Wright[1], Suresh Jagannathan[2], Cristian Ungureanu[2], and
Aaron Hertzmann[3]

[1] STAR Laboratory, InterTrust Technologies Corp., 460 Oakmead Parkway,
Sunnyvale, CA 94086, wright@intertrust.com
[2] NEC Research Institute, 4 Independence Way, Princeton, NJ 08540,
{suresh,cristian}@research.nj.nec.com
[3] Media Research Laboratory, New York University, 715 Broadway,
NewYork, NY 10003, hertzman@mrl.nyu.edu

## 1   Introduction

A typical compiler for Java translates source code into machine-independent
byte code. The byte code may be either interpreted by a Java Virtual Machine, or further compiled to native code by a just-in-time compiler. The byte
code architecture provides platform independence at the cost of execution speed.
When Java is used as a tool for writing applets—small ultra-portable programs
that migrate across the web on demand—this tradeoff is justified. However, as
Java gains acceptance as a mainstream programming language, performance
rather than platform independence becomes a prominent issue. To obtain high-
performance code for less mobile applications, we are developing an optimizing
compiler for Java that bypasses byte code, and, just like optimizing compilers
for C or Fortran, translates Java directly to native code.

Our approach to building an optimizing compiler for Java has two novel
aspects: we use an intermediate language based on *lambda-calculus*, and this
intermediate language is *typed*. Intermediate representations based on lambda-
calculi have been instrumental in developing high-quality implementations of
functional languages such Scheme [13, 19] and Standard ML [3]. By using an
intermediate language based on lambda-calculus to compile Java, we hope to
gain the same organizational benefits in our compiler.

The past few years have also seen the development in the functional programming community of a new approach to designing compilers for languages
like ML and Haskell based on *typed intermediate languages* [15, 20]. By emphasizing formal definition of a compiler's intermediate languages with associated
type systems, this approach yields several benefits. First, properties such as type
safety of the intermediate languages can be studied mathematically outside the
sometimes messy environment of compiler source code. Second, type checkers
can be implemented for the intermediate languages, and by running these type
checkers on the intermediate programs after various transformations, we can detect a large class of errors in transformations. Indeed, by running a type checker

after each transformation, we may be able to localize a bug causing incorrect code to a specific transformation, without even running the generated code. Finally, a formal definition of a typed intermediate language serves as complete and precise documentation of the interface between two compiler passes. In short, using typed intermediate languages leads to higher levels of confidence in the correctness of compilers.

Our compiler first performs ordinary Java type checking on the source program, and then translates the Java program into an intermediate language (IL) of records and first-order procedures. The translation (1) converts an object into a record containing mutable fields for instance variables and immutable procedures for methods; (2) replaces a method call with a combination of record field selections and a first-order procedure call; (3) makes the implicit *self* parameter of a method explicit by adding an additional parameter to the procedure representing that method and passing the record representing the object as an additional argument at calls; and (4) replaces Java's complex name resolution mechanisms with ordinary static scoping. The resulting IL program typechecks since the source program did, but its typing derivation uses record subtyping where the derivation for the Java program used inheritance subtyping.

In contrast to our approach, traditional compilers for object-oriented languages typically perform analyses and optimizations on a graphical representation of a program. Nodes represent arithmetic operations, assignments, conditional branches, control merges, and message sends [8]. In later stages of optimization, message send nodes may be replaced with combinations of more primitive operations to permit method dispatch optimization. In earlier stages of optimization, program graphs satisfy an informal type system which is essentially that of the source language. In later stages, program graphs are best viewed as untyped, like the representations manipulated by conventional compilers for procedural languages.

By compiling Java using a typed lambda-calculus, we hope to gain increased confidence in the correctness of the generated code. Indeed, for languages like Java that are used to write web-based applications, whether mobile or not, correctness is vital. Incorrect code generated by the compiler could lead to a security breach with serious consequences. Additionally, by translating Java into an intermediate language of records and procedures, we hope to leverage not only optimizations developed for object-oriented languages [8], but also optimizations developed for functional languages [3, 15, 20] such as Standard ML and Haskell, as well as classical optimizations for static-single-assignment representations of imperative languages [7]. In particular, representing objects as records exposes their representations to optimization. The representations of objects can be changed by transformations on IL programs, and the type system ensures that the resulting representations are consistent. Even for optimizations like inlining and copy propagation that do not explicitly change object representations, the type system provides valuable assurance that representations remain consistent.

Unfortunately, the problem of designing a sound type system that incorporates object-oriented features into a record-based language appears to have no simple solution. With a straightforward translation of objects into records and a natural type system, contravariance in the subtyping rule for function types foils the necessary subtyping relation between the types of records that represent Java objects. The problem is that making the implicit recursion through an object's self parameter explicit as an additional argument to each method leads to function types that are recursive in both covariant and contravariant positions, and hence permit no subtyping. More sophisticated type systems that can express the necessary subtyping exist [2, 5, 16], but these type systems require more complex encodings of objects and classes. Object calculi that keep self-recursion implicit [1, 5] are more complex than record calculi and do not expose representations in a manner suitable for an intermediate language.

Rather than devise an unwieldy IL and translation, we take a more pragmatic approach. We assume that a Java program is first type-checked by the Java type-checker before it is translated into the IL. Now, optimizations and transformations performed on the IL must ensure that (1) IL typing is preserved, and (2) safety invariants provided by the Java type-checker are not violated. To satisfy the first requirement, self parameters in the IL are assigned type ⊤ (top), the type that is the supertype of any record type. To satisfy the second requirement, **typecase** operations are inserted within method bodies to recover the appropriate type of self parameters as dictated by the Java type system. The resulting IL program is typable and performs runtime checks at **typecase** expressions to ensure it is safe with respect to Java typing. However, since the source program has passed the Java type-checker, these checks should never fail. Failure indicates a compiler bug. During compiler development, these checks remain in the generated object code. For production code, the code generator simply omits the checks. In either case, we lose the ability to statically detect errors in transformations that misuse self parameters. On the other hand, we can still detect a large class of type errors involving misuse of other parameters and variables, and we gain the benefit of a simple, typed intermediate language that is easy to work with.

The remainder of the paper is organized as follows. The next section presents a core IL of records and procedures. Following that, Section 3 illustrates the translation from Java to our IL with several examples. Section 4 concludes with a summary of related work.

## 2 Language

The following grammar defines the types of our explicitly-typed intermediate language for Java:

$$t ::= pt \mid rt \mid t^* \to t \mid tag$$

$$rt ::= [\mu\alpha].\{[\text{tag} : tag] [x : ft]^*\} \mid [\mu\alpha].\{\!\!\{\text{tag} : tag [x : ft]^*\}\!\!\} \mid \alpha$$

$$ft ::= pt \; array \mid rt \; array \mid vt$$

$$vt ::= t \; var \mid t$$

$$pt ::= boolean \mid byte \mid short \mid int \mid long \mid char \mid float \mid double \mid void$$

where $x \in Var$ is a set of *variables* and $\alpha \in TyVar$ is a set of *type variables* used for recursive type definitions. There are four kinds of types $t$: *primitive types* $pt$, *function types* $t_1 \cdots t_n \to t$, *ordered record types* $\{x_1 : ft_1 \ \cdots \ x_n : ft_n\}$, and *unordered record types* $\{\!\!\{x_1 : ft_1 \ \cdots \ x_n : ft_n\}\!\!\}$. Two additional kinds, mutable variable types $t$ *var* and mutable array types $pt$ *array* and $rt$ *array*, are not full-fledged types in their own right, but may be used as types of fields in records and as types of variables. Several restrictions, which are motivated below, apply to the formation of types. The field names $x_1 \ldots x_n$ of a record type must be distinct. The first field of an unordered record type must be named **tag** and of type *tag*. Tags encode the static type of an object, and are used to inspect the type of a record at runtime. An ordered record type need not include a field named **tag** of type *tag*, but if it does, this field must appear first. Unordered record types are considered equal under different orderings of their second through last fields; that is,

$$\{\!\!\{\textbf{tag} : tag, \ x_2 : ft_2 \ \cdots \ x_n : ft_n\}\!\!\} \ = \ \{\!\!\{\textbf{tag} : tag, \ permute(x_2 : ft_2, \ldots, x_n : ft_n)\}\!\!\}$$

where *permute* yields an arbitrary permutation of its arguments. The fields of ordered record types may not be rearranged. Both kinds of record types may be recursive if prefixed by the binding operator $\mu$, hence

$$t = \mu\alpha.\{x_1 : ft_1 \ \cdots \ x_n : ft_n\} = \{x_1 : ft_1[\alpha \mapsto t] \ \cdots \ x_n : ft_n[\alpha \mapsto t]\}$$

and

$$t = \mu\alpha.\{\!\!\{x_1 : ft_1 \ \cdots \ x_n : ft_n\}\!\!\} = \{\!\!\{x_1 : ft_1[\alpha \mapsto t] \ \cdots \ x_n : ft_n[\alpha \mapsto t]\}\!\!\}$$

where $t'[\alpha \mapsto t]$ denotes the substitution of $t$ for free occurrences of $\alpha$ in $t'$.

Figure 1 defines the subtyping relation on types. The relation allows a longer ordered record type to be a subtype of a shorter record type, provided the sequence of field names of the shorter type is a prefix of the sequence of field names of the longer type, and provided that the types of like-named fields are subtypes. Since the fields of unordered record types can be reordered arbitrarily (except for the first), a longer unordered record type is a subtype of any shorter unordered record type with a subset of the longer type's fields. An ordered record type is also a subtype of an unordered record type with the same fields. The subtyping relation includes the usual contravariant rule for function types, as well as a covariant rule for array types.

Our translation uses ordered record types to represent Java classes. In the intermediate language, subtyping on ordered record types expresses Java's single inheritance class hierarchy. Because field offsets for ordered record types can be computed statically, the translation can implement access to a member of a Java object with efficient record-field selection operations. For example, our translation could represent objects of the following Java classes:

```
class A {                           class B extends A {
    int i;                              int get_i() { return i; }
    A f( A x ) { i = 0; return x; }  }
}
```

$$pt <: pt \qquad t \ var <: t \ var \qquad \frac{t_1 <: t_2 \qquad t_2 <: t_3}{t_1 <: t_3}$$

$$\frac{t'_1 <: t_1 \ \cdots \ t'_n <: t_n \qquad t <: t'}{t_1 \cdots t_n \to t <: t'_1 \cdots t'_n \to t'} \qquad \frac{t <: t'}{t \ array <: t' \ array}$$

$$\frac{ft_1 <: ft'_1 \ \cdots \ ft_n <: ft'_n}{\{x_1 : ft_1 \ \cdots \ x_n : ft_n \ \cdots \ x_{n+m} : ft_{n+m}\} <: \{x_1 : ft'_1 \ \cdots \ x_n : ft'_n\}}$$

$$\frac{ft_1 <: ft'_1 \ \cdots \ ft_n <: ft'_n}{\{\!\{x_1 : ft_1 \ \cdots \ x_n : ft_n \ \cdots \ x_{n+m} : ft_{n+m}\}\!\} <: \{\!\{x_1 : ft'_1 \ \cdots \ x_n : ft'_n\}\!\}}$$

$$\{x_1 : ft_1 \ \cdots \ x_n : ft_n\} <: \{\!\{x_1 : ft_1 \ \cdots \ x_n : ft_n\}\!\}$$

$$\frac{\alpha <: \alpha' \Rightarrow t <: t' \qquad \alpha \notin t' \qquad \alpha' \notin t}{\mu\alpha.t <: \mu\alpha'.t'}$$

**Fig. 1.** Subtyping relation.

with the following IL types:

$$t_A = \mu\alpha. \{\, \mathsf{tag} : tag,$$
$$\qquad \mathsf{i} : int \ var,$$
$$\qquad \mathsf{f} : \{\!\{ \mathsf{tag} : tag \}\!\} \times \alpha \to \alpha$$
$$\}$$

$$t_B = \{\, \mathsf{tag} : tag,$$
$$\qquad \mathsf{i} : int \ var,$$
$$\qquad \mathsf{f} : \{\!\{ \mathsf{tag} : tag \}\!\} \times t_A \to t_A,$$
$$\qquad \mathsf{get\_i} : \{\!\{ \mathsf{tag} : tag \}\!\} \to int$$
$$\}$$

(In fact the translated types are not quite this simple; see Section 3.) The type $\{\!\{\mathsf{tag} : tag\}\!\}$ plays the role of $\top$ discussed in the introduction since any record type containing a **tag** field is a subtype of this type. The Java typing rules permit an object of class B to be passed to methods like f that expect an A. Since $t_B <: t_A$, values of type $t_B$ can be passed to both IL functions f. A reference to any field of a record of type $t_A$ or $t_B$ is implemented as a fixed-offset access into the record.

Since Java interfaces permit multiple inheritance, ordered record types cannot support the necessary subtyping for interface types. Hence our translation uses unordered record types to represent interfaces. Accessing a particular field of a record of unordered type is more expensive as record values with different field orders can belong to the same unordered record type. The field access operation for unordered record types determines the actual order of a value's fields from the initial tag field required of the unordered type. For example, consider the following Java interface and its corresponding IL type:

```
Interface J {
    int get_i();
    A f( A x );
}
```

$$t_J = \{\!\{\, \mathsf{tag} : tag,$$
$$\qquad \mathsf{get\_i} : \{\!\{ \mathsf{tag} : tag \}\!\} \to int,$$
$$\qquad \mathsf{f} : \{\!\{ \mathsf{tag} : tag \}\!\} \times t_A \to t_A$$
$$\}\!\}$$

$$
\begin{array}{lll}
e & ::= & v & \text{syntactic value} \\
& | & \text{let } d^* \text{ in } e & \text{binding} \\
& | & \{[x:ft=f]^*\} & \text{record construction} \\
& | & x & \text{variable reference} \\
& | & x := e & \text{variable update} \\
& | & e.x & \text{ordered record field selection} \\
& | & e.x := e & \text{ordered record field update} \\
& | & e@x & \text{unordered record field selection} \\
& | & e@x := e & \text{unordered record field update} \\
& | & e; e & \text{sequencing} \\
& | & e(e^*) & \text{procedure invocation} \\
& | & r(e^*) & \text{primitive invocation} \\
& | & \text{if } e \text{ then } e \text{ else } e & \text{conditional} \\
& | & \text{typecase } e \text{ of } [[g \text{ as } x \Rightarrow e]]^* \text{ [else } e] & \text{type conditional} \\
& | & \text{try } e\, e & \text{exception handler} \\
& | & \text{raise } e & \text{exception raise} \\
& | & e[e] & \text{array element selection} \\
& | & e[e] := e & \text{array update for primitive types} \\
& | & e[e] :=^{\{\}} e & \text{array update for record types} \\
\\
v & ::= & c & \text{simple constant} \\
& | & g & \text{tag} \\
& | & \lambda\,[x:t]^*.\,e & \text{first-order procedure} \\
& | & \{[x:ft=v]^*\} & \text{record of values} \\
\\
f & ::= & e & \text{initial value} \\
& | & [e^*] & \text{array construction} \\
\\
d & ::= & x:vt = e & \text{value declaration} \\
& | & \text{rec } [[x:t=v]^*] & \text{set of recursive value declarations} \\
& | & g \approx t\,[\prec: g^*] & \text{tag declaration}
\end{array}
$$

**Fig. 2.** Expression syntax.

If we amend class B to implement interface J, type $t_B$ does not change, and we have $t_B <: t_J$. (Again, the translated types are not quite this simple; see Section 3.)

Figure 2 specifies the expressions $e$, values $v$, and declarations $d$ of our intermediate language, where $g \in \textit{Tag}$ are tags, $c \in \textit{Const}$ are basic constants, and $r \in \textit{Prim}$ are primitive operations. Constants, tags, and procedures are values, as well as records where all initializers are values. Primitive operations can only appear in call position. Procedures are called by value, bind their arguments as usual, and must be *first-order*: the only free variables a procedure is allowed are *global* variables bound by top-level let-expressions. A declaration $d_i \equiv (x : vt = e)$ appearing in an expression let $d_1 \cdots d_n$ in $e'$ binds $x$ of type $vt$ in $d_{i+1}$ through $d_n$ and $e'$. A recursive declaration $d_i \equiv$ rec $[x_a : t_a = v_a \cdots x_z : t_z = v_z]$ binds $x_a \ldots x_z$ of types $t_a \ldots t_z$ in all of $v_a \ldots v_z$ and $e'$. A tag declaration $d_i \equiv g \approx t \prec: g_1 \cdots g_n$ introduces tag $g$ and associates it with type $t$ and tags $g_1 \cdots g_n$. Tags $g_1 \cdots g_n$ are called *supertags* of $g$. Conversely, $g$ is a *subtag* of $g_1 \cdots g_n$. The translation places a tag in a record field named **tag** when the type a record was constructed with may need to be recovered by a language operation like **typecase**. In a record construction, a field type $t$ *var* indicates that the field is mutable, but its initializer must be a value of type $t$. Similarly, declarations of type $t$ *var* introduce mutable variables must have initializers of type $t$. Mutable fields and variables are automatically "dereferenced" when accessed. (There are no values of type $t$ *var*.) The expressions $e.x$ and $e@x$ access fields of records of ordered and unordered type, respectively. The expressions $e.x := e$ and $e@x := e$ update such fields. The unordered record operations $e@x$ and $e@x := e$ use the initial tag field of a record to determine the appropriate offset into the record. Ordinary if-expressions provide boolean conditionals, and **typecase** tests the tag of a record-valued expression. A **typecase** expression evaluates the first clause $[g \text{ as } x \Rightarrow e]$ for which $g$ is a supertag of the record's tag. In the clause body $e$, $x$ is bound to the record, but with a more precise type. The expression try $e_1 \, e_2$ evaluates $e_1$ with $e_2$ as an exception handler. If $e_1$ raises no exception, its value is returned as the value of the try-expression. If $e_1$ raises exception $v$, the expression $e_2(v)$ is evaluated and its value becomes the value of the try-expression. The expression **raise** $e$ evaluates $e$ to a record $v$ and raises an exception.

Since arrays can only appear within records in our IL, the three expressions for accessing and updating arrays actually operate on records. These operations retrieve or modify array elements associated with a record field named **array**. Another field named **length** stores an array's size. The assignment operation $e_1[e_2] :=^{\{\}} e_3$ for arrays whose elements are records sets the element of $e_1$.**array** at index $e_2$ to the value of $e_3$. Due to the covariant rule for array subtyping, this operation must also perform a runtime check to ensure that the value of $e_3$ is a subtype of the runtime array component type. Hence a third field named **elemtag** holds a tag representing the component type of the array. Since Java arrays are implicitly subtypes of the Java class **Object**, our translation places additional fields such as **clone** and **getClass** in records that represent arrays. We explain our rationale for this treatment of arrays below.

IL expressions must obey a collection of type checking rules. To simplify the presentation, we describe these rules in two groups. Figure 3 defines the first group of rules which concern simple expressions and procedures. The function $\mathcal{D}$ strips *var* off a type:

$$\mathcal{D}(\mathit{ft}) = \begin{cases} t & \text{if } \mathit{ft} = t \text{ } var \, ; \\ \mathit{ft} & \text{otherwise.} \end{cases}$$

$$\frac{\text{TypeOf}(c) = pt}{A \vdash c : pt} \qquad \frac{A[x_1 \mapsto t_1] \cdots [x_n \mapsto t_n] \vdash e : t}{A \vdash \lambda x_1 : t_1 \cdots x_n : t_n . e \ : \ t_1 \cdots t_n \to t}$$

$$\frac{A(x) = vt}{A \vdash x : \mathcal{D}(vt)} \qquad \frac{A(x) = t \ var \qquad A \vdash e : t}{A \vdash x := e : void}$$

$$\frac{A \vdash e_0 : t_1 \cdots t_n \to t \qquad A \vdash e_1 : t_1 \quad \cdots \quad A \vdash e_n : t_n}{A \vdash e_0(e_1 \cdots e_n) : t}$$

$$\frac{\text{TypeOf}(r) = pt_1 \cdots pt_n \to t \qquad A \vdash e_1 : pt_1 \quad \cdots \quad A \vdash e_n : pt_n}{A \vdash r(e_1 \cdots e_n) : t}$$

$$\frac{A \vdash e_1 : boolean \qquad A \vdash e_2 : t \qquad A \vdash e_3 : t}{A \vdash \text{if } e_1 \text{ then } e_2 \text{ else } e_3 : t} \qquad \frac{A \vdash e_1 : t_1 \qquad A \vdash e_2 : t_2}{A \vdash e_1; e_2 : t_2}$$

$$\frac{A \vdash d_1 \Rightarrow A_1 \quad \cdots \quad A + A_1 + \cdots + A_{n-1} \vdash d_n \Rightarrow A_n \qquad A + A_1 + \cdots + A_n \vdash e : t}{A \vdash \text{let } d_1 \cdots d_n \text{ in } e : t}$$

$$\frac{A \vdash e : \mathcal{D}(vt)}{A \vdash x : vt = e \Rightarrow [x \mapsto vt]}$$

$$\frac{t <: T(g_1) \quad \cdots \quad t <: T(g_n) \qquad T(g) = t \qquad G(g) = \{g_1, \ldots, g_n\}}{A \vdash g \approx t \prec: g_1 \cdots g_n \Rightarrow []}$$

$$\frac{A[x_1 \mapsto t_1 \cdots x_n \mapsto t_n] \vdash v_1 : t_1 \quad \cdots \quad A[x_1 \mapsto t_1 \cdots x_n \mapsto t_n] \vdash v_n : t_n}{A \vdash \text{rec } [x_1 : t_1 = v_1 \quad \cdots \quad x_n : t_n = v_n] \Rightarrow [x_1 \mapsto t_1 \cdots x_n \mapsto t_n]}$$

$$\frac{A \vdash e : t \qquad t <: t'}{A \vdash e : t'}$$

**Fig. 3.** Typing rules for simple expressions.

$A$ is a type assignment that maps variables to types. The rules also refer to two global maps $T$ and $G$. Map $T : Tag \xrightarrow{\text{fin}} Type$ associates types with tags, and map $G : Tag \xrightarrow{\text{fin}} \mathcal{P}(Tag)$ associates sets of tags with tags. An IL expression $e$ is typable if there exist maps $T$ and $G$ and a typing derivation concluding $[] \vdash e : t$.

Most of the typing rules for simple expressions are standard; we discuss only the exceptions. The last three rules produce environments for declarations. The rule for a tag declaration $g \approx t \prec: g_1 \cdots g_n$ requires the global map $T$ to associate $g$ with type $t$, and the map $G$ to associate $g$ with the set $\{g_1, \ldots, g_n\}$. $T$ allows the type associated with $g$ to be recovered by language operations such as typecase. $G$ abstracts the Java type hierarchy and allows language operations such as typecase to test relations in this hierarchy. For soundness, the typing rule requires that the types associated with tags related in $G$ be similarly related under subtyping; that is, if $g$ is declared to be a subtag of $g'$, then $T(g) <: T(g')$.

Figure 4 defines the typing rules for records and related expressions. We explain only the non-standard rules here. A tag has type $tag$, provided that $T$

$$\frac{g \in \mathrm{Dom}(T) \qquad g \in \mathrm{Dom}(G)}{A \vdash g : tag}$$

$$\frac{A \vdash e_1 : ft_1 \quad \cdots \quad A \vdash e_n : ft_n}{A \vdash \{x_1 : ft_1 = e_1 \quad \cdots \quad x_n : ft_n = e_n\} : \{x_1 : ft_1 \quad \cdots \quad x_n : ft_n\}},$$

if $x_1 = $ tag and $ft_1 = tag$ then
$\qquad e_1 = g$ and $T(g) = \{x_1 : ft_1 \quad \cdots \quad x_n : ft_n\}$
if $x_i = $ array and $ft_i = t$ array then
$\qquad e_i = [e'_1 \cdots e'_m]$ and $x_j = $ length and $e_j = \mathsf{m}$ and $i < j$
if $x_i = $ array and $ft_i = rt$ array then
$\qquad x_k = $ elemtag and $e_k = g'$ and $T(g') = rt$ and $k < i < j$

$$\frac{A \vdash e : \mathcal{D}(vt)}{A \vdash e : vt} \qquad \frac{A \vdash e_1 : t \quad \cdots \quad A \vdash e_n : t}{A \vdash [e_1 \cdots e_n] : t \; array}$$

$$\frac{A \vdash e : \{\cdots \; x : ft\}}{A \vdash e.x : \mathcal{D}(ft)} \qquad \frac{A \vdash e : \{\cdots \; x : t \; var\} \qquad A \vdash e_2 : t}{A \vdash e_1.x := e_2 : void}$$

$$\frac{A \vdash e : \{\!\{\mathsf{tag} : tag, \; x : ft\}\!\}}{A \vdash e@x : \mathcal{D}(ft)} \qquad \frac{A \vdash e : \{\!\{\mathsf{tag} : tag, \; x : t \; var\}\!\} \qquad A \vdash e_2 : t}{A \vdash e_1@x := e_2 : void}$$

$$\frac{A \vdash e_1 : \{\cdots \; \mathsf{array} : t \; array \; \cdots \; \mathsf{length} : int\} \qquad A \vdash e_2 : int}{A \vdash e_1[e_2] : t}$$

$$\frac{A \vdash e_1 : \{\cdots \; \mathsf{array} : pt \; array \; \cdots \; \mathsf{length} : int\} \qquad A \vdash e_2 : int \qquad A \vdash e_3 : pt}{A \vdash e_1[e_2] := e_3 : void}$$

$$\frac{A \vdash e_1 : \{\cdots \; \mathsf{elemtag} : tag \; \cdots \; \mathsf{array} : t \; array \; \cdots \; \mathsf{length} : int\}}{A \vdash e_2 : int \quad A \vdash e_3 : t \quad t <: \{\!\{\mathsf{tag} : tag\}\!\}}{A \vdash e_1[e_2] :=^{\{\}} e_3 : void}$$

$$\frac{A \vdash e_0 : \{\!\{\mathsf{tag} : tag\}\!\}}{A[x_1 \mapsto T(g_1)] \vdash e_1 : t \quad \cdots \quad A[x_n \mapsto T(g_n)] \vdash e_n : t \qquad A \vdash e_{n+1} : t}{\mathsf{typecase} \; e_0 \; \mathsf{of} \; [g_1 \; \mathsf{as} \; x_1 \Rightarrow e_1] \; \cdots \; [g_n \; \mathsf{as} \; x_n \Rightarrow e_n] \; [\mathsf{else} \; e_{n+1}] : t}$$

$$\frac{A \vdash e_1 : t \qquad A \vdash e_2 : \{\!\{\mathsf{tag} : tag\}\!\} \to t}{A \vdash \mathsf{try} \; e_1 \; e_2 : t} \qquad \frac{A \vdash e : \{\!\{\mathsf{tag} : tag\}\!\}}{A \vdash \mathsf{raise} \; e : void}$$

**Fig. 4.** Typing rules for records and related expressions.

and $G$ associate it with appropriate types and supertags. Record expressions receive ordered record types with several restrictions. First, if the first field is named **tag** and has type $tag$, then its initializer must be a tag $g$ whose type in $T$ is the type of the entire record. This ensures that a record's type can be recovered from its tag. Second, a field may have an array initializer of length $m$ if and only if the field's name is **array** and there is a field named **length** whose initializer is the constant m. This restriction ensures that the length field can be used for bounds checking accesses to the array. Third, if an array field is present of type *rt array* where *rt* is a record type, then the record must include a field named elemtag whose initializer is a tag corresponding to *rt*. Array update uses the elemtag field to perform its runtime type check. The third and fourth typing rules handle initializers for fields. The rules for array access and update require $e_1$ to be a record containing array and length fields. The rule for update where the component type is a record type additionally requires an elemtag field. The rule for typecase requires that the expression being tested have a record type including a tag field. For each clause $[g_i$ as $x_i \Rightarrow e_i]$, variable $x_i$ is bound in $e_i$ to $T(g_i)$, since the typing rule for record construction ensures that any record containing tag $g_i$ will have type $T(g_i)$. Finally, the typing rules for exception constructs require the exception be a tagged record as the translation uses typecase within handlers to distinguish different exceptions.

Provided that array access and update operations perform bounds checks, this type system is sound. But to achieve high performance code, we need to lift array bounds checks out of loops or eliminate them entirely. Our IL is designed so that a safe array access operation can be replaced with a combination of an explicit test and a corresponding unsafe operation. For instance, we replace $e_1[e_2]$ with

$$
\begin{aligned}
&\text{let } a = e_1 \\
&\quad\ i = e_2 \\
&\text{in if } i \geq 0 \ \& \ i < a.\text{length then } {}_{unsafe}[a]i \\
&\quad\ \text{else raise IndexOutOfBoundsException}
\end{aligned}
$$

The explicit tests so introduced can then be optimized as usual.

## 3  Translation

The translation from Java to our intermediate language of records and procedures:

- replaces method dispatch with simple record accesses and a first-order procedure call;
- passes object state explicitly through this parameters that are treated no differently from any other function parameter;
- supports efficient implementation of member access by representing objects as ordered records;
- replaces Java's complex mechanisms for name resolution (visibility keywords, overloading, super, inner classes, and packages) with ordinary static scoping;
- flattens the class inheritance hierarchy by explicitly including record fields defined by superclasses;
- expresses method sharing among objects of the same class by placing procedures that implement the methods in a shared record;
- accommodates subtyping between Java classes by assigning type T to this and using typecase to recover the appropriate type;

```
class Point {
    int x;
    int y = 3;
    Point() { x = 2;};
    public void mv( int dx, int dy ) { x += dx; y += dy; };
    public boolean eq( Point other ) { return (x == other.x && y == other.y); }
    Point like() { Point p = new Point(); p.x = x; p.y = y; return p; }
}

class ColorPoint extends Point {
    int c;
    public boolean eq( Point other ) {
        if ( other instanceof ColorPoint )
            return super.eq( other ) && c == ((ColorPoint) other).c;
        else
            return false;
    }
    ColorPoint sc( int c ) { this.c = c; return this; }
    ColorPoint() { super(); }
    ColorPoint( int c ) { super(); this.c = c; }
}
```

**Fig. 5.** Example Java classes.

- uses type tags on records to support runtime type tests and casts;
- accommodates interface subtyping by using unordered record types;
- lifts static methods and constructor and initialization procedures out of classes and represents them as top-level procedures;
- expresses class initialization as explicit tests and calls that can be optimized;
- replaces implicit conversions on primitive types with explicit operations, eliminates widening conversions in favor of implicit subtyping, and expresses narrowing conversions with typecase;
- expresses local control constructs (for, while, break, etc.) with uses of tail-recursive procedures;
- places lock and unlock instructions where control enters or leaves synchronized blocks.

In this section, we illustrate some aspects of this translation with examples. All Java objects implicitly extend class Object and hence have members such as clone and getClass, but we omit such members in these examples to simplify the presentation.

Figure 5 presents Java code defining two classes Point and ColorPoint. In the example, a Point object contains x and y coordinate fields, and methods to move a point (mv), test whether two points are the same (eq), and clone a new point from the current one (like). Class ColorPoint inherits from Point and adds a color field c. ColorPoint overrides the eq method of Point and also provides a

$$t_P = \mu\alpha. \{ \text{ tag: } tag,$$

$$\text{methods: } \{$$

$$\text{mv: } \{\!\!\{\text{tag} : tag\}\!\!\} \times int \times int \rightarrow void,$$

$$\text{eq: } \{\!\!\{\text{tag} : tag\}\!\!\} \times \alpha \rightarrow boolean,$$

$$\text{like: } \{\!\!\{\text{tag} : tag\}\!\!\} \rightarrow \alpha$$

$$\},$$

$$\text{x: } int \; var,$$

$$\text{y: } int \; var$$

$$\}$$

$$t_C = \mu\beta. \{ \text{ tag: } tag,$$

$$\text{methods: } \{$$

$$\text{mv: } \{\!\!\{\text{tag} : tag\}\!\!\} \times int \times int \rightarrow void,$$

$$\text{eq: } \{\!\!\{\text{tag} : tag\}\!\!\} \times t_P \rightarrow boolean,$$

$$\text{like: } \{\!\!\{\text{tag} : tag\}\!\!\} \rightarrow t_P,$$

$$\text{sc: } \{\!\!\{\text{tag} : tag\}\!\!\} \times int \rightarrow \beta$$

$$\},$$

$$\text{x: } int \; var,$$

$$\text{y: } int \; var,$$

$$\text{c: } int \; var$$

$$\}$$

**Fig. 6.** Types for Point and ColorPoint objects in the IL.

new method sc to set its color. The ColorPoint class declares two constructors. The first initializes a new ColorPoint object with a default color; the second sets the color field explicitly to the color supplied as an argument.

Figure 6 presents the record types corresponding to Point and ColorPoint. In general, records corresponding to objects include a tag field, a methods field, and fields for the instance variables, both explicit and inherited. The methods field contains a record of functions corresponding to the instance methods of the class, both explicit and inherited. Initially, this record is shared by all objects of the class, although optimizations may replace it with a record of specialized functions in certain objects. The functions take an additional first argument which is the object record itself. The IL types do not include fields for constructors or static methods as these procedures are called directly without selecting them from an object.

The types of mv and eq in $t_C$ and $t_P$ are the *same*. This is because Java requires that an overriding method be of the same type as the overridden one. Since $t_C$ has at least the same fields as $t_P$, and since the members in the shared prefix have the same type, we have $t_C <: t_P$. Hence a record denoting a ColorPoint can be passed to a function that expects a record denoting a Point.

A program in our intermediate language consists of a set of mutually recursive values corresponding to methods, constructors, and method tables. Other than references to other top-level definitions, these procedures have no free variables. Notably, this is supplied as an explicit argument, unlike its treatment in

```
    let tagP ≈ t_P
      rec [newP: → t_P =
              λ. { tag:tag = tagP, methods:... = Pmethods,
                   x:int var = 0, y:int var = 0 }
            initP: t_P → void =
              λthis:t_P . this.y := 3; this.x := 2
            Pmethods: ... =
              { mv: ... = mvP, eq: ... = eqP, like: ... = likeP }
            mvP: {tag : tag} × int × int → void =
              λthis:{tag : tag}, dx:int, dy:int .
                  typecase this of
                     [tagP as this ⇒ this.x := this.x + dx; this.y := this.y + dy]
                     [else raise CompilerError]
            eqP: {tag : tag} × t_P → boolean =
              λthis:{tag : tag}, other:t_P .
                  typecase this of
                     [tagP as this ⇒ if not(this.x == other.x) then false
                                     else this.y == other.y]
                     [else raise CompilerError]
            likeP: {tag : tag} → t_P =
              λthis:{tag : tag} .
                  typecase this of
                     [tagP as this ⇒ let it = newP() in initP(it); it ]
                     [else raise CompilerError]
       ]
    in ...
```

**Fig. 7.** Translation of Point class.

Java and other object-based languages. This property facilitates code-movement optimizations on our IL such as inlining.

Figure 7 shows the translation of the Point class. We elide some types that are obvious from context. The translation generates a procedure newP for constructing new Point objects, a procedure initP for initializing them, a record of functions corresponding to the methods of the class, and the functions themselves. Each method function dispatches on the type of its first argument. A tag encodes the static type of an object; this type is examined at runtime using typecase. Thus, if mv is invoked by an object that is not a Point, the argument tag supplied in the call will not be a subtag of tagP, and a runtime exception will be raised. Such an error will not be caught at compile-time because the type expected by mv for this argument is $\top = \{tag : tag\}$. Indeed, $\top$ is the *self* type expected by all translated methods.

Figure 8 shows the translation of the ColorPoint class. An interesting aspect of ColorPoint's definition is its use of super. Calls to super in ColorPoint constructors are translated to calls to initP. The call super.eq( other ) becomes a direct call to eqP since Java's semantics dictate that such uses of super bypass the usual

```
     let  ... code for Point ...
  in let
     tagC ≈ tP
     rec [newC: → tC =
             λ. { tag:tag = tagC, methods:... = Cmethods,
                   x:int var = 0, y:int var = 0, c:int var = 0 }
          initC₁: tC → void =
                  λthis:tC. initP(this)
          initC₂: tC × int → void =
                  λthis:tC, c:int. initP(this); this.c := c
          Cmethods: ... =
                  { mv: ... = mvP, eq: ... = eqC, like: ... = likeP, sc : ... = scC }
          eqC: {tag : tag} × tP → boolean =
                  λthis:{tag : tag}, other: tP .
                     typecase this of
                        [tagC as this ⇒ if (typecase other of
                                            [tagC as other ⇒ true]
                                            [else false]) then
                                         (if not(eqP(this, other)) then false
                                         else this.c == (typecase other of
                                                          [tagC as other ⇒ other]
                                                          [else raise CastException]).c)
                                     else false]
                        [else raise CompilerError]
          scC: {tag : tag} × int → tC =
                  λthis:{tag : tag}, c:int .
                     typecase this of
                        [tagC as this ⇒ this.c := c; this]
                        [else raise CompilerError]
  in ...
```

**Fig. 8.** Translation of ColorPoint class

dynamic method dispatch. Uses of **typecase** capture the runtime behavior of **instanceof** and narrowing conversions. In particular, (**typecase** other ...) takes the **tagC** branch if other.tag is **tagC** or any subtag of **tagC**. All records containing such a tag are guaranteed to represent ColorPoints, or belong to subclasses of ColorPoint.

Figure 9 illustrates a Java interface **Widget** and its corresponding type $t_W$ in our IL. Since the classes that implement **Widget** may have methods in different orders, the methods field of $t_W$ has an unordered record type. If we amend **Point** to implement **Widget**, the translated types $t'_P$ and $t'_C$ for **Point** and **ColorPoint**, also shown in Figure 9, include a **tag** field in their **methods** record to achieve the subtyping $t'_C <: t'_P <: t_W$.

```
interface Widget {
        boolean eq( Point other );
        void mv( int dx, int dy );
}
```

$t_W = \{$ tag: $tag$,
       methods: $\{\!\{$ tag: $tag$,
                eq: $\{\!\{$tag $: tag\}\!\} \times t'_P \to boolean$,
                mv: $\{\!\{$tag $: tag\}\!\} \times int \times int \to void$
       $\}\!\}$
       $\}$

$t'_P = \mu\alpha. \{$ tag: $tag$,
        methods: $\{$
         tag: $tag$,
         mv: $\{\!\{$tag $: tag\}\!\} \times int \times int \to void$,
         eq: $\{\!\{$tag $: tag\}\!\} \times \alpha \to boolean$,
         like: $\{\!\{$tag $: tag\}\!\} \to \alpha$
        $\}$,
        x: $int\ var$,
        y: $int\ var$
       $\}$

$t'_C = \mu\beta. \{$ tag: $tag$,
        methods: $\{$
         tag: $tag$,
         mv: $\{\!\{$tag $: tag\}\!\} \times int \times int \to void$,
         eq: $\{\!\{$tag $: tag\}\!\} \times t'_P \to boolean$,
         like: $\{\!\{$tag $: tag\}\!\} \to t'_P$,
         sc: $\{\!\{$tag $: tag\}\!\} \times int \to \beta$
        $\}$,
        x: $int\ var$,
        y: $int\ var$,
        c: $int\ var$
       $\}$

**Fig. 9.** Interface Widget and types for Widget, Point, and ColorPoint.

## 4 Related Work

Optimizations for object-oriented languages, type systems for object-oriented languages, and typed intermediate languages are three topics that have been investigated independently by other researchers and relate to the work presented here.

### Optimizations for Objects

An important issue addressed by optimizing compilers for object-oriented languages is reducing the overhead introduced by encoding polymorphism. Statically-typed object-oriented languages such as Java support polymorphism through subclassing. Subclasses share implementations with their parents. Because methods can be overridden to provide alternative implementations, the exact method invoked at a call site may not be easily determined at compile time. Indeed, without aggressive analyses, compilers are unlikely to determine the control flow of a program that makes any significant use of inheritance. On the other hand, relying only on intraprocedural optimization may not be effective because methods are usually short and make frequent calls to other methods.

There are two main ways of eliminating the dispatch at a call $x.f(\ldots)$. Either (i) the value of the receiver $x$ can be of only one type $T$, in which case we can call $T$'s method $f$ directly, or (ii) $x$ can be of any of the types in a set $S$, but all types in $S$ share the same implementation of $f$, in which case we can call $f$ directly. Concrete type inference and class hierarchy analysis are two well-known analyses that have been devised to address the issue of dispatch elimination.

*Concrete Type Inference* [14, 17, 9, 10] is a form of flow analysis that identifies, for each expression, the set of possible types its values may belong to. When a receiver is found to have only one possible type, the method dispatch can be replaced by a direct function call to that type's method.

*Class Hierarchy Analysis* [9, 4, 10] is a program analysis that, based solely on the program's class structure, identifies a set of types $S$ that share the same implementation of method $f$. An example of such a set is the set containing class $C$ and all subclasses of $C$ that do not override $f$. Such sets can be computed either from programmer's annotations ("final" in Java) or from inspection of the complete class hierarchy. The analysis can be adapted to work, although less beneficially, in the presence of separate compilation, where *implementations* are separated from *interfaces*. In such cases it is still possible to eliminate method dispatch at link time [11].

Even if the above analyses are unable to identify a call site as calling a unique function, it may still be possible to optimize the program by using a *type-case* statement with execution branching on the exact type of the value to code specific to each possible type [6]. Message splitting is a variation of this technique which consists of duplicating not only the method call on each branch of the type case, but subsequent statements as well, whenever this enables further optimizations.

Dynamically typed languages, and to a lesser extent statically typed languages, could benefit from *type feedback*—information about the set of concrete types that a receiver is observed to have during program's execution. Comparison of type feedback with either class hierarchy analysis [9] or concrete type inference [12] shows it to be a valuable technique.

In contrast to our typed intermediate language, the intermediate language on which these optimizations have typically been performed is an untyped control-flow graph. Low-level nodes in the graph are used to represent arithmetic operations, assignments, conditional branches, etc. High-level nodes are used to represent the semantics of method calls [6]. High-level nodes help the compiler postpone code-generation decisions for method dispatch until after optimizations aimed at replacing method calls with direct function calls are performed. Remaining method dispatches are then translated into more primitive operations, and the code is then subject to further intra-procedural optimizations. This approach is well-suited for implementing dynamically typed languages, where a method dispatch can be a rather heavy-weight construct. On the other hand, in a statically typed language with single inheritance such as Java, method dispatch consists of fetching a function pointer from a record from a known offset, and calling that function. We believe that in such a setting, an intermediate language based on first order functions and records is a viable alternative. All the complicated constructs of the source language, including method dispatch, are translated into simpler operations. Flow analysis techniques used to drive interprocedural optimizations for functional languages can be directly applied to our intermediate language and need not be modified to understand the nuances of method dispatch. By having available the function tables constructed for each type, analyses can still compute a reasonably precise conservative approximation to the set of methods called at a call site, facilitating optimizations like inlining.

**Type Systems for Objects**

In designing our typed IL for Java, we considered and rejected several alternatives. A naive attempt to translate Java into a record-based IL uses the same language and type system as ours, but gives self parameters the object's record type rather than $\top$. That is, mv, eq, and like in class Point all expect a value of type $t_P$ for their first argument. This solution fails because, translating ColorPoint the same way, we no longer have $t_C <: t_P$ due to contravariant subtyping of functions. Hence many Java-typable programs are not typable under such a translation.

Several object calculi have most of the language features found in Java and support the necessary subtyping [1, 5]. However, in these calculi, self parameters are implicitly bound, and method dispatch is not broken down into separate function selection and procedure call mechanisms. Consequently it would be difficult to adapt existing techniques for optimizing procedural languages to such calculi. Moreover, the complexity of these calculi make them inappropriate as the foundation for an IL.

Finally languages that employ a *split-self* semantics represent an object as a pair of a record containing the object's state and a record containing the object's code [16]. They use existential types to achieve subtyping, and include pack and unpack operations to manipulate values of existential type. The encoding of objects in this style is complex and unwieldy for use in a compiler.

**Typed Intermediate Languages**

Several advanced functional language implementations have embraced the use of a typed intermediate language to express optimizations and transformations [18, 20]. The motivation for using a typed intermediate language holds equally well in the context of a Java implementation. Like most functional languages, Java has a rich type system and requires aggressive compiler optimization to achieve acceptable performance. However, while the intermediate language type systems developed for functional language implementations have been based on a polymorphic $\lambda$-calculus, the type system in our IL more closely reflects features found in Java. Thus, it provides record subtyping to express single inheritance, unordered record types to express interfaces, and a **tag** type to express runtime type inspection.

To summarize, our typed intermediate language for Java serves three major roles: (1) it gives us increased confidence in the correctness of optimizations; (2) it exposes salient properties of an object's representation that may be then optimized; and (3) it facilitates type-specific decisions throughout the compiler and runtime system. We are confident that a typed intermediate language of this kind will be instrumental in realizing a high-performance Java implementation.

# References

1. ABADI, M., AND CARDELLI, L. *A Theory of Objects*. Springer-Verlag, 1996.
2. ABADI, M., CARDELLI, L., AND VISWANATHAN, R. An Interpretation of Objects and Object Types. In *Proceedings of the Conference on Principles of Programming Languages* (1996), pp. 392–406.
3. APPEL, A. W. *Compiling with Continuations*. Cambridge University Press, 1991.
4. BACON, D., AND SWEENEY, P. Fast static analysis of C++ virtual function calls. *OOPSLA'96 Conference on Object-Oriented Programming Systems, Languages, and Applications* (1996).
5. BRUCE, K. B., CARDELLI, L., AND PIERCE, B. C. Comparing Object Encodings. In *Theoretical Aspects of Computer Software (TACS), Sendai, Japan* (Sept. 1997).
6. CHAMBERS, C. *The Design and Implementation of the SELF Compiler, an Optimizing Compiler for Object-Oriented Programming Languages*. PhD thesis, Stanford University, March 1992.
7. CYTRON, R., FERRANTE, J., ROSEN, B. K., WEGMAN, M. N., AND ZADECK, F. K. Efficiently Computing Static Single Assignment Form and the Control Dependence Graph. *TOPLAS 13*, 4 (October 1991), 451–490.
8. DEAN, J., DEFOUW, G., GROVE, D., LITVINOV, V., AND CHAMBERS, C. Vortex: An optimizing compiler for object-oriented languages. *OOPSLA'96 Conference on Object-Oriented Programming Systems, Languages, and Applications* (1996), 83–100.
9. DEAN, J., GROVE, D., AND CHAMBERS, C. Optimization of object-oriented programs using static class hierarchy analysis. *ECOOP* (1995).
10. DIWAN, A., MOSS, E., AND MCKINLEY, K. Simple and effective analysis of statically-typed object-oriented programs. *OOPSLA'96 Conference on Object-Oriented Programming Systems, Languages, and Applications* (1996).
11. FERNANDEZ, M. F. Simple and effective link-time optimization of modula-3 programs. *Proceedings of the Conference on Programming Language Design and Implementation* (1995), 103–115.
12. HÖLZLE, U., AND AGESEN, O. Dynamic versus static optimization techniques for object-oriented languages. *OOPSLA'95 Conference on Object-Oriented Programming Systems, Languages, and Applications* (1995).
13. KRANZ, D., KELSEY, R., REES, J. A., HUDAK, P., PHILBIN, J., AND ADAMS, N. I. Orbit: An optimizing compiler for scheme. *ACM SIGPLAN Conference Proceedings* (1986).

14. PALSBERG, J., AND SCHWARTZBACH, M. I. Object-oriented type inference. *OOP-SLA '91 Conference on Object-Oriented Programming Systems, Languages, and Applications* (1991), 146–161.

15. PEYTON-JONES, S., LAUNCHBURY, J., SHIELDS, M., AND TOLMACH, A. Briding the gulf: A common intermediate language for ML and Haskell. In *Proceedings of the Conference on Principles of Programming Languages* (1998), ACM Press, pp. 49–61.

16. PIERCE, B. C., AND TURNER, D. N. Simple type-theoretic foundations for object-oriented programming. *Journal of Functional Programming 4*, 2 (Apr. 1994), 207–247. A preliminary version appeared in Principles of Programming Languages, 1993, and as University of Edinburgh technical report ECS-LFCS-92-225, under the title "Object-Oriented Programming Without Recursive Types".

17. PLEVYAK, J., AND CHIEN, A. A. Precise concrete type inference for object-oriented languages. *OOPSLA '94 Object-Oriented Programming Systems, Language, and Applications* (1994), 324–340.

18. SHAO, Z. Flexible Representation Analysis. In *Proceedings of the International Conference on Functional Programming* (1997), ACM Press, pp. 85–98.

19. STEELE JR., G. L. Rabbit: a compiler for scheme. Master's thesis, Massachusetts Institute of Technology, May 1977.

20. TARDITI, D., MORRISETT, G., CHENG, P., STONE, C., HARPER, R., AND LEE, P. TIL: A Type-Directed Optimizing Compiler for ML. In *Proceedings of the Conference on Programming Language Design and Implementation* (1996), ACM Press, pp. 181–192.

# Stack-Based Typed Assembly Language *

Greg Morrisett, Karl Crary, Neal Glew, and David Walker

Cornell University

**Abstract.** In previous work, we presented a *Typed Assembly Language* (TAL). TAL is sufficiently expressive to serve as a target language for compilers of high-level languages such as ML. This work assumed such a compiler would perform a *continuation-passing style* transform and eliminate the control stack by heap-allocating activation records. However, most compilers are based on stack allocation. This paper presents STAL, an extension of TAL with stack constructs and stack types to support the stack allocation style. We show that STAL is sufficiently expressive to support languages such as Java, Pascal, and ML; constructs such as exceptions and displays; and optimizations such as tail call elimination and callee-saves registers. This paper also formalizes the typing connection between CPS-based compilation and stack-based compilation and illustrates how STAL can formally model calling conventions by specifying them as formal translations of source function types to STAL types.

## 1 Introduction and Motivation

Statically typed source languages have efficiency and software engineering advantages over their dynamically typed counterparts. Modern type-directed compilers [19, 25, 7, 32, 20, 29, 12] exploit the properties of typed languages more extensively than their predecessors by preserving type information computed in the front end through a series of typed intermediate languages. These compilers use types to direct sophisticated transformations such as closure conversion [18, 31, 17, 1, 21], region inference [8], subsumption elimination [9, 11], and unboxing [19, 22, 28]. Without types these transformations are, in many cases, less effective or impossible. Furthermore, the type translation partially specifies the corresponding term translation and often captures the critical concerns in an elegant and succinct fashion. Strong type systems not only describe but also enforce many important invariants. Consequently, developers of type-based compilers may invoke a type-checker after each code transformation, and if the output fails to type-check, the developer knows that the compiler contains an internal error. Although type-checkers for decidable type systems will not catch all compiler errors, they have proven themselves valuable debugging tools in practice [24].

---

* This material is based on work supported in part by the AFOSR grant F49620-97-1-0013, ARPA/RADC grant F30602-96-1-0317, ARPA/AF grant F30602-95-1-0047, and AASERT grant N00014-95-1-0985. Any opinions, findings, and conclusions or recommendations expressed in this publication are those of the authors and do not reflect the views of these agencies.

Despite the numerous advantages of compiling with types, until recently, no compiler propagated type information through the final stages of code generation. The TIL/ML compiler, for instance, preserves types through approximately 80% of compilation but leaves the remaining 20% untyped. Many of the complex tasks of code generation including register allocation and instruction scheduling are left unchecked; types are not used to specify or explain these low-level code transformations.

These observations motivated our exploration of very low-level type systems and corresponding compiler technology. In Morrisett et al. [23], we presented a *typed assembly language* (TAL) and proved that its type system was sound with respect to an operational semantics. We demonstrated the expressiveness of this type system by sketching a type-preserving compiler from an ML-like language to TAL. The compiler ensured that well-typed source programs were always mapped to well-typed assembly language programs and that they preserved source level abstractions such as user-defined abstract data types and closures. Furthermore, we claimed that the type system of TAL did not interfere with many traditional compiler optimizations including inlining, loop-unrolling, register allocation, instruction selection, and instruction scheduling.

However, the compiler we presented was critically based on a *continuation-passing style* (CPS) transform, which eliminated the need for a control stack. In particular, activation records were represented by heap-allocated closures as in the SML of New Jersey compiler (SML/NJ) [2,3]. For example, Figure 1 shows the TAL code our heap-based compiler would produce for the recursive factorial computation. Each function takes an additional argument which represents the control stack as a continuation closure. Instead of "returning" to the caller, a function invokes its continuation closure by jumping directly to the code of the closure, passing the environment of the closure and the result in registers.

Allocating continuation closures on the heap has many advantages over a conventional stack-based implementation. First, it is straightforward to implement control primitives such as exceptions, first-class continuations, or user-level lightweight coroutine threads [3, 31, 34]. Second, Appel and Shao [5] have shown that heap allocation of closures can have better space properties, primarily because it is easier to share environments. Third, there is a unified memory management mechanism (namely the garbage collector) for allocating and collecting all kinds of objects, including activation frames. Finally, Appel and Shao [5] have argued that, at least for SML/NJ, the locality lost by heap-allocating activation frames is negligible.

Nevertheless, there are also compelling reasons for providing support for stacks. First, Appel and Shao's work did not consider imperative languages, such as Java, where the ability to share environments is greatly reduced, nor did it consider languages that do not require garbage collection. Second, Tarditi and Diwan [14, 13] have shown that with some cache architectures, heap allocation of continuations (as in SML/NJ) can have substantial overhead due to a loss of locality. Third, stack-based activation records can have a smaller memory footprint than heap-based activation records. Finally, many machine architectures have hardware mechanisms that expect programs to behave in a stack-like fashion. For example, the Pentium Pro processor has an internal stack that it uses to predict return addresses for procedures so that instruction pre-fetching will not be stalled [16]. The internal stack is guided by the use of call/return primitives which use the standard control stack.

Clearly, compiler writers must weigh a complex set of factors before choosing stack allocation, heap allocation, or both. The target language must not constrain these design decisions. In this paper, we explore the addition of a stack to our typed assembly language in order to give compiler writers the flexibility they need. Our stack typing discipline is remarkably simple, but powerful enough to compile languages such as Pascal, Java, or ML without adding high-level primitives to the assembly language. More specifically, the typing discipline supports stack allocation of temporary variables and values that do not escape, stack allocation of procedure activation frames, exception handlers, and displays, as well as optimizations such as callee-saves registers. Unlike the JVM architecture [20], our system does not constrain the stack to have the same size at each control-flow point, nor does it require new high-level primitives for procedure call/return. Instead, our assembly language continues to have low-level RISC-like primitives such as loads, stores, and jumps. However, source-level stack allocation, general source-level stack pointers, general pointers into either the stack or heap, and some advanced optimizations cannot be typed.

A key contribution of the type structure is that it provides a unifying declarative framework for specifying procedure calling conventions regardless of the allocation strategy. In addition, the framework further elucidates the connection between a heap-based continuation-passing style compiler, and a conventional stack-based compiler. In particular, this type structure makes explicit the notion that the only differences between the two styles are that, instead of passing the continuation as a boxed, heap-allocated tuple, a stack-based compiler passes the continuation unboxed in registers and the environments for continuations are allocated on the stack. The general framework makes it easy to transfer transformations developed for one style to the other. For instance, we can easily explain the callee-saves registers of SML/NJ [2–4] and the callee-saves registers of a stack-based compiler as instances of a more general CPS transformation that is independent of the continuation representation.

## 2 Overview of TAL and CPS-Based Compilation

In this section, we briefly review our original proposal for typed assembly language (TAL) and sketch how a polymorphic functional language, such as ML, can be compiled to TAL in a continuation-passing style, where continuations are heap-allocated.

Figure 2 gives the syntax for TAL. Programs ($P$) are triples consisting of a heap, register file, and instruction sequence. Heaps map labels to heap values which are either tuples of word-sized values or code sequences. Register files map registers to word-sized values. Instruction sequences are lists of instructions

$(H, \{\}, I)$ where
$H$ = l_fact:

```
        code[]{r1:⟨⟩,r2:int,r3:τₖ}.
          bneq r2,l_nonzero
          unpack [α,r3],r3              % zero branch: call k (in r3) with 1
          ld r4,r3(0)                   % project k code
          ld r1,r3(1)                   % project k environment
          mov r2,1
          jmp r4                        % jump to k
      l_nonzero:
        code[]{r1:⟨⟩,r2:int,r3:τₖ}.
          sub r4,r2,1                   % n − 1
          malloc r5[int,τₖ]            % create environment for cont in r5
          st r5(0),r2                   % store n into environment
          st r5(1),r3                   % store k into environment
          malloc r3 [∀[].{r1:⟨int¹,τₖ¹⟩,r2:int},⟨int¹,τₖ¹⟩]   % create cont closure
          mov r2,l_cont
          st r3(0),r2                   % store cont code
          st r3(1),r5                   % store environment ⟨n,k⟩
          mov r2,r4                     % arg := n − 1
          mov r3,pack [⟨int¹,τₖ¹⟩,r3] as τₖ  % abstract environment type
          jmp l_fact                    % recursive call
      l_cont:
        code[]{r1:⟨int¹,τₖ¹⟩,r2:int}.    % r2 contains (n − 1)!
          ld r3,r1(0)                   % retrieve n
          ld r4,r1(1)                   % retrieve k
          mul r2,r3,r2                  % n × (n − 1)!
          unpack [α,r4],r4              % unpack k
          ld r3,r4(0)                   % project k code
          ld r1,r4(1)                   % project k environment
          jmp r3                        % jump to k
      l_halt:
        code[]{r1:⟨⟩,r2:int}.
          mov r1,r2
          halt[int]                     % halt with result in r1
```

and $I$ =

```
      malloc r1[]                      % create empty environment (⟨⟩)
      malloc r2[]                      % create empty environment
      malloc r3[∀[].{r1:⟨⟩,r2:int},⟨⟩]  % create halt closure in r3
      mov r4,l_halt
      st r3(0),r4                      % store cont code
      st r3(1),r2                      % store environment ⟨⟩
      mov r2,6                         % load argument (6)
      mov r3,pack [⟨⟩,r3] as τₖ        % abstract environment type
      jmp l_fact                       % begin fact with
                                       % {r1 = ⟨⟩, r2 = 6, r3 = haltcont}
```

and $\tau_k = \exists\alpha.\langle\forall[].\{r1{:}\alpha, r2{:}int\}^1, \alpha^1\rangle$

**Fig. 1.** Typed Assembly Code for Factorial

| | |
|---|---|
| *types* | $\tau ::= \alpha \mid int \mid \forall[\Delta].\Gamma \mid \langle \tau_1^{\varphi_1}, \ldots, \tau_n^{\varphi_n} \rangle \mid \exists \alpha.\tau$ |
| *initialization flags* | $\varphi ::= 0 \mid 1$ |
| *label assignments* | $\Psi ::= \{\ell_1{:}\tau_1, \ldots, \ell_n{:}\tau_n\}$ |
| *type assignments* | $\Delta ::= \cdot \mid \alpha, \Delta$ |
| *register assignments* | $\Gamma ::= \{r_1{:}\tau_1, \ldots, r_n{:}\tau_n\}$ |
| | |
| *registers* | $r ::= \mathtt{r1} \mid \cdots \mid \mathtt{rk}$ |
| *word values* | $w ::= \ell \mid i \mid ?\tau \mid w[\tau] \mid pack\ [\tau, w]\ as\ \tau'$ |
| *small values* | $v ::= r \mid w \mid v[\tau] \mid pack\ [\tau, v]\ as\ \tau'$ |
| *heap values* | $h ::= \langle w_1, \ldots, w_n \rangle \mid \mathtt{code}[\Delta]\Gamma.I$ |
| *heaps* | $H ::= \{\ell_1 \mapsto h_1, \ldots, \ell_n \mapsto h_n\}$ |
| *register files* | $R ::= \{r_1 \mapsto w_1, \ldots, r_n \mapsto w_n\}$ |
| | |
| *instructions* | $\iota ::= aop\ r_d, r_s, v \mid bop\ r, v \mid \mathtt{ld}\ r_d, r_s(i) \mid \mathtt{malloc}\ r[\vec{\tau}] \mid$ |
| | $\quad \mathtt{mov}\ r_d, v \mid \mathtt{st}\ r_d(i), r_s \mid \mathtt{unpack}\ [\alpha, r_d], v \mid$ |
| *arithmetic ops* | $aop ::= \mathtt{add} \mid \mathtt{sub} \mid \mathtt{mul}$ |
| *branch ops* | $bop ::= \mathtt{beq} \mid \mathtt{bneq} \mid \mathtt{bgt} \mid \mathtt{blt} \mid \mathtt{bgte} \mid \mathtt{blte}$ |
| *instruction sequences* | $I ::= \iota; I \mid \mathtt{jmp}\ v \mid \mathtt{halt}\ [\tau]$ |
| *programs* | $P ::= (H, R, I)$ |

**Fig. 2.** Syntax of TAL

terminated by either a jmp or halt instruction. The context $\Delta$ ʟ ᴀds the free type variables of $\Gamma$ in $\forall[\Delta].\Gamma$, and of both $\Gamma$ and $I$ in $\mathtt{code}[\Delta]\Gamma.I$. The instruction unpack $[\alpha, r], v$ binds $\alpha$ in the following instructions. We consider syntactic objects to be equivalent up to alpha-conversion, and consider label assignments, register assignments, heaps, and register files equivalent up to reordering of labels and registers. Register names do not alpha-convert. The notation $\vec{X}$ denotes a sequence of zero or more $X$s, and $|\cdot|$ denotes the length of a sequence.

The instruction set consists mostly of conventional RISC-style assembly operations, including arithmetic, branches, loads, and stores. One exception, the unpack instruction, strips the quantifier from the type of an existentially typed value and introduces a new type variable into scope. On an untyped machine, this is implemented by an ordinary move. The other non-standard instruction is malloc, which is explained below. Evaluation is specified as a deterministic rewriting system that takes programs to programs (see Morrisett et al. [23] for details).

The types for TAL consist of type variables, integers, tuple types, existential types, and polymorphic code types. Tuple types contain initialization flags (either 0 or 1) that indicate whether or not components have been initialized. For example, if register $r$ has type $\langle int^0, int^1 \rangle$, then it contains a label bound in the heap to a pair that can contain integers, where the first component may not have been initialized, but the second has. In this context, the type system allows the second component to be loaded, but not the first. If an integer value is stored into $r(0)$ then afterwards $r$ has the type $\langle int^1, int^1 \rangle$, reflecting the fact that the first component is now initialized. The instruction $\text{malloc } r[\tau_1, \ldots, \tau_n]$ heap-allocates a new tuple with uninitialized fields and places its label in register $r$.

TAL code types $(\forall[\alpha_1, \ldots, \alpha_n].\Gamma)$ describe code blocks $(\text{code}[\alpha_1, \ldots, \alpha_n]\Gamma.I)$, which are instruction sequences, that expect a register file of type $\Gamma$ and in which the type variables $\alpha_1, \ldots, \alpha_n$ are held abstract. In other words, $\Gamma$ serves as a register file pre-condition that must hold before control may be transferred to the code block. Code blocks have no post-condition because control is either terminated via a $\text{halt}$ instruction or transferred to another code block.

The type variables that are abstracted in a code block provide a means to write polymorphic code sequences. For example, the polymorphic code block

```
code[α]{r1:α, r2:∀[].{r1:⟨α¹, α¹⟩}}.
     malloc r3[α, α]
     st      r3(0), r1
     st      r3(1), r1
     mov     r1, r3
     jmp     r2
```

roughly corresponds to a CPS version of the ML function $\text{fn}\,(x{:}\alpha) \Rightarrow (x, x)$. The block expects upon entry that register $r1$ contains a value of the abstract type $\alpha$, and $r2$ contains a return address (or continuation label) of type $\forall[].\{r1 : \langle\alpha^1, \alpha^1\rangle\}$. In other words, the return address requires register $r1$ to contain an initialized pair of values of type $\alpha$ before control can be returned to this address. The instructions of the code block allocate a tuple, store into the tuple two copies of the value in $r1$, move the pointer to the tuple into $r1$ and then jump to the return address in order to "return" the tuple to the caller. If the code block is bound to a label $\ell$, then it may be invoked by simultaneously instantiating the type variable and jumping to the label (e.g., $\text{jmp}\,\ell[int]$).

Source languages like ML have nested higher-order functions that might contain free variables and thus require *closures* to represent functions. At the TAL level, we represent closures as a pair consisting of a code block label and a pointer to an environment data structure. The type of the environment must be held abstract in order to avoid typing difficulties [21], and thus we *pack* the type of the environment and the pair to form an existential type.

All functions, including continuation functions introduced during CPS conversion, are thus represented as existentials. For example, once CPS converted, a source function of type $int \to \langle\rangle$ has type $(int, (\langle\rangle \to void)) \to void$.[1] After closures are introduced, the code will have type:

$$\exists\alpha_1.\langle(\alpha_1, int, \exists\alpha_2.\langle(\alpha_2, \langle\rangle) \to void, \alpha_2\rangle) \to void, \alpha_1\rangle$$

Finally, at the TAL level the function will be represented by a value with the type:

$$\exists\alpha_1.\langle\forall[].\{r1{:}\alpha_1, r2{:}int, r3{:}\exists\alpha_2.\langle\forall[].\{r1{:}\alpha_2, r2{:}\langle\rangle\}^1, \alpha_2^1\rangle\}^1, \alpha_1^1\rangle$$

---

[1] The *void* return types are intended to suggest the non-returning aspect of CPS code.

Here, $\alpha_1$ is the abstracted type of the closure's environment. The code for the closure requires that the environment be passed in register r1, the integer argument in r2, and the continuation in r3. The continuation is itself a closure where $\alpha_2$ is the abstracted type of its environment. The code for the continuation closure requires that the environment be passed in r1 and the unit result of the computation in r2.

To apply a closure at the TAL level, we first use the **unpack** operation to open the existential package. Then the code and the environment of the closure pair are loaded into appropriate registers, along with the argument to the function. Finally, we use a jump instruction to transfer control to the closure's code.

Figure 1 gives the CPS-based TAL code for the following ML expression which computes six factorial:

```
let fun fact n = if n = 0 then 1 else n * (fact(n - 1)) in
   fact 6
end
```

## 3 Adding Stacks to TAL

In this section, we show how to extend TAL to achieve a Stack-based Typed Assembly Language (STAL). Figure 3 defines the new syntactic constructs for the language. In what follows, we informally discuss the dynamic and static semantics for the modified language, leaving formal treatment to Appendix A.

| | | |
|---|---|---|
| *types* | $\tau$ | $::= \cdots \mid ns$ |
| *stack types* | $\sigma$ | $::= \rho \mid nil \mid \tau{::}\sigma$ |
| *type assignments* | $\Delta$ | $::= \cdots \mid \rho, \Delta$ |
| *register assignments* | $\Gamma$ | $::= \{r_1{:}\tau_1, \ldots, r_n{:}\tau_n, \mathrm{sp}{:}\sigma\}$ |
| *word values* | $w$ | $::= \cdots \mid w[\sigma] \mid ns$ |
| *small values* | $v$ | $::= \cdots \mid v[\sigma]$ |
| *register files* | $R$ | $::= \{r_1 \mapsto w_1, \ldots, r_n \mapsto w_n, \mathrm{sp} \mapsto S\}$ |
| *stacks* | $S$ | $::= nil \mid w{::}S$ |
| *instructions* | $\iota$ | $::= \cdots \mid \mathtt{salloc}\ n \mid \mathtt{sfree}\ n \mid \mathtt{sld}\ r_d, \mathrm{sp}(i) \mid \mathtt{sst}\ \mathrm{sp}(i), r_s$ |

**Fig. 3.** Additions to TAL for Simple Stacks

Operationally, we model stacks ($S$) as lists of word-sized values. Uninitialized stack slots are filled with nonsense ($ns$). Register files now include a distinguished register, sp, which represents the current stack. There are four new instructions that manipulate the stack. The $\mathtt{salloc}\ n$ instruction places $n$ words of nonsense on the top of the stack. In a conventional machine, assuming stacks grow towards lower addresses, an $\mathtt{salloc}$ instruction would correspond to subtracting $n$ from the current value of the stack pointer. The $\mathtt{sfree}\ n$ instruction removes the top $n$ words from the stack, and corresponds to adding $n$ to the current stack pointer. The sld $r$, sp$(i)$ instruction loads the $i^{\text{th}}$ word of the stack into register $r$, whereas the sst sp$(i)$, $r$ stores register $r$ into the $i^{\text{th}}$ word. Note, the instructions ld and st cannot be used with the stack pointer.

A program becomes *stuck* if it attempts to execute:

- sfree $n$ and the stack does not contain at least $n$ words,
- sld $r$, sp$(i)$ and the stack does not contain at least $i + 1$ words or else the $i^{\text{th}}$ word of the stack is *ns*, or
- sst sp$(i)$, $r$ and the stack does not contain at least $i + 1$ words.

As in the original TAL, the typing rules for the modified language prevent well-formed programs from becoming stuck.

Stacks are described by *stack types* ($\sigma$), which include *nil* and $\tau{::}\sigma$. The latter represents a stack of the form $w{::}S$ where $w$ has type $\tau$ and $S$ has type $\sigma$. Stack slots filled with nonsense have type *ns*. Stack types also include stack type variables ($\rho$) which may be used to abstract the tail of a stack type. The ability to abstract stacks is critical for supporting procedure calls and is discussed in detail later.

As before, the register file for the abstract machine is described by a register file type ($\Gamma$) mapping registers to types. However, $\Gamma$ also maps the distinguished register sp to a stack type $\sigma$. Finally, code blocks and code types support polymorphic abstraction over both types and stack types.

One of the uses of the stack is to save temporary values during a computation. The general problem is to save on the stack $n$ registers, say $r_1$ through $r_n$, of types $\tau_1$ through $\tau_n$, perform some computation $e$, and then restore the temporary values to their respective registers. This would be accomplished by the following instruction sequence where the comments (delimited by %) show the stack's type at each step of the computation.

$$
\begin{aligned}
&\qquad\qquad\qquad\qquad \text{\% } \sigma \\
&\texttt{salloc } n \qquad\qquad \text{\% } ns{::}ns{::}\cdots{::}ns{::}\sigma \\
&\texttt{sst}\quad \texttt{sp}(0), r_1 \qquad \text{\% } \tau_1{::}ns{::}\cdots{::}ns{::}\sigma \\
&\vdots \\
&\texttt{sst}\quad \texttt{sp}(n-1), r_n \ \text{\% } \tau_1{::}\tau_2{::}\cdots{::}\tau_n{::}\sigma \\
&\texttt{code for } e \qquad\quad \text{\% } \tau_1{::}\tau_2{::}\cdots{::}\tau_n{::}\sigma \\
&\texttt{sld}\quad r_1, \texttt{sp}(0) \qquad \text{\% } \tau_1{::}\tau_2{::}\cdots{::}\tau_n{::}\sigma \\
&\vdots \\
&\texttt{sld}\quad r_n, \texttt{sp}(n-1) \ \text{\% } \tau_1{::}\tau_2{::}\cdots{::}\tau_n{::}\sigma \\
&\texttt{sfree}\quad n \qquad\qquad \text{\% } \sigma
\end{aligned}
$$

If, upon entry, $r_i$ has type $\tau_i$ and the stack is described by $\sigma$, and if the code for $e$ leaves the state of the stack unchanged, then this code sequence is well-typed. Furthermore, the typing discipline does not place constraints on the order in which the stores or loads are performed.

It is straightforward to model higher-level primitives, such as push and pop. The former can be seen as simply salloc 1 followed by a store to sp$(0)$, whereas the latter is a load from $sp(0)$ followed by sfree 1. Also, a "jump-and-link" or "call" instruction which automatically moves the return address into a register or onto the stack can be synthesized from our primitives. To simplify the presentation, we did not include these instructions in STAL; a practical implementation, however, would need a full set of instructions appropriate to the architecture.

The stack is commonly used to save the current return address, and temporary values across procedure calls. Which registers to save and in what order is usually specified by a compiler-specific calling convention. Here we consider a simple calling convention where it is assumed there is one integer argument and one unit result, both of which are passed in register r1, and the return address is passed in the register ra. When invoked, a procedure may choose to place temporaries on the stack as shown above, but when it jumps to the return address, the stack should be in the same state as it was upon entry. Naively, we might expect the code for a function obeying this calling convention to have the following STAL type:

$$\forall[].\{\texttt{r1}{:}int, \texttt{sp}{:}\sigma, \texttt{ra}{:}\forall[].\{\texttt{r1}{:}\langle\rangle, \texttt{sp}{:}\sigma\}\}$$

Notice that the type of the return address is constrained so that the stack must have the same shape upon return as it had upon entry. Hence, if the procedure pushes any arguments onto the stack, it must pop them off.

However, this typing is unsatisfactory for two reasons. The first problem is that there is nothing preventing the procedure from popping off values from the stack and then pushing new values (of the appropriate type) onto the stack. In other words, the caller's stack frame is not protected from the function's code. The second problem is much worse: such a function can only be invoked from states where the stack is exactly described by $\sigma$. This effectively prevents invocation of the procedure from two different points in the program. For example, there is no way for the procedure to push its return address on the stack and jump to itself.

The solution to both problems is to abstract the type of the stack using a stack type variable:

$$\forall[\rho].\{\texttt{r1}{:}int, \texttt{sp}{:}\rho, \texttt{ra}{:}\forall[].\{\texttt{r1} : int, \texttt{sp}{:}\rho\}\}$$

To invoke a function with this type, the caller must instantiate the bound stack type variable $\rho$ with the current type of the stack. As before, the function can only jump to the return address when the stack is in the same state as it was upon entry. However, the first problem above is addressed because the type checker treats $\rho$ as an abstract stack type while checking the body of the code. Hence, the code cannot perform an sfree, sld, or sst on the stack. It must first allocate its own space on the stack, only this space may be accessed by the function, and the space must be freed before returning to the caller.[2] The second problem is solved because the stack type variable may be instantiated

---

[2] Some intuition on this topic may be obtained from Reynolds' theorem on parametric polymorphism [26] but a formal proof is difficult.

in different ways. Hence multiple call sites with different stack states, including recursive calls, may now invoke the function. In fact, a recursive call will usually instantiate the stack variable with a different type than the original call because, unless it is a tail call, it will need to store its return address on the stack.

---

$(H, \{\text{sp} \mapsto nil\}, I)$ where

$H = $ l_fact:

```
    code[ρ]{r1 : ⟨⟩, r2 : int, sp : ρ, ra : τ_ρ}.
        bneq r2,l_nonzero[ρ]              % if n = 0 continue
        mov r1,1                          % result is 1
        jmp ra                            % return
    l_nonzero:
    code[ρ]{r1 : ⟨⟩, r2 : int, sp : ρ, ra : τ_ρ}.
        sub r3,r2,1                       % n − 1
        salloc 2                          % save n and return address to stack
        sst sp(0),r2
        sst sp(1),ra
        mov r2,r3                         % recursive call fact(n − 1)
        mov ra,l_cont[ρ]
        jmp l_fact[int::τ_ρ::ρ]
    l_cont:
    code[ρ]{r1 : int, sp : int::τ_ρ::ρ}.
        sld r2,sp(0)                      % restore n and return address
        sld ra,sp(1)
        sfree 2
        mul r1,r2,r1                      % result is n × fact(n − 1)
        jmp ra                            % return
    l_halt:
    code[]{r1 : int, sp : nil}.
        halt [int]
```

and $I = $

```
    malloc r1[]                           % environment
    mov r2,6                              % argument
    mov ra,l_halt                         % return address for initial call
    jmp l_fact[nil]
```

and $\tau_\rho = \forall[].\{r1 : int, sp : \rho\}$

**Fig. 4.** STAL Factorial Example

---

Figure 4 gives stack-based code for the factorial example of the previous section. The function is invoked by moving its environment (an empty tuple) into r1, the argument into r2, and the return address label into ra and jumping to the label l_fact. Notice that the nonzero branch must save the argument and current return address on the stack before jumping to the fact label in a recursive call. It is interesting to note that the stack-based code is quite similar to the heap-based code of Figure 1. Indeed, the code remains in a continuation-passing style, but instead of passing the continuation as a heap-allocated tuple, the environment of the continuation is passed in the stack pointer and the code of the continuation is passed in the return address register.

To more fully appreciate the correspondence, consider the type of the TAL version of 1_fact from Figure 1:

$$\forall[].\{r1:\langle\rangle, r2:int, r3:\exists\alpha.\langle\forall[].\{r1:\alpha, r2:int\}^1, \alpha^1\rangle\}$$

We could have used an alternative approach where we pass the components of the continuation closure unboxed in separate registers. To do so, the caller must unpack the continuation and the function must abstract the type of the continuation's environment resulting in a quantifier rotation:

$$\forall[\alpha].\{r1:\langle\rangle, r2:int, r3:\forall[].\{r1:\alpha, r2:int\}, r4:\alpha\}$$

Now, it is clear that the STAL code, which has type

$$\forall[\rho].\{r1:\langle\rangle, r2:int, ra:\forall[].\{sp:\rho, r1:int\}, sp:\rho\}$$

is essentially the same! Indeed, the only difference between a CPS-based compiler, such as SML/NJ, and a conventional stack-based compiler, is that for the latter, continuation environments are allocated on a stack. Our type system describes this well-known connection elegantly.

Our techniques can be applied to other calling conventions and do not appear to inhibit most optimizations. For instance, tail calls can be eliminated in CPS simply by forwarding a continuation closure to the next function. If continuations are allocated on the stack, we have the mechanisms to pop the current activation frame off the stack and to push any arguments before performing the tail call. Furthermore, the type system is expressive enough to type this resetting and adjusting for any kind of tail call, not just a self tail call. As another example, some CISC-style conventions push the arguments, the environment, and then the return address on the stack, and return the result on the stack. With this convention, the factorial code would have type:

$$\forall[\rho].\{sp:\forall[]\{sp:int::\rho\}::\langle\rangle::int::\rho\}$$

Callee-saves registers (registers whose values must be preserved across function calls) can be handled in the same fashion as the stack pointer. In particular, the function holds abstract the type of the callee-saves register and requires that the register have the same type upon return. For instance, if we wish to preserve register r3 across a call to factorial, we would use the type:

$$\forall[\rho, \alpha].\{r1:\langle\rangle, r2:int, r3:\alpha, ra:\forall[]\{sp:\rho, r1:int, r3:\alpha\}, sp:\rho\}$$

Translating this type back in to a boxed, heap allocated closure, we obtain:

$$\forall[\alpha].\{r1:\langle\rangle, r2:int, r3:\alpha, ra:\exists\beta.\langle\forall[]\{r1:\beta, r2:int, r3:\alpha\}^1, \beta^1\rangle\}$$

This is the type of the callee-saves approach of Appel and Shao [4]. Thus we see how our correspondence enables transformations developed for heap-based compilers to be used in traditional stack-based compilers and vice versa. The generalization to multiple callee-saves registers and other calling conventions should be clear. Indeed, we have found that the type system of STAL provides a concise way to declaratively specify a variety of calling conventions.

# 4 Exceptions

We now consider how to implement exceptions in STAL. We will find that a calling convention for function calls in the presence of exceptions may be derived from the heap-based CPS calling convention, just as was the case without exceptions. However, implementing this calling convention will require that the type system be made more expressive by adding *compound* stack types. This additional expressiveness will turn out to have uses beyond exceptions, allowing most compiler-introduced uses of pointers into the midst of the stack.

## 4.1 Exception Calling Conventions

In a heap-based CPS framework, exceptions are implemented by passing two continuations: the usual continuation and an *exception continuation*. Code raises an exception by jumping to the latter. For an integer to unit function, this calling convention is expressed as the following TAL type (ignoring the outer closure and environment):

$$\forall[\,].\{r1{:}int, ra{:}\exists\alpha_1.\langle\forall[\,].\{r1{:}\alpha_1, r2{:}\langle\rangle\}^1, \alpha_1^1\rangle, re{:}\exists\alpha_2.\langle\forall[\,].\{r1{:}\alpha_2, r2{:}exn\}^1, \alpha_2^1\rangle\}$$

Again, the caller might unpack the continuations:

$$\forall[\alpha_1, \alpha_2].\{r1{:}int, ra{:}\forall[\,].\{r1{:}\alpha_1, r2{:}\langle\rangle\}, ra'{:}\alpha_1, re{:}\forall[\,].\{r1{:}\alpha_2, r2{:}exn\}, re'{:}\alpha_2\}$$

Then the caller might (erroneously) attempt to place the continuation environments on stacks, as before:

$$\forall[\rho_1, \rho_2].\{r1{:}int, ra{:}\forall[\,].\{sp{:}\rho_1, r1{:}\langle\rangle\}, sp{:}\rho_1, re{:}\forall[\,].\{sp{:}\rho_2, r1{:}exn\}, sp'{:}\rho_2\}$$

Unfortunately, this calling convention uses two stack pointers, and STAL has only one stack.[3] Observe, though, that the exception continuation's stack is necessarily a tail of the ordinary continuation's stack. This observation leads to the following calling convention for exceptions with stacks:

$$\forall[\rho_1, \rho_2].\{\, sp{:}\rho_1 \circ \rho_2, r1{:}int, ra{:}\forall[\,].\{sp{:}\rho_1 \circ \rho_2, r1{:}\langle\rangle\},$$
$$re'{:}ptr(\rho_2), re{:}\forall[\,].\{sp{:}\rho_2, r1{:}exn\}\}$$

---

[3] Some language implementations use a separate exception stack; with some minor modifications, this calling convention would be satisfactory for such implementations.

This type uses two new constructs we now add to STAL (see Figure 5). When $\sigma_1$ and $\sigma_2$ are stack types, the stack type $\sigma_1 \circ \sigma_2$ is the result of appending the two types. Thus, in the above type, the function is presented with a stack with type $\rho_1 \circ \rho_2$, all of which is expected by the regular continuation, but only a tail of which ($\rho_2$) is expected by the exception continuation. Since $\rho_1$ and $\rho_2$ are quantified, the function may still be used for any stack so long as the exception continuation accepts some tail of that stack.

To raise an exception, the exception is placed in r1 and the control is transfered to the exception continuation. This requires cutting the actual stack down to just that expected by the exception continuation. Since the length of $\rho_1$ is unknown, this can not be done by sfree. Instead, a pointer to the desired position in the stack is supplied in re', and is moved into sp. The type $ptr(\sigma)$ is the type of pointers into the stack at a position where the stack has type $\sigma$. Such pointers are obtained simply by moving sp into a register.

## 4.2 Compound Stacks

The additional syntax to support exceptions is summarized in Figure 5. The new type constructors were discussed above. The word value $ptr(i)$ is used by the operational semantics to represent pointers into the stack; the element pointed to is $i$ words from the bottom of the stack. (See Figure 7 for details.) Of course, on a real machine, these would be implemented by actual pointers. The instructions mov $r_d$, sp and mov sp, $r_s$ save and restore the stack pointer, and the instructions sld $r_d, r_s(i)$ and sst $r_d(i), r_s$ allow for loading from and storing to pointers.

---

$$
\begin{array}{lll}
types & \tau ::= \cdots \mid ptr(\sigma) \\
stack\ types & \sigma ::= \cdots \mid \sigma_1 \circ \sigma_2 \\
word\ values & w ::= \cdots \mid ptr(i) \\
instructions\ \iota & ::= \cdots \mid \text{mov } r_d, \text{sp} \mid \text{mov sp}, r_s \mid \text{sld } r_d, r_s(i) \mid \text{sst } r_d(i), r_s
\end{array}
$$

**Fig. 5.** Additions to TAL for Compound Stacks

---

The introduction of pointers into the stack raises a delicate issue for the typing system. When the stack pointer is copied into a register, changes to the stack are not reflected in the type of the copy, and can invalidate a pointer. Consider the following incorrect code:

```
% begin with sp : τ::σ, sp ↦ w::S (τ ≠ ns)
mov r1, sp    % r1 : ptr(τ::σ)
sfree 1       % sp : σ, sp ↦ S
salloc 1      % sp : ns::σ, sp ↦ ns::S
sld r2, r1(0) % r2 : τ but r2 ↦ ns
```

When execution reaches the final line, r1 still has type $ptr(\tau::\sigma)$, but this type is no longer consistent with the state of the stack; the pointer in r1 points to $ns$.

To prohibit erroneous loads of this sort, the type system requires that the pointer $r_s$ be *valid* in the instructions sld $r_d, r_s(i)$, sst $r_d(i), r_s$, and mov sp, $r_s$. An invariant of our system is that the type of sp always describes the current stack, so using a pointer into the stack will be sound if that pointer's type is consistent with sp's type. Suppose sp has type $\sigma_1$ and $r$ has type $ptr(\sigma_2)$, then $r$ is valid if $\sigma_2$ is a tail of $\sigma_1$ (formally, if there exists some $\sigma'$ such that $\sigma_1 = \sigma' \circ \sigma_2$). If a pointer is invalid, it may be neither loaded from nor moved into the stack pointer. In the above example the load will be rejected because r1's type $\tau::\sigma$ is not a tail of sp's type, $ns::\sigma$.

### 4.3  Using Compound Stacks

Recall the type for a function in the presence of exceptions:

$$\forall[\rho_1, \rho_2].\{\, \text{sp}:\rho_1 \circ \rho_2, \text{r1}:int, \text{ra}:\forall[\,].\{\text{sp}:\rho_1 \circ \rho_2, \text{r1}:\langle\rangle\},$$
$$\text{re}':ptr(\rho_2), \text{re}:\forall[\,].\{\text{sp}:\rho_2, \text{r1}:exn\}\}$$

An exception may be raised within the body of such a function by restoring the handler's stack from re′ and jumping to the handler. A new exception handler may be installed by copying the stack pointer to re′ and making forthcoming function calls with the stack type variables instantiated to *nil* and $\rho_1 \circ \rho_2$. Calls that do not install new exception handlers would attach their frames to $\rho_1$ and pass on $\rho_2$ unchanged.

Since exceptions are probably raised infrequently, an implementation could save a register by storing the exception continuation's code pointer on the stack, instead of in its own register. If this convention were used, functions would expect stacks with the type $\rho_1 \circ (\tau_{\text{handler}}::\rho_2)$ and exception pointers with the type $ptr(\tau_{\text{handler}}::\rho_2)$ where $\tau_{\text{handler}} = \forall[\,].\{\text{sp}:\rho_2, \text{r1}:exn\}$.

This last convention illustrates a use for compound stacks that goes beyond implementing exceptions. We have a general tool for locating data of type $\tau$ amidst the stack by using the calling convention:

$$\forall[\rho_1, \rho_2].\{\text{sp}:\rho_1 \circ (\tau::\rho_2), \text{r1}:ptr(\tau::\rho_2), \ldots\}$$

One application of this tool would be for implementing Pascal with displays. The primary limitation of this tool is that if more than one piece of data is stored amidst the stack, although quantification may be used to avoid specifying the precise locations of that data, function calling conventions would have to specify in what *order* data appears on the stack. It appears that this limitation could be removed by introducing a limited form of intersection type, but we have not yet explored the ramifications of this enhancement.

## 5  Related and Future Work

Our work is partially inspired by Reynolds [27], which uses functor categories to "replace continuations by instruction sequences and store shapes by descriptions of the structure of the run-time stack." However, Reynolds was primarily concerned with using functors to express an intermediate language of a semantics-based compiler for Algol, whereas we are primarily concerned with type structure for general-purpose target languages.

Stata and Abadi [30] formalize the Java bytecode verifier's treatment of subroutines by giving a type system for a subset of the Java Virtual Machine language. In particular, their type system ensures that for any program control point, the Java stack is of the same size each time that control point is reached during execution. Consequently, procedure call must be a primitive construct (which it is in JVML). In contrast, our treatment supports polymorphic stack recursion, and hence procedure calls can be encoded with existing assembly-language primitives.

Tofte and others [8, 33] have developed an allocation strategy involving regions. Regions are lexically scoped containers that have a LIFO ordering on their lifetimes, much like the values on a stack. As in our approach, polymorphic recursion on abstracted region variables plays a critical role. However, unlike the objects in our stacks, regions are variable-sized, and objects need not be allocated into the region which was most recently created. Furthermore, there is only one allocation mechanism in Tofte's system (the stack of regions) and no need for a garbage collector. In contrast, STAL only allows allocation at the top of the stack and assumes a garbage collector for heap-allocated values. However, the type system for STAL is considerably simpler than the type system of Tofte et al., as it requires no effect information in types.

Bailey and Davidson [6] also describe a specification language for modeling procedure calling conventions and checking that implementations respect these conventions. They are able to specify features such as a variable number of arguments that our formalism does not address. However, their model is explicitly tied to a stack-based calling convention and does not address features such as exception handlers. Furthermore, their approach does not integrate the specification of calling conventions with a general-purpose type system.

Although our type system is sufficiently expressive for compilation of a number of source languages, it falls short in several areas. First, it cannot support general pointers into the stack because of the ordering requirements; nor can stack and heap pointers be unified so that a function taking a tuple argument can be passed either a heap-allocated or a stack-allocated tuple. Second, threads and advanced mechanisms for implementing first-class continuations such as the work by Hieb et al. [15] cannot be modeled in this system without adding new primitives.

However, we claim that the framework presented here is a practical approach to compilation. To substantiate this claim, we are constructing a compiler called TALC that maps the KML language [10] to a variant of STAL described here, suitably adapted for the Intel IA32 architecture. We have found it straightforward to enrich the target language type system to include support for other type constructors, such as references, higher-order constructors, and recursive types. The compiler uses an unboxed stack allocation style of continuation passing.

Although we have discussed mechanisms for typing stacks at the assembly language level, our techniques generalize to other languages. The same mechanisms, including the use of polymorphic recursion to abstract the tail of a stack, can be used to introduce explicit stacks in higher level calculi. An intermediate language with explicit stacks would allow control over allocation at a point where more information is available to guide allocation decisions.

## 6 Summary

We have given a type system for a typed assembly language with both a heap and a stack. Our language is flexible enough to support the following compilation techniques: CPS using both heap allocation and stack allocation, a variety of procedure calling conventions, displays, exceptions, tail call elimination, and callee-saves registers.

A key contribution of the type system is that it makes procedure calling conventions explicit and provides a means of specifying and checking calling conventions that is grounded in language theory. The type system also makes clear the relationship between heap allocation and stack allocation of continuation closures, capturing both allocation strategies in one calculus.

## References

1. Andrew W. Appel and Trevor Jim. Continuation-passing, closure-passing style. In *Sixteenth ACM Symposium on Principles of Programming Languages*, pages 293–302, Austin, January 1989.
2. Andrew W. Appel and David B. MacQueen. Standard ML of New Jersey. In Martin Wirsing, editor, *Third International Symposium on Programming Language Implementation and Logic Programming*, pages 1–13, New York, August 1991. Springer-Verlag. Volume 528 of *Lecture Notes in Computer Science*.
3. Andrew W. Appel. *Compiling with Continuations*. Cambridge University Press, 1992.
4. Andrew Appel and Zhong Shao. Callee-saves registers in continuation-passing style. *Lisp and Symbolic Computation*, 5:189–219, 1992.
5. Andrew Appel and Zhong Shao. An empirical and analytic study of stack vs. heap cost for languages with clsoures. *Journal of Functional Programming*, 1(1), January 1993.
6. Mark Bailey and Jack Davidson. A formal model of procedure calling conventions. In *Twenty-Second ACM Symposium on Principles of Programming Languages*, pages 298–310, San Francisco, January 1995.
7. Lars Birkedal, Nick Rothwell, Mads Tofte, and David N. Turner. The ML Kit (version 1). Technical Report 93/14, Department of Computer Science, University of Copenhagen, 1993.
8. Lars Birkedal, Mads Tofte, and Magnus Vejlstrup. From region inference to von Neumann machines via region representation inference. In *Twenty-Third ACM Symposium on Principles of Programming Languages*, pages 171–183, St. Petersburg, January 1996.
9. Val Breazu-Tannen, Thierry Coquand, Carl A. Gunter, and Andre Scedrov. Inheritance as implicit coercion. *Information and Computation*, 93:172–221, 1991.

44

10. Karl Crary. *KML Reference Manual*. Department of Computer Science, Cornell University, 1996.
11. Karl Crary. Foundations for the implementation of higher-order subtyping. In *ACM SIGPLAN International Conference on Functional Programming*, pages 125–135, Amsterdam, June 1997.
12. Allyn Dimock, Robert Muller, Franklyn Turbak, and J. B. Wells. Strongly typed flow-directed reprsentation transformations. In *ACM SIGPLAN International Conference on Functional Programming*, pages 11–24, Amsterdam, June 1997.
13. Amer Diwan, David Tarditi, and Eliot Moss. Memory subsystem performance of programs using copying garbage collection. In *Twenty-First ACM Symposium on Principles of Programming Languages*, pages 1–14, January 1994.
14. Amer Diwan, David Tarditi, and Eliot Moss. Memory system performance of programs with intensive heap allocation. *ACM Transactions on Computer Systems*, 13(3):244–273, August 1995.
15. Robert Hieb, R. Kent Dybvig, and Carl Bruggeman. Representing control in the presence of first-class continuations. In *ACM SIGPLAN Conference on Programming Language Design and Implementation*, pages 66–77, June 1990. Published as *SIGPLAN Notices*, 25(6).
16. Intel Corporation. *Intel Architecture Optimization Manual*. Intel Corporation, P.O. Box 7641, Mt. Prospect, IL, 60056-7641, 1997.
17. David Kranz, R. Kelsey, J. Rees, P. R. Hudak, J. Philbin, and N. Adams. ORBIT: An optimizing compiler for Scheme. In *Proceedings of the ACM SIGPLAN '86 Symposium on Compiler Construction*, pages 219–233, June 1986.
18. P. J. Landin. The mechanical evaluation of expressions. *Computer J.*, 6(4):308–20, 1964.
19. Xavier Leroy. Unboxed objects and polymorphic typing. In *Nineteenth ACM Symposium on Principles of Programming Languages*, pages 177–188, Albuquerque, January 1992.
20. Tim Lindholm and Frank Yellin. *The Java Virtual Machine Specification*. Addison-Wesley, 1996.
21. Y. Minamide, G. Morrisett, and R. Harper. Typed closure conversion. In *Twenty-Third ACM Symposium on Principles of Programming Languages*, pages 271–283, St. Petersburg, January 1996.
22. Gregory Morrisett. *Compiling with Types*. PhD thesis, Carnegie Mellon University, 1995. Published as CMU Technical Report CMU-CS-95-226.
23. Greg Morrisett, David Walker, Karl Crary, and Neal Glew. From System F to typed assembly language. In *Twenty-Fifth ACM Symposium on Principles of Programming Languages*, San Diego, January 1998. Extended version published as Cornell University technical report TR97-1651, November 1997.
24. G. Morrisett, D. Tarditi, P. Cheng, C. Stone, R. Harper, and P. Lee. The TIL/ML compiler: Performance and safety through types. In *Workshop on Compiler Support for Systems Software*, Tucson, February 1996.
25. Simon L. Peyton Jones, Cordelia V. Hall, Kevin Hammond, Will Partain, and Philip Wadler. The Glasgow Haskell compiler: a technical overview. In *Proc. UK Joint Framework for Information Technology (JFIT) Technical Conference*, July 1993.
26. John C. Reynolds. Types, abstraction and parametric polymorphism. In *Information Processing '83*, pages 513–523. North-Holland, 1983. Proceedings of the IFIP 9th World Computer Congress.

27. John Reynolds. Using functor categories to generate intermediate code. In *Twenty-Second ACM Symposium on Principles of Programming Languages*, pages 25–36, San Francisco, January 1995.

28. Zhong Shao. Flexible representation analysis. In *ACM SIGPLAN International Conference on Functional Programming*, pages 85–98, Amsterdam, June 1997.

29. Z. Shao. An overview of the FLINT/ML compiler. In *Workshop on Types in Compilation*, Amsterdam, June 1997. ACM SIGPLAN. Published as Boston College Computer Science Dept. Technical Report BCCS-97-03.

30. Raymie Stata and Martín Abadi. A type system for java bytecode subroutines. In *Twenty-Fifth ACM Symposium on Principles of Programming Languages*, San Diego, January 1998.

31. Guy L. Steele Jr. Rabbit: A compiler for Scheme. Master's thesis, MIT, 1978.

32. D. Tarditi, G. Morrisett, P. Cheng, C. Stone, R. Harper, and P. Lee. TIL: A type-directed optimizing compiler for ML. In *ACM SIGPLAN Conference on Programming Language Design and Implementation*, pages 181–192, Philadelphia, May 1996.

33. Mads Tofte and Jean-Pierre Talpin. Implementation of the typed call-by-value $\lambda$-calculus using a stack of regions. In *Twenty-First ACM Symposium on Principles of Programming Languages*, pages 188–201, January 1994.

34. Mitchell Wand. Continuation-based multiprocessing. In *Proceedings of the 1980 LISP Conference*, pages 19–28, August 1980.

# A    Formal STAL Semantics

This appendix contains a complete technical description of our calculus, STAL. The STAL abstract machine is very similar to the TAL abstract machine (described in detail in Morrisett et al. [23]). The syntax appears in Figure 6. The operational semantics is given as a deterministic rewriting system in Figure 7. The notation $a[b/c]$ denotes capture avoiding substitution of $b$ for $c$ in $a$. The notation $a\{b \mapsto c\}$ represents map update:

$$\{b_1 \mapsto c_1, b_2 \mapsto c_2, \ldots, b_n \mapsto c_n\}\{b \mapsto c\} = \begin{cases} \{b \mapsto c, b_1 \mapsto c_1, \ldots, b_n \mapsto c_n\}, \\ \quad \text{if } b \notin \{b_1, \ldots, b_n\} \\ \{b_1 \mapsto c, b_2 \mapsto c_2, \ldots, b_n \mapsto c_n\}, \\ \quad \text{if } b = b_1 \end{cases}$$

To make the presentation simpler for the branching rules, some extra notation is used for expressing sequences of type and stack type instantiations. We introduce a new syntactic class ($\psi$) for type sequences:

$$\psi ::= \cdot \mid \tau, \psi \mid \sigma, \psi$$

The notation $w[\psi]$ stands for the obvious iteration of instantiations; the substitution notation $I[\psi/\Delta]$ is defined by:

$$I[\cdot/\cdot] = I$$
$$I[\tau, \psi/\alpha, \Delta] = I[\tau/\alpha][\psi/\Delta]$$
$$I[\sigma, \psi/\rho, \Delta] = I[\sigma/\rho][\psi/\Delta]$$

The static semantics is similar to TAL's but requires extra judgments for definitional equality of types, stack types, and register file types and uses a more compositional style for instructions. Definitional equality is needed because two stack types (such as $(int::nil) \circ (int::nil)$ and $int::int::nil$) may be syntactically different but represent the same type. The judgments are summarized in Figure 8, the rules for type judgments appear in Figure 9, and the rules for term judgments appear in Figures 10 and 11. The notation $\Delta', \Delta$ denotes appending $\Delta'$ to the front of $\Delta$, that is:

$$\cdot, \Delta = \Delta$$
$$(\alpha, \Delta'), \Delta = \alpha, (\Delta', \Delta)$$
$$(\rho, \Delta'), \Delta = \rho, (\Delta', \Delta)$$

As with TAL, STAL is type sound:

**Proposition A1 (Type Soundness)** *If $\vdash P$ and $P \longmapsto^* P'$ then $P'$ is not stuck.*

This proposition is proved using the following two lemmas.

**Lemma 1 (Subject Reduction).** *If $\vdash P$ and $P \longmapsto P'$ then $\vdash P'$.*

A well-formed terminal state has the form $(H, R\{r1 \mapsto w\}, \text{halt } [\tau])$ where there exists a $\Psi$ such that $\vdash H : \Psi$ and $\Psi; \cdot \vdash w : \tau$ wval.

**Lemma 2 (Progress).** *If $\vdash P$ then either $P$ is a well-formed terminal state or there exists $P'$ such that $P \longmapsto P'$.*

| | |
|---|---|
| *types* | $\tau ::= \alpha \mid int \mid ns \mid \forall[\Delta].\Gamma \mid \langle \tau_1^{\varphi_1}, \ldots, \tau_n^{\varphi_n} \rangle \mid \exists\alpha.\tau \mid ptr(\sigma)$ |
| *stack types* | $\sigma ::= \rho \mid nil \mid \tau::\sigma \mid \sigma_1 \circ \sigma_2$ |
| *initialization flags* | $\varphi ::= 0 \mid 1$ |
| *label assignments* | $\Psi ::= \{\ell_1{:}\tau_1, \ldots, \ell_n{:}\tau_n\}$ |
| *type assignments* | $\Delta ::= \cdot \mid \alpha, \Delta \mid \rho, \Delta$ |
| *register assignments* | $\Gamma ::= \{r_1{:}\tau_1, \ldots, r_n{:}\tau_n, \mathbf{sp}{:}\sigma\}$ |
| | |
| *registers* | $r ::= \mathtt{r1} \mid \cdots \mid \mathtt{rk}$ |
| *word values* | $w ::= \ell \mid i \mid ns \mid ?\tau \mid w[\tau] \mid w[\sigma] \mid pack\ [\tau, w]\ as\ \tau' \mid ptr(i)$ |
| *small values* | $v ::= r \mid w \mid v[\tau] \mid v[\sigma] \mid pack\ [\tau, v]\ as\ \tau'$ |
| *heap values* | $h ::= \langle w_1, \ldots, w_n \rangle \mid \mathbf{code}[\Delta]\Gamma.I$ |
| *heaps* | $H ::= \{\ell_1 \mapsto h_1, \ldots, \ell_n \mapsto h_n\}$ |
| *register files* | $R ::= \{r_1 \mapsto w_1, \ldots, r_n \mapsto w_n, \mathbf{sp} \mapsto S\}$ |
| *stacks* | $S ::= nil \mid w::S$ |
| | |
| *instructions* | $\iota ::= aop\ r_d, r_s, v \mid bop\ r, v \mid \mathtt{ld}\ r_d, r_s(i) \mid \mathtt{malloc}\ r[\vec{\tau}] \mid$ |
| | $\quad \mathtt{mov}\ r_d, v \mid \mathtt{mov}\ \mathbf{sp}, r_s \mid \mathtt{mov}\ r_d, \mathbf{sp} \mid \mathtt{salloc}\ n \mid$ |
| | $\quad \mathtt{sfree}\ n \mid \mathtt{sld}\ r_d, \mathbf{sp}(i) \mid \mathtt{sld}\ r_d, r_s(i) \mid$ |
| | $\quad \mathtt{sst}\ \mathbf{sp}(i), r_s \mid \mathtt{sst}\ r_d(i), r_s \mid \mathtt{st}\ r_d(i), r_s \mid$ |
| | $\quad \mathtt{unpack}\ [\alpha, r_d], v$ |
| *arithmetic ops* | $aop ::= \mathtt{add} \mid \mathtt{sub} \mid \mathtt{mul}$ |
| *branch ops* | $bop ::= \mathtt{beq} \mid \mathtt{bneq} \mid \mathtt{bgt} \mid \mathtt{blt} \mid \mathtt{bgte} \mid \mathtt{blte}$ |
| *instruction sequences* | $I ::= \iota; I \mid \mathtt{jmp}\ v \mid \mathtt{halt}\ [\tau]$ |
| *programs* | $P ::= (H, R, I)$ |

**Fig. 6.** Syntax of STAL

| $(H, R, I) \longmapsto P$ where | |
|---|---|
| if $I =$ | then $P =$ |
| add $r_d, r_s, v; I'$ | $(H, R\{r_d \mapsto R(r_s) + \hat{R}(v)\}, I')$ |
| | and similarly for mul and sub |
| beq $r, v; I'$ | $(H, R, I')$ |
|       when $R(r) \neq 0$ | and similarly for bneq, blt, etc. |
| beq $r, v; I'$ | $(H, R, I''[\psi/\Delta])$ |
|       when $R(r) = 0$ | where $\hat{R}(v) = \ell[\psi]$ and $H(\ell) = \text{code}[\Delta]\Gamma.I''$ |
| | and similarly for bneq, blt, etc. |
| jmp $v$ | $(H, R, I'[\psi/\Delta])$ |
| | where $\hat{R}(v) = \ell[\psi]$ and $H(\ell) = \text{code}[\Delta]\Gamma.I'$ |
| ld $r_d, r_s(i); I'$ | $(H, R\{r_d \mapsto w_i\}, I')$ |
| | where $R(r_s) = \ell$ and $H(\ell) = \langle w_0, \ldots, w_{n-1}\rangle$ and $0 \leq i < n$ |
| malloc $r_d[\tau_1, \ldots, \tau_n]; I'$ | $(H\{\ell \mapsto \langle ?\tau_1, \ldots, ?\tau_n\rangle\}, R\{r_d \mapsto \ell\}, I')$ |
| | where $\ell \notin H$ |
| mov $r_d, v; I'$ | $(H, R\{r_d \mapsto \hat{R}(v)\}, I')$ |
| mov $r_d, \text{sp}; I'$ | $(H, R\{r_d \mapsto ptr(|S|)\}, I')$ |
| mov $\text{sp}, r_s; I'$ | $(H, R\{\text{sp} \mapsto w_j :: \cdots :: w_1 :: nil\}, I')$ |
| | where $R(\text{sp}) = w_n :: \cdots :: w_1 :: nil$ |
| | and $R(r_s) = ptr(j)$ with $0 \leq j \leq n$ |
| salloc $n; I'$ | $(H, R\{\text{sp} \mapsto \underbrace{ns :: \cdots :: ns}_{n} :: R(\text{sp})\}, I')$ |
| sfree $n; I'$ | $(H, R\{\text{sp} \mapsto S\}, I')$ |
| | where $R(\text{sp}) = w_1 :: \cdots :: w_n :: S$ |
| sld $r_d, \text{sp}(i); I'$ | $(H, R\{r_d \mapsto w_i\}, I')$ |
| | where $R(\text{sp}) = w_0 :: \cdots :: w_{n-1} :: nil$ and $0 \leq i < n$ |
| sld $r_d, r_s(i); I'$ | $(H, R\{r_d \mapsto w_{j-i}\}, I')$ |
| | where $R(r_s) = ptr(j)$ and $R(\text{sp}) = w_n :: \cdots :: w_1 :: nil$ |
| | and $0 \leq i < j \leq n$ |
| sst $\text{sp}(i), r_s; I'$ | $(H, R\{\text{sp} \mapsto w_0 :: \cdots :: w_{i-1} :: R(r_s) :: S\}, I')$ |
| | where $R(\text{sp}) = w_0 :: \cdots :: w_i :: S$ and $0 \leq i$ |
| sst $r_d(i), r_s; I'$ | $(H, R\{\text{sp} \mapsto w_n :: \cdots :: w_{j-i+1} :: R(r_s) :: w_{j-i-1} :: \cdots :: w_1 :: nil\}, I')$ |
| | where $R(r_d) = ptr(j)$ and $R(\text{sp}) = w_n :: \cdots :: w_1 :: nil$ |
| | and $0 \leq i < j \leq n$ |
| st $r_d(i), r_s; I'$ | $(H\{\ell \mapsto \langle w_0, \ldots, w_{i-1}, R(r_s), w_{i+1}, \ldots, w_{n-1}\rangle\}, R, I')$ |
| | where $R(r_d) = \ell$ and $H(\ell) = \langle w_0, \ldots, w_{n-1}\rangle$ and $0 \leq i < n$ |
| unpack $[\alpha, r_d], v; I'$ | $(H, R\{r_d \mapsto w\}, I'[\tau/\alpha])$ |
| | where $\hat{R}(v) = pack\ [\tau, w]\ as\ \tau'$ |

$$\text{Where } \hat{R}(v) = \begin{cases} R(r) & \text{when } v = r \\ w & \text{when } v = w \\ \hat{R}(v')[\tau] & \text{when } v = v'[\tau] \\ pack\ [\tau, \hat{R}(v')]\ as\ \tau' & \text{when } v = pack\ [\tau, v']\ as\ \tau' \end{cases}$$

**Fig. 7.** Operational Semantics of STAL

| Judgement | Meaning |
|---|---|
| $\Delta \vdash \tau$ | $\tau$ is a valid type |
| $\Delta \vdash \sigma$ | $\sigma$ is a valid stack type |
| $\vdash \Psi$ | $\Psi$ is a valid heap type |
| | (no context is used because heap types must be closed) |
| $\Delta \vdash \Gamma$ | $\Gamma$ is a valid register file type |
| $\Delta \vdash \tau_1 = \tau_2$ | $\tau_1$ and $\tau_2$ are equal types |
| $\Delta \vdash \sigma_1 = \sigma_2$ | $\sigma_1$ and $\sigma_2$ are equal stack types |
| $\Delta \vdash \Gamma_1 = \Gamma_2$ | $\Gamma_1$ and $\Gamma_2$ are equal register file types |
| $\Delta \vdash \tau_1 \leq \tau_2$ | $\tau_1$ is a subtype of $\tau_2$ |
| $\Delta \vdash \Gamma_1 \leq \Gamma_2$ | $\Gamma_1$ is a register file subtype of $\Gamma_2$ |
| $\vdash H : \Psi$ | the heap $H$ has type $\Psi$ |
| $\Psi \vdash S : \sigma$ | the stack $S$ has type $\sigma$ |
| $\Psi \vdash R : \Gamma$ | the register file $R$ has type $\Gamma$ |
| $\Psi \vdash h : \tau$ hval | the heap value $h$ has type $\tau$ |
| $\Psi; \Delta \vdash w : \tau$ wval | the word value $w$ has type $\tau$ |
| $\Psi; \Delta \vdash w : \tau^\varphi$ fwval | the word value $w$ has flagged type $\tau^\varphi$ |
| | (i.e., $w$ has type $\tau$ or $w$ is $?\tau$ and $\varphi$ is 0) |
| $\Psi; \Delta; \Gamma \vdash v : \tau$ | the small value $v$ has type $\tau$ |
| $\Psi; \Delta; \Gamma \vdash \iota \Rightarrow \Delta'; \Gamma'$ | given a context of type $\Psi; \Delta; \Gamma$, $\iota$ is a well formed instruction and produces a context of type $\Psi; \Delta'; \Gamma'$ |
| $\Psi; \Delta; \Gamma \vdash I$ | $I$ is a valid sequence of instructions |
| $\vdash P$ | $P$ is a valid program |

**Fig. 8.** Static Semantics of STAL (judgments)

$$\boxed{\Delta \vdash \tau \quad \Delta \vdash \sigma \quad \vdash \Psi \quad \Delta \vdash \Gamma}$$

$$\frac{\Delta \vdash \tau = \tau}{\Delta \vdash \tau} \qquad \frac{\Delta \vdash \sigma = \sigma}{\Delta \vdash \sigma} \qquad \frac{\cdot \vdash \tau_i}{\vdash \{\ell_1 \mapsto \tau_1, \ldots, \ell_n \mapsto \tau_n\}} \qquad \frac{\Delta \vdash \Gamma = \Gamma}{\Delta \vdash \Gamma}$$

$$\boxed{\Delta \vdash \tau_1 = \tau_2 \quad \Delta \vdash \sigma_1 = \sigma_2 \quad \Delta \vdash \Gamma_1 = \Gamma_2}$$

$$\frac{\Delta \vdash \tau_2 = \tau_1}{\Delta \vdash \tau_1 = \tau_2} \qquad \frac{\Delta \vdash \tau_1 = \tau_2 \quad \Delta \vdash \tau_2 = \tau_3}{\Delta \vdash \tau_1 = \tau_3}$$

$$\frac{\Delta \vdash \sigma_2 = \sigma_1}{\Delta \vdash \sigma_1 = \sigma_2} \qquad \frac{\Delta \vdash \sigma_1 = \sigma_2 \quad \Delta \vdash \sigma_2 = \sigma_3}{\Delta \vdash \sigma_1 = \sigma_3}$$

$$\frac{}{\Delta \vdash \alpha = \alpha} \; (\alpha \in \Delta) \qquad \frac{}{\Delta \vdash int = int}$$

$$\frac{\Delta', \Delta \vdash \Gamma_1 = \Gamma_2}{\Delta \vdash \forall[\Delta'].\Gamma_1 = \forall[\Delta'].\Gamma_2} \qquad \frac{\Delta \vdash \tau_i = \tau_i'}{\Delta \vdash \langle \tau_1^{\varphi_1}, \ldots, \tau_n^{\varphi_n} \rangle = \langle \tau_1'^{\varphi_1}, \ldots, \tau_n'^{\varphi_n} \rangle}$$

$$\frac{\alpha, \Delta \vdash \tau_1 = \tau_2}{\Delta \vdash \exists \alpha.\tau_1 = \exists \alpha.\tau_2} \qquad \frac{}{\Delta \vdash ns = ns} \qquad \frac{\Delta \vdash \sigma_1 = \sigma_2}{\Delta \vdash ptr(\sigma_1) = ptr(\sigma_2)}$$

$$\frac{}{\Delta \vdash \rho = \rho} \; (\rho \in \Delta) \qquad \frac{}{\Delta \vdash nil = nil}$$

$$\frac{\Delta \vdash \tau_1 = \tau_2 \quad \Delta \vdash \sigma_1 = \sigma_2}{\Delta \vdash \tau_1 {::} \sigma_1 = \tau_2 {::} \sigma_2} \qquad \frac{\Delta \vdash \sigma_1 = \sigma_1' \quad \Delta \vdash \sigma_2 = \sigma_2'}{\Delta \vdash \sigma_1 \circ \sigma_2 = \sigma_1' \circ \sigma_2'}$$

$$\frac{\Delta \vdash \sigma}{\Delta \vdash nil \circ \sigma = \sigma} \qquad \frac{\Delta \vdash \sigma}{\Delta \vdash \sigma \circ nil = \sigma}$$

$$\frac{\Delta \vdash \tau \quad \Delta \vdash \sigma_1 \quad \Delta \vdash \sigma_2}{\Delta \vdash (\tau {::} \sigma_1) \circ \sigma_2 = \tau {::} (\sigma_1 \circ \sigma_2)}$$

$$\frac{\Delta \vdash \sigma_1 \quad \Delta \vdash \sigma_2 \quad \Delta \vdash \sigma_3}{\Delta \vdash (\sigma_1 \circ \sigma_2) \circ \sigma_3 = \sigma_1 \circ (\sigma_2 \circ \sigma_3)}$$

$$\frac{\Delta \vdash \sigma = \sigma' \quad \Delta \vdash \tau_i = \tau_i'}{\Delta \vdash \{\mathbf{sp}{:}\sigma, r_1 \mapsto \tau_1, \ldots, r_n \mapsto \tau_n\} = \{\mathbf{sp}{:}\sigma', r_1{:}\tau_1', \ldots, r_n{:}\tau_n'\}}$$

$$\boxed{\Delta \vdash \tau_1 \leq \tau_2 \quad \Delta \vdash \Gamma_1 \leq \Gamma_2}$$

$$\frac{\Delta \vdash \tau_1 = \tau_2}{\Delta \vdash \tau_1 \leq \tau_2} \qquad \frac{\Delta \vdash \tau_1 \leq \tau_2 \quad \Delta \vdash \tau_2 \leq \tau_3}{\Delta \vdash \tau_1 \leq \tau_3}$$

$$\frac{\Delta \vdash \tau_i}{\Delta \vdash \langle \tau_1^{\varphi_1}, \ldots, \tau_{i-1}^{\varphi_{i-1}}, \tau_i^1, \tau_{i+1}^{\varphi_{i+1}}, \ldots, \tau_n^{\varphi_n} \rangle \leq \langle \tau_1^{\varphi_1}, \ldots, \tau_{i-1}^{\varphi_{i-1}}, \tau_i^0, \tau_{i+1}^{\varphi_{i+1}}, \ldots, \tau_n^{\varphi_n} \rangle}$$

$$\frac{\Delta \vdash \sigma = \sigma' \quad \Delta \vdash \tau_i = \tau_i' \; (\text{for } 1 \leq i \leq n) \quad \Delta \vdash \tau_i \; (\text{for } n < i \leq m)}{\Delta \vdash \{\mathbf{sp}{:}\sigma, r_1{:}\tau_1, \ldots, r_m{:}\tau_m\} \leq \{\mathbf{sp}{:}\sigma', r_1{:}\tau_1', \ldots, r_n{:}\tau_n'\}} \; (m \geq n)$$

**Fig. 9.** Static Semantics of STAL, Judgments for Types

$$\boxed{\vdash P \quad \vdash H : \Psi \quad \Psi \vdash S : \sigma \quad \Psi \vdash R : \Gamma}$$

$$\frac{\vdash H : \Psi \quad \Psi \vdash R : \Gamma \quad \Psi; \cdot; \Gamma \vdash I}{\vdash (H, R, I)}$$

$$\frac{\vdash \Psi \quad \Psi \vdash h_i : \tau_i \ \text{hval}}{\vdash \{\ell_1 \mapsto h_1, \dots, \ell_n \mapsto h_n\} : \Psi} \ (\Psi = \{\ell_1 : \tau_1, \dots, \ell_n : \tau_n\})$$

$$\frac{}{\Psi \vdash nil : nil} \qquad \frac{\Psi; \cdot \vdash w : \tau \ \text{wval} \quad \Psi \vdash S : \sigma}{\Psi \vdash w :: S : \tau :: \sigma}$$

$$\frac{\Psi \vdash S : \sigma \quad \Psi; \cdot \vdash w_i : \tau_i \ \text{wval} \quad (\text{for } 1 \le i \le n)}{\Psi \vdash \{\mathbf{sp} \mapsto S, r_1 \mapsto w_1, \dots, r_m \mapsto w_m\} : \{\mathbf{sp} : \sigma, r_1 : \tau_1, \dots, r_n : \tau_n\}} \ (m \ge n)$$

$$\boxed{\Psi \vdash h : \tau \ \text{hval} \quad \Psi; \Delta \vdash w : \tau \ \text{wval} \quad \Psi; \Delta \vdash w : \tau^\varphi \ \text{fwval} \quad \Psi; \Delta; \Gamma \vdash v : \tau}$$

$$\frac{\Psi; \cdot \vdash w_i : \tau_i^{\varphi_i} \ \text{fwval}}{\Psi \vdash \langle w_1, \dots, w_n \rangle : \langle \tau_1^{\varphi_1}, \dots, \tau_n^{\varphi_n} \rangle \ \text{hval}} \qquad \frac{\Delta \vdash \Gamma \quad \Psi; \Delta; \Gamma \vdash I}{\Psi \vdash \mathbf{code}[\Delta]\Gamma.I : \forall[\Delta].\Gamma \ \text{hval}}$$

$$\frac{\Delta \vdash \tau_1 \le \tau_2}{\Psi; \Delta \vdash \ell : \tau_2 \ \text{wval}} \ (\Psi(\ell) = \tau_1) \qquad \frac{}{\Psi; \Delta \vdash i : int \ \text{wval}}$$

$$\frac{\Delta \vdash \tau \quad \Psi; \Delta \vdash w : \forall[\alpha, \Delta'].\Gamma \ \text{wval}}{\Psi; \Delta \vdash w[\tau] : \forall[\Delta'].\Gamma[\tau/\alpha] \ \text{wval}} \qquad \frac{\Delta \vdash \sigma \quad \Psi; \Delta \vdash w : \forall[\rho, \Delta'].\Gamma \ \text{wval}}{\Psi; \Delta \vdash w[\sigma] : \forall[\Delta'].\Gamma[\sigma/\rho] \ \text{wval}}$$

$$\frac{\Delta \vdash \tau \quad \Psi; \Delta \vdash w : \tau'[\tau/\alpha] \ \text{wval}}{\Psi; \Delta \vdash pack \ [\tau, w] \ as \ \exists \alpha.\tau' : \exists \alpha.\tau' \ \text{wval}} \qquad \frac{}{\Psi; \Delta \vdash ns : ns \ \text{wval}}$$

$$\frac{\Delta \vdash \sigma}{\Psi; \Delta \vdash ptr(i) : ptr(\sigma) \ \text{wval}} \ (|\sigma| = i) \qquad \frac{\Delta \vdash \tau}{\Psi; \Delta \vdash ?\tau : \tau^0 \ \text{fwval}}$$

$$\frac{\Psi; \Delta \vdash w : \tau \ \text{wval}}{\Psi; \Delta \vdash w : \tau^\varphi \ \text{fwval}} \qquad \frac{}{\Psi; \Delta; \Gamma \vdash r : \tau} \ (\Gamma(r) = \tau) \qquad \frac{\Psi; \Delta \vdash w : \tau \ \text{wval}}{\Psi; \Delta; \Gamma \vdash w : \tau}$$

$$\frac{\Delta \vdash \tau \quad \Psi; \Delta; \Gamma \vdash v : \forall[\alpha, \Delta'].\Gamma'}{\Psi; \Delta; \Gamma \vdash v[\tau] : \forall[\Delta'].\Gamma'[\tau/\alpha]} \qquad \frac{\Delta \vdash \sigma \quad \Psi; \Delta; \Gamma \vdash v : \forall[\rho, \Delta'].\Gamma'}{\Psi; \Delta; \Gamma \vdash v[\sigma] : \forall[\Delta'].\Gamma'[\sigma/\rho]}$$

$$\frac{\Delta \vdash \tau \quad \Psi; \Delta; \Gamma \vdash v : \tau'[\tau/\alpha]}{\Psi; \Delta; \Gamma \vdash pack \ [\tau, v] \ as \ \exists \alpha.\tau' : \exists \alpha.\tau'}$$

$$\frac{\cdot \vdash \tau_1 = \tau_2 \quad \Psi \vdash h : \tau_2 \ \text{hval}}{\Psi \vdash h : \tau_1 \ \text{hval}} \qquad \frac{\Delta \vdash \tau_1 = \tau_2 \quad \Psi; \Delta \vdash w : \tau_2 \ \text{wval}}{\Psi; \Delta \vdash w : \tau_1 \ \text{wval}}$$

$$\frac{\Delta \vdash \tau_1 = \tau_2 \quad \Psi; \Delta; \Gamma \vdash v : \tau_2}{\Psi; \Delta; \Gamma \vdash v : \tau_1}$$

$$\boxed{\Psi; \Delta; \Gamma \vdash I}$$

$$\frac{\Psi; \Delta; \Gamma \vdash \iota \Rightarrow \Delta'; \Gamma' \quad \Psi; \Delta'; \Gamma' \vdash I}{\Psi; \Delta; \Gamma \vdash \iota; I} \qquad \frac{\Delta \vdash \Gamma_1 \le \Gamma_2 \quad \Psi; \Delta; \Gamma_1 \vdash v : \forall[].\Gamma_2}{\Psi; \Delta; \Gamma_1 \vdash \mathbf{jmp} \ v}$$

$$\frac{\Delta \vdash \tau \quad \Psi; \Delta; \Gamma \vdash \mathbf{r1} : \tau}{\Psi; \Delta; \Gamma \vdash \mathbf{halt} \ [\tau]}$$

**Fig. 10.** STAL Static Semantics, Term Constructs except Instructions

$$\boxed{\Psi; \Delta; \Gamma \vdash \iota \Rightarrow \Delta'; \Gamma'}$$

$$\frac{\Psi; \Delta; \Gamma \vdash r_s : int \quad \Psi; \Delta; \Gamma \vdash v : int}{\Psi; \Delta; \Gamma \vdash aop\ r_d, r_s, v \Rightarrow \Delta; \Gamma\{r_d{:}int\}}$$

$$\frac{\Psi; \Delta; \Gamma_1 \vdash r : int \quad \Psi; \Delta; \Gamma_1 \vdash v : \forall[].\Gamma_2 \quad \Delta \vdash \Gamma_1 \leq \Gamma_2}{\Psi; \Delta; \Gamma_1 \vdash bop\ r, v \Rightarrow \Delta; \Gamma_1}$$

$$\frac{\Psi; \Delta; \Gamma \vdash r_s : \langle \tau_0^{\varphi_0}, \ldots, \tau_{n-1}^{\varphi_{n-1}} \rangle}{\Psi; \Delta; \Gamma \vdash ld\ r_d, r_s(i) \Rightarrow \Delta; \Gamma\{r_d{:}\tau_i\}} \ (\varphi_i = 1 \wedge 0 \leq i < n)$$

$$\frac{\Delta \vdash \tau_i}{\Psi; \Delta; \Gamma \vdash malloc\ r[\tau_1, \ldots, \tau_n] \Rightarrow \Delta; \Gamma\{r{:}\langle \tau_1^0, \ldots, \tau_n^0 \rangle\}}$$

$$\frac{\Psi; \Delta; \Gamma \vdash v : \tau}{\Psi; \Delta; \Gamma \vdash mov\ r_d, v \Rightarrow \Delta; \Gamma\{r_d{:}\tau\}}$$

$$\frac{}{\Psi; \Delta; \Gamma \vdash mov\ r_d, sp \Rightarrow \Delta; \Gamma\{r_d{:}ptr(\sigma)\}} \ (\Gamma(sp) = \sigma)$$

$$\frac{\Psi; \Delta; \Gamma \vdash r_s : ptr(\sigma_2) \quad \Delta \vdash \sigma_1 = \sigma_3 \circ \sigma_2}{\Psi; \Delta; \Gamma \vdash mov\ sp, r_s \Rightarrow \Delta; \Gamma\{sp{:}\sigma_2\}} \ (\Gamma(sp) = \sigma_1)$$

$$\frac{}{\Psi; \Delta; \Gamma \vdash salloc\ n \Rightarrow \Delta; \Gamma\{sp: \underbrace{ns::\cdots::ns}_{n}::\sigma\}} \ (\Gamma(sp) = \sigma)$$

$$\frac{\Delta \vdash \sigma_1 = \tau_0::\cdots::\tau_{n-1}::\sigma_2}{\Psi; \Delta; \Gamma \vdash sfree\ n \Rightarrow \Delta; \Gamma\{sp{:}\sigma_2\}} \ (\Gamma(sp) = \sigma_1)$$

$$\frac{\Delta \vdash \sigma_1 = \tau_0::\cdots::\tau_i::\sigma_2}{\Psi; \Delta; \Gamma \vdash sld\ r_d, sp(i) \Rightarrow \Delta; \Gamma\{r_d{:}\tau_i\}} \ (\Gamma(sp) = \sigma_1 \wedge 0 \leq i)$$

$$\frac{\Psi; \Delta; \Gamma \vdash r_s : ptr(\sigma_3) \quad \Delta \vdash \sigma_1 = \sigma_2 \circ \sigma_3 \\ \Delta \vdash \sigma_3 = \tau_0::\cdots::\tau_i::\sigma_4}{\Psi; \Delta; \Gamma \vdash sld\ r_d, r_s(i) \Rightarrow \Delta; \Gamma\{r_d{:}\tau_i\}} \ (\Gamma(sp) = \sigma_1 \wedge 0 \leq i)$$

$$\frac{\Delta \vdash \sigma_1 = \tau_0::\cdots::\tau_i::\sigma_2 \quad \Psi; \Delta; \Gamma \vdash r_s : \tau}{\Psi; \Delta; \Gamma \vdash sst\ sp(i), r_s \Rightarrow \Delta; \Gamma\{sp{:}\tau_0::\cdots::\tau_{i-1}::\tau::\sigma_2\}} \ (\Gamma(sp) = \sigma_1 \wedge 0 \leq i)$$

$$\frac{\Psi; \Delta; \Gamma \vdash r_d : ptr(\sigma_3) \quad \Psi; \Delta; \Gamma \vdash r_s : \tau \\ \Delta \vdash \sigma_1 = \sigma_2 \circ \sigma_3 \quad \Delta \vdash \sigma_3 = \tau_0::\cdots::\tau_i::\sigma_4 \\ \Delta \vdash \sigma_5 = \tau_0::\cdots::\tau_{i-1}::\tau::\sigma_4}{\Psi; \Delta; \Gamma \vdash sst\ r_d(i), r_s \Rightarrow \Delta; \Gamma\{sp{:}\sigma_2 \circ \sigma_5, r_d{:}ptr(\sigma_5)\}} \ (\Gamma(sp) = \sigma_1 \wedge 0 \leq i)$$

$$\frac{\Psi; \Delta; \Gamma \vdash r_d : \langle \tau_0^{\varphi_0}, \ldots, \tau_{n-1}^{\varphi_{n-1}} \rangle \quad \Psi; \Delta; \Gamma \vdash r_s : \tau_i}{\Psi; \Delta; \Gamma \vdash st\ r_d(i), r_s \Rightarrow \Delta; \Gamma\{r_d{:}\langle \tau_0^{\varphi_0}, \ldots, \tau_{i-1}^{\varphi_{i-1}}, \tau_i^1, \tau_{i+1}^{\varphi_{i+1}}, \ldots, \tau_{n-1}^{\varphi_{n-1}} \rangle\}} \ (0 \leq i < n)$$

$$\frac{\Psi; \Delta; \Gamma \vdash v : \exists \alpha.\tau}{\Psi; \Delta; \Gamma \vdash unpack\ [\alpha, r_d], v \Rightarrow \alpha, \Delta; \Gamma\{r_d{:}\tau\}} \ (\alpha \notin \Delta)$$

**Fig. 11.** STAL Static Semantics, Instructions

# How Generic is a Generic Back End?
# Using MLRISC as a Back End for the TIL
# Compiler*
# (Preliminary Report)

Andrew Bernard**, Robert Harper, and Peter Lee

School of Computer Science
Carnegie Mellon University
Pittsburgh, PA 15213

**Abstract.** We describe the integration of MLRISC, a "generic" compiler back end, with TIL, a type-directed compiler for Standard ML. The
TIL run-time system uses a form of type information to enable partially
tag-free garbage collection. We show how we propagate this information
through the final phases of the compiler, even though the back end is
unaware of the existence of this information. Additionally, we identify
the characteristics of MLRISC that enable us to use it with TIL and
suggest ways in which it might better support our compiler. Preliminary
performance measurements show that we pay a significant cost for using
MLRISC, relative to a custom back end.

## 1 Introduction

We describe how we integrated *MLRISC*, a "generic" compiler back end, with
*TIL*, a type-directed compiler for the Standard ML (SML) programming language. A *type-directed compiler* uses variable type information to guide succes-
sive translations between intermediate languages [13]. Type-directed compilers
rely on complete variable type information for most or all phases of compilation—
thus, types are preserved by intermediate code transformations during each
phase. A *generic compiler back end* translates a low-level intermediate language

* This research was sponsored in part by the Advanced Research Projects Agency
CSTO under the title "The Fox Project: Advanced Languages for Systems Software",
ARPA Order No. C533, issued by ESC/ENS under Contract No. F19628-95-C-0050,
and in part by the National Science Foundation under Grant No. CCR-9502674. The
views and conclusions contained in this document are those of the authors and should
not be interpreted as representing official policies, either expressed or implied, of the
Defense Advanced Research Projects Agency, the National Science Foundation, or
the U.S. Government.
** This material is based on work supported under under a National Science Foundation Graduate Fellowship. Any opinions, findings, conclusions or recommendations
expressed in this publication are those of the author(s) and do not necessarily reflect
the views of the National Science Foundation.

into machine code—the intention is that the back end does not depend on a particular source language or front-end implementation technology. A compiler back end could itself be type directed—both Typed Assembly Language [12] and Proof-Carrying Code [14] [15] encode variable type information at the assembly-language level—although this is not common practice, and, as a matter of fact, MLRISC is not type directed.

TIL translates a source program through a succession of typed intermediate languages until it arrives at conventional assembly code. The typed intermediate languages used in TIL specify types explicitly at all variable binding sites. Thus, TIL can always determine the type of a variable without having to resort to type inference. The universal availability of type information permits TIL to check types after any phase of compilation—this helps to ensure the correctness of compiler optimizations during development. Type information also allows TIL to perform additional optimizations that are not directly available to conventional compilers [13] [10].

A principal benefit of type-directed compilation is that it facilitates sound *tag-free garbage collection* [18]. Sound garbage collection requires that the heap pointers used by an executing program be identified unambiguously. Tag-free garbage collection permits these heap pointers to be identified without perturbing the run-time representations of values.

In TIL's run-time model, word-sized values (*e.g.*, integers and heap pointers) are not tagged, whereas composite values contain tags for their constituent locations. The *location* of a word-sized value is tagged instead of the value itself—this "out-of-band" tagging scheme allows a single location tag, or *trace value*, to identify many different run-time values. A *trace table* is a static encoding of trace values either for a given procedure activation or for a set of static storage locations. A procedure activation requires trace values for the machine registers used by the procedure as well as its stack frame slots. A complete set of trace tables can be synthesized at compile time for a program because all the possible procedure activation shapes can be statically determined.

*RTL* (Register Transfer Language) is the lowest-level intermediate language used in TIL. A back end for TIL thus translates RTL to assembly language. RTL is an imperative language that resembles the instruction set of a RISC processor, but it also provides complex primitives that are tailored to SML. An RTL *pseudo register* identifies a procedure-local, word-sized storage location: pseudo registers are mapped to machine registers and stack slots by the back end. RTL is not a typed intermediate language, but RTL does annotate pseudo registers with trace values; these are similar to, but distinct from, run-time trace values (the latter are a translation of the former).

There are actually two versions of the TIL compiler: *TIL1* [17] [13] is the first-generation compiler; its successor is called *TILT*. We will refer to the *TIL* compiler when the discussion applies to either compiler interchangeably. Both compilers share a common RTL language: the back end of TIL1 translates RTL directly to assembly language. This back end operates on RTL itself and explicitly propagates trace values through the spilling and register allocation phases.

As only the trace value component of this back end was customized for TIL1, it largely duplicates other work.

MLRISC[1], on the other hand, is a compiler back end implemented in SML that transforms an abstract intermediate language into the assembly language for a particular processor architecture. Taking RTL, MLRISC, and the TIL run-time system as given, our task is to transform RTL code into MLRISC code, and to make the object code generated by MLRISC compatible with the TIL run-time system. We impose an additional constraint on our implementation: we may not customize the interface of MLRISC specifically for TIL, as this would make it necessary to track such customizations across new versions of MLRISC.

As MLRISC does not propagate trace information, we cannot use it as a "drop in" replacement for the TIL1 back end—we must have an additional mechanism that derives run-time trace values from RTL trace values. Run-time trace values are encoded with references to machine register numbers and stack slots. This means that our mechanism must operate in concert with MLRISC, because the global register allocation and spilling phases of MLRISC assign these locations. This is the principal difficulty addressed by our work: how do we translate abstract trace values to concrete trace values "in parallel" with the abstract-to-concrete code translation performed by MLRISC?

Note that significant correctness questions are inevitably raised by the specification of such a translation, because trace values represent invariants—much in the same way that types represent invariants—that may be perturbed by the back end. Trace tables betray an implicit expectation by the run-time system that the object code produced by the back end will (loosely) reflect the original type structure of the program. As the back end is presented with no explicit type structure, how can we expect its code transformations to respect such a type structure? Another contribution of our work is that we describe the implicit constraints that we expect MLRISC to satisfy to ensure the soundness of the trace value translation.

In the remainder of this paper, we focus on how TIL communicates trace information to the run-time system by way of MLRISC. In Section 2 we detail the compiler and run-time system, whereas in Section 3 we present MLRISC. We discuss in Section 4 the techniques we use to marry MLRISC to RTL and the TIL run-time system, and Section 5 is an assessment of our experience. In Section 6 we propose improvements to the current implementation, and in Section 7 we draw together summarizing conclusions.

## 2  TIL

The TIL compiler is characterized by its aggressive use of type information. TIL compiles programs written in the Standard ML '97 programming language to DEC Alpha assembly language. All transformations (i.e., compiler phases)

---

[1] We chose to use MLRISC as a back end for our compiler because our research does not directly address back end implementation technology. With MLRISC, we hope to leverage the work of a larger group of researchers.

in TIL are based on explicitly typed intermediate languages. However, RTL, the lowest-level intermediate language used in TIL, is not typed in the same sense that the other intermediate languages are typed. RTL pseudo registers are tagged with trace values that represent a degenerate form of type information that is tailored to the run-time system. Figure 1 is a depiction of the intermediate languages used in TILT; see Morrisett [13] for a description of the intermediate languages used in TIL1.

SML ➤ Abstract Syntax ➤ HIL ➤ MIL ➤ RTL ➤ MLRISC ➤ Assembly Language

**Fig. 1.** Intermediate Languages in TILT

## 2.1 HIL and MIL

The TILT elaborator translates programs from abstract syntax to *HIL* (High-level Intermediate Language). HIL is an explicitly-typed refinement of the SML programming language, including the module system; a detailed discussion of HIL is beyond the scope of this paper (see Harper and Stone [11] for further details). HIL is translated to *MIL* (Mid-level Intermediate Language) by the *phase splitter*, which is responsible for eliminating modules and breaking abstraction barriers. MIL is a lower-level, explicitly-typed, polymorphic intermediate language that does not provide modules.

## 2.2 RTL

TILT translates MIL to *RTL* (Register Transfer Language) after performing closure conversion, determining data representations, and making heap allocation explicit, among other things. RTL resembles an abstract assembly language in which there are an unbounded supply of local *pseudo registers* for each procedure. Pseudo registers are identified by positive integers and are automatically mapped to machine registers and stack slots by the back end. Each pseudo register is annotated with a trace value that classifies the kinds of values that the register can contain—one can think of trace values as degenerate type information that is present only for the benefit of the run-time system. RTL trace values are derived directly from MIL variable types.

Figure 3 contains one possible RTL translation[2] of the SML function in Figure 2[3]. Pseudo registers are given names (*e.g.*, x) in this example to clarify

---

[2] This is not the actual RTL code currently produced by TILT for this function: it has been simplified by hand to clarify its correspondence to the original SML code. This correspondence is obscured by the poor RTL code that TILT currently generates.

[3] This function was not written to compute anything interesting. Rather, the particular intermediate code it translates to helps to illustrate points later in this paper.

the presentation; in an actual RTL program, pseudo registers are identified by positive integers. Variables introduced by the compiler are prefixed by an underscore. Pseudo register trace values are written following the pseudo-register name in parentheses—trace values encode the "traceability" of a pseudo register, perhaps by projecting the contents of another pseudo register (Table 1). Trace values identify pointers into the heap to the run-time system—we explain the role of run-time trace values in Section 2.3. Section 2.3 also contains a discussion of type environments, of which _tenv1(trace) is one example.

```
fun f(x, n: int, 1: int list, 12: int list) =
    g(x, n, if length 1>0 then hd 1 else 1)
```

**Fig. 2.** An SML Function to Take the Head of a List

| | |
|---|---|
| trace | A pointer into the heap |
| notrace_int | An integer |
| notrace_code | A pointer to machine code |
| notrace_real | A floating-point number |
| label | A pointer to data, but not into the heap |
| compute *path* | May be a pointer into the heap: *path* is an expression that evaluates (at run time) to the actual trace value |
| unset | Uninitialized |
| locative | A pointer into the middle of an item in the heap (cannot be traced) |

**Table 1.** Trace Values for an RTL Pseudo Register

On entry to the body of the procedure, the argument pseudo registers listed in the procedure header contain the values of the actual arguments passed to the procedure. Similarly, on exit from the body, the result pseudo register listed in the procedure header will be copied into the actual machine-level result register, if necessary. The arguments and results of each procedure call are simply listed in order, as RTL uses an implicit calling convention. When a given pseudo register needs to be moved to/from a specific argument/result machine register according to a particular calling convention, this code is generated as part of the call/entry/exit sequence.

## 2.3  The Run-Time System

**Run-time Type Information**  Certain benefits arise from the use of typed intermediate languages: for example, types can be checked after compiler passes to help ensure correctness. Additionally, type-based information can be used at

```
procedure f:
  arguments = [_tenv1(trace),                  ; arguments to f
              x(compute _tenv1(trace).0),
              n(notrace_int),
              l(trace),
              l2(trace)]
  results   = [_t3(notrace_int)]               ; result of f
{
  call     "length"                            ; _t1 <- length(l)
           arguments = [l(trace)]              ; (call #1)
           results   = [_t1(notrace_int)]
  bcndi2   le, _t1(notrace_int), 0, _L1         ; if _t1<=0 goto _L1
  call     "hd"                                ; _t2 <- hd(l)
           arguments = [l(trace)]              ; (call #2)
           results   = [_t2(notrace_int)]
  br       _L2                                 ; goto _L2
_L1:
  mv       1, _t2(notrace_int)                  ; _t2 <- 1
_L2:
  call     "g"                                 ; _t3 <- g(x, n, _t2)
           arguments =                         ; (call #3)
             [_tenv1(trace),
             x(compute _tenv1(trace).0),
             n(notrace_int),
             _t2(notrace_int)]
           results   = [_t3(notrace_int)]
}
```

**Fig. 3.** A Translation of the code in Figure 2 to RTL

run time for dynamic type dispatch and tag-free garbage collection[13]. In TIL, the main ramification for the back end is that the run-time system uses a simple form of type information to reclaim storage.

The TIL run-time system uses a tracing, copying garbage collector to reclaim unused values in the heap. When the garbage collector is invoked, it must determine the locations of all the heap pointers that are in use so that it does not reclaim accessible memory. The garbage collector is said to *trace* these pointers to determine the layout of the objects they address, and to copy these objects to new locations. Traceable pointers may reside in registers, on the stack, in the data segment, or in the heap. However, these locations may also contain a variety of non-pointer values (*e.g.*, word-sized integers) that *cannot* be safely traced. The "traceability" of a given location is determined by its type: trace values, which are derived directly from types, specify to the garbage collector which locations should be traced. Machine registers and stack frame slots are tagged with trace values according to a static table that is indexed by the return address of an active procedure. Static (*i.e.*, global) storage locations are tagged by a corresponding set of static tables. The header of a heap value contains trace values for its slots. Tagging locations is potentially more efficient than tagging values because a single location tag can be shared for many values.

Note that the usual run-time model for garbage collection is *not* tag free. A typical implementation of tagged garbage collection makes the representations of heap pointers and non-heap pointers disjoint by encoding "tags" in the low-order bits of each word. This approach introduces extra overhead, constrains the range of representable values, and complicates interoperability with other languages. Part of the purpose of TIL is to determine whether these pitfalls can be avoided in a garbage-collected programming language implementation.

**Representing Type Information** At run time, vestigial type information is represented as *type environments* and *trace tables*. Type environments supply type information for variables whose types cannot be resolved at compile time (*e.g.*, polymorphic variables). For example, in Figure 2, the type of x is polymorphic and thus cannot be statically determined by the compiler—x could take the value 3, "three", [1, 1, 1], or any of a number of values that have distinct representations at run time. A type environment for f has the caller pass an explicit representation of x's type so that both the run-time system and f can operate on it [18] [10]. Type environments are needed only for functions such as f where complete type information is not available at compile time. A type environment is a record of values that encode properties of types that are important to the run-time system. Note that type environments are unlike the explicit value descriptors used in many other language implementations, in that type environments are constructed only in contexts where they are specifically needed, as opposed to being an integral part of every value.

Trace tables map machine registers, stack slots, and static locations to trace values. A trace table gives a value of yes to those locations that are known to contain pointers into the heap. Other trace values allow the status of a location to depend on a type environment or on the dynamic caller's trace table: the trace values that can be attached to a storage location by a trace table are documented in Table 2. This table resembles Table 1 because run-time trace values are derived from the corresponding RTL trace values. By contrast, objects in the heap have special headers that specify trace values for locations in the object.

| | |
|---|---|
| `yes` | Contains a pointer into the heap |
| `no` | Does not contain a pointer into the heap |
| `callee` *id* | Contains the *saved value* of a callee-save register: *id* identifies a machine register in the dynamic caller's activation whose trace value should be used for this location. |
| `stack` *offset, index* | A polymorphic location: *offset* is the offset in the current stack frame of a pointer to a type environment that contains the trace value of this location at index *index*. |
| `global` *label, index* | A polymorphic location: *label* is the label of a type environment in the data segment that contains the trace value of this location at index *index*. |
| `unset` | Uninitialized |
| `impossible` | Contains a heap pointer, but cannot be traced |

**Table 2.** Trace Values for a Trace Table Storage Location

**Locating Pointers** Trace tables are consulted by the run-time system only when the garbage collector is invoked. This invocation takes the form of a library call from an active procedure that is unable to allocate storage. At this time, the collector must locate and trace all pointers into the heap: this process is nontrivial because pointers can potentially reside in any machine register, stack location, or static variable, and because the pointers themselves contain no identifying information (*e.g.*, tags). For static variables, we create a table in a known location that points to the trace tables for all static regions. Tracing the stack is more difficult because the stack depends on the dynamic behavior of the program. However, there are only a statically computable number of distinct activations, each of which can be determined by the compiler. Thus, we index a static table for each activation record according to the return address of a call site in the corresponding procedure. Because the collector is invoked via a procedure call, we simply use the return address in its activation record to locate the trace table of the most recent stack frame. Each trace table includes the size of its stack frame, so we can use these offsets to "walk up" the stack. This means that we need to generate a trace table for each direct call to the collector and for each call to another procedure that might indirectly call the collector[4].

At collection time, a callee-save register initialized by an active procedure may have had its value saved on the stack by another procedure, or the original

---

[4] In practice, we simply assume that all procedures might indirectly call the collector.

value may be left intact. The trace table of the most recent procedure activation holds the correct trace values for the machine register file at the time the collector is invoked. If any callee-save registers are not allocated by the most recently called procedure, then their trace values are determined according to the trace table of the next most recently called procedure: this is the function of the callee trace value. A callee trace value is also possible when a callee-save register is saved to the stack (and the register is presumably overwritten)—in this case, the proper stack location is given the callee trace value and the trace table of the next most recent activation record is consulted to determine the status of the stack location. This process can continue as long as the trace value of a location is specified as callee.

**Example** In Figure 4, we show a possible DEC Alpha Assembly Language translation of the example function of Figure 2, whereas in Figure 5 we document the registers used in Figure 4. $_tenv, $x, $n, $1, and $12 are assigned to callee-save temporaries in this procedure (*e.g.*, $11, $12, etc. according to the standard calling convention). $_tenv1 contains the type environment for the function. The procedure begins by allocating a stack frame of size 32 and saving the return address and the callee-save registers on the stack. The arguments to the procedure are then moved from registers defined by the calling convention into the corresponding callee-save temporaries. Next, a call is made to length with the value of l as an argument (the standard calling convention requires all calls to jump through $pv). The result of the length call is then compared against zero and a branch is taken to _L1 if it is not strictly positive. Assuming the branch is not taken, a call is made to hd and the result is saved in $t2; otherwise $t2 gets the value 1. The two control paths next converge at a call to g with arguments x, n, and $t2—the result of this call becomes the result of f after it restores the caller's register file from the stack frame. The ldgp instructions are a peculiarity of the Alpha standard calling convention.

The important things to notice in Figure 4 are the three call sites (commented (call #*n*)) for which we must construct trace tables. These trace tables must correctly identify the trace status of values in the register file and the local stack frame at the time of the corresponding call. In Figure 6, we show a trace table for call #2—notice that the trace values of stack slots saving callee-save registers depend on the dynamic caller's trace table (these slots are given trace status callee *n*).

## 3  MLRISC

MLRISC [8] is a generic compiler back end developed by Lal George at Bell Laboratories. MLRISC is "generic" in the sense that it can be used to compile many different programming languages. The interface language to MLRISC, also called "MLRISC", is essentially an architecture-independent assembly language: MLRISC is thus suited to compiling programming languages for which a translation to assembly language is feasible; to date, MLRISC has been used to compile SML

```
f:      ldgp    $gp, 0($pv)        ; set global pointer
        subl    $sp, 32, $sp       ; alloc frame
        stl     $ra, 0($sp)        ; save return address
        stl     $_tenv, 8($sp)     ; save callee save
        stl     $x, 12($sp)
        stl     $n, 16($sp)
        stl     $1, 20($sp)
        stl     $12, 24($sp)
        mov     $arg0, $_tenv      ; get arguments
        mov     $arg1, $x
        mov     $arg2, $n
        mov     $arg3, $1
        mov     $arg4, $12
        stl     $_tenv, 28($sp)    ; save type environment
        mov     $1, $arg0          ; $t1 <- length(1)
        lda     $pv, length
        jsr     $ra, ($pv)         ; (call #1)
        ldgp    $gp, 0($ra)        ; set global pointer
        cmple   $res, 0, $t0       ; if $t1<=0 goto _L1
        bne     $t0, _L1
        mov     $1, $arg0          ; $t2 <- hd(1)
        lda     $pv, hd
        jsr     $ra, ($pv)         ; (call #2)
        ldgp    $gp, 0($ra)        ; set global pointer
        mov     $res, $t2
        br      $zero, _L2         ; goto _L2
_L1:    lda     $t2, 1             ; $t2 <- 1
_L2:    mov     $_tenv, $arg0      ; $t3 <- g(x, n, $t2)
        mov     $x, $arg1
        mov     $n, $arg2
        mov     $t2, $arg3
        lda     $pv, g
        jsr     $ra, ($pv)         ; (call #3)
        ldgp    $gp, 0($ra)        ; set global pointer
        ldl     $ra, 0($sp)        ; restore return address
        ldl     $_tenv, 8($sp)     ; restore callee save
        ldl     $x, 12($sp)
        ldl     $n, 16($sp)
        ldl     $1, 20($sp)
        ldl     $12, 24($sp)
        addl    $sp, 32, $sp       ; dealloc frame
        jmp     $zero, ($ra)       ; return
```

**Fig. 4.** A Translation of the SML function in Figure 2 to DEC Alpha Assembly Language

$sp Stack pointer
$pv Call address
$ra Return address

$argn Argument $n$
$res Result
$tn Caller-save temporary $n$
$zero Always zero

**Fig. 5.** Registers Used in Figure 4

| $_tenv | yes | | Always trace |
|---|---|---|---|
| $x | stack 28, | 0 | Trace according to $_tenv |
| $n | no | | Never trace |
| | | | |
| 8($sp) | callee | $_tenv | Use dynamic caller's trace value for $_tenv |
| 12($sp) | callee | $x | Use dynamic caller's trace value for $x |
| 16($sp) | callee | $n | Use dynamic caller's trace value for $n |
| 20($sp) | callee | $1 | Use dynamic caller's trace value for $1 |
| 24($sp) | callee | $12 | Use dynamic caller's trace value for $12 |
| 28($sp) | yes | | Always trace |

**Fig. 6.** A Trace Table for Call #2 of Figure 4

and Tiger [3]. Our compiler differs from other compilers using MLRISC [4] [2] [3], however, in that TIL does not use dynamic tag bits to distinguish heap pointers from other word-sized values.

In MLRISC, as in RTL, local storage locations are identified by numbered *pseudo registers*. Pseudo registers are transparently mapped to machine registers or spilled to the stack by MLRISC. Pseudo registers in MLRISC, however, carry no trace values or other type information; there are distinct classes of integer, floating-point, and condition-code pseudo registers, but an integer pseudo register that happens to be used as a heap pointer is not distinguished in any way. The principal challenge in integrating MLRISC with TIL, then, is to propagate pseudo-register trace values to the run-time system in the form of run-time trace values. Because pseudo registers are transformed into machine registers and stack slots, trace values for these locations will be based on the code transformations performed by MLRISC (*e.g.*, register allocation, spilling).

In Figure 7, we show the SML function in Figure 2 as it might be translated to MLRISC. Pseudo registers are given names (*e.g.*, x) in this example to clarify the presentation; in an actual MLRISC program, pseudo registers are identified by positive integers (*e.g.*, 500). Machine registers are referred to by a small positive integer (*e.g.*, 16) and can be used interchangeably with pseudo registers in MLRISC code. Names generated by the compiler are prefixed by an underscore; _tenv1 contains the type environment (see Section 2.3) for the function and cs1 through cs5 are used to hold the saved values of the callee-save registers. Following the Alpha standard calling convention, this code uses machine registers 16 through 20 to hold arguments and register 0 to hold the result; in MLRISC, unlike RTL, calling conventions are explicitly specified in terms of primitive op-

erations. An MLRISC procedure is a sequence of imperative *statements*, each
of which may refer to applicative *expressions*; the terms "statement" and "expression" have the normal connotations of programming language terminology.
In Table 3 and Table 4, we document the MLRISC constructs used in this example. Expressions can be nested to an arbitrary depth, so, in general, a single
statement can generate many assembly language instructions.

| | |
|---|---|
| bcc *cexp, label* | Branch to label *label* if the result of evaluating conditional expression *cexp* is true. |
| call *addr* | Call the procedure at the address formed by evaluating expression *addr*. |
| copy *dst, src* | Copy the registers listed in *src* into the corresponding registers listed in *dst*; this is a "parallel" operation: no register can appear more than once in the union of *src* and *dst*. copy statements are coalesced [9] by MLRISC whenever possible. |
| mv *dst, exp* | Move the result of evaluating expression *exp* into register *dst*. |
| jmp *addr* | Jump to the code at the address formed by evaluating expression *addr*. |
| ret | Return from the current procedure. |
| store32 *addr, exp* | Store the result of evaluating expression *exp* as a 32-bit value at the address formed by evaluating expression *addr*. |

**Table 3.** Selected MLRISC Statements

# 4 Techniques

This section discusses the translation techniques we use to integrate MLRISC
with TIL. In Section 4.1 we touch on the technology that translates RTL code
to MLRISC code, whereas in Section 4.2 we outline how we construct trace
tables for MLRISC from RTL trace values. Finally, in Section 4.3 we justify the
correctness of trace values for translated code.

## 4.1 From RTL to MLRISC

Translating RTL "instructions" to MLRISC "statements" is relatively straightforward—the principal difficulty lies in generating efficient code for conditional
branches. RTL provides two forms of conditional branch instruction: one that
compares a pseudo register against zero, and one that compares two pseudo
registers. The current translation from MIL to RTL favors the former kind of
branch, even for comparisons between two pseudo registers. It does this by storing the boolean result of each comparison in a third pseudo register and then
testing the third pseudo register against zero. Although this idiom matches the
use of conditionals in certain RISC architectures (*e.g.*, the Alpha), it cannot

```
f:
    mv       gp, reg pv                       ; set global pointer
    mv       sp, sub(reg sp, const frame)     ; alloc frame
    store32  add(reg sp, li 0), reg ra        ; save return address
    copy     [cs1, cs2, cs3, cs4, cs5],
             [11, 12, 13, 14, 15]             ; save callee save
    copy     [_tenv1, x, n, 1, 12],
             [16, 17, 18, 19, 20]             ; get arguments
    store32  add(reg sp,
                 const _tenv1_offset),
             reg _tenv1                       ; save type environment
    copy     [16], [1]                        ; _t1 <- length(1)
    mv       pv, label "length"
    call     reg pv                           ; (call #1)
    mv       gp, reg pv                       ; set global pointer
    copy     [_t1], [0]
    bcc      cmp(le, reg _t1, li 0), _L1      ; if _t1<=0 goto _L1
    copy     [16], [1]                        ; _t2 <- hd(1)
    mv       pv, label "hd"
    call     reg pv                           ; (call #2)
    mv       gp, reg pv                       ; set global pointer
    copy     [_t2], [0]
    jmp      label _L2                        ; goto _L2
_L1:
    mv       _t2, li 1                        ; _t2 <- 1
_L2:
    copy     [16, 17, 18, 19],
             [_tenv1, x, n, _t2]              ; _t3 <- g(x, n, _t2)
    mv       pv, label "g"
    call     reg pv                           ; (call #3)
    mv       gp, reg pv                       ; set global pointer
    copy     [_t3], [0]
    copy     [0], [_t3]
    mv       ra, add(reg sp, li 0),           ; restore return address
    copy     [11, 12, 13, 14, 15],
             [cs1, cs2, cs3, cs4, cs5]        ; restore callee save
    mv       sp, add(reg sp, const frame)     ; dealloc frame
    ret                                       ; return
```

**Fig. 7.** A Translation of the SML function in Figure 2 to MLRISC

| | |
|---|---|
| add (*exp1*, *exp2*) | Evaluates to the result of adding the results of evaluating *exp1* and *exp2*. |
| cmp (*cmp*, *exp1*, *exp2*) | Evaluates to true if the result of evaluating *exp1* and *exp2* are ordered according to comparison *cmp*. This expression evaluates to a condition code, as opposed to an integer. |
| const *fn* | Evaluates to the result of calling the function *fn* during the final code generation phase. const allows constants in the final assembly language program to depend on the results of earlier phases (*e.g.*, spilling). |
| label *string* | Evaluates to the address of label *string*. |
| li *n* | Evaluates to the integer *n*. |
| load32 *addr* | Evaluates to the result of loading a 32-bit value from the address formed by evaluating expression *addr*. |
| reg *id* | Evaluates to the contents of pseudo register *id*. |
| sub (*exp1*, *exp2*) | Evaluates to the result of subtracting the result of evaluating *exp2* from the result of evaluating *exp1*. |

**Table 4.** Selected MLRISC Expressions

be expressed efficiently in MLRISC, because there is no statement to move the result of a comparison directly into an integer pseudo register. We address this problem by "preprocessing" the RTL code into two-operand conditional branch form whenever the result of a compare instruction is used by an immediately following branch instruction, *and* the boolean result is not used anywhere else in the procedure.

Although RTL and MLRISC treat pseudo registers in much the same way (*i.e.*, as local storage locations for a procedure), one cannot interchange the two notions. For example, the MLRISC translation of an RTL instruction that refers to pseudo register 500 cannot simply refer to pseudo register 500, because pseudo registers in MLRISC code must be allocated explicitly through MLRISC. To overcome this difficulty, we maintain a mapping from RTL pseudo registers to MLRISC pseudo registers and allocate a new pseudo register from MLRISC whenever we see an RTL pseudo register that does not have an existing mapping. As MLRISC pseudo registers, unlike RTL pseudo registers, carry no explicit trace values, we construct a separate mapping from MLRISC pseudo registers to run-time trace values. Storing the trace values "off to the side" allows us to forget about RTL pseudo registers entirely for the later phases of the translation.

Our translation "forces" certain pseudo registers to spill by manually replacing them with memory accesses; this transformation is accomplished as a separate pass over the MLRISC code just before we pass it to MLRISC. Pseudo registers that are forced to spill include those holding type environments referred to by trace values, those saving callee-save registers in the presence of exception handlers, as well as any global registers that do not fit in the machine register file. Because the trace value of a given pseudo register can refer to a type environment on the stack to resolve its status (*e.g.*, stack in Table 2), we must ensure that these type environments are in fact on the stack and not being held in a machine register. The callee-save registers must be restored to their former values at the end of an exception handler, so we force the pseudo registers that are used to save these registers to be spilled to the stack so that we can later restore them. Finally, for performance, TIL reserves a small number of machine registers to hold global values that are used by most procedures (*e.g.*, the current heap and limit pointers). Unfortunately, certain machine architectures (most notably, the Intel x86) do not have enough registers for this scheme to be feasible, so we rewrite code using these registers with references to global memory locations.

## 4.2 Constructing Trace Tables

The most interesting part of the translation from RTL to MLRISC is constructing trace tables for call sites. As MLRISC does not explicitly propagate type information, we construct trace tables by passing trace values "around" MLRISC's code generator. Trace tables are represented as *data* pseudo operations that are compiled into the data segment of the program.

Because trace tables are encoded in terms of machine register numbers and stack offsets, and because trace values are attached indirectly to pseudo registers, we must account for the results of spilling and register allocation during trace table generation. For example, if pseudo register 500 has the run-time trace value **yes** and is mapped to machine register 12, then a trace table should contain a **yes** entry for machine register 12. This implies that we must generate code and trace table data in separate phases—first we translate the code to obtain a pseudo-register mapping, then we generate trace table data based on this mapping. We must also generate a single trace table for all the static locations in a module: this is accomplished by mapping the RTL label for each static location to a corresponding MLRISC label. In Figure 8 we illustrate how an RTL module containing procedures and static variables is transformed into MLRISC code statements and data directives. Note that for reasons of expediency, trace tables are generated first in terms of RTL data directives which are then translated to MLRISC data directives. This allows us to reuse the trace table module from the TIL1 back end.

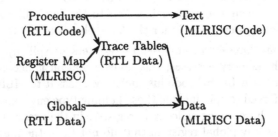

**Fig. 8.** Generating MLRISC Code and Trace Tables from RTL

The results of register allocation and spilling are not difficult to obtain from MLRISC. The mapping from pseudo registers to machine registers is exported as a data structure by the MLRISC interface. We can construct the mapping from spilled pseudo registers to stack offsets because MLRISC spills pseudo registers via a "call back" to our code. It is important to understand that the mappings used by these phases must be accessible for our technique to work—for a back end that does not export this information, we cannot determine how the pseudo registers are represented at run time, and therefore cannot construct trace tables from pseudo-register trace values. This problem is explored further in Section 5.2

## 4.3  Register Allocation

Suppose that in Figure 7, pseudo-registers 12 (trace value **yes**) and _t2 (trace value **no**) have both been mapped to machine register 4 by MLRISC's register allocator. Which trace value should we give machine register 4 when constructing a trace table? Obviously, we cannot resolve this conflict with just the pseudo-register mapping—we should look at the code to determine which pseudo register was *defined* most recently on the control path to the call site in question. However, because the code may contain arbitrary branches and loops, a linear scan will not resolve this ambiguity in general. Notice that pseudo registers can be mapped to the same machine register only if they have non-overlapping live ranges: otherwise, definitions of the pseudo registers would interfere with each other. Thus, for a given call site we can resolve a conflicting register assignment by choosing the trace value of the pseudo register that is live across the call site [7], as there can be only one.

Figure 7 additionally illustrates a deeper problem, in that the correct trace value for machine register 4 at `call #3` depends on the run-time contents of pseudo-register _t1: if _t1 is greater than zero, then machine register 4 will be overwritten by the result of `call #2`. This example suggests that there are cases where the code generation transformations induced by the back end will make it impossible to give a fixed trace value to a particular machine register. Fortunately, such unpredictable trace values can only arise when none of the pseudo registers in question are live across the call site—otherwise, the generated code would be incorrect, because the definition of one pseudo register could interfere with the later use of another.

Returning to our example, we know that neither 12 nor _t2 can be used after `call #3`, because such a use might read the value of the wrong pseudo register. This observation suggests that we must take into account the next *use* of a pseudo register *after* the call site as well as its *definition before* the call site—it is not sufficient to simply note the trace value at the most recent definition. We can give a machine register the trace value **no** if the contents of that register will not be used after the corresponding call site: because the register will not be used, its contents need not be retained by the garbage collector. This happy coincidence allows us to give the trace value **no** to machine register 4 for our example.

Thus, to construct a trace table for a given call site, we map the pseudo registers live across the site through the pseudo-register mapping and pair the resulting machine registers with the trace values for the corresponding pseudo registers. All other machine registers are given the trace value no. Liveness analysis has the added benefit of minimizing storage retained during garbage collection. This, in turn, enhances performance by reducing the load on the collector and also enables certain programs to terminate that would not otherwise [16]. Our liveness analysis is based on well-understood data-flow techniques [1]. Note that the call-site liveness analysis must be at least as precise as the register-allocation liveness analysis for this technique to work.

We give trace values to stack slots holding spilled pseudo registers with an analogous technique—in Figure 9 we show the construction of a trace table for call #2 of Figure 7 from the live pseudo-register set, a run-time trace value mapping, and a sample MLRISC register mapping.

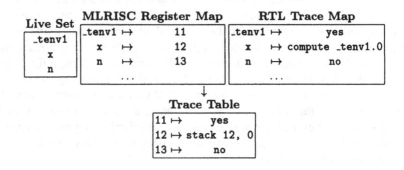

**Fig. 9.** Constructing a Trace Table

# 5    Assessment

## 5.1    TIL

RTL is not well-suited as a source language for MLRISC because the languages are similar enough that the translation between them is essentially wasted work. The principal difference between RTL and MLRISC is that RTL pseudo registers are annotated with trace information; as we describe in Section 4.1, it is not difficult to simulate this capability for MLRISC pseudo registers, so there is no compelling reason to use RTL as a separate translation step. We thus see the use of RTL as an intermediate language as vestigial: we plan to translate directly from the MIL intermediate language in the future. We originally decided to translate from RTL to expedite development of the compiler, as MIL was in a fluid state of development at the time.

## 5.2 MLRISC

This section seeks to identify the specific features of MLRISC that made it possible for us to integrate it with TIL. We also suggest additional features not found in MLRISC that would have made our job easier, or would have resulted in more efficient code generation. We speculate that our experience may be of use to designers of other generic back-ends [5] [6].

We divide the relevant features into two classes: those that are essential to the propagation of type information, and those that can enhance performance or simplify translation when using type-directed techniques. An underlying theme of our characterization is that the back end needs to do more than simply emit assembly code on behalf of the client—it should also return information about *how* the translation was accomplished.

We first present a brief summary of our conclusions. These are the key features of MLRISC that enable the type-directed translation techniques of our compiler:

- A visible pseudo-register-to-machine-register mapping
- A machine-register mapping that is unique for a given pseudo register
- A visible pseudo-register-to-stack-slot mapping
- A spilled pseudo register will not also be mapped to a machine register

These are features not found in MLRISC that might enhance the performance of our translation:

- Visible liveness information
- An extensible spill mechanism

**Essential Features** As the TIL run-time system uses trace tables that contain machine register numbers, a client-accessible pseudo-register mapping is needed to propagate trace values. Input trace values are attached to pseudo registers, so we must be able to uncover which pseudo registers are mapped to which machine registers if we are to encode trace value mappings for the latter. Although it might be possible to deduce the pseudo-register mapping by comparing the output object code with the input pseudo code, this is likely to be difficult for a back end that performs aggressive optimizations (*e.g.*, global instruction scheduling).

The shape of the mapping to machine registers can also present problems to the implementor. MLRISC maps each pseudo register to at most one machine register [9]; thus, when an unspilled pseudo register is live across a call site, we can always precisely identify which machine register it is mapped to. If a single pseudo register might be mapped to one of several machine registers at different points in the code, then MLRISC would need to tell us the mapping ranges for each register. Again, it might be possible to deduce this information from the object code—or even from the pseudo code, if we know the back end's register allocation algorithm—but such a deduction algorithm is likely to be complex and correspondingly inefficient.

Given the mapping to machine registers, we must have a similar mapping to stack slots for pseudo registers that have been spilled transparently by the back end. For MLRISC, there is no special interface to this information, but because we implement the spill mechanism ourselves[5], we can easily reconstruct it. If a back end does not provide a customizable spill mechanism, it must allow the client to query the spill status and location of a given pseudo register so that trace value mappings can be constructed for the stack.

Note that to simplify trace table generation, we ensure that a spilled pseudo register will never be mapped to a machine register (*i.e.*, a spilled pseudo register is always on the stack for its entire lifetime). This is accomplished by allocating a new temporary and rewriting the instruction referring to the spilled pseudo register with a reference to the temporary instead; a store instruction (or load in the case of a reload) is then appended (or prepended) to the rewritten instruction. Because the lifetime of the temporary is only between the rewritten instruction and the store (or load), we can assume that it will never be live across a call site [7], and thus need not be traced. Although such a temporary will never be traced, the stack slot containing the original value still might be traced if it is live across the call site in question. Making the "spilled to the stack" and "mapped to a machine register" states exclusive for a given pseudo register simplifies the process of constructing trace tables—if we could not assume this, then we would have to track *where* the pseudo register is moved to or from the stack and which location(s) (stack slot or register) its next use(s) expect it to be in. As this information is not exported by MLRISC, it is not clear how we would recover it.

Our assumption about the lifetimes of spill temporaries may not hold in the presence of global instruction scheduling, but as MLRISC does not currently perform global instruction scheduling, our implementation is sound for the moment. To implement our translation in the presence of global instruction scheduling, we would need access to the liveness analysis of the back end, or we would need to be able to constrain the scheduling of instructions referring to potentially traceable values. Note that the former solution has the added benefit of reducing the overhead incurred by our translation.

**Desirable Features** It is unfortunate that we must perform a data-flow analysis to determine liveness across call sites, because this work will be largely duplicated by MLRISC's register allocator. It would be more efficient if we could derive call site liveness from the register allocator's own liveness information. This might be accomplished in a hypothetical version of MLRISC by returning the pseudo registers that are live into and out of each basic block as part of the translation to assembly language. Additionally, each call site must be isolated in its own basic block: this could be done by TIL if MLRISC were to provide a way to explicitly delimit basic blocks. Note that because spilling is performed in a pass prior to register allocation, liveness information may be lost for spilled pseudo

---

[5] When MLRISC decides to spill a pseudo register, it calls a client-supplied function to return an architecture-specific code sequence for the spill.

registers when they are replaced by memory accesses—unless MLRISC retains information showing that they cannot be aliased, it will have to assume that they are always live after the first definition. It might be possible to deduce the liveness of spilled pseudo registers by analyzing the spill and reload patterns via another data-flow analysis, but this seems counterproductive. It is not correct to simply assume that spilled pseudo registers are always live, because the contents of a given stack slot may not be initialized until after the first call site.

Our translation to MLRISC includes a "forced spill" pass (see Section 4.1) that replaces certain pseudo registers with memory accesses. As MLRISC implements a similar spilling pass, it would save implementation time if MLRISC were to allow the client to provide an additional spill set as a part of code generation. This would avoid the extra spill pass that currently handles our special spill cases.

## 5.3 Performance

**Benchmarks** Because the optimizer in the TILT compiler is still under construction, we cannot yet take meaningful performance measurements of the object code produced by MLRISC in conjunction with TILT. However, because TILT and TIL1 use the same RTL intermediate language, we can use MLRISC as a back end for the TIL1 compiler: in Table 5, we present the relative execution times of some of the benchmark programs from Tarditi *et al.* [17]. These measurements show that by using MLRISC as a back end for TIL1, we introduce a significant amount of overhead into the generated code. We believe that this overhead is due to complications in the translation of RTL code to MLRISC code, and is not due to MLRISC itself.

| Program | TIL1 | TIL1-MLRISC | TIL1-MLRISC/TIL1 |
|---------|------|-------------|------------------|
| FFT | 2.02 | 2.49 | 1.23 |
| Knuth-Bendix | 2.28 | 2.70 | 1.18 |
| Lexgen | 2.66 | 3.09 | 1.16 |
| Life | 2.07 | 2.51 | 1.21 |
| Matmult | 2.66 | 2.61 | 0.98 |
| Simple | 11.91 | 14.03 | 1.18 |

**Table 5.** TIL1-MLRISC Execution Time Relative to TIL1

The execution times in Table 5 are the time in seconds required to execute the programs on a DEC Alpha 3000/600 workstation with 96mb of RAM. This workstation has a 175MHz Alpha 21064 processor with 8k primary instruction and data caches and a 2mb unified secondary cache. Each figure is the arithmetic mean of ten consecutive runs of the corresponding program. See Tarditi *et al.* [17] for descriptions of the benchmark programs.

We made one change to MLRISC for the purpose of benchmarking: MLRISC ordinarily generates floating-point arithmetic instructions with the sud flags set in the instruction word. Because these instructions are emulated in software on our workstation, we replaced them with the equivalent "garden-variety" instructions (e.g. addt instead of addt/sud). The sud flags control the precise semantics of floating-point operations—see the *Alpha Architecture Handbook* for more information. As use of the sud flags makes the FFT benchmark about 300 times slower on our workstation, it is not meaningful to take performance measurements with them set.

We used a calling convention without integer callee-save registers for these benchmarks because, when used with TIL1, MLRISC often allocates pseudo registers to callee-save registers in such a way that violates the constraints of our trace table encoding. In particular, our encoding requires that the contents of a callee-save register either be saved on the stack or be left in the original machine register during the activation of a procedure. When used with TIL1, however, MLRISC often allocates the pseudo registers used to save the callee-save registers to other (different) callee-save registers—this is not expressible in our trace table encoding. We have encountered this problem with much less frequency when using MLRISC as a back end for TILT, but it remains unresolved.

**Target Code** The principal techniques outlined in this paper for interfacing MLRISC to TIL operate only on type information, and therefore should not have a direct effect on object code quality. However, there are sources of inefficiency in the code transformations performed by our translation. Additionally, the limitations of these techniques may introduce performance-limiting constraints when used with other back ends.

To elaborate on the former point, the details of the translation from RTL to MLRISC has a significant effect on the ultimate quality of the object code, as is indicated by the discussion of conditional branch translation in Section 4.1. It is clear, however, that this particular difficulty arises as an artifact of an unfortunate mismatch between the semantics of conditional values in RTL and MLRISC, and does not represent a general problem with the interaction between TIL and MLRISC.

Another valid question might arise about whether the "forced spill" phase outlined in Section 5.2 will introduce so many new spills as to significantly degrade performance. Although it seems unlikely that the indiscriminate spilling of type environments will have a measurable effect on performance, one cannot so easily dismiss the spilling of the callee-save registers and the pervasive global registers. Note, however, that in each of these cases, spilling is introduced as a consequence of constraints imposed by the run-time system, and not as a consequence of a poor interaction between the compiler and the back end. Thus, the forced spill phase is really a function of the run-time architecture used with TIL and will be required in some form whether or not the object code is generated by MLRISC. A general discussion of the performance of type-directed run-time architectures is beyond the scope of this paper, but see Tarditi *et al.* [17] and Morrisett [13].

A potential performance problem that *is* directly related to the use of ML-RISC as a back end for TIL concerns the constraints that our techniques impose on a back end to simplify trace table generation. These restrictions are discussed in Section 5.2, and although none of them appear to be especially restrictive, it will be difficult to demonstrate this without measurements. Unfortunately, this is particularly awkward to do for our technology, as only one of these constraints (spilled pseudo registers) can be alleviated in MLRISC. Even if we were to remove this limitation, however, we would not be able to execute the resulting code because of the absence of trace tables. It might be more productive to examine individual measurements of these code generation features on other compiler platforms and then use the results as a guide to forming conclusions about the potential drawbacks of our techniques.

**Compilation Speed** A final performance consideration relates to how the use of our techniques affects the speed of compilation. Because we perform an extra liveness analysis before code generation (see Section 4.3), there is a potential for inefficiency here. Preliminary measurements show that our use of MLRISC has a significant performance cost: the combined RTL-to-MLRISC translation and the subsequent MLRISC code generation phases together perform at less than half the speed of the TIL1 back end when used with TILT. These same measurements also indicate that the bulk of the time is being spent in translation code external to MLRISC; MLRISC on its own is usually faster than the TIL1 back end. Unfortunately, we have not yet isolated the source of this inefficiency: the extra liveness analysis by itself only accounts for a fraction of the translation overhead—it typically consumes less than 5 percent of the total compilation time. It is certainly possible that most of the translation overhead is caused by unoptimized code on our end. In our opinion, it is too early to draw meaningful conclusions about the performance of the translation itself, as there may still be room for substantial optimization.

# 6 Future Work

In this section, we discuss features of MLRISC that are currently underutilized.

MLRISC is able to perform inter-procedural register allocation on procedures in the same call graph. We do not currently take advantage of this feature, but hope to utilize it once we fully understand the complications with regard to trace table construction. Because ML programs typically use function calls for looping, the performance benefits of this optimization may be significant when the compiler has not entirely optimized away procedure calls.

MLRISC does not currently perform any global instruction scheduling, but we expect that it will eventually do so. We anticipate that this optimization will introduce complications into our call-site liveness analysis because the live ranges of pseudo registers will be perturbed across basic blocks. For example, if the first definition of a traceable pseudo register is moved forward past a call site, then the garbage collector will trace an uninitialized value at that call site if no corrective action is taken. Because basic blocks in ML programs tend to be so small that local instruction scheduling has little benefit, we think it will be important to find a solution to this problem that does not unduly constrain the back end. This topic is also discussed in Section 5.2

MLRISC provides condition-code pseudo registers in addition to integer and floating-point pseudo registers. We currently do not use these pseudo registers because RTL does not distinguish condition codes from integers. A direct translation from MIL might make it easier to take advantage of these registers and also to correct some additional inefficiencies in the translation of conditional branches.

Finally, we hope to isolate the source of the current translation inefficiency so that using MLRISC with TILT is not significantly slower than using the TIL1 back end. We also hope to improve the performance of the object code generated by MLRISC once implementation of the TILT optimizer is complete.

## 7 Conclusion

We have presented our approach to integrating MLRISC, a generic back end, with TIL, a type-directed compiler. Our work is a solution to a specific instance of a more general problem: how can abstract trace information be mapped to concrete trace information, given that the correct mapping is a function of a parallel code translation performed by the back end? Register allocation and spilling are the critical code translations that must be reproduced to translate trace information. MLRISC exports its register and spill mappings: it is this property of MLRISC that makes it possible to use it with our compiler.

As important parts of TILT are still being developed, we cannot draw definitive conclusions yet about the merits of our approach. It is currently unclear if the use of MLRISC will give us a significant improvement in object code quality. It is also unclear whether the "scaffolding" we have constructed around MLRISC can be made efficient enough not to seriously degrade compilation time.

It is reasonable to object to our use of RTL as an intermediate language between MIL and MLRISC, because RTL serves essentially the same purpose as MLRISC. We chose to retain RTL from TIL1 only to better compartmentalize our development effort. One could argue that some of the problems we have encountered are due more to the use of RTL than to the use of MLRISC. In particular, we expect that in a hypothetical translation from MIL to MLRISC, a redundant liveness analysis on MIL code would be less onerous due to its more structured control flow. This would appear to undermine our contention that the back end should export the results of its liveness analysis for use by the rest of the compiler. However, we do not believe that simply performing the call-site liveness analysis on MIL code is an adequate long-term solution, because it is not clear that liveness of variables in MIL code necessarily corresponds to liveness of machine registers and stack slots in machine code—we even know that this correspondence will not hold in the presence of global instruction scheduling. For this reason, we think that the availability of liveness information from MLRISC will be crucial to the long-term success of this effort.

Our work attests that MLRISC is "generic enough" to be reused as the back end of our compiler, even though TIL is substantially different from Standard ML of New Jersey [4], the compiler for which MLRISC was originally developed. Reuse has attendant costs, however, and the most significant of these appear to be related to the speed of compilation. We suggest that generic compiler technology is a valuable asset, but that more developers will benefit from it if interfaces are made flexible enough to encompass dissimilar compilation strategies.

## Acknowledgements

Special thanks to Lal George for his helpful insights during the integration of MLRISC and TIL.

## References

1. A. V. Aho, R. Sethi, and J. D. Ullman. *Compilers: principles, techniques, tools.* Addison-Wesley, 1986.
2. Andrew W. Appel. A runtime system. *Lisp and Symbolic Computation 3*, pages 343–380, 1990.
3. Andrew W. Appel. *Modern Compiler Implementation in ML.* Cambridge University Press, 1998.
4. Andrew W. Appel and David B. MacQueen. Standard ML of new jersey. In *Third International Symposium on Programming Language Implementation and Logic Programming*, pages 1–13. Springer-Verlag, August 1991.
5. Andrew W. Appel et al. The national compiler infrastructure project.
6. Robert P. Wilson et al. SUIF: An infrastructure for research on parallelizing and optimizing compilers. Technical report, Computer Systems Laboratory, Stanford University.
7. Lal George. Personal Communication.
8. Lal George. MLRISC: Customizable and reusable code generators. Technical report, Bell Labs, December 1996. submitted to PLDI.
9. Lal George and Andrew W. Appel. Iterated register coalescing. *ACM Transactions on Programming Languages and Systems*, 18(3):300–324, May 1996.
10. Robert Harper and Greg Morrisett. Compiling polymorphism using intensional type analysis. In *Conference Record of the 22nd Annual ACM SIGPLAN-SIGACT Symposium on Principles of Programming Languages*, pages 130–141. ACM, January 1995.
11. Robert Harper and Chris Stone. A type-theroretic interpretation of standard ML. Technical report, Carnegie Mellon University, 1997. submitted for publication.
12. Greg Morrisett, David Walker, Karl Crary, and Neal Glew. From system F to typed assembly language. In *Conference Record of the 25th ACM SIGPLAN-SIGACT Symposium on Principles of Programming Languages*, pages 85–97. ACM, January 1998.

13. J. Gregory Morrisett. *Compiling with Types*. PhD thesis, Carnegie Mellon University, December 1995. Published as CMU Technical Report CMU-CS-95-226.
14. George C. Necula. Proof-carrying code. In *Conference Record of the 24th Annual ACM SIGPLAN-SIGACT Symposium on Principles of Programming Languages*. ACM, January 1997.
15. George C. Necula and Peter Lee. The design and implementation of a certifying compiler. In *Proceedings of the ACM SIGPLAN Conference on Programming Language Design and Implemantation*, New York, 1998. ACM Press.
16. Zhong Shao and Andrew W. Appel. Space-efficient closure representations. In *Conference on Lisp and Functional programming*, June 94.
17. D. Tarditi, G. Morrisett, P. Cheng, C. Stone, R. Harper, and P. Lee. TIL : A type-directed optimizing compiler for ML. In *Proceedingsof the ACM SIGPLAN Conference on Programming Language Design and Implemantation*, pages 181–192, New York, May21–24 1996. ACM Press.
18. Andrew Tolmach. Tag-free garbage collection using explicit type parameters. In *Proceedings 1994 ACM Conference on Lisp and Functional Programming*, June 1994.

# A Toolkit for Constructing Type- and Constraint-Based Program Analyses

Alexander Aiken, Manuel Fähndrich, Jeffrey S. Foster, Zhendong Su

University of California, Berkeley* **

**Abstract.** BANE (the *Berkeley Analysis Engine*) is a publicly available toolkit for constructing type- and constraint-based program analyses.[1] We describe the goals of the project, the rationale for BANE's overall design, some examples coded in BANE, and briefly compare BANE with other program analysis frameworks.

## 1 Introduction

Automatic program analysis is central to contemporary compilers and software engineering tools. Program analyses are also arguably the most difficult components of such systems to develop, as significant theoretical and practical issues must be addressed in even relatively straightforward analyses.

Program analysis poses difficult semantic problems, and considerable effort has been devoted to understanding what it means for an analysis to be correct [CC77]. However, designing a theoretically well-founded analysis is necessary but not sufficient for obtaining a useful analysis. Demonstrating utility requires implementation and experimentation, preferably with large programs. Many plausible analyses are not beneficial in practice, and others require substantial modification and tuning before producing useful information at reasonable cost.

It is important to prototype and realistically test analysis ideas, usually in several variations, to judge the cost/performance trade-offs of multiple design points. We know of no practical analytical method for showing utility, because the set of programs that occur in practice is a very special, and not easily modeled, subset of all programs. Unfortunately, experiments are relatively rare because of the substantial effort involved.

BANE (for the *Berkeley ANalysis Engine*) is a toolkit for constructing type- and constraint-based program analyses. A goal of the project is to dramatically lower the barriers to experimentation and to make it relatively easy for researchers to realistically prototype and test new program analysis ideas (at

* Authors' address: Electrical Engineering and Computer Science Department, University of California, Berkeley, 387 Soda Hall #1776, Berkeley, CA 94720-1776 Email: {aiken,manuel,jfoster,zhendong}@cs.berkeley.edu

** Supported in part by an NDSEG fellowship, NSF National Young Investigator Award CCR-9457812, NSF Grant CCR-9416973, and gifts from Microsoft and Rockwell.

[1] The distribution may be obtained from the BANE homepage at http://bane.cs.berkeley.edu.

least type- and constraint-based ideas). To this end, in addition to providing constraint specification and resolution components, the BANE distribution also provides parsers and interfaces for popular languages (currently C and ML) as well as test suites of programs ranging in size from a few hundred to tens of thousands of lines of code.

BANE has been used to implement several realistic program analyses, including an uncaught exception inference system for ML programs [FA97,FFA98], points-to analyses for C [FFA97,FFSA98], and a race condition analysis for a factory control language [AFS98]. Each of these analyses also scales to large programs—respectively at least 20,000 lines of ML, 100,000 lines of C, and production factory control programs. These are the largest programs we have available (the peculiar syntax of the control language precludes counting lines of code).

## 2 System Architecture

Constraint-based analysis is appealing because elaborate analyses can be expressed with a concise and simple set of constraint generation rules. These rules separate analysis specification (constraint generation) from implementation (constraint resolution). Implementing an analysis using BANE involves only writing code to (1) generate the appropriate constraints from the program text and (2) interpret the solutions of the constraints. Part (1) is usually a simple recursive walk of the abstract-syntax tree, and part (2) is usually testing for straightforward properties of the constraint solutions. The system takes care of constraint representation, resolution, and transformation. Thus, BANE frees the analysis designer from writing a constraint solver, usually the most difficult portion of a constraint-based analysis to design and engineer.

In designing a program analysis toolkit one soon realizes that no single formalism covers both a large fraction of interesting analyses and provides uniformly good performance in an implementation. BANE provides a number of different constraint *sorts*: constraint languages and associated resolution engines that can be reused as appropriate for different applications. Each sort is characterized by a language of expressions, a constraint relation, a solution space, and an implementation strategy. In some cases BANE provides multiple implementations of the same constraint language as distinct sorts because the different implementations provide different engineering trade-offs to the user. Extending BANE with new sorts is straightforward.

An innovation in BANE is support for *mixed constraints*: the use of multiple sorts of constraints in a single application [FA97]. In addition to supporting naturally multi-sorted applications, we believe the ability to change constraint languages allows analysis designers to explore fine-grain engineering decisions, targeting subproblems of an analysis with the constraint system that gives the best efficiency/precision properties for the task at hand. Section 3 provides an example of successively refining an analysis through mixed constraints.

$$\cup : \text{Set Set} \rightarrow \text{Set}$$
$$\cap : \text{Set Set} \rightarrow \text{Set}$$
$$\neg\{c_1, \ldots, c_n\} : \text{Set} \qquad \text{for any set of Set-constructors } c_i \in \Sigma_{Set}$$
$$0 : \text{Set}$$
$$1 : \text{Set}$$

**Fig. 1.** Operations in the sort Set.

Mixed constraint systems are formalized using a many-sorted algebra of expressions. Each sort $s$ includes a set of variables $V_s$, a set of constructors $\Sigma_s$, and possibly some other operations. Each sort has a constraint relation $\subseteq_s$. Constraints and resolution rules observe sorts; that is, a constraint $X \subseteq_s Y$ implies $X$ and $Y$ are $s$-expressions.

The user selects the appropriate mixture of constraints by providing constructor signatures. If $S$ is the set of sorts, each $n$-ary constructor $c$ is given a signature

$$c : \iota_1 \ldots \iota_n \rightarrow S$$

where $\iota_i$ is $s$ or $\bar{s}$ for some $s \in S$. Overlined sorts mark contravariant arguments of $c$; the rest are covariant arguments. For example, let sort Term be a set of constructors $\Sigma_{\text{Term}}$ and variables $V_{\text{Term}}$ with no additional operations. Pure terms over $\Sigma_{\text{Term}}$ and $V_{\text{Term}}$ are defined by giving constructor signatures

$$c : \underbrace{\text{Term} \ldots \text{Term}}_{arity(c)} \rightarrow \text{Term} \quad c \in \Sigma_{\text{Term}}$$

As another example, let Set be a sort with the set operators in Figure 1 (the set operations plus least and greatest sets). Pure set expressions are defined by the signatures

$$c : \underbrace{\text{Set} \ldots \text{Set}}_{arity(c)} \rightarrow \text{Set} \quad c \in \Sigma_{\text{Set}}$$

There are many examples of program analyses based on equations between Terms (e.g., [DM82,Hen92,Ste96]) and based on inclusion constraints between Set expressions (e.g., [And94,AWL94,EST95,FFK+96,Hei94]). The literature also has natural examples of mixed constraint systems, although they have not been recognized previously as a distinct category. For example, many *effect systems* [GJSO92] use a function space constructor

$$\cdot \rightarrow \cdot : \; \overline{\text{Term}} \; \text{Set} \; \text{Term} \rightarrow \text{Term}$$

where the Set expressions are used only to carry the set of latent effects of the function.

These three examples—terms, set expressions, and a mixed language with set and term components—illustrate that by altering the signatures of constructors a range of analysis domains can be realized. For example, a flow-based analysis using set expressions can be coarsened to a unification-based analysis using terms. Similarly, a term-based analysis can be refined to an effect analysis by adding a Set component to the $\rightarrow$ constructor.

## 2.1 The Framework

From the user's point of view, our framework consists of a number of sorts of expressions together with resolution rules for constraints over those expressions. In addition, the user must provide constructor signatures specifying how the different sorts are combined. In this section we focus on the three sorts Term, FlowTerm, and Set. The distributed implementation also supports a Row sort [Rém89] for modeling records.

Besides constructors and variables a sort may have arbitrary operations peculiar to that sort; for example, sort Set includes set operations. Each sort $s$ has a constraint relation $\subseteq_s$ and resolution rules. Constraints and resolution rules preserve sorts, so that $X \subseteq_s Y$ implies $X$ and $Y$ are $s$-expressions. For example, for the Term sort, the constraint relation $\subseteq_{\text{Term}}$ is equality, and the resolution rules implement term unification for constructors with signatures Term...Term $\rightarrow$ Term. For clarity we write the constraint relation of term unification as "$=_t$" instead of $\subseteq_{\text{Term}}$.

The resolution rules in Figure 2 are read as left-to-right rewrite rules. The left- and right-hand sides of rules are conjunctions of constraints. Sort FlowTerm has the expressions of sort Term but a different set of resolution rules (see Figure 2b). FlowTerm uses inclusion instead of equality constraints. The inclusion constraints are more precise, but also more expensive to resolve, requiring exponential time in the worst case. For certain applications, however, FlowTerm is very efficient [HM97]. We write $\subseteq_{\text{ft}}$ for the FlowTerm constraint relation.

The constructor rules connect constraints of different sorts. For example, in sort FlowTerm the rule

$$S \wedge c(T_1, \ldots, T_n) \subseteq_{\text{ft}} c(T'_1, \ldots, T'_n) \equiv S \wedge T_1 \subseteq_{\iota_1} T'_1 \wedge \cdots \wedge T_n \subseteq_{\iota_n} T'_n$$
$$\text{if } c : \iota_1 \cdots \iota_n \rightarrow \text{FlowTerm}$$

says constraints propagate structurally to constructor arguments; this is where FlowTerm has a precision advantage over Term (see below). Note this rule preserves sorts. The rule for constructors of sort Term (Figure 2a) is slightly different because $\subseteq_{\text{Term}}$ is equality, a symmetric relation. Thus, constraints on constructor arguments are also symmetric:

$$S \wedge f(T_1, \ldots, T_n) =_t f(T'_1, \ldots, T'_n) \equiv S \wedge T_1 \subseteq_{\iota_1} T'_1 \wedge T'_1 \subseteq_{\iota_1} T_1 \wedge \cdots \wedge$$
$$T_n \subseteq_{\iota_n} T'_n \wedge T'_n \subseteq_{\iota_n} T_n$$
$$\text{if } f : \iota_1 \cdots \iota_n \rightarrow \text{Term}$$

Figure 2c shows the rules for the Set sort. In addition to the standard rules [AW93], Set includes special rules for set complement, which is problematic in the presence of contravariant constructors. We deal with set complement using

$$S \wedge f(T_1, \ldots, T_n) =_t f(T'_1, \ldots, T'_n) \equiv S \wedge T_1 \subseteq_{\iota_1} T'_1 \wedge T'_1 \subseteq_{\iota_1} T_1 \wedge \cdots \wedge$$
$$T_n \subseteq_{\iota_n} T'_n \wedge T'_n \subseteq_{\iota_n} T_n \quad \text{if } f : \iota_1 \cdots \iota_n \to \textbf{Term}$$
$$S \wedge f(\ldots) =_t g(\ldots) \equiv \text{inconsistent} \quad \text{if } f \neq g$$

(a) Resolution rules for sort **Term**.

$$S \wedge c(T_1, \ldots, T_n) \subseteq_{tt} c(T'_1, \ldots, T'_n) \equiv S \wedge T_1 \subseteq_{\iota_1} T'_1 \wedge \cdots \wedge T_n \subseteq_{\iota_n} T'_n$$
$$\text{if } c : \iota_1 \cdots \iota_n \to \textbf{FlowTerm}$$
$$S \wedge c(\ldots) \subseteq_{tt} d(\ldots) \equiv \text{inconsistent} \quad \text{if } c \neq d$$
$$S \wedge \alpha \subseteq_{tt} c(T_1, \ldots, T_n) \equiv S \wedge \alpha = c(\alpha_1, \ldots, \alpha_n) \wedge \alpha_i \subseteq_{\iota_i} T_i$$
$$\alpha_i \text{ fresh}, \quad c : \iota_1 \cdots \iota_n \to \textbf{FlowTerm}$$
$$S \wedge c(T_1, \ldots, T_n) \subseteq_{tt} \alpha \equiv S \wedge \alpha = c(\alpha_1, \ldots, \alpha_n) \wedge T_i \subseteq_{\iota_i} \alpha_i$$
$$\alpha_i \text{ fresh}, \quad c : \iota_1 \cdots \iota_n \to \textbf{FlowTerm}$$

(b) Resolution rules for sort **FlowTerm**.

$$S \wedge 0 \subseteq_s T \equiv S$$
$$S \wedge T \subseteq_s 1 \equiv S$$
$$S \wedge c(T_1, \ldots, T_n) \subseteq_s c(T'_1, \ldots, T'_n) \equiv S \wedge T_1 \subseteq_{\iota_1} T'_1 \wedge \cdots \wedge T_n \subseteq_{\iota_n} T'_n$$
$$\text{if } c : \iota_1 \cdots \iota_n \to \textbf{Set}$$
$$S \wedge c(\ldots) \subseteq_s d(\ldots) \equiv \text{inconsistent} \quad \text{if } c \neq d$$
$$S \wedge T_1 \cup T_2 \subseteq_s T \equiv S \wedge T_1 \subseteq_s T \wedge T_2 \subseteq_s T$$
$$S \wedge T \subseteq_s T_1 \cap T_2 \equiv S \wedge T \subseteq_s T_1 \wedge T \subseteq_s T_2$$
$$S \wedge \alpha \subseteq_s \alpha \equiv S$$
$$S \wedge \alpha \cap T \subseteq_s \alpha \equiv S$$
$$S \wedge T_1 \subseteq_s Pat(T_2, T_3) \equiv S \wedge T_1 \cap T_3 \subseteq_s T_2$$
$$S \wedge \alpha \cap T_1 \subseteq_s T_2 \equiv S \wedge \alpha \subseteq_s Pat(T_2, T_1)$$
$$S \wedge \neg\{c_1, \ldots, c_n\} \subseteq_s \neg\{d_1, \ldots, d_m\} \equiv S \quad \text{if } \{d_1, \ldots, d_m\} \subseteq \{c_1, \ldots, c_n\}$$
$$S \wedge c(\ldots) \subseteq_s \neg\{d_1, \ldots, d_m\} \equiv S \quad \text{if } c \notin \{d_1, \ldots, d_m\}$$

(c) Resolution rules for sort **Set**.

$$S \wedge X \subseteq_\iota \alpha \wedge \alpha \subseteq_\iota Y \equiv S \wedge X \subseteq_\iota \alpha \wedge \alpha \subseteq_\iota Y \wedge X \subseteq_\iota Y$$
$$S \wedge T_1 \subseteq_\tau T_2 \equiv S \wedge T_2 \subseteq_\iota T_1$$

(d) General rules.

**Fig. 2.** Resolution rules for constraints.

two mechanisms. First, explicit complements have the form $\neg\{c_1, \dots, c_n\}$, which has all values of sort Set except those with head constructor $c_1, \dots, c_n$. Second, more general complements are represented implicitly. Define $\neg R$ to be the set such that $R \cap \neg R = 0$ and $R \cup \neg R = 1$ (in all solutions). Now define

$$Pat(T, R) = (T \cap R) \cup \neg R$$

The operator $Pat$ [2] encapsulates a disjoint union involving a complement. $Pat$ is equivalent to in power to disjoint union, but constraint resolution involving $Pat$ does not require computing complements. Of course, wherever $Pat(T, R)$ is used the set $\neg R$ must exist; this is an obligation of the analysis designer (see [FA97] for details). Given the definitions of $Pat$ and $\neg\{c_1, \dots, c_n\}$, basic set theory shows the rules in Figure 2c are sound.

Our specification of sort Set is incomplete. We have omitted some rules for simplifying intersections and some restrictions on the form of solvable constraints. The details may be found in [AW93,FA97].

Figure 2d gives two general rules that apply to all sorts. The first rule expresses that $\subseteq_\iota$ is transitive. The second flips constraints that arise from contravariant constructor arguments.

We now present a small example of a mixed constraint system. Consider an effect system where each function type carries a set of atomic effects (e.g., the set of globally visible variables that may be modified by invoking the function). Let the constructors have signatures

$$\cdot \xrightarrow{\overline{\cdot}} \cdot : \overline{\texttt{FlowTerm}} \ \texttt{Set} \ \texttt{FlowTerm} \to \texttt{FlowTerm}$$
$$\texttt{int} : \texttt{FlowTerm}$$
$$\texttt{a}_1, \dots, \texttt{a}_n : \texttt{Set} \qquad\qquad \text{(the atomic effects)}$$

The following constraint

$$\alpha \xrightarrow{\texttt{a}_1 \cup \texttt{a}_2} \beta \subseteq_{\texttt{ft}} \texttt{int} \xrightarrow{\gamma} \texttt{int}$$

is resolved as follows:

$$\alpha \xrightarrow{\texttt{a}_1 \cup \texttt{a}_2} \beta \subseteq_{\texttt{ft}} \texttt{int} \xrightarrow{\gamma} \texttt{int}$$
$$\Rightarrow \alpha \subseteq_{\overline{\texttt{tf}}} \texttt{int} \wedge \texttt{a}_1 \cup \texttt{a}_2 \subseteq_\texttt{s} \gamma \wedge \beta \subseteq_{\texttt{ft}} \texttt{int}$$
$$\Rightarrow \texttt{int} \subseteq_{\texttt{tf}} \alpha \wedge \texttt{a}_1 \cup \texttt{a}_2 \subseteq_\texttt{s} \gamma \wedge \beta \subseteq_{\texttt{ft}} \texttt{int}$$
$$\Rightarrow \alpha = \texttt{int} \wedge \texttt{a}_1 \cup \texttt{a}_2 \subseteq_\texttt{s} \gamma \wedge \beta = \texttt{int}$$

Thus in all solutions $\alpha$ and $\beta$ are both int and $\gamma$ is a superset of $\texttt{a}_1 \cup \texttt{a}_2$.

## 2.2 Scalability

The main technical challenge in BANE is to develop methods for scaling constraint-based analyses to large programs. Designing for scalability has led to

---

[2] $Pat$ stands for "pattern," because it is used most often to express pattern matching.

a system with a significantly different organization than other program analysis systems [Hei94,AWL94].

To handle very large programs it is essential that the implementation be structured so that independent program components can be analyzed separately first and the results combined later. Consider the following generic inference rule where expressions are assigned types under some set of assumptions $A$ and constraints $C$

$$\frac{A, C \vdash e_1 : \tau_1 \quad A, C \vdash e_2 : \tau_2}{A, C \vdash E[e_1, e_2] : \tau}$$

where $E[e_1, e_2]$ is a compound expression with subexpressions $e_1$ and $e_2$. In all other implementations we know of, such inference systems are realized by accumulating a set of global constraints $C$. In BANE one can write rules as above, but the following alternative is also provided:

$$\frac{A, C_1 \vdash e_1 : \tau_1 \quad A, C_2 \vdash e_2 : \tau_2}{A, C_1 \wedge C_2 \vdash E[e_1, e_2] : \tau}$$

$C_1$ contains only the constraints required to type $e_1$ (similarly for $C_2$ and $e_2$). This structure has advantages. First, separate analysis of program components is trivial by design rather than added as an afterthought. Second, the running time of algorithms that examine the constraints (e.g., *constraint simplification*, which replaces constraint systems by equivalent, and smaller, systems) is guaranteed to be a function only of the expression being analyzed; in particular, the running time is independent of the rest of the program. Note that this design changes the primitive operation for accumulating constraints from adding individual constraints to a global system to combining independent constraint systems. Because this latter operation is more expensive, BANE applications tend to use a mixture of the two forms of rules to obtain good overall performance and scalability.

Many other aspects of the BANE architecture have been engineered primarily for scalability [FA96]. The emphasis on scalability, plus the overhead of supporting general user-specified constructor signatures, has a cost in runtime performance, but this cost appears to be small. For example, a BANE implementation of the type inference system for core Standard ML performs within a factor of two of the hand-written implementation in the SML/NJ compiler.

In other cases a well-engineered constraint library can substantially outperform hand-written implementations. BANE implementations of a class of cubic-time flow analyses can be orders of magnitude faster than special-purpose systems because of optimizations implemented in the solver for BANE's set constraint sort [FFSA98].

## 3   The BANE Interface by Example

This section presents a simple analysis written in BANE. We show by example how an analysis can be successively refined using mixed constraints. BANE is a library written in Standard ML of New Jersey [MTH90]. Writing a program analysis using BANE requires ML code to traverse abstract syntax while generating constraints and ML code to extract the desired information from the solutions of the constraints.

For reasons of efficiency, BANE's implementation is stateful. BANE provides the notion of a *current constraint system* (CCS) into which all constraints are added. Functionality to create new constraint systems and to change the CCS are provided, so one is not limited to a single global constraint system. For simplicity, the examples in this section use only a single constraint system.

## 3.1 A Trivial Example: Simple Type Inference for a Lambda Calculus

This example infers types for a lambda calculus with the following abstract syntax:

```
datatype ast =
    Var of string
  | Int of int
  | Fn of {formal:string, body:ast}
  | App of {function:ast, argument:ast}
```

The syntax includes identifiers (strings), primitive integers, abstraction, and application. The language of types consists of the primitive type int, a function type →, as well as type variables $v$.

$$\tau ::= v \mid \text{int} \mid \tau \to \tau$$

The first choice is the sort of expressions and constraints to use for the type inference problem. All that is needed in this case are terms and term equality; the appropriate sort is Term (structure Bane.Term). To make the code more readable, we rebind this structure as structure TypeSort.

```
structure TypeSort = Bane.Term
```

BANE uses distinct ML types for expressions of distinct sort. In this case, type expressions have ML type

```
type ty = TypeSort.T Bane.expr
```

Next, we need the type constructors for integers and functions. The integer type constructor can be formed using a constant signature, and a standard function type constructor is predefined.

```
val int_tycon = Cons.new {name="int", signa=TypeSort.constSig}
val fun_tycon = TypeSort.funCon
```

The constant integer type is created by applying the integer constructor to an empty list of arguments. We also define a function to apply the function type constructor to the domain and range, using the generic function Bane.Common.cons : 'a constructor * genE list -> 'a expr that applies a constructor of sort

$$\frac{}{A \vdash x : A[x]} \quad \text{[VAR]} \qquad \frac{}{A \vdash i : \texttt{int}} \quad \text{[INT]}$$

$$\frac{\alpha \text{ fresh}}{A[x \mapsto \alpha] \vdash e : \tau} \quad \text{[ABS]} \qquad \frac{\begin{array}{c} A \vdash e_1 : \tau_1 \\ A \vdash e_2 : \tau_2 \\ \alpha \text{ fresh} \\ \tau_1 = \tau_2 \to \alpha \end{array}}{A \vdash e_1\, e_2 : \alpha} \quad \text{[APP]}$$

**Fig. 3.** Type inference rules for example lambda calculus

'a to a list of arguments. In general, constructor arguments can have a variety of distinct sorts with distinct ML types. Since ML only allows homogeneously typed lists, BANE uses an ML type genE for expressions of any sort. The lack of subtyping in ML forces us to use conversion functions TypeSort.toGenE to convert the domain and range from TypeSort.T Bane.expr to Bane.genE.

```
val intTy = Bane.Common.cons (int_tycon, [])
fun funTy (domain,range) = Common.cons (fun_tycon,
                                    [TypeSort.toGenE domain,
                                     TypeSort.toGenE range])
```

Finally, we define a function for creating fresh type variables by specializing the generic function Bane.Var.freshVar : 'a Bane.sort -> 'a Bane.expr. We also bind operator == to the equality constraint of TypeSort.

```
fun freshTyVar () = Bane.Var.freshVar TypeSort.sort
infix ==
val op == = TypeSort.unify
```

With these auxiliary bindings, the standard type inference rules in Figure 3 are translated directly into a case analysis on the abstract syntax. Type environments are provided by a module with the following signature:

```
signature ENV =
  sig
      type name = string

      type 'a env

      val empty  : 'a env
      val insert : 'a env * name * 'a -> 'a env
      val find   : 'a env * name -> 'a option
  end
```

The type of identifiers is simply looked up in the environment. If the environment contains no assumption for an identifier, an error is reported.

```
fun elaborate env ast =
  case ast of
```

```
Var x => (case Env.find (env, x) of
              SOME ty => ty
            | NONE => <report error: free variable>)
```

The integer case is even simpler:

```
| Int i => intTy
```

Abstractions are typed by creating a fresh unconstrained type variable for the lambda bound formal, extending the environment with a binding for the formal, and typing the body in the extended environment.

```
| Fn {formal,body} =>
    let val v = freshTyVar ()
        val env' = Env.insert (env,formal,v)
        val body_ty = elaborate env' body
    in
        funTy (v, body_ty)
    end
```

For applications we obtain the function type ty1 and the argument type ty2 via recursive calls. A fresh type variable result stands for the result of the application. Type ty1 must be equal to a function type with domain ty2 and range result. The handler around the equality constraint catches inconsistent constraints in the case where ty1 is not a function, or the domain and argument don't agree.

```
| App {function,argument} =>
    let val ty1 = elaborate env function
        val ty2 = elaborate env argument

        val result = freshTyVar ()
        val fty = funTy (ty2, result)
    in
        (ty1 == fty) handle exn =>
                       <report type error>;
        result
    end
```

We haven't specified whether our type language for lambda terms includes recursive types. The Term sort allows recursive solutions by default. If only non-recursive solutions are desired, an occurs check can be enabled via a BANE option:

```
Bane.Flags.set (SOME TypeSort.sort) "occursCheck";
```

As an example, consider the Y combinator

$$Y = \lambda f.(\lambda x.f\ (x\ x))(\lambda x.f\ (x\ x))$$

Its inferred type is

$$(\alpha \to \alpha) \to \alpha$$

where the type variable $\alpha$ is unconstrained. With the occurs check enabled, type inference for Y fails.

## 3.2 Type Inference with Flow Information

The simple type inference described above yields type information for each lambda term or fails if the equality constraints have no solution. Suppose we want to augment type inference to gather information about the set of lambda abstractions to which each lambda expression may evaluate. We assume the abstract syntax is modified so that lambda abstractions are labeled:

```
| Fn of {formal:string, body:ast, label:string}
```

Our goal is to refine function types to include a label-set, so that the type of a lambda term not only describes the domain and the range, but also an approximation of the set of syntactic abstractions to which it may evaluate. The function type constructor thus becomes a ternary constructor fun(*dom, rng, labels*). The resulting analysis is similar to the flow analysis described in [Mos96]. The natural choice of constraint language for label-sets is obviously set constraints, and we bind the structure LabelSet to one particular implementation of set constraints:

```
structure LabelSet = Bane.SetIF
```

We define the new function type constructor containing an extra field for the label-set by building a signature with three argument sorts, the first two being Type sorts and the last being a LabelSet sort. Note how the variance of each constructor argument is specified in the signature through the use of functions TypeSort.ctv_arg (contravariance) and TypeSort.cov_arg (covariance). Resolution of equality constraints itself does not require variance annotations, but other aspects of BANE do.

```
val funSig = TypeSort.newSig {args=[TypeSort.ctv_arg TypeSort.genSort,
                                    TypeSort.cov_arg TypeSort.genSort,
                                    TypeSort.cov_arg LabelSet.genSort],
                              attributes=[]}

val fun_tycon = Bane.Cons.new {name="fun", signa=funSig}
```

We are now using a mixed constraint language: types are terms with embedded label-sets. Constraints between types are still equality constraints, and as a result, induced constraints between label sets are also equalities.

The type rules for abstraction and application are easily modified to include label information.

$$
\frac{\begin{array}{c} \alpha \text{ fresh} \\ A[x \mapsto \alpha] \vdash e : \tau \\ \{l\} \subseteq \epsilon \qquad \epsilon \text{ fresh} \end{array}}{A \vdash \lambda^l x.e : \mathrm{fun}(\alpha, \tau, \epsilon)} \; [\mathrm{ABS}]
\qquad
\frac{\begin{array}{c} A \vdash e_1 : \tau_1 \\ A \vdash e_2 : \tau_2 \\ \alpha, \epsilon \text{ fresh} \\ \tau_1 = \mathrm{fun}(\tau_2, \alpha, \epsilon) \end{array}}{A \vdash e_1 \, e_2 : \alpha} \; [\mathrm{APP}]
$$

Because Term constraints generate equality constraints on the embedded Sets, the label-sets of distinct abstractions may be equated during type inference. As a result, the [ABS] rule introduces a fresh label-set variable $\epsilon$ along with a constraint $\{l\} \subseteq \epsilon$ to correctly model that the lambda abstraction evaluates to itself. (Note that this inclusion constraint is between Set expressions.) Using a constrained variable rather than a constant set $\{l\}$ allows the label-set to be merged with other sets through equality constraints. The handling of arrow-effects in region inference is similar [TT94].

The label-set variable $\epsilon$ introduced by each use of the [APP] rule stands for the set of abstractions potentially flowing to that application site.

The code changes required to accommodate the new rules are minimal. For abstractions, the label is converted into a constant set constructor with the same name through Cons.new. A constant set expression is then built from the constructor and used to constrain the fresh label-set variable labelvar. Finally, the label-set variable is used along with the domain and range to build the function type of the abstraction.

```
| Fn {formal,body,label} =>
    let val v = freshTyVar ()
        val env' = Env.insert (env,formal,v)
        val body_ty = elaborate env' body
        (* create a new constant constructor *)
        val c = Cons.new {name=label, signa=LabelSet.constSig}
        val lab = Common.cons (c,[])
        val labelvar = freshLabelVar ()
    in
        (lab <= labelvar);
        funTy (v, body_ty, labelvar)
    end
```

The changes to the implementation of [APP] are even simpler, requiring only the introduction of a fresh label-set variable. The label-set variable may be stored in a map for later inspection of the set of abstractions flowing to particular application sites.

```
| App {function,argument} =>
        let val ty1 = elaborate env function
            val ty2 = elaborate env argument

            val result = freshTyVar ()
            val labels = freshLabelVar ()
            val fty = funTy (ty2, result, labels)
        in
            (ty1 == fty) handle exn =>
                            <report type error>;
            result
        end
```

We now provide a number of examples showing the information gathered by the flow analysis. Consider the standard lambda encodings for values true, false, nil, and cons, and their inferred types.

$$\text{true} = \lambda^{\text{true}}x.\lambda^{\text{true}_1}y.x \qquad \alpha \xrightarrow{\epsilon_1} \beta \xrightarrow{\epsilon_2} \alpha \setminus \text{true} \subseteq \epsilon_1 \wedge \text{true}_1 \subseteq \epsilon_2$$

$$\text{false} = \lambda^{\text{false}}x.\lambda^{\text{false}_1}y.y \qquad \alpha \xrightarrow{\epsilon_1} \beta \xrightarrow{\epsilon_2} \beta \setminus \text{false} \subseteq \epsilon_1 \wedge \text{false}_1 \subseteq \epsilon_2$$

$$\text{nil} = \lambda^{\text{nil}}x.\lambda^{\text{nil}_1}y.x \qquad \alpha \xrightarrow{\epsilon_1} \beta \xrightarrow{\epsilon_2} \alpha \setminus \text{nil} \subseteq \epsilon_1 \wedge \text{nil}_1 \subseteq \epsilon_2$$

$$\text{cons} = \lambda^{\text{cons}}hd.\lambda^{c_1} tl.\lambda^{c_2}x.\lambda^{c_3}y.y \; hd \; tl \qquad \alpha \xrightarrow{\epsilon_1} \beta \xrightarrow{\epsilon_2} \gamma \xrightarrow{\epsilon_3} (\alpha \xrightarrow{\epsilon_4} \beta \xrightarrow{\epsilon_5} \delta) \xrightarrow{\epsilon_6} \delta \setminus$$
$$\text{cons} \subseteq \epsilon_1 \wedge c_1 \subseteq \epsilon_2 \wedge$$
$$c_2 \subseteq \epsilon_3 \wedge c_3 \subseteq \epsilon_6$$

The analysis yields constrained types $\tau \setminus C$, where the constraints $C$ describe the label-set variables embedded in type $\tau$. (To improve the readability of types, function types are written using the standard infix form with label-sets on the arrow.) For example, the type of nil

$$\alpha \xrightarrow{\epsilon_1} \beta \xrightarrow{\epsilon_2} \alpha \setminus \text{nil} \subseteq \epsilon_1 \wedge \text{nil}_1 \subseteq \epsilon_2$$

has the label-set $\epsilon_1$ on the first arrow, and associated constraint $\text{nil} \subseteq \epsilon_1$. The label-set is extracted from the final type using the following BANE code fragment:

```
val ty = elaborate error baseEnv e
val labels = case Common.deCons (fun_tycon, ty) of
             SOME [dom,rng,lab] =>
                 LabelSet.tlb (LabelSet.fromGenE lab)
             | NONE => []
```

The function `Common.deCons` is used to decompose constructed expressions. In this case we match the final type expression against the pattern $fun(dom, rng, lab)$. If the match succeeds, `deCons` returns the list of arguments to the constructor. In this case we are interested in the least solution of the label component `lab`. We obtain this information via the function `LabelSet.tlb`, which returns the *transitive lower-bound* (TLB) of a given expression. The TLB is a list of constructed expressions $c(\ldots)$, in our case a list of constants corresponding to abstraction labels.

A slightly more complex example using the lambda expressions defined above is

$$\text{head} = \lambda^{\text{head}}l.l \; \text{nil} \; (\lambda^{\text{head}_1}x.\lambda^{\text{head}_2}y.x) \qquad ((\alpha \xrightarrow{\epsilon_1} \iota_1 \xrightarrow{\epsilon_2} \alpha) \xrightarrow{\epsilon_3}$$
$$(\beta \xrightarrow{\epsilon_4} \iota_2 \xrightarrow{\epsilon_5} \beta) \xrightarrow{\epsilon_6} \gamma)$$
$$\xrightarrow{\epsilon_7} \gamma \setminus$$
$$\text{head} \subseteq \epsilon_7 \wedge$$
$$\text{nil} \subseteq \epsilon_1 \wedge$$
$$\text{nil}_1 \subseteq \epsilon_2 \wedge$$
$$\text{head}_1 \subseteq \epsilon_4 \wedge$$
$$\text{head}_2 \subseteq \epsilon_5$$

$$\text{head (cons true nil)} : \alpha \xrightarrow{\epsilon_1} \beta \xrightarrow{\epsilon_2} \alpha \setminus \text{true} \subseteq \epsilon_1 \wedge \text{true}_1 \subseteq \epsilon_2$$

The expression head (cons true nil) takes the head of the list containing true. Even though the function head is defined to return nil if the argument is the empty list, the flow analysis correctly infers that the result in this case is true.

The use of equality constraints may cause undesired approximations in the flow information. Consider an example taken from Section 3.1 of Mossin's thesis [Mos96]

$$\text{select} = \lambda^{\text{select}} x.\lambda^{\text{sel}_1} y.\lambda^{\text{sel}_2} f.\text{if } x \text{ then } f\,x \text{ else } f\,y$$

The select function takes three arguments, $x$, $y$, and $z$, and depending on the truth value of $x$, returns the result of applying $f$ to either $x$ or $y$. The abbreviation if $p$ then $e_1$ else $e_2$ stands for the application $p\,e_1\,e_2$. The type constraints for the two applications of $f$ cause the flow information of $x$ and $y$ to be merged. As a result, the application

$$\text{select true false } (\lambda z.z)$$

does not resolve the condition of the if-then-else to true. To observe the approximation directly in the result type, we modify the example slightly:

$$\text{select}' = \lambda^{\text{select}} x.\lambda^{\text{sel}_1} y.\lambda^{\text{sel}_2} f.\text{if } x \text{ then } f\,x\,x \text{ else } f\,y\,x$$

Now $f$ is applied to two arguments, the first being either $x$ or $y$, the second being $x$ in both cases. We modify the example use of select such that $f$ now ignores its first argument and simply returns the second, i.e. $x$. The expression thus evaluates to true.

$$\text{select}' \text{ true false } (\lambda z.\lambda w.w)$$

The inferred type for this application is

$$\tau \setminus \tau = \tau \xrightarrow{\epsilon_1} \tau \xrightarrow{\epsilon_2} \tau$$
$$\text{true} \cup \text{false} \subseteq \epsilon_1$$
$$\text{true}_1 \cup \text{false}_1 \subseteq \epsilon_2$$

where the label-set of the function type indicates that the result can be either true or false. This approximation can be overcome through the use of subtyping.

## 3.3 Type Inference with Flow Information and Subtyping

The inclusion relation on label-sets embedded within types can be lifted to a natural subtyping relation on structural types. This idea has been described in the context of control-flow analysis in [HM97], for a more general flow analysis in [Mos96], and for more general set expressions in [FA97]. A subtype-based analysis where sets are embedded within terms can be realized in BANE through the use of the FlowTerm sort. The FlowTerm sort provides inclusion constraints instead of equality for the same language and solution space as the Term sort. To take advantage of the extra precision of subtype inference in our example, we first change the TypeSort structure to use the FlowTerm sort.

```
structure TypeSort = Bane.FlowTerm
```

The definition of the function type constructor with labels remains the same, although the domain and range are now of sort FlowTerm.

```
val funSig = TypeSort.newSig {args=[TypeSort.ctv_arg TypeSort.genSort,
                                    TypeSort.cov_arg TypeSort.genSort,
                                    TypeSort.cov_arg LabelSet.genSort],
                              attributes=[]}

val fun_tycon = Bane.Cons.new {name="fun", signa=funSig}
```

The inference rules for abstraction and application change slightly. In the [ABS] rule, it is no longer necessary to introduce a fresh label-set variable, since label sets are no longer merged in the subtype approach. Instead the singleton set can be directly embedded within the function type. In the [APP] rule, we simply replace the equality constraint with an inclusion.

$$\frac{A[x \mapsto \alpha] \vdash e : \tau}{A \vdash \lambda^l x.e : \text{fun}(\alpha, \tau, \{l\})} \; [\text{ABS}] \qquad \frac{\begin{array}{c} A \vdash e_1 : \tau_1 \\ A \vdash e_2 : \tau_2 \\ \tau_1 \subseteq \text{fun}(\tau_2, \alpha, \epsilon) \end{array}}{A \vdash e_1 \, e_2 : \alpha} \; [\text{APP}]$$

Note that the inclusion constraint in the [APP] rule allows subsumption not only on the label-set of the function, but also on the domain and the range, since

$$\text{fun}(dom, range, labels) \subseteq \text{fun}(\tau_2, \alpha, \epsilon) \Leftrightarrow \begin{array}{l} \tau_2 \subseteq dom \; \wedge \\ range \subseteq \alpha \; \wedge \\ labels \subseteq \epsilon \end{array}$$

We return to the example of the previous section where flow information was merged:

$$\text{select' true false } (\lambda z.\lambda w.w)$$

Using subtype inference, the type of this expression is

$$\tau \setminus \tau = \tau \xrightarrow{\epsilon_1} \tau \xrightarrow{\epsilon_2} \tau$$
$$\text{true} \subseteq \epsilon_1$$
$$\text{true}_1 \subseteq \epsilon_2$$

The flow information now precisely models the fact that only true is passed as the second argument to $\lambda z.\lambda w.w$.

## 4  Analysis Frameworks

We conclude by comparing BANE with other program analysis frameworks. There have been many such frameworks in the past; see for example [ATGL96,AM95,Ass96,CDG96,DC96,HMCCR93,TH92,Ven89,YH93]. Most frameworks are based on standard dataflow analysis, as first proposed by Cocke [Coc70] and developed by Kildall [Kil73] and Kam and Ullman [KU76], while others are based on more general forms of abstract interpretation [Ven89,YH93].

In previous frameworks the user specifies a lattice and a set of transfer functions, either in a specialized language [AM95], in a Yacc-like system [TH92], or as a module conforming to a certain interface [ATGL96,CDG96,DC96,HMCCR93]. The framework traverses a program representation (usually a control flow graph) either forwards or backwards, calling user-defined transfer functions until the analysis reaches a fixed point.

A fundamental distinction between BANE and these frameworks is the interface with a client analysis. In BANE, the interface is a system of constraints, which is an explicit data structure that the framework understands and can inspect and transform for best effect. In other frameworks the interface is the transfer and lattice functions, all of which are defined by the client. These functions are opaque—their effect is unknown to the framework—which in general means that the dataflow frameworks have less structure that can be exploited by the implementation. For example, reasoning about termination of the framework is impossible without knowledge of the client. Additionally, using transfer functions implies that information can flow conveniently only in one direction, which gives rise to the restriction in dataflow frameworks that analyses are either forwards or backwards. An analysis that is neither forwards nor backwards (e.g., most forms of type inference) is at best awkward to code in this model.

On the other hand, dataflow frameworks provide more support for the task of implementing traditional dataflow analyses than BANE, since they typically manage the control flow graph and its traversal as well as the computation of abstract values. With BANE the user must write any needed traversal of the program structure, although this is usually a simple recursive walk of the abstract syntax tree. Since BANE has no knowledge of the program from which constraints are generated, BANE cannot directly exploit any special properties of program structure that might make constraint solving more efficient.

While there is very little experimental evidence on which to base any conclusion, it is our impression that an analysis implemented using the more general frameworks with user-defined transfer functions suffers a significant performance penalty (perhaps an order of magnitude) compared with a special-purpose implementation of the same analysis. Note that the dataflow frameworks target a different class of applications than BANE, and we do not claim that BANE is particularly useful for traditional dataflow problems. However, as discussed in Section 2.2, we do believe for problems with a natural type or constraint formulation that BANE provides users with significant benefits in development time together with good scalability and good to excellent performance compared with hand-written implementations of the same analyses.

# 5 Conclusions

BANE is a toolkit for constructing type- and constraint-based program analyses. An explicit goal of the project is to make realistic experimentation with program analysis ideas much easier than is now the case. We hope that other researchers find BANE useful in this way. The BANE distribution is available on the World Wide Web from http://bane.cs.berkeley.edu.

# References

[AFS98]     A. Aiken, M. Fähndrich, and Z. Su. Detecting Races in Relay Ladder Logic Programs. In *Tools and Algorithms for the Construction and Analysis of Systems, 4th International Conference, TACAS'98*, volume 1384 of *LNCS*, pages 184–200, Lisbon, Portugal, 1998. Springer.

[AM95]      M. Alt and F. Martin. Generation of efficient interprocedural analyzers with PAG. *Lecture Notes in Computer Science*, 983:33–50, 1995.

[And94]     L. Andersen. *Program Analysis and Specialization for the C Programming Language*. PhD thesis, DIKU, University of Cophenhagen, May 1994.

[Ass96]     U. Assmann. How to Uniformly Specify Program Analysis and Transformation with Graph Rewrite Systems. In *Proceedings of the Sixth International Conference on Compiler Construction (CC '96)*, pages 121–135. Springer-Verlag, April 1996.

[ATGL96]    A. Adl-Tabatabai, T. Gross, and G. Lueh. Code Reuse in an Optimizing Compiler. In *Proceedings of the ACM Conference on Object-Oriented Programming Systems, Languages, and Applications (OOPSLA '96)*, pages 51–68, October 1996.

[AW93]      A. Aiken and E. Wimmers. Type Inclusion Constraints and Type Inference. In *Proceedings of the 1993 Conference on Functional Programming Languages and Computer Architecture*, pages 31–41, Copenhagen, Denmark, June 1993.

[AWL94]     A. Aiken, E. Wimmers, and T.K. Lakshman. Soft Typing with Conditional Types. In *Twenty-First Annual ACM Symposium on Principles of Programming Languages*, pages 163–173, January 1994.

[CC77]      P. Cousot and R. Cousot. Abstract Interpretation: A Unified Lattice Model for Static Analysis of Programs by Contruction or Approximation of Fixed Points. In *Fourth Annual ACM Symposium on Principles of Programming Languages*, pages 238–252, January 1977.

[CDG96]     C. Chambers, J. Dean, and D. Grove. Frameworks for Intra- and Interprocedural Dataflow Analysis. Technical Report 96-11-02, Department of Computer Science and Engineering, University of Washington, November 1996.

[Coc70]     J. Cocke. Global Common Subexpression Elimination. *ACM SIGPLAN Notices*, 5(7):20–24, July 1970.

[DC96]      M. Dwyer and L. Clarke. A Flexible Architecture for Building Data Flow Analyzers. In *Proceedings of the 18th International Conference on Software Engineering (ICSE-18)*, Berlin, Germany, March 1996.

[DM82]      L. Damas and R. Milner. Principle Type-Schemes for Functional Programs. In *Ninth Annual ACM Symposium on Principles of Programming Languages*, pages 207–212, January 1982.

[EST95]     J. Eifrig, S. Smith, and V. Trifonov. Sound Polymorphic Type Inference for Objects. In *OOPSLA '95*, pages 169–184, 1995.

[FA96]      M. Fähndrich and A. Aiken. Making Set-Constraint Based Program Analyses Scale. In *First Workshop on Set Constraints at CP'96*, Cambridge, MA, August 1996. Available as Technical Report CSD-TR-96-917, University of California at Berkeley.

[FA97]      M. Fähndrich and A. Aiken. Program Analysis Using Mixed Term and Set Constraints. In *Proceedings of the 4th International Static Analysis Symposium*, pages 114–126, 1997.

[FFA97]     J. Foster, M. Fähndrich, and A. Aiken. Flow-Insensitive Points-to Analysis with Term and Set Constraints. Technical Report UCB//CSD-97-964, University of California, Berkeley, July 1997.

[FFA98]     M. Fähndrich, J. Foster, and A. Aiken. Tracking down Exceptions in Standard ML Programs. Technical Report UCB/CSD-98-996, EECS Department, UC Berkeley, February 1998.

[FFK+96]    C. Flanagan, M. Flatt, S. Krishnamurthi, S. Weirich, and M. Felleisen. Catching Bugs in the Web of Program Invariants. In *Proceedings of the 1996 ACM SIGPLAN Conference on Programming Language Design and Implementation*, pages 23–32, May 1996.

[FFSA98]    M. Fähndrich, J. Foster, Z. Su, and A. Aiken. Partial Online Cycle Elimination in Inclusion Constraint Graphs. In *Proceedings of the ACM SIGPLAN '98 Conference on Programming Language Design and Implementation*, 1998.

[GJSO92]    D. Gifford, P. Jouvelot, M. Sheldon, and J. O'Toole. Report on the FX-91 Programming Language. Technical Report MIT/LCS/TR-531, Massachusetts Institute of Technology, February 1992.

[Hei94]     N. Heintze. Set Based Analysis of ML Programs. In *Proceedings of the 1994 ACM Conference on LISP and Functional Programming*, pages 306–17, June 1994.

[Hen92]     F. Henglein. Global Tagging Optimization by Type Inference. In *Proceedings of the 1992 ACM Conference on Lisp and Functional Programming*, pages 205–215, July 1992.

[HM97]      N. Heintze and D. McAllester. Linear-Time Subtransitive Control Flow Analysis. In *Proceedings of the 1997 ACM SIGPLAN Conference on Programming Language Design and Implementation*, June 1997.

[HMCCR93]   M. Hall, J. Mellor-Crummey, A. Carle, and R. Rodríguez. FIAT: A Framework for Interprocedural Analysis and Transformation. In U. Banerjee, D. Gelernter, A. Nicolau, and D. Padua, editors, *Proceedings of the 6th International Workshop on Parallel Languages and Compilers*, pages 522–545, Portland, Oregon, August 1993. Springer-Verlag.

[Kil73]     G. A. Kildall. A Unified Approach to Global Program Optimization. In *ACM Symposium on Principles of Programming Languages*, pages 194–206, Boston, MA, October 1973. ACM, ACM.

[KU76]      J. Kam and J. Ullman. Global Data Flow Analysis and Iterative Algorithms. *Journal of the ACM*, 23(1):158–171, January 1976.

[Mos96]     Christian Mossin. *Flow Analysis of Typed Higher-Order Programs*. PhD thesis, DIKU, Department of Computer Science, University of Copenhagen, 1996.

[MTH90]     Robin Milner, Mads Tofte, and Robert Harper. *The Definition of Standard ML*. MIT Press, 1990.

[Rém89]     D. Rémy. Typechecking records and variants in a natural extension of ML. In *Conference Record of the Sixteenth Annual ACM Symposium on Principles of Programming Languages, Austin, Texas*, pages 60–76, January 1989.

[Ste96]     B. Steensgaard. Points-to Analysis in Almost Linear Time. In *Proceedings of the 23rd Annual ACM SIGPLAN-SIGACT Symposium on Principles of Programming Languages*, pages 32–41, January 1996.

[TH92]     S. Tjiang and J. Hennessy. Sharlit – A tool for building optimizers. In
           *Proceedings of the ACM SIGPLAN '92 Conference on Programming Lan-*
           *guage Design and Implementation*, pages 82–93, July 1992.

[TT94]     M. Tofte and J.-P. Talpin. Implementation of the Typed Call-by-Value
           λ-Calculus using a Stack of Regions. In *Twenty-First Annual ACM Sym-*
           *posium on Principles of Programming Languages*, pages 188–201, 1994.

[Ven89]    G. A. Venkatesh. A framework for construction and evaluation of high-
           level specifications for program analysis techniques. In *Proceedings of the*
           *ACM SIGPLAN '89 Conference on Programming Language Design and*
           *Implementation*, pages 1–12, 1989.

[YH93]     K. Yi and W. Harrison, III. Automatic Generation and Management
           of Interprocedural Program Analyses. In *Proceedings of the Twnetieth*
           *Annual ACM Symposium on Principles of Programming Languages*, pages
           246–259, January 1993.

# Optimizing ML
# Using a Hierarchy of Monadic Types

Andrew Tolmach[*]

Pacific Software Research Center
Portland State University & Oregon Graduate Institute
Dept. of Computer Science, P.S.U., P.O. Box 751, Portland, OR 97207, USA
apt@cs.pdx.edu

**Abstract.** We describe a type system and typed semantics that use a
hierarchy of monads to describe and delimit a variety of effects, including
non-termination, exceptions, and state, in a call-by-value functional language. The type system and semantics can be used to organize and justify
a variety of optimizing transformations in the presence of effects. In addition, we describe a simple monad inferencing algorithm that computes
the minimum effect for each subexpression of a program, and provides
more accurate effects information than local syntactic methods.

## 1   Introduction

Optimizers are often implemented as engines that repeatedly apply improving
transformations to programs. Among the most important transformations are
*propagation* of values from their defining site to their use site, and *hoisting* of
invariant computations out of loops. If we use a pure (side-effect-free) language
based on the lambda calculus as our compiler intermediate language, these transformations can be neatly described by the simple equations for beta-reduction

(Beta) $$\text{let } x = e_1 \text{ in } e_2 = e_2[e_1/x]$$

and for the exchange and hoisting of bindings

(Exchange)
$$\text{let } x_1 = e_1 \text{ in (let } x_2 = e_2 \text{ in } e_3) = \\ \text{let } x_2 = e_2 \text{ in (let } x_1 = e_1 \text{ in } e_3) \\ (x_1 \notin FV(e_2); x_2 \notin FV(e_1))$$

(RecHoist)
$$\text{letrec } f\ x = (\text{let } y = e_1 \text{ in } e_2) \text{ in } e_3 = \\ \text{let } y = e_1 \text{ in (letrec } f\ x = e_2 \text{ in } e_3) \\ (x, f \notin FV(e_1); y \notin FV(e_3))$$

where $FV(e)$ is the set of free variables of $e$. The side conditions nicely express
the data dependence conditions under which the equations are valid. Either

---

[*] Supported, in part, by the US Air Force Materiel Command under contract F19628-
93-C-0069 and by the National Science Foundation under grant CCR-9503383.

orientation of the equation generates a valid transformation.[1] Effective compilers for pure, lazy functional languages (e.g., [14]) have been conceived and built on the basis of such transformations, with considerable advantages for modularity and correctness.

It would be nice to apply similar methods to the optimization of languages like ML, which have side effects such as I/O, mutable state, and exceptions. Unfortunately, these "rearranging" transformations are not generally valid for such languages. For example, if we apply (Beta) (oriented left-to-right) in a situation where evaluating $e_1$ performs output and $x$ is mentioned twice in $e_2$, evaluating the resulting expression might produce the output twice. In fact, once an eager evaluation order is fixed, even non-termination becomes a "side effect." For example, (RecHoist) is not valid unless $e_1$ is known to be terminating (and free of other effects too, of course).

A similar challenge long faced *lazy* functional languages at the source level: how could one obtain the power of side-effecting operations without invalidating simple "equational reasoning" based on (Beta) and similar rules? The effective solution discovered in that context is to use *monads* [9,13]. An obvious idea, therefore, is to use monads in an internal representation (IR) for compilers of call-by-value languages. Some initial steps in this direction were recently taken by Peyton Jones, Launchbury, Shields, and Tolmach [11]. The aim of that work was to design an IR suitable for both eager and lazy source languages. In this paper we pursue the use of monads with particular reference to eager languages (only), and address the question of how to discover and record several *different sorts* of effects in a single, unified monadic type system. We introduce a *hierarchy* of monads, ordered by increasing "strength of effect," and an inference algorithm for annotating source program subexpressions with their minimal effect.

Past approaches to coping with effects have fallen into two main camps. One approach (used, e.g., by SML of New Jersey [1] and the TIL compiler [17]) is to fall back on a weaker form of (Beta), called (Beta$_v$), which *is* valid in eager settings. (Beta$_v$) restricts the bound expression $e$ to variables, constants, and $\lambda$-abstractions; since "evaluating" these expressions never actually causes any computation, they can be moved and substituted with impunity. To augment this rule, these compilers use local syntactic analysis to discover expressions that are demonstrably pure and terminating. Local syntactic analysis must assume that calls to unknown functions may be impure and non-terminating. Still, this form of analysis can be quite effective, particularly if the compiler inlines functions enthusiastically. The other approach (used, e.g., by the ML Kit compiler [4]) uses a sophisticated *effect inference* system [15] to track the latent effects of functions on a very detailed basis. The goals of this school are typically more far-reaching; the aim is to use effects information to provide more generous

---

[1] Of course, the fact that a transformation is valid doesn't mean that applying it will necessarily improve the program. For example, (Beta) (oriented left-to-right) is not an improving transformation if $e_1$ is expensive to compute and $x$ appears many times in $e_2$; similarly, (RecHoist) (oriented left-to-right) is not improving if $f$ is not applied in $e_3$.

polymorphic generalization rules (e.g., as in [21, 16]), or to perform significantly more sophisticated optimizations, such as automatic parallelization [6] or stack-allocation of heap-like data [18]. In support of these goals, effect inference has generally been used to track store effects at a fine-grained level.

Our approach is essentially a simple monomorphic variant of effect inference applied to a wider variety of effects (including non-termination, exceptions, and IO), cast in monadic form, and intended to support transformational code-motion optimizations. We infer information about latent effects, but we do not attempt to calculate effects at a very fine level of granularity. In return, our inference system is particularly simple to state and implement. However, there is nothing fundamentally new about our system as compared with that of Talpin and Jouvelot [15], except our decision to use a monadic syntax and validate it using a typed monadic semantics. A practical advantage of the monadic syntax is that it makes it easy to reflect the results of the effect inference in the program itself, where they can be easily consulted (and kept up to date) by subsequent optimizations, rather than in an auxiliary data structure. An advantage of the monadic semantics is that it provides a natural foundation for probing and proving the correctness of transformations in the presence of a variety of effects.

In related work, Wadler [20] has recently and independently shown that Talpin and Jouvelot's effect inference system can be applied in a monadic framework; he uses an untyped semantics, and considers only store effects. In another independent project, Benton and Kennedy are prototyping an ML compiler with an IR that describes effects using a monadic encoding similar to ours [3].

## 2   Source Language

This section briefly describes an ML-like source language we use to explain our approach. The call-by-value source language is presented in Fig. 1. It is a simple, monomorphic variant of ML, expressed in A-normal form [5], which names the result of each computation and makes evaluation order completely explicit. The class **const** includes primitive functions as well as constants. The **Let** construct is monomorphic; that is, $\text{Let}(x, e_1, e_2)$ has the same semantics and typing properties as would $\text{App}(\text{Abs}(x, e_2), e_1)$ (were this legal A-normal form). The restriction to a monomorphic language is not essential (see Sect. 5). All functions are unary; primitives like **Plus** take a two-element tuple as argument. For simplicity of presentation, we restrict **Letrec** to single functions.

The types of constants are given in Fig. 2. Exceptions carry values of type **Exn**, which are nullary exception constructors. **Raise** takes an exception constructor; rather than providing a means for declaring such constructors, we assume an arbitrary pool of constructor constants. **Handle** catches *all* exceptions that are raised while evaluating its first argument and passes the associated exception value to its second argument, which must be a handler function expecting an **Exn**. The body of the handler function may or may not choose to reraise the exception depending on its value, which may be tested using **EqExn**.

```
datatype typ =                          type varty = var * typ
   Int
 | Bool                                 datatype value =
 | Exn                                     Var of var
 | Tup of typ list                       | Const of const
 | -> of typ * typ

datatype const =                        datatype exp =
   Integer of int                          Val of value
 | True | False                          | Abs of varty * exp
 | DivByZero | ...                       | App of value * value
 | Plus | Minus | Times                  | If of value * exp * exp
 | Divide                                | Let of varty * exp * exp
 | EqInt | LtInt                         | Letrec of varty * varty * exp * exp
 | EqBool | EqExn                        | Tuple of value list
 | WriteInt                              | Project of int * value
 | ...                                   | Raise of value
                                         | Handle of exp * value
```

**Fig. 1.** Abstract syntax for source language (presented as ML datatype)

```
                    Integer _ : Int
                  True,False : Bool
                   DivByZero : Exn
  Plus,Minus,Times,Divide : Tup[Int,Int] -> Int
              EqInt,LtInt : Tup[Int,Int] -> Bool
                     EqBool : Tup[Bool,Bool] -> Bool
                      EqExn : Tup[Exn,Exn] -> Bool
                   WriteInt : Int -> Tup[]
```

**Fig. 2.** Typings for constants in initial environment

The primitive function Divide has the potential to raise a particular exception DivByZero. We supply WriteInt as a paradigmatic state-altering primitive; internal side-effects such as ML reference manipulations would be handled similarly. All other primitives are pure and guaranteed to terminate. The semantics of the remainder of the language are completely ordinary.

## 3   Intermediate Representation with Monadic Types

Figure 3 shows the abstract syntax of our monadic intermediate representation (IR). (For an example of the code, look ahead to Fig. 11.) For the most part, terms are the same as in the source language, but with the addition of monad annotations on Let and Handle constructs and a new Up construct; these are described in detail below.

```
datatype monad = ID | LIFT | EXN | ST

datatype mtyp = M of monad * vtyp
and vtyp =
  Int
| Bool
| Exn
| Tup of vtyp list
| -> of vtyp * mtyp

type varty = var * vtyp

datatype value =
  Var of var
| Const of const

datatype exp =
  Val of value
| Abs of varty * exp
| App of value * value
| If of value * exp * exp
| Let of monad * monad * varty * exp * exp
| Letrec of varty * varty * exp * exp
| Tuple of value list
| Project of int * value
| Raise of mtyp * value
| Handle of monad * exp * value
| Up of monad * monad * exp
```

**Fig. 3.** Abstract syntax for monadic typed intermediate representation

```
         Integer _ : Int
        True,False : Bool
         DivByZero : Exn
  Plus,Minus,Times : Tup[Int,Int] -> M(ID,Int)
            Divide : Tup[Int,Int] -> M(EXN,Int)
       EqInt,LtInt : Tup[Int,Int] -> M(ID,Bool)
            EqBool : Tup[Bool,Bool] -> M(ID,Bool)
             EqExn : Tup[Exn,Exn] -> M(ID,Bool)
          WriteInt : Int -> M(ST,Tup[])
```

**Fig. 4.** Monadic typings for constants in initial environment

Values have ordinary value types (vtyps); expressions have monadic types (mtyps), which incorporate a vtyp and a monad (possibly the identity monad, ID). Since this is a call-by-value language, the domain of each arrow types is a vtyp, but the codomain is an arbitrary mtyp. The monadic types for the constants are specified in Fig. 4. The typing rules are given in Fig. 5. In this figure, and throughout our discussion, $t$ ranges value types, $m$ over monads, $v$ over values, $c$ over constants, $x,y,z,f$ over variables, and $e$ over expressions.

For this presentation, we use four monads arranged in a simple linear order. In order of "increasing effect," these are:

- ID, the identity monad, which describes pure, terminating computations.
- LIFT, the lifting monad, which describes pure but potentially non-terminating computations.
- EXN, the monad of exceptions and lifting, which describes computations that may raise an (uncaught) exception, and are potentially non-terminating.
- ST, the monad of state, exceptions, and lifting, which describes computations that may write to the "outside world," may raise an exception, and are potentially non-terminating.

We write $m_1 < m_2$ iff $m_1$ precedes $m_2$ on this list. Intuitively, $m_1 < m_2$ implies that computations in $m_2$ are "more effectful" than those in $m_1$; they can provoke any of the effects in $m_1$ and then some. This particular hierarchy captures a number of distinctions that are useful for transforming ML programs. We discuss the extension of our approach to more elaborately stratified monadic structures in Sect. 6.

More formally, suppose for each monad $m$ we are given the standard operations $unit_m$, which turns values into null computations in $m$, and $bind_m$, which composes computations in $m$, and that the usual monad laws hold:

(Left) $$bind_m \ (unit_m x) \ k = k \ x$$

(Right) $$bind_m \ e \ unit_m = e$$

(Assoc) $$bind_m \ e \ (\lambda x.bind_m \ (k \ x) \ h) = bind_m (bind_m \ e \ k) \ h$$

Moreover, suppose that for each value type $t$ and monad $m$, $\mathcal{M}[m](\mathcal{T}[t])$ gives the domain of values of type $M(m,t)$. Then $m_1 < m_2$ implies that there exists an unique embedding $up_{m_1 \to m_2}$ which, for every value type $t$, maps $\mathcal{M}[m_1](\mathcal{T}[t])$ to $\mathcal{M}[m_2](\mathcal{T}[t])$. The $up$ functions, sometimes called monad morphisms or lifting functions [10], obey these laws:

(Unit) $$up_{m_1 \to m_2} \circ unit_{m_1} = unit_{m_2}$$

(Bind) $$up_{m_1 \to m_2}(bind_{m_1} \ e \ k) = bind_{m_2}(up_{m_1 \to m_2} \ e) \ (up_{m_1 \to m_2} \circ k)$$

The $up$ functions can also be viewed as generalizations of $unit$ operations, since, by (Unit), $up_{\text{ID} \to m} = unit_m$. Fig. 6 gives semantic interpretations for types as

$$\frac{E(v) = t}{E \vdash_v \mathtt{Var}\ v : t}$$

$$\frac{\mathtt{Typeof}(c) = t}{E \vdash_v \mathtt{Const}\ c : t}$$

$$\frac{E \vdash_v v : t}{E \vdash \mathtt{Val}\ v : \mathtt{M(ID},t)}$$

$$\frac{E + \{x : t_1\} \vdash e : \mathtt{M}(m_2,t_2)}{E \vdash \mathtt{Abs}(x : t_1,e) : \mathtt{M(ID},t_1 \mathtt{\ ->\ M}(m_2,t_2))}$$

$$\frac{E \vdash_v v_1 : t_1 \mathtt{\ ->\ M}(m_2,t_2) \quad E \vdash_v v_2 : t_1}{E \vdash \mathtt{App}(v_1,v_2) : \mathtt{M}(m_2,t_2)}$$

$$\frac{E \vdash_v v : \mathtt{Bool} \quad E \vdash e_1 : \mathtt{M}(m,t) \quad E \vdash e_2 : \mathtt{M}(m,t)}{E \vdash \mathtt{If}(v,e_1,e_2) : \mathtt{M}(m,t)}$$

$$\frac{E \vdash e_1 : \mathtt{M}(m_1,t_1) \quad E + \{x : t_1\} \vdash e_2 : \mathtt{M}(m_2,t_2) \quad (m_1 \leq m_2)}{E \vdash \mathtt{Let}(m_1,m_2,x : t_1,e_1,e_2) : \mathtt{M}(m_2,t_2)}$$

$$\frac{\begin{array}{c}E + \{f : t_0 \mathtt{\ ->\ M}(m_1,t_1), x : t_0\} \vdash e_1 : \mathtt{M}(m_1,t_1) \\ E + \{f : t_0 \mathtt{\ ->\ M}(m_1,t_1)\} \vdash e_2 : \mathtt{M}(m_2,t_2)\end{array} \quad (\mathtt{LIFT} \leq m_1)}{E \vdash \mathtt{Letrec}(f : t_0 \mathtt{\ ->\ M}(m_1,t_1), x : t_0,e_1,e_2) : \mathtt{M}(m_2,t_2)}$$

$$\frac{E \vdash_v v_1 : t_1 \quad \ldots \quad E \vdash_v v_n : t_n}{E \vdash \mathtt{Tuple}(v_1,\ldots,v_n) : \mathtt{M(ID,Tup}[t_1,\ldots,t_n])}$$

$$\frac{E \vdash_v v : \mathtt{Tup}[t_1,\ldots,t_n] \quad (1 \leq i \leq n)}{E \vdash \mathtt{Project}(i,v) : \mathtt{M(ID},t_i)}$$

$$\frac{E \vdash_v v : \mathtt{Exn}}{E \vdash \mathtt{Raise(M(EXN},t),v) : \mathtt{M(EXN},t)}$$

$$\frac{E \vdash e : \mathtt{M}(m,t) \quad E \vdash_v v : \mathtt{Exn\ ->\ M}(m,t) \quad (\mathtt{EXN} \leq m)}{E \vdash \mathtt{Handle}(m,e,v) : \mathtt{M}(m,t)}$$

$$\frac{E \vdash e : \mathtt{M}(m_1,t) \quad (m_1 \leq m_2)}{E \vdash \mathtt{Up}(m_1,m_2,e) : \mathtt{M}(m_2,t)}$$

**Fig. 5.** Typing rules for intermediate language

complete partial orders ($\mathcal{CPO}$'s), and for our monads, together with the associated *up* and *bind* functions. Note that the following laws hold under these semantics:

(Id) $$up_{m \to m} = id$$

(Compose) $$up_{m_0 \to m_2} = up_{m_1 \to m_2} \circ up_{m_0 \to m_1} \quad (m_0 \leq m_1 \leq m_2)$$

A typed semantics for terms is given in Figs. 7 and 8. Environments $\rho$ map identifiers to values. This semantics is largely predictable. However, the Let construct now serves to make the composition of monadic computations explicit, and the Up construct makes monadic coercions explicit. Intuitively,

$$\text{Let} (m_1, m_2, (x, t_1), e_1, e_2)$$

evaluates $e_1$, which has monadic type $\text{M}(m_1, t)$, performing any associated effects, binds the resulting value to $x : t_1$, and then evaluates $e_2$, which has monadic type $\text{M}(m_2, t_2)$. Thus, it essentially plays the role of the usual monadic *bind* operation; in particular, if $m_1 = m_2$, the semantic interpretation of the above expression in environment $\rho$ is just

$$bind_{m_1} (\mathcal{E}[\![e_1]\!]\rho)(\lambda y.\mathcal{E}[\![e_2]\!]\rho[x := y])$$

However, our typing rules (Fig. 5) require only that $m_2 \geq m_1$; i.e., $e_2$ may be in a more effectful monad than $e_1$ The semantics of a general "mixed-monad" Let is

$$bind_{m_2} (up_{m_1 \to m_2} (\mathcal{E}[\![e_1]\!]\rho))(\lambda y.\mathcal{E}[\![e_2]\!]\rho[x := y])$$

The term $\text{Let} (\text{Up}(m_1, m_2, e_1), m_2, (x, t), e_1, e_2)$ has the same semantics, so the more general form of Let is strictly redundant. But this form is useful, because it makes it easier to state (and recognize left-hand sides for) many interesting *transformations* involving Let whose validity depends on the monad $m_1$ rather than on $m_2$. For example, a "non-monadic" Let, for which (Beta) is always valid, is simply one in which $m_1 = \text{ID}$. Further examples will be shown in Sect. 4.

The semantics of the "non-proper morphism" $\text{Handle}(e, v)$ deserve special attention. Expression $e$ may be in either EXN or ST, and the meaning of Handle depends on which; the ST version must manipulate the state component. Note that there are two plausible ways to combine state with exceptions. In the semantics we have given (as in ML), handling an exception does not alter the state, but it would be equally reasonable to revert the state on handle. Incidentally, we don't have to give a semantics when $e$ is in ID or LIFT, because the typing rule for Handle disallows these cases. Of course, such cases might appear in source code; to generate monadic IR for them, $e$ can be coerced into EXN with an explicit Up, or the Handle can be omitted altogether in favor of $e$, which by its type cannot raise an exception! A Raise expression is handled similarly; the typing rules force it into monad EXN, so semantics need only be given for that case, but the whole expression may be coerced into ST by an explicit Up if necessary.

$$\mathcal{T} : \text{vtyp} \to \mathcal{CPO}$$
$$\mathcal{T}[\![\text{Int}]\!] = \mathcal{Z}$$
$$\mathcal{T}[\![\text{Bool}]\!] = \mathcal{Z} \qquad\qquad (0 \text{ represents false})$$
$$\mathcal{T}[\![\text{Exn}]\!] = \mathcal{Z}$$
$$\mathcal{T}[\![\text{Tup}[t_1,\ldots,t_n]]\!] = \mathcal{T}[\![t_1]\!] \times \ldots \times \mathcal{T}[\![t_n]\!] \qquad\qquad (n > 0)$$
$$\mathcal{T}[\![\text{Tup}[]]\!] = \mathbf{1}$$
$$\mathcal{T}[\![t_1 \text{ -> } \text{M}(m_2,t_2)]\!] = \mathcal{T}[\![t_1]\!] \to \mathcal{M}[\![m_2]\!](\mathcal{T}[\![t_2]\!])$$

$$\mathcal{M} : \text{monad} \to \mathcal{CPO} \to \mathcal{CPO}$$
$$\mathcal{M}[\![\text{ID}]\!]c = c$$
$$\mathcal{M}[\![\text{LIFT}]\!]c = c_\perp$$
$$\mathcal{M}[\![\text{EXN}]\!]c = (\mathbf{Ok}(c) + \mathbf{Fail}(\mathcal{Z}))_\perp$$
$$\mathcal{M}[\![\text{ST}]\!]c = \mathbf{State} \to ((\mathbf{Ok}(c) + \mathbf{Fail}(\mathcal{Z})) \times \mathbf{State})_\perp$$

$$bind_{\text{ID}} \; x \; k = k \; x$$
$$
\begin{aligned}
bind_{\text{LIFT}} \; x \; k &= k \; a && \text{if } x = a_\perp \\
&\quad \perp && \text{if } x = \perp \\
bind_{\text{EXN}} \; x \; k &= k \; a && \text{if } x = \mathbf{Ok}(a)_\perp \\
&\quad \mathbf{Fail}(b)_\perp && \text{if } x = \mathbf{Fail}(b)_\perp \\
&\quad \perp && \text{if } x = \perp \\
bind_{\text{ST}} \; x \; k \; s &= k \; a \; s' && \text{if } x \; s = (\mathbf{Ok}(a), s')_\perp \\
&\quad (\mathbf{Fail}(b), s')_\perp && \text{if } x \; s = (\mathbf{Fail}(b), s')_\perp \\
&\quad \perp && \text{if } x \; s = \perp
\end{aligned}
$$

$$
\begin{aligned}
up_{m \to m} \; x &= x \\
up_{\text{ID} \to \text{LIFT}} \; x &= x_\perp \\
up_{\text{ID} \to \text{EXN}} \; x &= \mathbf{Ok}(x)_\perp \\
up_{\text{ID} \to \text{ST}} \; x \; s &= (\mathbf{Ok}(x), s)_\perp \\
up_{\text{LIFT} \to \text{EXN}} \; x &= \mathbf{Ok}(a)_\perp && \text{if } x = a_\perp \\
&\quad \perp && \text{if } x = \perp \\
up_{\text{LIFT} \to \text{ST}} \; x \; s &= (\mathbf{Ok}(a), s)_\perp && \text{if } x = a_\perp \\
&\quad \perp && \text{if } x = \perp \\
up_{\text{EXN} \to \text{ST}} \; x \; s &= (\mathbf{Ok}(a), s)_\perp && \text{if } x = \mathbf{Ok}(a)_\perp \\
&\quad (\mathbf{Fail}(b), s)_\perp && \text{if } x = \mathbf{Fail}(b)_\perp \\
&\quad \perp && \text{if } x = \perp
\end{aligned}
$$

**Fig. 6.** Semantics of types and monads

$$\mathcal{V} : (\text{value} : t) \to Env \to \mathcal{T}[t]$$
$$\mathcal{V}[\text{Var } v]\rho = \rho(v)$$
$$\mathcal{V}[\text{Const (Integer } i)]\rho = i$$
$$\mathcal{V}[\text{Const True}]\rho = 1$$
$$\mathcal{V}[\text{Const False}]\rho = 0$$
$$\mathcal{V}[\text{Const Plus}]\rho = plus$$
$$\ldots \mathcal{V}[\text{Const Divide}]\rho = divideby$$
$$\ldots \mathcal{V}[\text{Const WriteInt}]\rho = writeint$$
$$\mathcal{V}[\text{Const DivByZero}]\rho = divby0$$

$$\cdots$$

$$plus\ (a_1, a_2) = a_1 + a_2$$
$$divideby\ (a_1, a_2) = \mathbf{Ok}(a_1/a_2)_\perp \qquad\qquad \text{if } a_2 \neq 0$$
$$\mathbf{Fail}(divby0)_\perp \qquad\qquad \text{if } a_2 = 0$$
$$State = [\mathcal{Z}] \qquad\qquad (\text{sequence written out so far})$$
$$writeint\ a\ s = (\mathbf{Ok}(), append(s, [a]))_\perp$$
$$divby0 = 42 \qquad\qquad (\text{arbitrary fixed integer})$$

**Fig. 7.** Semantics of values

$$\mathcal{E} : (\text{exp} : \text{M}(m,t)) \to Env \to \mathcal{M}[m](\mathcal{T}[t])$$
$$\mathcal{E}[\text{Val } v]\rho = \mathcal{V}[v]\rho$$
$$\mathcal{E}[\text{Abs}(x,e)]\rho = \lambda y.\mathcal{E}[e]\rho[x := y]$$
$$\mathcal{E}[\text{App}(v_1,v_2)]\rho = (\mathcal{V}[v_1]\rho)\ (\mathcal{V}[v_2]\rho)$$
$$\mathcal{E}[\text{If}(v,e_1,e_2)]\rho = if\ (\mathcal{V}[v]\rho)\ (\mathcal{E}[e_1]\rho)\ (\mathcal{E}[e_2]\rho)$$
$$\mathcal{E}[\text{Letrec}(f,x,e_1,e_2)]\rho = \mathcal{E}[e_2](\rho[f := fix(\lambda f'.\lambda v.\mathcal{E}[e_1](\rho[f := f', x := v]))])$$
$$\mathcal{E}[\text{Tuple}(v_1,\ldots,v_n)]\rho = (\mathcal{V}[v_1]\rho,\ldots,\mathcal{V}[v_n]\rho)$$
$$\mathcal{E}[\text{Project}(i,v)]\rho = proj_i(\mathcal{V}[v]\rho)$$
$$\mathcal{E}[\text{Raise}(\text{M}(\text{EXN},t),v)]\rho = (\mathbf{Fail}(\mathcal{V}[v]\rho))_\perp$$
$$\mathcal{E}[\text{Handle}(m,e,v)]\rho = handle_m(\mathcal{E}[e]\rho)(\mathcal{V}[v]\rho)$$
$$\mathcal{E}[\text{Let}(m_1,m_2,x,e_1,e_2)]\rho = bind_{m_2}(up_{m_1 \to m_2}(\mathcal{E}[e_1]\rho))(\lambda y.\mathcal{E}[e_2]\rho[x := y])$$
$$\mathcal{E}[\text{Up}(m_1,m_2,e)]\rho = up_{m_1 \to m_2}(\mathcal{E}[e]\rho)$$

$$if\ v\ a_t\ a_f = a_t \qquad\qquad \text{if } v \neq 0$$
$$a_f \qquad\qquad \text{if } v = 0$$
$$proj_i(v_1,\ldots,v_n) = v_i$$
$$handle_{\text{EXN}}\ x\ h = \mathbf{Ok}(a)_\perp \qquad\qquad \text{if } x = \mathbf{Ok}(a)_\perp$$
$$h\ a \qquad\qquad \text{if } x = \mathbf{Fail}(a)_\perp$$
$$\perp \qquad\qquad \text{if } x = \perp$$
$$handle_{\text{ST}}\ x\ h\ s = (\mathbf{Ok}(a), s')_\perp \qquad\qquad \text{if } x\ s = (\mathbf{Ok}(a), s')_\perp$$
$$h\ a\ s' \qquad\qquad \text{if } x\ s = (\mathbf{Fail}(a), s')_\perp$$
$$\perp \qquad\qquad \text{if } x\ s = \perp$$

**Fig. 8.** Semantics of expressions

$$\text{(LetLeft)} \quad \frac{\texttt{Let}(m_2,m_3,x,\texttt{Up}(m_1,m_2,e_1),e_2) = \texttt{Let}(m_1,m_3,x,e_1,e_2)}{(m_1 \leq m_2 \leq m_3)}$$

$$\text{(LetRight)} \quad \frac{\texttt{Let}(m_1,m_2,x,e,\texttt{Up}(\texttt{ID},m_2,\texttt{Val}(\texttt{Var }x))) = \texttt{Up}(m_1,m_2,e)}{(m_1 \leq m_2)}$$

$$\text{(LetAssoc)} \quad \begin{array}{c} \texttt{Let}(m_2,m_3,x,\texttt{Let}(m_1,m_2,y,e_1,e_2),e_3) = \\ \texttt{Let}(m_1,m_3,y,e_1,\texttt{Let}(m_2,m_3,x,e_2,e_3)) \\ (m_1 \leq m_2 \leq m_3; y \notin FV(e_3)) \end{array}$$

$$\text{(IdentUp)} \quad \texttt{Up}(m,m,e) = e$$

$$\text{(ComposeUp)} \quad \frac{\texttt{Up}(m_1,m_3,e) = \texttt{Up}(m_2,m_3,(\texttt{Up}(m_1,m_2,e)))}{(m_1 \leq m_2 \leq m_3)}$$

$$\text{(LetUp)} \quad \begin{array}{c} \texttt{Up}(m_2,m_4,\texttt{Let}(m_1,m_2,x,e_1,e_2)) = \\ \texttt{Let}(m_3,m_4,x,\texttt{Up}(m_1,m_3,e_1),\texttt{Up}(m_2,m_4,e_2)) \\ (m_1 \leq m_2, m_3 \leq m_4) \end{array}$$

**Fig. 9.** Generalized monad laws

## 4 Transformation Rules

In this section we attempt to motivate our IR, and in particular our choice of monads, by presenting a number of useful transformation laws. These laws can can be proved correct with respect to the denotational semantics of Sect. 3. The proofs are straightforward but tedious, so are omitted here. Of course, this is by no means a complete set of rules needed by an optimizer; there are many others, both general-purpose and specific to particular operators. Also, as noted earlier, not all valid transformations are improvements.

Figure 9 gives general rules for manipulating monadic expressions. (LetLeft), (LetRight), and (LetAssoc) are generalizations of the usual (Left), (Right), and (Assoc) laws for a single monad, which can be recovered from these rules by setting $m_1 = \text{ID}$ and $m_2 = m_3$ in (LetLeft), setting $m_1 = m_2$ in (LetRight), and setting $m_1 = m_2 = m_3$ in (LetAssoc). (IdentUp) and (ComposeUp) are just the (Ident) and (Compose) laws stated in IR syntax; they let us do housekeeping on coercions. Law (Unit) is the special case of (ComposeUp) obtained by setting $m_1 = \text{ID}$. (LetUp) permits us to move expressions with suitably weak effects in and out of coercions; (Bind) is the special case of (LetUp) obtained by setting $m_1 = m_2$ and $m_3 = m_4$, All these laws have variants involving Letrec, in which $\texttt{Letrec}(f,x,e_1,e_2):M(m,t)$ behaves just like $\texttt{Let}(\texttt{ID},m,f,\texttt{Abs}(x,e_1),e_2)$; we omit the details of these.

Figure 10 lists some valid laws for altering execution order. We have full beta reduction for variables bound in the ID monad (BetaID). In general, the order of two bindings can be exchanged if there is no data dependence between them, *and* if either of them is in the ID monad (ExchangeID) or both are in or below the LIFT monad (ExchangeLIFT). The intuition for the latter rule is that it harmless to reorder two expressions even if one or both may not terminate, because we cannot detect which one causes the non-termination. On the other hand, there is no similar rule for the EXN monad, because we *can* distinguish different raised exceptions according to the constructor value they carry. This is the principal difference between LIFT and EXN for the purposes of code motion.

Rule (RecHoistID) states that it always valid to lift a pure expression out of a Letrec (if no data dependence is violated). (RecHoistEXN) reflects a much stronger property: it is valid to lift a non-terminating or exception-raising expression of a Letrec *if* the recursive function is guaranteed to be executed at least once. This is the principal advantage of distinguishing EXN from the more general ST monad, for which the transform is not valid. Although the left-hand side of (RecHoistEXN) may seem a crude way to characterize functions guaranteed to be called at least once, and unlikely to appear in practice, it arises naturally if we systematically introduce loop headers for recursions [2], according to the following law:

$$\text{Letrec}(f,x,e_1,e_2):M(m,t) =$$

(Hdr) $\quad \text{Let}(\text{ID},m,f,\text{Abs}(z,\text{Letrec}(f',x,e_1[f'/f],\text{App}(f',z))),e_2)$
$$(f' \notin FV(e_1); f' \neq z)$$

(HandleHoistExn) says that an expression that cannot raise an exception can always be hoisted out of a Handle. Finally, (IfHoistID), (ThenHoistID), and (AbsHoistID) show the flexibility with which ID expressions can be manipulated; these are more likely to be useful when oriented right-to-left ("hoisting down" into conditionally executed code). As before, all these rules have variants involving Letrec in place of Let(ID,...), which we omit here.

As a (rather artificial) example of the power of these transformations, consider the code in Fig. 11. The computation of w is invariant, so we would like to hoist it above recursive function r. Because the binding for w is marked as pure and terminating, it can be lifted out of the if using (IfHoistID), and can then be exchanged with the pure bindings for s and t using (ExchangeID). This positions it to be lifted out of r using (RecHoistID). Note that the monad annotations tell us that w is pure and terminating even though it invokes the unknown function g, which is actually bound to h.

The example also exposes the limitations of monomorphic effects: if f were also applied to an impure function, then g and hence w would be marked as impure, and the binding for w would not be hoistable. In practice, it might be desirable to clone separate copies of f, specialized according to the effectfulness of their g argument. Worse yet, consider a function that is naturally parametric in its effect, such as map. Such a function will always be pessimistically annotated with an effect reflecting the most-effectful function passed to it within the program. The obvious solution is to give functions like map a generic type abstracted over a monad variable, analogous to an effect variable in the system of Talpin and Jouvelot [15]. We believe our system can be extended to handle such generic types, but we have not examined the semantic issues involved in detail.

(BetaID) $\quad\quad\quad\quad\quad\quad$ $\text{Let}(\text{ID},m,x,e_1,e_2) = e_2[e_1/x]$

(ExchangeID)
$$\text{Let}(m_1,m_3,x_1,e_1,\text{Let}(m_2,m_3,x_2,e_2,e_3)) =$$
$$\text{Let}(m_2,m_3,x_2,e_2,\text{Let}(m_1,m_3,x_1,e_1,e_3))$$
$$(m_1 = \text{ID} \textit{or } m_2 = \text{ID}; x_1 \notin FV(e_2); x_2 \notin FV(e_1))$$

(ExchangeLIFT)
$$\text{Let}(m_1,m_3,x_1,e_1,\text{Let}(m_2,m_3,x_2,e_2,e_3)) =$$
$$\text{Let}(m_2,m_3,x_2,e_2,\text{Let}(m_1,m_3,x_1,e_1,e_3))$$
$$(m_1,m_2 \leq \text{LIFT}; x_1 \notin FV(e_2); x_2 \notin FV(e_1))$$

(RecHoistID)
$$\text{Letrec}(f,x,\text{Let}(\text{ID},m_2,y,e_1,e_2),e_3):\text{M}(m_3,t) =$$
$$\text{Let}(\text{ID},m_3,y,e_1,\text{Letrec}(f,x,e_2,e_3))$$
$$(f,x \notin FV(e_1); y \notin FV(e_3))$$

(RecHoistEXN)
$$\text{Letrec}(f,x,\text{Let}(m_1,m_2,y,e_1,e_2),\text{App}(f,v)) =$$
$$\text{Let}(m_1,m_2,y,e_1,\text{Letrec}(f,x,e_2,\text{App}(f,v)))$$
$$(m_1 \leq \text{EXN}; f,x \notin FV(e_1); y \neq v)$$

(HandleHoistEXN)
$$\text{Handle}(m_2,\text{Let}(m_1,m_2,x,e_1,e_2),v) =$$
$$\text{Let}(m_1,m_2,x,e_1,\text{Handle}(m_2,e_2,v))$$
$$(m_1 \leq \text{EXN}; x \neq v)$$

(IfHoistID)
$$\text{If}(v,\text{Let}(\text{ID},m,x,e_1,e_2),e_3) =$$
$$\text{Let}(\text{ID},m,x,e_1,\text{If}(v,e_2,e_3))$$
$$(x \notin FV(e_3); x \neq v)$$

(ThenHoistID)
$$\text{If}(v,e_1,\text{Let}(\text{ID},m,x,e_2,e_3)) =$$
$$\text{Let}(\text{ID},m,x,e_2,\text{If}(v,e_1,e_3))$$
$$(x \notin FV(e_1); x \neq v)$$

(AbsHoistID)
$$\text{Abs}(x:t,\text{Let}(\text{ID},m,y,e_1,e_2)) =$$
$$\text{Let}(\text{ID},\text{ID},y,e_1,\text{Abs}(x:t,e_2))$$
$$(x \notin FV(e_1); y \neq x)$$

**Fig. 10.** Code motion laws for monadic expressions

```
let f:(Int -> M(ID,Int * Int)) -> M(ST,Int) =
    fn (g:Int->M(ID,Int * Int)) =>
        letrec r (x:Int) : M(ST,Int) =
            letID t:Int * Int = (x,1)
            in letID s:Bool = EqInt(t)
                in if s then
                        Up(ID,ST,0)
                    else
                        letID w:Int * Int = g(3)
                        in letID y:Int = Plus(w)
                            in letID z:Int * int = (x,y)
                                in letEXN x':Int = Divide(z)
                                    in letST dummy:() = WriteInt(x')
                                        in r(x')
            in r(10)
in let h:Int->M(ID,Int * Int) = fn (p:Int) => (p,p)
    in f(h)
```

**Fig. 11.** Example of intermediate code, presented in an obvious concrete analogue of the abstract syntax

## 5   Monad Inference

It would be possible to translate source programs into type-correct IR programs by simply assuming that *every* expression falls into the maximally-effectful monad (ST in our case). Every source Let would become a LetST, every variable and constant would be coerced into ST, and every primitive would return a value in ST. Peyton Jones *et al.* [11] suggest performing such a translation, and then using the monad laws (analogous to those in Fig. 9) and the worker-wrapper transform [12] to simplify the result, hopefully resulting in some less-effectful expression bindings. The main objection to this approach is that it doesn't allow calls to unknown functions (for which worker-wrapper doesn't apply) to return non-ST results. For example, in the code of Fig. 11, no local syntactic analysis could discover that argument function g is pure and terminating.

To obtain better control over effects, we have developed an inference algorithm for computing the minimal monadic effect of each subexpression in a program. Pure, provably terminating expressions are placed in ID, pure but potentially non-terminating expressions in LIFT, and so forth. The algorithm deals with the latent monadic effects in functions, by recording them in the result types. As an example, it produces the annotations shown in Fig. 11.

The input to the algorithm is an typed program in the source language; the output is a program in the monadically typed IR. The term translation is essentially trivial, since the source and target have identical term structure, except for the possible need for Up terms in the target. Consider, for example, the source term If($x$,Val $y$,Raise $z$). Since Val $y$ is a value, its translation is in the ID monad, whereas the translation of Raise $z$ must be in the EXN or ST

$$\frac{E \vdash_v v : \texttt{Bool} \quad E \vdash e_1 \Rightarrow e_1' : \texttt{M}(m_1,t) \quad E \vdash e_2 \Rightarrow e_2' : \texttt{M}(m_1,t) \quad (m_1 \leq m_2)}{E \vdash \texttt{If}(v,e_1,e_2):t \Rightarrow \texttt{Up}(m_1,m_2,\texttt{If}(v,e_1',e_2')) : \texttt{M}(m_2,t)}$$

$$\frac{E \vdash e_1 \Rightarrow e_1' : \texttt{M}(m_1,t_1) \quad E + \{x:t_1\} \vdash e_2 \Rightarrow e_2' : \texttt{M}(m_2,t_2) \quad (m_1 \leq m_2 \leq m_3)}{E \vdash \texttt{Let}(x:t_1,e_1,e_2):t_2 \Rightarrow \texttt{Up}(m_2,m_3,\texttt{Let}(m_1,m_2,x:t_1,e_1',e_2')) : \texttt{M}(m_3,t_2)}$$

$$\frac{E \vdash_v v : \texttt{Exn} \quad (\texttt{EXN} \leq m)}{E \vdash \texttt{Raise}(t,v):t \Rightarrow \texttt{Up}(\texttt{EXN},m,\texttt{Raise}(\texttt{M}(\texttt{EXN},t),v)) : \texttt{M}(m,t)}$$

**Fig. 12.** Selected translation rules

monad. To glue together these subterm translations we must insert a coercion around the translation of the Val term. Up terms serve exactly this purpose; they add the necessary flexibility to the system to permit all monad constraints to be met. Such a coercion is potentially needed around each subterm in the program.

To develop a deterministic, syntax-directed, translation, we turn each typing rule in Fig. 5 (*except* Up) into a translation rule, simply by recording the inferred type and monad information in the appropriate annotation slots of the output, combining the translations of subterms in the obvious manner, and wrapping an Up term around the result. As examples, Fig. 12 shows the translation rules corresponding to the typing rules for If, Let, and Raise. Each free type and monad in the translated typed term is initially set to a fresh variable; the translation algorithm generates a set of constraints relating these variables just as in an ordinary type inference algorithm. We discuss the solution of these constraints below. As specified here, the translation is profligate in its introduction of Up coercion terms, most of which will prove (after constraint resolution) to be unnecessary identity coercions. We use a postprocessing step to remove unneeded coercions using the (IdentUp) rule.

The translation algorithm generates constraints between types and between monads. Type constraints can be solved using ordinary unification, except that unifying the codomain mtyps of two arrow types requires that their monad components be equated as well as their vtyp components. The interesting question is how to record and resolve constraints on the monad variables. Such constraints are introduced explicitly by the side conditions in the Let, Letrec, and Up rules, implicitly by the equating of monads from subexpressions in the If and Handle rules, and (even more) implicitly as a result of ordinary unification of arrow types, which mention monads in their codomains. The side-condition constraints are all inequalities of the form $m_1 \geq m_2$, where $m_1$ is a monad variable and $m_2$ is a variable or an explicit monad. The implicit constraints are all equalities $m_1 = m_2$; for uniformity, we replace these by a pair of inequalities: $m_1 \geq m_2$ and $m_2 \geq m_1$. We collect constraints as a side-effect of the translation process, simply by adding them to a global list.

It is very common for there to be circularities among the monad constraints. To solve the constraint system, we view it as a directed graph with a node for each monad and monad variable, and an edge from $m_1$ to $m_2$ for each constraint $m_1 \geq m_2$. We then partition the graph into its strongly connected components, and sort the components into reverse topological order. We process one component at a time, in this order. Since $\geq$ is anti-symmetric, all the nodes in a given component must be assigned the same monad; once this has been determined, it is assigned to all the variables in the component before proceeding to the next component. To determine the minimum possible correct assignment for a component, we consult all the edges from nodes in that component to nodes *outside* the component; because of the order of processing, these nodes must already have received a monad assignment. The maximum of these assignments is the minimum correct assignment for this component. If there are no such edges, the minimum correct assignment is ID. This algorithm is linear in the number of constraints, and hence in the size of the source program.

To summarize, we perform monad inference by first translating the source program into a form padded with coercion operators and annotated with monad variables, meanwhile collecting constraints on these variables, and then solving the resulting constraint system to fill in the variables in the translated program. The resulting program will contain many null coercions of the form $\mathrm{Up}(m,m,e)$; these can be removed by a single postprocessing pass.

Our algorithm is very similar to a that of Talpin and Jouvelot [15], restricted to a monomorphic source language. Both algorithms generate essentially the same sets of constraints. Talpin and Jouvelot solve the effect constraints using an extended form of unification rather than by a separate mechanism.

It would be natural to extend our algorithm to handle Hindley-Milner polymorphism for both types and monads in the Talpin-Jouvelot style. The idea is to generalize all free type and effect variables in `let` definitions and allow different uses of the bound identifier to instantiate these in different ways. In particular, parametric functions like `map` could be used with many different monads, without one use "polluting" the others. Functions not wholly parametric in their effects would place a minimum effect bound on permissible instantiations for monad variables. Supporting this form of monad polymorphism seems desirable even if there is no type polymorphism (e.g., because the program has already been explicitly monomorphized [19]).

In whole-program compilation of a monad-polymorphic program, the complete set of effect instantiations for each polymorphic definition would be known. This set could be used to put an upper effect bound on monad variables within the definition body and hence determine what transformations are legal there. Alternatively, it could be used to guide the generation of effect-specific clones as suggested in the previous section. In a separate-compilation setting, monad polymorphism in a library definition would still be useful for client code, but not for the library code: in the absence of complete information about uses of a definition, any variable monad in the body of the definition would need to be treated as ST, the most "effectful" monad, for the purposes of performing transformations within the body.

# 6 Extending the Monad Hierarchy

Our basic approach is not restricted to the linearly-ordered set of monads presented in Sect. 3. It extends naturally to any collection of monads and *up* embedding operations that form a *lattice*, with ID as the lattice bottom element. It is clearly reasonable to require a partial order; this is equivalent to requiring that (Ident) and (Compose) hold. From the partial order requirement, the distinguished role for ID, and the assumption that each monad obeys (Left), (Right), and (Assoc), and each *up* operation obeys (Unit) and (Bind), we can prove the laws of Fig. 9. (The validity of the laws in Fig. 10 naturally depends on the specific semantics of the monads involved.) By also insisting that any two monads in the collection have a least upper bound under embedding, we guarantee that any two arbitrary expressions (e.g., the two arms of an if) can be coerced into a (unique) common monad, and hence that the monad inference mechanism of Sect. 5 will work.

One might be tempted to describe such a lattice by specifying a set of "primitive" monads encapsulating individual effects, and then assuming the existence of arbitrary "union" monads representing combinations of effects. As the Handle discussion in Sect. 3 indicates, however, there is often more than one way to combine two effects, so it makes no sense to talk in a general way about the "union" of two monads. Instead, it appears necessary to specify explicitly, for every monad $m$ in the lattice,

- a semantic interpretation for $m$;
- a definition for $bind_m$;
- a definition of $up_{m \to m'}$ for each $m \leq m'$;[2]
- for each non-proper morphism NP introduced in $m$, a definition of $np_{m'}$ for every $m' \geq m$.

The lack of a generic mechanism for combining monads is rather unfortunate, since it turns the proofs of many transformation laws into lengthy case analyses. We conjecture that restricting attention to *up* operations that represent *natural* monad transformers [10] might help organize such proofs into simpler form.

# 7 Status and Conclusions

We believe our approach to inferring and recording effects shows promise in its simplicity and its semantic clarity. It remains to be seen whether effects information of the kind described here can be used to improve the performance of ML code in any significant way. To answer this question, we have extended the IR described here to a version that supports full Standard ML; we have implemented the monad inference algorithm for this version, and are currently measuring its effectiveness using the backend of our RML compiler system [19].

---

[2] Since the (Ident) and (Compose) laws must hold in a partial order, it suffices to define $up_{m \to m'}$ for just enough choices of $m, m'$ to guarantee the existence of least upper bounds, since these definitions will imply the definition for other pairs of monads.

# Acknowledgements

We have benefitted from conversations with John Launchbury and Dick Kieburtz, and from exposure to the ideas in their unpublished papers [7, 8]. The comments of the anonymous referees also motivated us to clarify the relationship of our algorithm with the existing work of Talpin and Jouvelot. Phil Wadler made helpful commments on an earlier draft.

# References

1. A. Appel. *Compiling with Continuations*. Cambridge University Press, 1992.
2. A. Appel. Loop headers in λ-calculus or CPS. *Lisp and Symbolic Computation*, 7(4):337–343, 1994.
3. N. Benton, July 1997. Personal communication.
4. L. Birkedal, M. Tofte, and M. Vejlstrup. From region inference to von Neumann machines via region representation inference. In *23rd ACM Symposium on Principles of Programming Languages (POPL'96)*, pages 171–183. ACM Press, 1996.
5. C. Flanagan, A. Sabry, B. F. Duba, and M. Felleisen. The essence of compiling with continuations. *Proc. SIGPLAN Conference on Programming Language Design and Implementation*, 28(6):237–247, June 1993.
6. D. Gifford, P. Jouvelot, J. Lucassen, and M. Sheldon. FX-87 REFERENCE MANUAL. Technical Report MIT-LCS//MIT/LCS/TR-407, Massachusetts Institute of Technology, Laboratory for Computer Science, Sept. 1987.
7. R. Kieburtz and J. Launchbury. Encapsulated effects. (unpublished manuscript), Oct. 1995.
8. R. Kieburtz and J. Launchbury. Towards algebras of encapsulated effects. (unpublished manuscript), 1997.
9. J. Launchbury and S. Peyton Jones. State in Haskell. *Lisp and Symbolic Computation*, pages 293–351, Dec. 1995.
10. S. Liang, P. Hudak, and M. Jones. Monad transformers and modular interpreters. In *22nd ACM Symposium on Principles of Programming Languages (POPL '95)*, Jan. 1995.
11. S. Peyton Jones, J. Launchbury, M. Shields, and A. Tolmach. Bridging the gulf: a common intermediate language for ml and haskel. In *25th ACM Symposium on Principles of Programming Languages (POPL'98)*, pages 49–61, San Diego, Jan 1998.
12. S. Peyton Jones and J. Launchbury. Unboxed values as first class citizens. In *Proc. Functional Programming Languages and Computer Architecture (FPCA '91)*, pages 636–666, Sept. 191.
13. S. Peyton Jones and P. Wadler. Imperative functional programming. In *20th ACM Symposium on Principles of Programming Languages (POPL'93)*, pages 71–84, Jan. 1993.
14. S. Peyton Jones. Compiling Haskell by program transformation: A report from the trenches. In *Proceedings of ESOP'96*, volume 1058 of *Lecture Notes in Computer Science*, pages 18–44. Springer Verlag, 1996.
15. J.-P. Talpin and P. Jouvelot. Polymorphic type, region and effect inference. *Journal of Functional Programming*, 2:245–271, 1992.
16. J.-P. Talpin and P. Jouvelot. The type and effect discipline. *Information and Computation*, 111(2):245–296, June 1994.

17. D. Tarditi. *Design and Implementation of Code Optimizations for a Type-Directed Compiler for Standard ML*. PhD thesis, Carnegie Mellon University, Dec. 1996. Technical Report CMU-CS-97-108.

18. M. Tofte and J.-P. Talpin. Region-based memory management. *Information and Computation*, 132(2):109–176, 1 Feb. 1997.

19. A. Tolmach and D. Oliva. From ML to Ada: Strongly-typed language interoperability via source trans lation. *Journal of Functional Programming*, 1998. (to appear).

20. P. Wadler. The marriage of effects and monads. (unpublished manuscript), Mar. 1998.

21. A. Wright. Typing references by effect inference. In *Proc. 4th European Symposium on Programming (ESOP '92)*, volume 582 of *Lecture Notes in Computer Science*, Feb. 1992.

# Type-Directed Continuation Allocation[*]

Zhong Shao and Valery Trifonov

Dept. of Computer Science
Yale University
New Haven, CT 06520-8285
{shao,trifonov}@cs.yale.edu

**Abstract.** Suppose we translate two different source languages, $L_1$ and $L_2$, into the same intermediate language; can they safely interoperate in the same address space and under the same runtime system? If $L_1$ supports first-class continuations (call/cc) and $L_2$ does not, can $L_2$ programs call arbitrary $L_1$ functions? Would the fact of possibly calling $L_1$ impose restrictions on the implementation strategy of $L_2$? Can we compile $L_1$ functions that do not invoke call/cc using more efficient techniques borrowed from the $L_2$ implementation? Our view is that the implementation of a common intermediate language ought to support the so-called *pay-as-you-go efficiency*: first-order monomorphic functions should be compiled as efficiently as in C and assembly languages, even though they may be passed to arbitrary polymorphic functions that support advanced control primitives (e.g. call/cc). In this paper, we present a typed intermediate language with effect and resource annotations, ensuring the safety of inter-language calls while allowing the compiler to choose continuation allocation strategies.

## 1 Introduction

Safe interoperability requires resolving a host of issues including mixed data representations, multiple function calling conventions, and different implementation protocols. Existing approaches to language interoperability either separate code written in different languages into different address spaces or have the unsafe, ad hoc and insecure foreign function call interface.

We position our further discussion of language interoperability in the context of a system hosting multiple languages, each safe in isolation. The supported languages may range from first-order monomorphic (*e.g.* a safe subset of C, or safe-C for short) to higher-order languages with advanced control, *e.g.* ML with first-class continuations. We assume that all languages have type systems which ensure runtime safety of accepted programs. In other words, in this paper we do not attempt to solve the problem of cooperating safely with programs written in unsafe languages, which in general can

---

[*] This research was sponsored in part by the DARPA ITO under the title "Software Evolution using HOT Language Technology", DARPA Order No. D888, issued under Contract No. F30602-96-2-0232, and in part by an NSF CAREER Award CCR-9501624, and NSF Grant CCR-9633390. The views and conclusions contained in this document are those of the authors and should not be interpreted as representing the official policies, either expressed or implied, of the Defense Advanced Research Projects Agency or the U.S. Government.

only be achieved at the expense of "sandboxing" the unsafe calls or complex and incomplete analyses of the unsafe code.

We believe that interoperability requires a serious and more formal treatment. As a first step, this paper describes a novel type-based technique to support principled language interoperation among languages with different protocols for allocation of activation records. Our framework allows programs written in multiple languages with overlapping features to interact with each other safely and reliably, yet without restricting the expressiveness of each language.

An interoperability scheme for activation record allocation should be

- safe: it should not be possible to violate the runtime safety of a language by calling a foreign function;
- expressive: the scheme should allow inter-language function calls;
- efficient: a language implementation should not be forced to use suboptimal methods for its own features in order to provide support for other languages' features. For instance a language that does not use call/cc should not have to be implemented using heap-based allocation of activation records.

Our solution is to ensure safety by using a common typed intermediate language [22] into which all of the source languages are translated. To maintain safety in an expressive interoperability scheme the type system is extended with annotations of the *effects* of the evaluation of a term, e.g. an invocation of call/cc, and polymorphic types with effect variables, allowing a higher-order function to be invoked with arguments coming from languages with different sets of effects. The central novelty of our approach is the introduction of annotations of the *resources* necessary for the realization of the effects of an evaluation; for instance a continuation heap may be required when invoking call/cc. Thus our type system can be used to support implementation efficiency by keeping track of the available language-dependent resources, and safety by allowing semantically correct inter-language function calls but banning semantically incorrect ones. In addition to providing safety, making resource handling explicit also opens new opportunities for code optimization beyond what a foreign function call mechanism can offer.

A common intermediate language like FLINT [21, 22] will likely support a very rich set of features to accommodate multiple source languages. Some of these features may impose implementation restrictions; for example, a practical implementation of first-class continuations (as in SML/NJ or Scheme) often requires the use of advanced stack representations [8] or heap-based activation records [20]. However in some cases stack-based allocation may be more efficient, and ideally we would like to have a compiler that can take advantage of it as long as this does not interfere with the semantic correctness of first-class continuations. Similarly, when compiling a simple safe-C-like language with no advanced control primitives (e.g., call/cc) into FLINT, we may prefer to compile it to code that uses the simple sequential stack of standard C; programs written in ML or Scheme using these safe-C functions must then follow the same allocation strategy when invoking them. This corresponds to the typical case of writing low-level systems modules in C and providing for their use in other languages, therefore we assume this model in the sequel, but the dual problem of compiling safe-C functions calling arbitrary ML functions by selectively imposing heap allocation on safe-C is similarly represented and solved within our system.

Thus our goal is efficient and expressive interoperability between code fragments written in languages using possibly different allocation disciplines for activation records, for instance, ML with heap allocation and safe-C with stack allocation. The following properties of the interoperability framework are essential for achieving this goal:

- ML and safe-C code should interoperate safely with each other within the same address space.
- All invocations of safe-C functions in ML functions should be allowed (provided they are otherwise type-correct).
- Only the invocations of ML functions that do not capture continuations should be allowed in safe-C functions.
- Any activation record that can potentially be captured as part of a first-class continuation should always be allocated on the heap (or using some fancy stack-chunk-based representations [8]).
- It should be possible to use stack allocation for activation records of ML functions when they are guaranteed not to be captured with a first-class continuation.
- The selection of allocation strategy should be decoupled from the actual function call.

The last property gives the compiler the freedom to switch allocation strategies more efficiently, instead of following a fixed foreign function interface mechanism. For example, an implementation of ML may use heap allocation of activation records by default to provide support for continuation capture. However, in cases when the compiler can prove that a function's activation record is not going to be accessible from any captured continuation, its allocation discipline is ambiguous; stack allocation may be preferred if the function invokes, or is invoked by, safe-C functions which use stack allocation. This specialization of code to a different allocation strategy effectively creates regions of ML code compiled in "safe-C mode" with the aim of avoiding the switch between heap and stack allocation on every cross-language call. In general, the separation of the selection of allocation strategy from the call allows its treatment as a commodity primitive operation and subjects it to other code-motion optimizations, e.g. hoisting it out of loops.

The proposed method can be applied to achieving more efficient interoperability with existing foreign code as well, although obviously in this case the usual friction between safety and efficiency can only be eased but not removed. In particular the possibility to select the allocation strategy switch point remains, thus higher efficiency can still be achieved while satisfying a given safety policy by specializing safe code to "unsafe mode" (e.g. for running with stack allocation within a sand-box).

## 2 A Resourceful Intermediate Language

To satisfy the requirements for efficient interoperability, outlined in the previous section, we define an A-normal-form-based typed intermediate language *RL* (Figure 1) with types having effect and resource annotations. Intuitively, an effect annotation such as CC indicates that a computation may capture a continuation by performing call/cc; a resource annotation such as H (continuation heap) or S (continuation stack) means that the corresponding runtime resource must be available to the computation.[1] Nontrivial effects can be primitive, effect variables, or unions of effects; commutativity and associativity of the union with $\emptyset$ as a unit are consistent with the typing rules and we assume them for brevity of notation. Each effect can only occur when the proper resources are available, e.g. CC would require the use of heap-based activation record allocation. Both the effect and resource usage annotations are inferred during the translation from the source language to the intermediate language, and can be used to assist code generation and to check the validity of cross-language function calls.

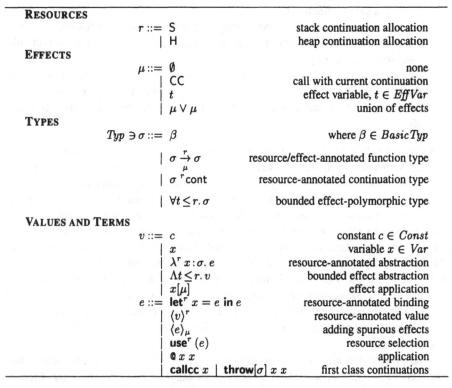

**Fig. 1.** Syntax of a resource-aware intermediate language *RL*

The resources required and effects produced by a function are made explicit in its type. A continuation can potentially produce all effects possible with the set of resources available at the point of its capture; for that reason continuation types only have a resource annotation.

---

[1] In this paper, we focus on application of this system to interoperability issues related to continuation allocation, but more diverse sets of resources will be necessary in a realistic language.

Function abstractions are annotated with the resources they may require and will maintain. In a higher-order language the effect of the evaluation of a function application may depend on the effects of its functional arguments; this dependence is expressed by means of effect polymorphism. Polymorphic abstractions introduce variables ranging over the set of possible effects of the term. Since the possible effects are determined by the available resources, we have *bounded effect polymorphism*; the relation $\mu \leq r$ (defined in the context of an effect environment in Figure 3) reflects the dependence between effects and resources, e.g. that **callcc** can only be performed if continuations are heap-allocated. The effect application $x[\mu]$ instantiates the body of the polymorphic abstraction to which $x$ is bound. The language construct **use$^r$** $(e)$ serves to mark the point where a change in the allocation strategy for activation records is required. Instead of having effect subsumption the language is equipped with a construct $\langle e \rangle_\mu$ for explicitly increasing the set of effects of $e$ to include $\mu$.

*Example 1.* The use of resource annotations to select allocation strategies is shown in the *RL* code below which includes extra type annotations for clarity.

$$
\begin{aligned}
&\textbf{let}^{\text{H}} \\
&\quad \text{applyToInt} \quad = \langle \Lambda t \leq \text{H}.\ \lambda^{\text{H}} f : \text{Int} \xrightarrow[t]{\text{H}} \text{Int}.\ \text{\o}\ f\ 42 \rangle^{\text{H}} \\
&\qquad\qquad\qquad : \forall t \leq \text{H}.\ (\text{Int} \xrightarrow[t]{\text{H}} \text{Int}) \xrightarrow[t]{\text{H}} \text{Int} \\[4pt]
&\quad \text{add1\_CC} \quad = \langle \lambda^{\text{H}} x : \text{Int}. \\
&\qquad\qquad\qquad\qquad \textbf{let}^{\text{H}}\ c = \langle \lambda^{\text{H}} k : \text{Int}\ ^{\text{H}}\text{cont}. \\
&\qquad\qquad\qquad\qquad\qquad \textbf{let}^{\text{H}}\ z = \text{\o}\ \text{succ}\ x\ \textbf{in throw}[\text{Int}]\ k\ z \rangle^{\text{H}} \\
&\qquad\qquad\qquad \textbf{in callcc}\ c \rangle^{\text{H}} \\
&\qquad\qquad\qquad : \text{Int} \xrightarrow[\text{CC}]{\text{H}} \text{Int} \\[4pt]
&\quad \text{add1\_Pure} \quad = \langle \lambda^{\text{S}} x : \text{Int}.\ \text{\o}\ \text{succ}\ x \rangle^{\text{H}} \\
&\qquad\qquad\qquad : \text{Int} \xrightarrow[\emptyset]{\text{S}} \text{Int} \\[4pt]
&\quad \text{add1\_Wrapped} = \langle \lambda^{\text{H}} x : \text{Int}.\ \textbf{use}^{\text{S}}\ (\text{\o}\ \text{add1\_Pure}\ x) \rangle^{\text{H}} \\
&\qquad\qquad\qquad : \text{Int} \xrightarrow[\emptyset]{\text{H}} \text{Int} \\[4pt]
&\textbf{in}\ \text{\o}\ (\text{applyToInt}[\text{CC}])\ \text{add1\_CC}\ ; \\
&\quad \text{\o}\ (\text{applyToInt}[\emptyset])\ \text{add1\_Wrapped}
\end{aligned}
$$

The function applyToInt is polymorphic in the effect of its parameter, but the parameter's resource requirements are fixed – it must use heap allocation. We consider two applications of applyToInt. The argument in the first, add1\_CC, is a function invoking **callcc**, which consequently uses heap allocation; on the other hand the argument in the second application, add1\_Pure, is pure and uses stack allocation. It is therefore incorrect to apply applyToInt to add1\_Pure. We use a wrapper to coerce it to the proper type:

we apply applyToInt to add1_Wrapped whose activation record is heap-allocated, and whose function is to switch to stack allocation (via **use**$^S$) before calling add1_Pure. Heap allocation is resumed upon return from add1_Pure.

## 3   Two Source Languages

To further illustrate the advantages of this system we consider the problem of translating into *RL* two source languages (Figure 2): a language *HL* with control operators (**callcc** and **throw**), implemented using heap-based allocation of activation records, and a language *SL* which always uses stack allocation. *HL* also allows declaring at the top of a program the identifiers of entities imported from *SL* code. The type systems of these languages are assumed monomorphic for simplicity, since polymorphism in types is largely orthogonal to the effect polymorphism of *RL*.

| | |
|---|---|
| *SL* TYPES | $\tau_{SL} ::= \beta \mid \tau_{SL} \to \tau_{SL}$ |
| *SL* TERMS | $e_{SL} ::= c \mid x \mid \lambda x : \tau_{SL}. e_{SL} \mid e_{SL} e_{SL} \mid$ **let** $x = e_{SL}$ **in** $e_{SL}$ |
| *HL* TYPES | $\tau_{HL} ::= \beta \mid \tau_{HL} \to \tau_{HL} \mid \tau_{HL}$ **cont** |
| *HL* TERMS | $e_{HL} ::= c \mid x \mid \lambda x : \tau_{HL}. e_{HL} \mid e_{HL} e_{HL} \mid$ **let** $x = e_{HL}$ **in** $e_{HL}$ |
| | $\mid$ **callcc** $e_{HL} \mid$ **throw**$[\tau_{HL}]$ $e_{HL}$ $e_{HL}$ |
| *HL* PROGRAMS | $p_{HL} ::= e_{HL} \mid$ **external**(*SL*) $x : \tau_{SL}$ **in** $p_{HL}$ |

**Fig. 2.** Syntax of the source languages *SL* and *HL*

The resource annotations in *RL* provide information about handling of the stack and heap resources, necessary in the following situations:

- when calling from *HL* a function written in *SL*, which may require switching from heap allocation of activation records to allocation on the stack used by *SL*; the heap resource must be preserved for use upon return from *SL* code.
- when calling an *HL* function from *SL* code, which is only semantically sound when the evaluation of the function does not capture a continuation, since part of the continuation data is stack-allocated; the type system maintains information about the possible effects of the evaluation, in this case whether **callcc** might be invoked.
- when selecting an allocation strategy for *HL* functions called (directly or indirectly) from within *SL* code; either their activation records must be allocated on the *SL* stack, or the latter must be preserved and restored upon return to *SL*.
- when selecting an allocation strategy for *HL* code invoking *SL* functions but not **callcc**, in order to optimize resource handling.

*Example 2.* Consider a program consisting of a main fragment in *HL* invoking the **external** *SL* function applyToInt with the *HL* function add1 as an argument; the call is meaningful because add1 does not invoke **callcc**. Only the *SL* type of the external function is given to the *HL* program which is separately compiled without access to the detailed effect annotations inferred from the code of the *SL* fragment.

*SL* fragment applyToInt:

$\lambda$f : Int $\rightarrow$ Int. succ (f 42)

The result of its separate compilation into *RL*, which uses stack allocation (for details of the translation we refer the reader to Section 5) is

$$\text{applyToInt} = \Lambda t \leq S. \, \lambda^S f : \text{Int} \xrightarrow[t]{S} \text{Int}. \, \textbf{let}^S \, x = \text{@} \, f \, 42 \, \textbf{in} \, \text{@} \, \text{succ} \, x$$

$$: \forall t \leq S. \, (\text{Int} \xrightarrow[t]{S} \text{Int}) \xrightarrow[t]{S} \text{Int}$$

*HL* fragment main:

    **external**(*SL*) applyToInt : (Int $\rightarrow$ Int) $\rightarrow$ Int

    **in let** add1 = $\lambda$x : Int. succ x

    **in** applyToInt add1

The result of its separate compilation into *RL* is

$$\text{main} = \lambda^H \, \text{applyToInt} : \forall t \leq S. \, (\text{Int} \xrightarrow[t]{S} \text{Int}) \xrightarrow[\emptyset]{S} \text{Int}.$$

      $\textbf{let}^H$

          applyToInt_H $= \langle \Lambda t \leq S.$

                    $\lambda^H f : \text{Int} \xrightarrow[t]{H} \text{Int}.$

                        $\textbf{let}^H \, f\_S = \langle \lambda^S x : \text{Int}. \, \textbf{use}^H \, (\text{@} \, f \, x) \rangle^H$

                          $\textbf{in use}^S \, (\text{@} \, (\text{applyToInt}[t]) \, f\_S) \rangle^H$

                $: \forall t \leq S. \, (\text{Int} \xrightarrow[t]{H} \text{Int}) \xrightarrow[\emptyset]{H} \text{Int}$

          add1          $= \langle \lambda^H x : \text{Int}. \, \text{@} \, \text{succ} \, x \rangle^H$

                $: \text{Int} \xrightarrow[\emptyset]{H} \text{Int}$

      **in** @ applyToInt_H[$\emptyset$] add1

$$: \left( \forall t \leq S. \, (\text{Int} \xrightarrow[t]{S} \text{Int}) \xrightarrow[\emptyset]{S} \text{Int} \right) \xrightarrow[\emptyset]{H} \text{Int}$$

The translation infers polymorphic effect types using a simplified version[2] of standard effect inference [23]. The resource annotations are fixed by the source language; the type of an external *SL* function in an *HL* program is annotated with the *SL* resources. In the code produced after translation the external functions are coerced to match the resources of *HL* using automatically generated wrappers. In the above code, the parameter f of applyToInt_H is wrapped to f_S before passing it to applyToInt; the function of the wrapper is to switch from the stack allocation discipline used by *SL* to heap allocation before invoking the code for f, and resume stack allocation upon return. Dually, the call to applyToInt itself is wrapped to enable stack allocation inside *HL* code.

---

[2] As presented here our system does not keep track of regions associated with effects.

Since the full *RL* type of the *SL* fragment is not available to it, the effect inference must conservatively approximate the effects of the *SL* functions. It treats the external applyToInt in the *HL* fragment as an effect-polymorphic parameter in order to allow its invocations with arguments with different effects. The price we pay for inference with this polymorphism in the case of separate compilation is that we assume that the effects of these invocations are the maximal allowed with the resources shared between the languages (in Example 2 we lose no precision since *SL* has no effects, but the approximation is reflected in the effect annotation $\emptyset$ of the type of the parameter of main). The following code, constructed mechanically given the inferred and expected types of applyToInt, coerces the actual type of applyToInt to the approximation used in the typing of main and performs the top-level application, thus linking the modules.

$\mathbf{let}^H$

$\quad$ applyToInt_Glue $= \langle \Lambda t \leq S. \lambda^S f\colon \mathsf{Int} \xrightarrow{S}_{t} \mathsf{Int}. \langle @ \text{ applyToInt}[t] \text{ f}\rangle_\emptyset\rangle^H$

$\qquad\qquad : \forall t \leq S. (\mathsf{Int} \xrightarrow{S}_{t} \mathsf{Int}) \xrightarrow{S}_{\emptyset} \mathsf{Int}$

$\mathbf{in}$ @ main applyToInt_Glue

More precise inference of the resulting effects is possible when the external function is a pre-compiled library routine whose *RL* type (with its precise effect annotations) is available when compiling main. In those cases we can take advantage of the let-polymorphism in inferring a type of main (in a setting similar to that of Example 1). However even the approximated effects obtained during separate compilation carry information that can be exploited for the optimization of inter-language calls, observing that the range of effects of a function is limited by the resources of its source language. In Example 2, after inlining and applying results of Section 4.4 (Theorem 2), the code for main can be optimized to eliminate the unnecessary switch to heap allocation in the instance of f_S. This yields

$\quad$ main $= \langle \lambda^H$ applyToInt$\colon \forall t \leq S. (\mathsf{Int} \xrightarrow{S}_{t} \mathsf{Int}) \xrightarrow{S}_{\emptyset} \mathsf{Int}.$

$\qquad \mathbf{let}^H$

$\qquad\qquad$ add1 $\quad = \langle \lambda^H x\colon \mathsf{Int}. @ \text{ succ } x\rangle^H \qquad$ (* now dead code *)

$\qquad\qquad$ add1_S $= \langle \lambda^S x\colon \mathsf{Int}. @ \text{ succ } x\rangle^H$

$\qquad \mathbf{in}$ use$^S$ (@ (applyToInt$[\emptyset]$) add1_S))$^H$

Thus the *HL* function add1 has been effectively specialized for the stack allocation strategy used by *SL*.

*Example 3.* Another optimization is merging of regions with the same resource requirements, illustrated on the following *HL* code fragment.

$\quad$ **external**(*SL*) intFn $\colon$ Int $\to$ Int **in** intFn (intFn 42)

which is naively translated to the *RL* function (shown after inlining of the parameter wrapper)

$$\Lambda t \leq S. \; \lambda^H \, intFn : Int \xrightarrow[t]{S} Int.$$

$$\mathbf{let}^H \; x = \langle \mathbf{use}^S \, (\mathbf{0} \; intFn \; 42) \rangle^H$$

$$\mathbf{in} \; \mathbf{use}^S \, (\mathbf{0} \; intFn \; x)$$

After combining the two $\mathbf{use}^S \, (\cdot)$ constructs the equivalent $RL$ term is

$$\Lambda t \leq S. \; \lambda^H \, intFn : Int \xrightarrow[t]{S} Int.$$

$$\mathbf{use}^S \, ( \; \mathbf{let}^S \; x = \langle \mathbf{0} \; intFn \; 42 \rangle^S \; \mathbf{in} \; \mathbf{0} \; intFn \; x)$$

A generalization of this transformation makes possible lifting of $\mathbf{use}^r \, (\cdot)$ constructs out of a loop when the resources $r$ are sufficient for all effects of the loop. Since in general a resource wrapper must restore resources upon return, a tail call moved into its scope effectively becomes non-tail; thus lifting a wrapper's scope over a recursive tail call is only useful when the wrapper is lifted out of the enclosing function as well, i.e. out of the loop.

## 4   Semantics of $RL$

### 4.1   Static Semantics

Correctness of resource use is ensured by the type system shown in Figure 3, which keeps track of the resources necessary for the evaluation of a term and a conservative estimate of the effects of the evaluation.

An effect environment $\Delta$ specifies the resource bounds of effect variables introduced by effect abstractions and effect-polymorphic types. The rules for effect sequents reflect the dependence of effects on resources (in this language this boils down to the dependence of the call/cc effect CC on the heap allocation resource H) and form the basis of effect polymorphism. The function $MaxEff$ yields the maximal effect possible with a given resource; in this system we have $MaxEff(S) = \emptyset$ and $MaxEff(H) = CC$. Rule (Eff-max) effectively states that the resource $r'$ can be used instead of resource $r$ if $r'$ provides for all effects possible under $r$.

In the sequents assigning types to values and terms the type environment $\Gamma$ maps free variables to types. Type judgments for values associate with a value $v$ and a pair of environments $\Delta$ and $\Gamma$ only a type $\sigma$, since values have no effects and therefore their evaluation requires no resources of the kind we control. The function $\theta$ maps constants to their predefined types.

Sequents for terms have the form $r; \Delta; \Gamma \vdash e : {}_{\overline{\mu}}\sigma$, where $r$ represents the available allocation resource, $\sigma$ is the type of $e$, and $\mu$ represents the effects of its evaluation. Rules (Exp-let) and (Exp-val) establish the correspondence between the resource annotations in these constructs and the currently available allocation resource; the effect of lifting a value to a term is none, while the effect of sequencing two computations via **let** is the union of their effects. Any effect allowed with the current resource may be added to the effects of a term using rule (Exp-spurious).

The central novelty is the $\mathbf{use}^{r'} \, (\cdot)$ construct for resource manipulation; its typing rule (Exp-use) imposes the crucial restriction that the effect $\mu$ of the term $e$ must be

**EFFECT ENVIRONMENT FORMATION**

(Env-eff-empty)
$$\vdash^{\Delta} \emptyset$$

(Env-eff-ext)
$$\frac{\vdash^{\Delta} \Delta}{\vdash^{\Delta} \Delta_t, \, t \leq r}$$

**TYPE ENVIRONMENT FORMATION**

(Env-typ-empty)
$$\frac{\vdash^{\Delta} \Delta}{\Delta \vdash^{\Gamma} \emptyset}$$

(Env-typ-ext)
$$\frac{\Delta \vdash^{\Gamma} \Gamma \quad \Delta \vdash^{\sigma} \sigma}{\Delta \vdash^{\Gamma} \Gamma_x, \, x : \sigma}$$

**EFFECTS**

(Eff-empty)
$$\frac{\vdash^{\Delta} \Delta}{\Delta \vdash^{\mu} \emptyset \leq r}$$

(Eff-CC)
$$\frac{\vdash^{\Delta} \Delta}{\Delta \vdash^{\mu} \mathsf{CC} \leq \mathsf{H}}$$

(Eff-var)
$$\frac{\vdash^{\Delta} \Delta \quad \Delta(t) = r}{\Delta \vdash^{\mu} t \leq r}$$

(Eff-combine)
$$\frac{\vdash^{\mu} \mu' \leq r, \, \mu'' \leq r}{\Delta \vdash^{\mu} \mu' \vee \mu'' \leq r}$$

(Eff-max)
$$\frac{\Delta \vdash^{\mu} \mu \leq r \quad \Delta \vdash^{\mu} MaxEff(r) \leq r'}{\Delta \vdash^{\mu} \mu \leq r'}$$

**VALUES**

(Val-const)
$$\frac{\Delta \vdash^{\Gamma} \Gamma}{\Delta; \Gamma \vdash^{\nu} c : \theta(c)}$$

(Val-var)
$$\frac{\Delta \vdash^{\Gamma} \Gamma \quad \Gamma(x) = \sigma}{\Delta; \Gamma \vdash^{\nu} x : \sigma}$$

(Val-abs)
$$\frac{\Delta \vdash^{\Gamma} \Gamma \quad \Delta \vdash^{\sigma} \sigma \quad r; \Delta; \Gamma_x, \, x : \sigma \vdash^{e} e : \underset{\mu}{-}\sigma'}{\Delta; \Gamma_x \vdash^{\nu} \lambda^r x : \sigma. \, e : \sigma \xrightarrow[\mu]{r} \sigma'}$$

(Val-poly)
$$\frac{\Delta \vdash^{\Gamma} \Gamma \quad \Delta_t, \, t \leq r; \Gamma \vdash^{\nu} v : \sigma}{\Delta; \Gamma \vdash^{\nu} \Lambda t \leq r. \, v : \forall t \leq r. \, \sigma}$$

(Val-tapp)
$$\frac{\Gamma(x) = \forall t \leq r. \, \sigma \quad \Delta \vdash^{\mu} \mu \leq r}{\Delta; \Gamma \vdash^{\nu} x[\mu] : [\mu/t]\sigma}$$

**TYPES**

(Typ-basic)
$$\frac{\vdash^{\Delta} \Delta}{\Delta \vdash^{\sigma} \beta}$$

(Typ-fun)
$$\frac{\Delta \vdash^{\mu} \mu \leq r \quad \Delta \vdash^{\sigma} \sigma, \sigma'}{\Delta \vdash^{\sigma} \sigma \xrightarrow[\mu]{r} \sigma'}$$

(Typ-cont)
$$\frac{\Delta \vdash^{\sigma} \sigma \quad \emptyset \vdash^{\mu} \mathsf{CC} \leq r}{\Delta \vdash^{\sigma} \sigma^{\, r} \mathsf{cont}}$$

(Typ-poly)
$$\frac{\vdash^{\Delta} \Delta \quad \Delta_t, \, t \leq r \vdash^{\sigma} \sigma}{\Delta \vdash^{\sigma} \forall t \leq r. \, \sigma}$$

**TERMS**

(Exp-let)
$$\frac{r; \Delta; \Gamma \vdash^{e} e : \underset{\mu}{-}\sigma \quad r; \Delta; \Gamma_x, \, x : \sigma \vdash^{e} e' : \underset{\mu'}{-}\sigma'}{r; \Delta; \Gamma \vdash^{e} \mathsf{let}^r \, x = e \,\, \mathsf{in} \, e' : \underset{\mu \vee \mu'}{-}\sigma'}$$

(Exp-val)
$$\frac{\Delta; \Gamma \vdash^{\nu} v : \sigma}{r; \Delta; \Gamma \vdash^{e} \langle v \rangle^r : \underset{\emptyset}{-}\sigma}$$

(Exp-spurious)
$$\frac{r; \Delta; \Gamma \vdash^{e} e : \underset{\mu}{-}\sigma \quad \Delta \vdash^{\mu} \mu' \leq r}{r; \Delta; \Gamma \vdash^{e} \langle e \rangle_{\mu'} : \underset{\mu \vee \mu'}{-}\sigma}$$

(Exp-use)
$$\frac{r'; \Delta; \Gamma \vdash^{e} e : \underset{\mu}{-}\sigma \quad \Delta \vdash^{\mu} \mu \leq r}{r; \Delta; \Gamma \vdash^{e} \mathsf{use}^{r'}(e) : \underset{\mu}{-}\sigma}$$

(Exp-app)
$$\frac{\Delta \vdash^{\Gamma} \Gamma \quad \Gamma(x) = \sigma' \xrightarrow[\mu]{r} \sigma \quad \Gamma(x') = \sigma'}{r; \Delta; \Gamma \vdash^{e} @ \, x \, x' : \underset{\mu}{-}\sigma}$$

(Exp-callcc)
$$\frac{\Delta \vdash^{\Gamma} \Gamma \quad \Gamma(x) = \sigma^{\, r} \mathsf{cont} \xrightarrow[\mu]{r} \sigma}{r; \Delta; \Gamma \vdash^{e} \mathsf{callcc} \, x : \underset{\mu \vee \mathsf{CC}}{-}\sigma}$$

(Exp-throw)
$$\frac{\Delta \vdash^{\Gamma} \Gamma \quad \Delta \vdash^{\sigma} \sigma' \quad \Gamma(x) = \sigma^{\, r} \mathsf{cont} \quad \Gamma(x') = \sigma}{r; \Delta; \Gamma \vdash^{e} \mathsf{throw}[\sigma'] \, x \, x' : \underset{MaxEff(r)}{-}\sigma'}$$

**Fig. 3.** The *RL* type system

supported by the resource $r$ available before the alternative resource $r'$ is selected. This ensures the correctness of the propagation of $\mu$ outside the scope of the **use**$^{r'}$ ($\cdot$).

The rules for application and **callcc** set the correspondence between the available resource and the resource required by the invoked function. In addition, (Exp-callcc) and (Exp-throw) specify that the continuation type is annotated with the same resource, which is needed by the context captured in the continuation and therefore must be matched when it is reactivated. The effect of evaluating a **callcc** includes CC, while the effect of a **throw** is that of the rest of the computation, which we estimate as the maximal possible with the current resource.

By induction on the structure of a typing derivation it follows that if a term has a type in a given environment, it has exactly one type, and the presence of type annotations allows its effective computation, *i.e.* there exists a function *EffTypeOf* such that

$$EffTypeOf\ (r,\ \Delta,\ \Gamma,\ e) = \langle \mu, \sigma \rangle \text{ if and only if } r; \Delta; \Gamma \vdash e : \underset{\mu}{-\sigma}.$$

We will also use the function *TypeOf* with the same arguments, returning the type $\sigma$ only.

## 4.2 Dynamic Semantics

The operational semantics of *RL* (Figure 4) is defined by means of a variant of the tail-call-safe $C_a$EK machine (Flanagan *et al.* [4]). The machine configuration is a tuple $\langle e, E, O, \rho \rangle$ where $e$ is the current term to be evaluated, $E$ is the environment mapping variables to machine values, $O$ is a heap of objects (closures), and $\rho$ is a tuple of *machine resources*. Depending on the allocation strategy used, $\rho$ is either a continuation stack $S$, recording (as in the original $C_a$EK machine) the context of the evaluation as a sequence of activation records, or a pair of a current continuation $k$ and a continuation heap $K$. In the latter form $k$ is a continuation handle and $K$ is a mapping from *ContHandles* to activation records which offers non-sequential access. In neither case does a function application (app) perform additional allocations of activation records, so both strategies are tail-call safe.

Machine values are either small constants or pointers into other structures where larger objects are allocated. All closures are allocated on the heap (the function $\gamma$ at the bottom of the figure shows the details).

The activation records created when evaluating a **let**$^r$-expression may be allocated either on the continuation heap $K$ (transition rule (let$^H$)) or on the continuation stack $S$ (rule (let$^S$)). An activation record represents a continuation, and in our small language there are only three possibilities: the computation either halts or continues by binding a variable to a computed value or by restoring a resource. Rules (val$^H$) and (val$^S$) perform the binding, depending on the allocation mode.

The evaluation of **use**$^r$ ($e$) selects the activation record allocation strategy for $e$, *e.g.* **use**$^S$ ($e$) selects stack-based allocation for $e$ (transition rule (use$^S$)). When the current allocation resource is already $r$ we define **use**$^r$ ($\cdot$) as a no-op; if a change of resource is performed, an activation record is pushed on (the top of) the new allocation resource. Correspondingly, heap-based allocation is restored by transition rule (resume$^H$) after the evaluation of $e$.

**SEMANTIC DOMAINS**

| | | | |
|---|---|---|---|
| $MachineVal \ni w ::=$ | Const $c$ \| Ptr $h$ \| Cont $k$ | | machine values |
| $E$ | $\in$ | $Var \to MachineVal$ | environment |
| $h$ | $\in$ | $HeapLocs$ | heap locations |
| $Object \ni o ::=$ | Closure $\langle x, e, E \rangle$ \| TyAbs $\langle t, r, v \rangle$ | | closures (objects) |
| $O$ | $\in$ | $HeapLocs \to Object$ | object heap |
| $k$ | $\in$ | $ContHandles$ | continuation handles |
| $ActRcd \ni a ::=$ | Bind $\langle x, e, E, k \rangle$ \| Resume $S$ \| Halt | | activation records |
| $K$ | $\in$ | $ContHandles \to ActRcd$ | activation record heap |
| $S ::=$ | Bind $\langle x, e, E, S \rangle$ \| Resume $\langle k, K \rangle$ \| Halt | | activation record stack |

**TRANSITION RULES**

(app) $\qquad \langle @\ x_1\ x_2, E, O, \rho \rangle \mapsto_1 \langle e', E'[x' \mapsto E(x_2)], O, \rho \rangle$
$\qquad\qquad$ where $E(x_1) = $ Ptr $h$, $O(h) = $ Closure $\langle x', e', E' \rangle$

**FOR HEAP-ALLOCATED ACTIVATION RECORDS**

(let$^{\mathsf{H}}$) $\qquad \langle \mathbf{let^H}\ x = e_1\ \mathbf{in}\ e_2, E, H, \langle k, K \rangle \rangle \mapsto_1$
$\qquad\qquad\qquad \langle e_1, E, H, \langle k', K[k' \mapsto \mathsf{Bind}\ \langle x, e_2, E|_{FV(e_2)-x}, k \rangle] \rangle \rangle$

(val$^{\mathsf{H}}$) $\qquad \langle \langle v \rangle^{\mathsf{H}}, E, H, \langle k, K \rangle \rangle \mapsto_1 \langle e', E'[x' \mapsto w], O', \langle k', K \rangle \rangle$
$\qquad\qquad$ where $K(k) = \mathsf{Bind}\ \langle x', e', E', k' \rangle$, $\langle w, O' \rangle = \gamma(v, E, O)$

(callcc) $\qquad \langle \mathbf{callcc}\ x, E, H, \langle k, K \rangle \rangle \mapsto_1 \langle e', E'[x' \mapsto \mathsf{Cont}\ k], O, \langle k, K \rangle \rangle$
$\qquad\qquad$ where $E(x) = $ Ptr $h$, $O(h) = $ Closure $\langle x', e', E' \rangle$

(throw) $\qquad \langle \mathbf{throw}[\sigma]\ x_1\ x_2, E, H, \langle k, K \rangle \rangle \mapsto_1 \langle e', E'[x' \mapsto E(x_2)], O, \langle k', K \rangle \rangle$
$\qquad\qquad$ where $E(x_1) = \mathsf{Cont}\ k_1$, $K(k_1) = \mathsf{Bind}\ \langle x', e', E', k' \rangle$

(use$^{\mathsf{S}}$) $\qquad \langle \mathbf{use^S}\ (e), E, H, \langle k, K \rangle \rangle \mapsto_1 \langle e, E, H, \langle \mathsf{Resume}\ \langle k, K \rangle \rangle \rangle$

(resume$^{\mathsf{S}}$) $\qquad \langle \langle v \rangle^{\mathsf{H}}, E, H, \langle k, K \rangle \rangle \mapsto_1 \langle \langle v \rangle^{\mathsf{S}}, E, H, \langle S \rangle \rangle$
$\qquad\qquad\qquad\qquad\qquad\qquad\qquad\qquad\qquad\qquad\qquad$ where $K(k) = \mathsf{Resume}\ S$

**FOR STACK-ALLOCATED ACTIVATION RECORDS**

(let$^{\mathsf{S}}$) $\qquad \langle \mathbf{let^S}\ x = e_1\ \mathbf{in}\ e_2, E, H, \langle S \rangle \rangle \mapsto_1 \langle e_1, E, H, \langle \mathsf{Bind}\ \langle x, e_2, E|_{FV(e_2)-x}, S \rangle \rangle \rangle$

(val$^{\mathsf{S}}$) $\qquad \langle \langle v \rangle^{\mathsf{S}}, E, H, \langle \mathsf{Bind}\ \langle x', e', E', S \rangle \rangle \rangle \mapsto_1 \langle e', E'[x' \mapsto w], O', \langle S \rangle \rangle$
$\qquad\qquad$ where $\langle w, H' \rangle = \gamma(v, E, O)$

(use$^{\mathsf{H}}$) $\qquad \langle \mathbf{use^H}\ (e), E, H, \langle S \rangle \rangle \mapsto_1 \langle e, E, H, \langle k, [k \mapsto \mathsf{Resume}\ S] \rangle \rangle$

(resume$^{\mathsf{H}}$) $\qquad \langle \langle v \rangle^{\mathsf{S}}, E, H, \langle \mathsf{Resume}\ \langle k, K \rangle \rangle \rangle \mapsto_1 \langle \langle v \rangle^{\mathsf{H}}, E, H, \langle k, K \rangle \rangle$

**REPRESENTATION OF VALUES**

$\gamma(c, E, O) = \langle \mathsf{Const}\ c, O \rangle \qquad \gamma(\lambda^r\ x : \sigma.\ e, E, O) = \langle \mathsf{Ptr}\ h, O[h \mapsto \mathsf{Closure}\ \langle x, e, E|_{FV(e)-x} \rangle] \rangle$

$\gamma(x, E, O) = \langle E(x), O \rangle \qquad \gamma(\Lambda t \leq r.\ v, E, O) = \langle \mathsf{Ptr}\ h, O[h \mapsto \mathsf{TyAbs}\ \langle t, r, v \rangle] \rangle$

$\qquad\qquad\qquad\qquad\qquad\qquad\qquad\qquad\qquad\qquad\qquad$ where $h \notin Dom\ (O)$

$\gamma(x[\mu], E, O) = \gamma([\mu/t]v, E, O)$ if $E(x) = \mathsf{Ptr}\ h'$, $O(h') = \mathsf{TyAbs}\ \langle t, r, v \rangle$, and $\vdash \mu \leq r$

**Fig. 4.** Semantics of *RL*

Another no-op is the increase of effect sets $\langle\cdot\rangle_\mu$ which only serves type-checking purposes.

## 4.3  Soundness of the Type System

The type system maintains the property that the effects of well-typed programs are possible with their available resources, formalized in the following statement, proved by induction on the typing derivation.

**Lemma 1.** *If* $r; \Delta; \Gamma \vdash e : \frac{}{\mu}\sigma$ *is a valid typing judgment, then* $\Delta \vdash \mu \leq r$.

Semantically this behavior of well-typed programs is expressed as soundness with respect to resource use, extending the standard soundness for safety of the type system, in the following theorem.

**Theorem 1.** *If* $r; \emptyset; \emptyset \vdash e : \frac{}{\mu}\sigma$, *then the configuration* $\langle e, \emptyset, \emptyset, \mathsf{Halt}^{\,r}\rangle$ *either diverges or evaluates to the configuration* $\langle\langle v\rangle^r, E, O, \langle\mathsf{Halt}^{\,r}\rangle\rangle$ *(for some $v$, $E$ and $O$), where* $\mathsf{Halt}^{\,S} \triangleq \langle\mathsf{Halt}\,\rangle$, *and* $\mathsf{Halt}^{\,H} \triangleq \langle k, K\rangle$ *for some $k$ and $K$ such that $K(k) = \mathsf{Halt}$.*

This result is a corollary of the standard properties of progress and subject reduction of the system, the proofs of which we sketch below. To simplify the proofs, we introduce a type-annotated version of the semantics, which maintains type information embedded in the runtime representation. Thus the representation of an abstraction in the type-annotated version is

$$\gamma\left(\lambda^r\, x : \sigma.\, e,\, E,\, O\right) = \langle\mathsf{Ptr}\; h,\, O[h \mapsto \mathsf{Closure}'\; \langle r,\, x,\, \sigma,\, e,\, E|_{FV(e)-x}\rangle]\rangle$$

In addition, the runtime environment $E$ is extended to keep the type of each value in its codomain; the value component of $E$ is denoted by $^VE$ and the type component by $^TE$.

The following definitions are helpful in defining typability of configurations.

**Definition 1.** *The bottom $bot(\rho)$ of an allocation resource $\rho$ is defined as follows:*

1.  *if $\rho = \langle S\rangle$, then $bot(\rho) = bot(S')$, if $S = \mathsf{Bind}\;\langle x', e', E', S'\rangle$, and $bot(\rho) = S$ otherwise;*
2.  *if $\rho = \langle k, K\rangle$, then $bot(\rho) = bot(\langle k', K\rangle)$, if $K(k) = \mathsf{Bind}\;\langle x', e', E', k'\rangle$, and $bot(\rho) = K(k)$ otherwise.*

**Definition 2.** *The outermost continuation heap $outerCont(\rho)$ reachable from allocation resource $\rho$ is*

1.  *$K$ if $\rho = \langle k, K\rangle$ and $bot(\rho) = \mathsf{Halt}$;*
2.  *$outerCont(\langle S\rangle)$ if $\rho = \langle k, K\rangle$ and $bot(\rho) = \mathsf{Resume}\; S$;*
3.  *$\emptyset$, if $\rho = \langle S\rangle$ and $bot(\rho) = \mathsf{Halt}$;*
4.  *$outerCont(\langle k, K\rangle)$ if $\rho = \langle S\rangle$ and $bot(\rho) = \mathsf{Resume}\;\langle k, K\rangle$.*

**Definition 3.** *A configuration closed in type environment $\Gamma$ is typable under resource $r$ with a result type $\sigma$ and an effect $\mu$, written $r; \Gamma \vdash \langle e, E, O, \rho\rangle : \frac{}{\mu}\sigma$, if for some $\sigma', \mu'$*

1. $Dom\,(\Gamma) \cap Dom\,(E) = \emptyset$; and
2. $r; \emptyset; \Gamma,\, {}^T\!E \vdash e : {}_{\overline{\mu'}}\sigma'$; and
3. $\Gamma \vdash \langle \rho, E, O \rangle \in \sigma' \xrightarrow[\mu']{r} \sigma$; and
4. for each $x \in Dom\,(E)$,
   (a) if ${}^V\!E(x) = $ Const $c$, then ${}^T\!E(x) = \theta(c)$;
   (b) if ${}^V\!E(x) = $ Ptr $h$ and $O(h) = $ Closure' $\langle r_1, x_1, \sigma_1, e_1, E_1 \rangle$, then
   $\emptyset; {}^T\!E_1 \vdash \lambda^{r_1} x_1 : \sigma_1.\, e_1 : {}^T\!E(x)$, and similarly for type abstractions;
   (c) if ${}^V\!E(x) = $ Cont $k$, then ${}^T\!E(x) = \sigma_1 \, {}^{r_1}$cont and

$$\Gamma \vdash \langle k,\, outerCont(\rho) \rangle, E, O \in \sigma_1 \xrightarrow[\mu_1]{r_1} \sigma_1'$$

and $\mu = \mu_1 \vee \mu_1'$, for some $\sigma_1'$ and $\mu_1'$,

and $\Gamma \vdash \langle \rho, E, O \rangle \in \sigma' \xrightarrow[\mu]{r} \sigma$ if

1. $r = $ S and $\rho = \langle \text{Halt} \rangle$ (i.e. an empty stack) and $\sigma = \sigma'$ and $\mu = \emptyset$; or
2. $r = $ S and $\rho = \langle \text{Bind}\,\langle x_1, e_1, E_1, S_1 \rangle \rangle$ and S; $\Gamma,\, x_1 : \sigma' \vdash \langle e_1, E_1, O, S_1 \rangle : {}_{\overline{\mu}}\sigma$;
or
3. $r = $ S and $\rho = \langle \text{Resume}\,\langle k', K' \rangle \rangle$ and $\Gamma \vdash \langle\langle k', K' \rangle, E, O \rangle \in \sigma' \xrightarrow[\mu]{H} \sigma$,

and similarly for $r = $ H.

Note that the environment may contain reachable variables bound to continuations even when the current allocation resource is a stack. Type correctness of these continuations cannot be verified with the stack resource, instead we have to find the corresponding continuation heap. However in this case the type system guarantees that the only continuation heap to which there are references in the environment is the outermost continuation heap, if such exists. The reason is that although it is possible to switch to heap allocation after executing in stack allocation mode, there are no invocations of **callcc** allowed since they would introduce the CC effect, which is not possible under the stack resource (cf. typing rule (Exp-use) in Figure 3).

We can now formulate the progress and subject reduction properties.

**Lemma 2 (Progress).** If $r; \emptyset \vdash^c \langle e, E, O, \rho \rangle : {}_{\overline{\mu}}\sigma$ where $r$ corresponds to $\rho$ (i.e. $r = $ S if $\rho = \langle S \rangle$, $r = $ H if $\rho = \langle k, K \rangle$), and $\rho \neq $ Halt $^r$, then there exists $C$ such that $\langle e, E, O, \rho \rangle \mapsto_1 C$.

**Lemma 3 (Subject reduction).** If $C = \langle e, E, O, \rho \rangle$ and $r; \emptyset \vdash^c C : {}_{\overline{\mu}}\sigma$ where $r$ corresponds to $\rho$, and $C \mapsto_1 C' = \langle e', E', O', \rho' \rangle$, then $r'; \emptyset \vdash^c C' : {}_{\overline{\mu'}}\sigma$ where $r'$ corresponds to $\rho'$, $\mu = \mu' \vee \mu_1'$, and the rule for this transition is (callcc) only if $\mu = $ CC $\vee \mu''$, for some $\mu_1'$ and $\mu''$.

In brief, in the case when $e \neq \langle v \rangle^r$, the proofs proceed by examining the structure of the typing derivation for $r; \emptyset; \Gamma,\, {}^T\!E \vdash e : {}_{\overline{\mu'}}\sigma'$; together with condition 4 of Definition 3 this yields that the values in the environment and on the heaps have the correct shape for the appropriate transition rule. In the case when $e$ has the form $\langle v \rangle^r$ the proofs inspect the structure of the derivation of $\Gamma \vdash \langle \rho, E, O \rangle \in \sigma' \xrightarrow[\mu]{r} \sigma$, which parallels the decision tree for the transition rules (val) and (resume) and the halting state.

## 4.4 Resource Transformations

Effect inference and type correctness with respect to resource use allow the compiler to modify the continuation allocation strategy of a program fragment and preserve its meaning. The following definitions adapt the standard notions of ordering and observational equivalence of open terms to the resource-based system.

**Definition 4.** *A* context *$C$ is a term with a hole $\bullet$; the result of placing a term $e$ in the hole of $C$ is denoted by $C[e]$ and may result in capturing effect and lambda variables free in $e$. The hole of a context $C$ is of type $(r, \Delta, \Gamma) \Rightarrow {}_{\mu}^{-}\sigma$ if $C[e]$ is typeable whenever $r; \Delta; \Gamma \vdash e : {}_{\mu}^{-}\sigma$.*

**Definition 5.** *$S; \Delta; \Gamma \vdash e \sqsubseteq e' : {}_{\mu}^{-}\sigma$ if for all contexts $C$ with hole of type $(r, \Delta, \Gamma) \Rightarrow {}_{\mu}^{-}\sigma$, all typed environments $E$ closing $C[e]$ and heaps $O$ closing $E$, and continuation stacks $S$, the configuration $\langle C[e'], E, O, \langle S \rangle \rangle$ converges if $\langle C[e], E, O, \langle S \rangle \rangle$ converges. Furthermore, $S; \Delta; \Gamma \vdash e \approx e' : {}_{\mu}^{-}\sigma$ if $S; \Delta; \Gamma \vdash e \sqsubseteq e' : {}_{\mu}^{-}\sigma$ and $S; \Delta; \Gamma \vdash e' \sqsubseteq e : {}_{\mu}^{-}\sigma$.*

One possible optimization is the conversion of heap-allocating code to stack-based strategy provided the code does not invoke **callcc** or **throw**, as per the following theorem.

**Theorem 2.** *If $H; \Delta; \Gamma \vdash e : {}_{\emptyset}^{-}\sigma$, then $S; \Delta; \Gamma \vdash \textbf{use}^H (e) \approx StkCont_\Delta (e; \Gamma) : {}_{\emptyset}^{-}\sigma$, where StkCont is the transformation defined as follows.*

$$
\begin{aligned}
StkCont_\Delta (\langle v \rangle^H; \Gamma) &= \langle v \rangle^S \\
StkCont_\Delta (\langle e \rangle_\mu; \Gamma) &= \langle StkCont_\Delta (e; \Gamma) \rangle_\mu \\
StkCont_\Delta (\textbf{use}^H (e); \Gamma) &= StkCont_\Delta (e; \Gamma) \\
StkCont_\Delta (\textbf{use}^S (e); \Gamma) &= e \\
StkCont_\Delta (\texttt{@} \, x_1 \, x_2; \Gamma) &= \textbf{let}^S \, x_1' = \langle \lambda^S \, x_2' : \Gamma(x_2). \, \textbf{use}^H (\texttt{@} \, x_1 \, x_2') \rangle^S \\
&\quad \textbf{in} \, \texttt{@} \, x_1' \, x_2 \\
StkCont_\Delta (\textbf{let}^H \, x = e_1 \, \textbf{in} \, e_2; \Gamma) &= \textbf{let}^S \, x = StkCont_\Delta (e_1; \Gamma) \\
&\quad \textbf{in} \, StkCont_\Delta (e_2; \Gamma_x, x : TypeOf (H, \Delta, \Gamma, e_2))
\end{aligned}
$$

## 5 Translation from *HL* to *RL*

Programs in language $\mathcal{L} \in \{HL, SL\}$ are translated into *RL* by an algorithm shown in Figure 5. The algorithm infers the effect and resource annotations of a term using fairly standard techniques. It is presented in the form of an inference system for judgments of the form $\Delta; \Gamma \vdash_{\mathcal{L}} e_{HL} \Rightarrow \Delta' \vdash e : {}_{\mu}^{-}\sigma$, where $e_{HL}$, $\Delta$, and $\Gamma$ are inputs corresponding respectively to the $\mathcal{L}$ term to translate (also overloaded to *HL* top-level programs) and the inherited effect and type environments, initially empty. The outputs of the translation are $e$, $\Delta'$, $\mu$, and $\sigma$, which stand for the translated term, the inferred effect environment, and the effect and type of $e$ in environments $\Delta'$ and $\Gamma$; thus the output of the algorithm satisfies $H; \Delta'; \Gamma \vdash e : {}_{\mu}^{-}\sigma$. The function $\mathcal{R}$ maps a language name to the resources available to a program in this language: $\mathcal{R}(HL) = H$ and $\mathcal{R}(SL) = S$.

**(Translate-external)**

$$\sigma' = CloseAll\,(Max^S(Annotate^S(\tau,\,Dom\,(\Delta))),\,S)$$

$$\sigma'' = CloseAll\,(Annotate^H(\tau,\,Dom\,(\Delta)),\,S) \qquad \Delta;\Gamma_x, x:\sigma'' \vdash_{HL} p \Rightarrow \Delta' \vdash e':\frac{}{\mu}\sigma$$

$$\Delta;\Gamma \vdash_{HL} \textbf{external}(SL)\ x:\tau\ \textbf{in}\ p$$
$$\Rightarrow \Delta' \vdash \lambda^H x:\sigma'.\,\textbf{let}^H\,x = Wrap^H_S(\bullet,\,x,\,\sigma')\ \textbf{in}\ e':\,\tfrac{}{\emptyset}(\sigma' \xrightarrow[\mu]{H} \sigma)$$

where

$$Annotate^r\,(\beta,\,V) = \beta$$
$$Annotate^r\,(\tau\ \text{cont},\,V) = (Annotate^r\,(\tau,\,V))\ ^r\text{cont}$$
$$Annotate^r\,(\tau \to \tau',\,V) = \sigma \xrightarrow{r}_t \sigma'\ \text{where}\ t \in EffVar - V,$$
$$\sigma = Annotate^r\,(\tau,\,V \cup \{t\}),$$
$$\sigma' = Annotate^r\,(\tau,\,V \cup \{t\} \cup fev(\sigma))$$
$$Wrap^{r'}_r\,(C,\,x,\,\forall t \le r''.\,\sigma) = \Lambda t \le r''.\,Wrap^{r'}_r\,(C[\textbf{let}^{r'}\,x' = \langle x[t]\rangle^r\ \textbf{in}\ \bullet],\,x',\,\sigma)$$
$$Wrap^{r'}_r\,(C,\,x,\,\sigma_1 \xrightarrow{r}_\mu \sigma_2) = \lambda^{r'}\,x_1:\sigma'_1.\,\textbf{let}^{r'}\,x'_1 = \langle Wrap^r_{r'}\,(\bullet,\,x_1,\,\sigma'_1)\rangle^{r'}$$
$$\text{in}\ Wrap^{r'}_r\,(C[\textbf{let}^{r'}\,x_2 = \texttt{@}\,x\,x'_1\ \textbf{in}\ \bullet],\,x_2,\,\sigma_2)$$
$$\text{where}\ \sigma'_1 = ConvertType^{r'}_r\,(\sigma_1)$$
$$Wrap^{r'}_r\,(C,\,x,\,\beta) = C[\langle x\rangle^{r'}]$$

**(Translate-app)**

$$\Delta;\Gamma \vdash_{\mathcal{L}} e_1 \Rightarrow \Delta_1 \vdash e'_1:\frac{}{\mu_1}\sigma_1 \quad \Delta_1;\Gamma \vdash_{\mathcal{L}} e_2 \Rightarrow \Delta_2 \vdash e'_2:\frac{}{\mu_2}\sigma_2 \quad \Delta';S \vdash \sigma_1 \sim (\sigma_2 \xrightarrow[t]{H} \alpha)$$

$$t \notin fev(\sigma_1) \cup fev(\sigma_2) \cup Dom\,(\Delta_2) \qquad\qquad x_1 \notin FV(e'_2)$$

$$\overline{\Delta_2 \sqcap \Delta';\Gamma \vdash_{\mathcal{L}} e_1\,e_2 \Rightarrow \Delta' \vdash \textbf{let}^H\,x_1 = e'_1\ \textbf{in}\ \textbf{let}^H\,x_2 = e'_2\ \textbf{in}\ \texttt{@}\,x_1\,x_2 :\frac{}{\mu_1 \vee \mu_2 \vee St}S\alpha}$$

where

$$\emptyset;[\sigma/\alpha] \vdash \alpha \sim \sigma \qquad \frac{\Delta_1;S_1 \vdash \sigma_1 \sim \sigma'_1 \quad \Delta_2;S_2 \vdash S_1\sigma_2 \sim S_1\sigma'_2 \quad S = mgu(S_2\mu,\,S_2\mu')}{\Delta_1 \sqcap \Delta_2;S \vdash \sigma_1 \xrightarrow{r}_\mu \sigma_2 \sim \sigma'_1 \xrightarrow{r}_{\mu'} \sigma'_2}$$

$$\frac{\Delta;S \vdash \sigma_1 \sim \sigma_2}{\Delta;S \vdash \sigma_1\ ^r\text{cont} \sim \sigma_2\ ^r\text{cont}} \qquad \frac{\Delta;S \vdash \sigma \sim \sigma' \quad \Delta' = MinEnv(St \le r)}{\Delta \sqcap \Delta';S_{\backslash\{t\}} \vdash \forall t \le r.\,\sigma \sim \sigma'}$$

$$MinEnv\,(t \le r) = t \le r \quad MinEnv\,(\mu_1 \vee \mu_2 \le r) = MinEnv\,(\mu_1 \le r) \sqcap MinEnv\,(\mu_2 \le r)$$
$$MinEnv\,(\emptyset \le r) = \emptyset \qquad MinEnv\,(CC \le H) = \emptyset$$

**(Translate-let)**

$$\Delta;\Gamma \vdash_{\mathcal{L}} e_1 \Rightarrow \Delta_1 \vdash e'_1:\frac{}{\mu_1}\sigma_1$$
$$\langle \sigma'_1,\,\Delta_2\rangle = Close(\sigma_1,\,\Delta_1,\,\Gamma) \quad \Delta_2;\Gamma_x, x:\sigma'_1 \vdash_{\mathcal{L}} e_2 \Rightarrow \Delta' \vdash e'_2:\frac{}{\mu_2}\sigma_2$$

$$\overline{\Delta;\Gamma \vdash_{\mathcal{L}} \textbf{let}\,x = e_1\ \textbf{in}\ e_2 \Rightarrow \Delta' \vdash \textbf{let}^H\,x = e'_1\ \textbf{in}\ e'_2 :\frac{}{\mu_1 \vee \mu_2}\sigma_2}$$

**(Translate-abs)**

$$\frac{\sigma = Annotate^H(\tau,\,Dom\,(\Delta)) \quad \Delta;\Gamma_x, x:\sigma \vdash_{\mathcal{L}} e \Rightarrow \Delta' \vdash e':-\sigma'}{\Delta;\Gamma \vdash_{\mathcal{L}} \lambda x:\tau.\,e \Rightarrow \Delta' \vdash \langle \lambda^H x:\sigma.\,e'\rangle^H :\,\frac{}{\emptyset}(\sigma \xrightarrow[\mu]{H} \sigma')}$$

**(Translate-callcc)**

$$\frac{\Delta;\Gamma \vdash_{HL} e \Rightarrow \Delta' \vdash e':-(\sigma\ ^H\text{cont} \xrightarrow[\mu']{H} \sigma)}{\Delta;\Gamma \vdash_{HL} \textbf{callcc}\ e \Rightarrow \Delta' \vdash \textbf{let}^H\,x = e'\ \textbf{in}\ \textbf{callcc}\ x :\frac{}{\mu \vee \mu' \vee CC}\sigma}$$

**Fig. 5.** Typed translation from *HL* to *RL*

Several auxiliary functions are shown in the figure, and the definitions of several simpler functions are as follows. The lub of two resources is defined by $r \sqcup r = r$ and $\mathsf{S} \sqcup \mathsf{H} = \mathsf{H}$. The function $\sqcap$ for merging two effect environments is defined as $(\Delta_1 \sqcap \Delta_2)(t) = \Delta_1(t) \sqcup \Delta_2(t)$ if $t \in Dom\,(\Delta_1) \cap Dom\,(\Delta_2)$, and $(\Delta_1 \sqcap \Delta_2)(t) = \Delta_i(t)$ on the rest of $Dom\,(\Delta_1) \cup Dom\,(\Delta_2)$. The free effect variables of a type $\sigma$ are denoted by $fev(\sigma)$; the function $Close(\sigma, \Delta, \Gamma)$ returns the pair $\langle \forall t_i \leq \Delta(t_i).\,\sigma,\ \Delta \backslash_{\overline{\{t_i\}}} \rangle$, where $\{\overline{t_i}\} = fev(\sigma) - fev(\Gamma)$, and similarly we have $CloseAll\,(\sigma, r) = \forall t_i \leq r.\,\sigma$ where $\{\overline{t_i}\} = fev(\sigma)$.

Separately compiled **external** functions are treated as parameters of the compiled *HL* fragment and are wrapped to convert the *HL* resources (continuation heap) to *SL* resources (continuation stack). The wrapping is performed by an auxiliary function invoked as $Wrap_r^{r'}\,(C, x, \sigma)$, which produces a term coercing $x$ from type $\sigma$ to type $ConvertType_r^{r'}\,(\sigma)$ with resource annotations $r'$ in place of $r$, and places it in context $C$. When compiling separately, the effects of an **external** function are approximated conservatively by applying $Max^r$ to the effect-annotated declared type of the function; by definition $Max^r(\sigma)$ is $\sigma_1 \xrightarrow[MaxEff(r)]{r} Max^r\,(\sigma_2)$ when $\sigma = \sigma_1 \xrightarrow{r}_{\mu} \sigma_2$, and $\sigma$ otherwise. This allows the view of external functions as effect-polymorphic without restricting their actual implementations.

# 6  Related Work and Conclusions

The work presented in this paper is mainly inspired by recent research on effect inference [5, 10, 11, 23, 24], efficient implementation of first-class continuations [2, 8, 20, 1], monads and modular interpreters [30, 12, 29, 13], typed intermediate languages [7, 25, 21, 17, 16, 3], and foreign function call interface [9, 18]. In the following, we briefly explain the relationship of these work with our resource-based approach.

- **Effect systems.** The idea of using effect-based type systems to support language interoperation was first proposed by Gifford and Lucassen [6, 5]. Along this direction, many researchers have worked on various kinds of effect systems and effect inference algorithms [10, 11, 23, 24, 28]. The main novelty of our effect system is that we imposed a "resource-based" upper-bound to the effect variables. Effect variables in all previous effect systems are always *universally* quantified without any upper bounds, so they can be instantiated into any effect expressions. Our system limits the quantification over a finite set of resources—this allows us to take advantage of the effect-resource relationship to support advanced compilation strategies.
- **Efficient call/cc.** Many people have worked on designing various strategies to support efficient implementation of first-class continuations [2, 8, 20, 1]. To support a reasonably efficient call/cc, compilers today mostly use "stack chunks" (a linked list of smaller stacks) [2, 8] or they simply heap allocate all activation records [20]. Both of these representations are incompatible with those used by traditional languages such as C and C++ where activation records are allocated on a sequential stack. First-class continuations thus always impose restrictions and interoperability challenges to the underlying compiler. In fact, many existing compilers choose not to support call/cc, simply because call/cc is not compatible with standard C

133

calling conventions. The techniques presented in this paper provide opportunities to support both efficient call/cc and interoperability with code that use sequential stacks.

- **Threads.** Implementing threads does not necessarily require first-class continuations but only an equivalent of one-shot continuations [1]. A finer distinction between these classes of continuations is useful, however the issues of incorporating linearity in the type system to ensure safety in the presence of one-shot continuations are beyond the scope of this paper.

- **Monads and modular interpreters.** The idea of using *resources* and *effects* to characterize the run-time configuration of a function is inspired by recent work on monad-based interactions and modular interpreters [30, 12, 29, 13]. Unlike in the monadic approach, our system provides a way of switching the runtime context "horizontally" from one to another via the **use**$^r$ ($e$) construct.

- **Typed intermediate languages.** Typed intermediate languages have received much attention lately, especially in the HOT (i.e., higher-order and typed) language community. However, recent work [7, 15, 22, 17, 3, 16, 14] has mostly focused on the theoretical foundations and general language design issues. The type system in this paper focused on the problem of compiling multiple source languages into a common typed intermediate format. We plan to incorporate the resource and effect annotations into our FLINT intermediate language [22].

- **Foreign function call interface.** The interoperability problem addressed in this paper has much in common with frameworks for multi-lingual programming, such as ILU, CORBA [27], and Microsoft's COM [19]. It also relates to the foreign function call interfaces in most existing compilers [9, 18]. Although these work do address many of the low-level problems, such as converting data representations between languages or passing information to remote processes, their implementations do not provide any safety guarantees (or if they do, they would require external programs run in a separate address space). The work presented in this paper focuses on interfacing programs running in the single address space with much higher performance requirements. We emphasize building a *safe*, *efficient*, and *robust* interface across multiple HOT languages.

We believe what we have presented in this paper is a good first-step towards a fully formal investigation on the topic of safe fine-grain language interoperations. We have concentrated on the issues of first-class continuations in this paper, but the framework presented here should also apply to handle other language features such as states, exceptions, and non-termination. The effect system described in this paper is also very general and useful for static program analysis: because it supports effect polymorphism, effect information is accurately propagated through high-order functions. This is clearly much more informative than the single one-bit (or N-bit) information seen in the simple monad-based calculus [16, 26].

There are many hard problems that must be solved in order to support a safe and fine-grained interoperation between ML and safe-C, for instance, the interactions between garbage collection and explicit memory allocation, between type-safe and unsafe language features etc. We plan to pursue these problems in the future.

## Acknowledgment

We are grateful to the anonymous referees for their valuable comments.

# References

[1] C. Bruggeman, O. Waddell, and K. Dybvig. Representing control in the presence of one-shot continuations. In *Proc. ACM SIGPLAN '96 Conf. on Prog. Lang. Design and Implementation*, pages 99–107, New York, June 1996. ACM Press.

[2] W. D. Clinger, A. H. Hartheimer, and E. M. Ost. Implementation strategies for continuations. In *1988 ACM Conference on Lisp and Functional Programming*, pages 124–131, New York, June 1988. ACM Press.

[3] A. Dimock, R. Muller, F. Turbak, and J. B. Wells. Strongly typed flow-directed representation transformations. In *Proc. 1997 ACM SIGPLAN International Conference on Functional Programming (ICFP'97)*, pages 11–24. ACM Press, June 1997.

[4] C. Flanagan, A. Sabry, B. F. Duba, and M. Felleisen. The essence of compiling with continuations. In *Proc. ACM SIGPLAN '93 Conf. on Prog. Lang. Design and Implementation*, pages 237–247, New York, June 1993. ACM Press.

[5] D. K. Gifford *et al.* FX-87 reference manual. Technical Report MIT/LCS/TR-407, M.I.T. Laboratory for Computer Science, September 1987.

[6] D. Gifford and J. Lucassen. Integrating functional and imperative programming. In *1986 ACM Conference on Lisp and Functional Programming*, New York, August 1986. ACM Press.

[7] R. Harper and G. Morrisett. Compiling polymorphism using intensional type analysis. In *Twenty-second Annual ACM Symp. on Principles of Prog. Languages*, pages 130–141, New York, Jan 1995. ACM Press.

[8] R. Hieb, R. K. Dybvig, and C. Bruggeman. Representing control in the presence of first-class continuations. In *Proc. ACM SIGPLAN '90 Conf. on Prog. Lang. Design and Implementation*, pages 66–77, New York, 1990. ACM Press.

[9] L. Huelsbergen. A portable C interface for Standard ML of New Jersey. Technical memorandum, AT&T Bell Laboratories, Murray Hill, NJ, January 1996.

[10] P. Jouvelot and D. K. Gifford. Reasoning about continuations with control effects. In *Proc. ACM SIGPLAN '89 Conf. on Prog. Lang. Design and Implementation*, pages 218–226. ACM Press, 1989.

[11] P. Jouvelot and D. K. Gifford. Algebraic reconstruction of types and effects. In *Eighteenth Annual ACM Symp. on Principles of Prog. Languages*, pages 303–310, New York, Jan 1991. ACM Press.

[12] J. Launchbury and S. Peyton Jones. Lazy functional state threads. In *Proc. ACM SIGPLAN '94 Conf. on Prog. Lang. Design and Implementation*, pages 24–35, New York, June 1994. ACM Press.

[13] S. Liang, P. Hudak, and M. Jones. Monad transformers and modular interpreters. In *Proc. 22rd Annual ACM SIGPLAN-SIGACT Symp. on Principles of Programming Languages*, pages 333–343. ACM Press, 1995.

[14] G. Morrisett, D. Walker, K. Crary, and N. Glew. From system F to typed assembly language. In *Proc. 25rd Annual ACM SIGPLAN-SIGACT Symp. on Principles of Programming Languages*, page (to appear). ACM Press, 1998.

[15] G. Morrisett. *Compiling with Types*. PhD thesis, School of Computer Science, Carnegie Mellon University, Pittsburgh, PA, December 1995. Tech Report CMU-CS-95-226.

[16] S. Peyton Jones, J. Launchbury, M. Shields, and A. Tolmach. Bridging the gulf: a common intermediate language for ML and Haskell. In *Proc. 25rd Annual ACM SIGPLAN-SIGACT Symp. on Principles of Programming Languages*, page (to appear). ACM Press, 1998.

[17] S. Peyton Jones and E. Meijer. Henk: a typed intermediate language. In *Proc. 1997 ACM SIGPLAN Workshop on Types in Compilation*, June 1997.

[18] S. Peyton Jones, T. Nordin, and A. Reid. Green card: a foreign-language interface for Haskell. Available at http://www.dcs.gla.ac.uk:80/ simonpj/green-card.ps.gz, 1997.

[19] D. Rogerson. *Inside COM: Microsoft's Component Object Model*. Microsoft Press, 1997.

[20] Z. Shao and A. W. Appel. Space-efficient closure representations. In *1994 ACM Conference on Lisp and Functional Programming*, pages 150–161, New York, June 1994. ACM Press.

[21] Z. Shao. An overview of the FLINT/ML compiler. In *Proc. 1997 ACM SIGPLAN Workshop on Types in Compilation*, June 1997.

[22] Z. Shao. Typed common intermediate format. In *Proc. 1997 USENIX Conference on Domain Specific Languages*, pages 89–102, October 1997.

[23] J.-P. Talpin and P. Jouvelot. Polymorphic type, region, and effect inference. *Journal of Functional Programming*, 2(3), 1992.

[24] J.-P. Talpin and P. Jouvelot. The type and effect discipline. *Information and Computation*, 111(2):245–296, June 1994.

[25] D. Tarditi, G. Morrisett, P. Cheng, C. Stone, R. Harper, and P. Lee. TIL: A type-directed optimizing compiler for ML. In *Proc. ACM SIGPLAN '96 Conf. on Prog. Lang. Design and Implementation*, pages 181–192. ACM Press, 1996.

[26] D. Tarditi. *Design and Implementation of Code Optimizations for a Type-Directed Compiler for Standard ML*. PhD thesis, School of Computer Science, Carnegie Mellon University, Pittsburgh, PA, December 1996. Tech Report CMU-CS-97-108.

[27] The Object Management Group. The common object request broker: Architecture and specifications (CORBA). Revision 1.2., Object Management Group (OMG), Framingham, MA, December 1993.

[28] M. Tofte and J.-P. Talpin. Implementation of the typed call-by-value λ-calculus using a stack of regions. In *Proc. 21st Annual ACM SIGPLAN-SIGACT Symp. on Principles of Programming Languages*, pages 188–201. ACM Press, 1994.

[29] P. Wadler. The essence of functional programming (invited talk). In *Nineteenth Annual ACM Symp. on Principles of Prog. Languages*, New York, Jan 1992. ACM Press.

[30] P. Wadler. How to declare an imperative (invited talk). In *International Logic Programming Symposium*, Portland, Oregon, December 1995. MIT Press.

# Polymorphic Equality – No Tags Required

Martin Elsman

Department of Computer Science, University of Copenhagen
Universitetsparken 1, DK-2100 Copenhagen Ø, Denmark.
E-mail: mael@diku.dk

**Abstract.** Polymorphic equality is a controversial language construct. While being convenient for the programmer, it has been argued that polymorphic equality (1) invites to violation of software engineering principles, (2) lays a serious burden on the language implementor, and (3) enforces a runtime overhead due to the necessity of tagging values at runtime. We show that neither (2) nor (3) are inherent to polymorphic equality by showing that one can compile programs with polymorphic equality into programs without polymorphic equality in such a way that there is no need for tagging or for runtime type analysis. Also, the translation is the identity on programs that do not use polymorphic equality. Experimental results indicate that even for programs that use polymorphic equality, the translation gives good results.

## 1 Introduction

Often, statically typed languages, like ML, provide the programmer with a generic function for checking structural equality of two values of the same type. To avoid the possibility of testing functional values for equality, the type system of Standard ML [11] distinguishes between ordinary type variables, which may be instantiated to any type, and equality type variables, which may be instantiated only to types that admit equality (i.e., types not containing ordinary type variables or function types). In this paper, we show how polymorphic equality may be eliminated entirely in the front-end of a compiler by a type based translation called equality elimination. The translation is possible for expressions that are typable according to the Standard ML type discipline[11]. We make three main contributions:

1. Identification and application of equality elimination in a call-by-value language without garbage collection, including treatment of parametric datatypes and side effects. Equality elimination eliminates the last obligation for tagging values in Standard ML and opens for efficient data representations and easier foreign language interfacing.
2. Measurements of the effect of equality elimination in the ML Kit with Regions [23, 3, 5] (from hereon just the Kit) and a discussion of the possibilities for data representations made possible by the translation.
3. Demonstration of semantic correctness of the translation. It has been considered non-trivial to demonstrate semantic correctness for type classes in Haskell [13, Sect. 4].

As an example of equality elimination, consider the following ML program, which declares the function member using polymorphic equality to test if a given value is among the elements of a list:

```
let fun member y [] = false
    | member y (x::xs) = (y = x) orelse member y xs
in (member 5 [3,5], member true [false])
end
```

The function member gets type scheme $\forall \varepsilon. \varepsilon \to \varepsilon$ *list* $\to$ *bool*, where $\varepsilon$ is an *equality type variable* (i.e., a type variable that ranges over equality types). In the example, the function member is used with instances *int* and *bool*, which both admit equality.

On the other hand, the function map, presented below, gets type scheme $\forall \alpha \beta. (\alpha \to \beta) \to \alpha$ *list* $\to \beta$ *list*, where $\alpha$ and $\beta$ are ordinary type variables and hence may be instantiated to any particular type.

```
fun map f [] = []
  | map f (x::xs) = f x :: map f xs
```

To eliminate polymorphic equality, it is possible to pass extra arguments to equality polymorphic functions as member above – one for each abstracted equality type variable in the type scheme for the function. Using type information, the example is translated into the program

```
let fun member eq y [] = false
    | member eq y (x::xs) = eq (y,x) orelse member eq y xs
in (member eq_int 5 [3,5], member eq_bool true [false])
end
```

For each use of an equality polymorphic function, appropriate instances of the equality primitive are passed as arguments. In the translated program above, eq_int and eq_bool denote primitive equality functions for testing integers and booleans for equality. These primitive functions are functions on base types and can be implemented efficiently by the backend of a compiler without the requirement that values be tagged. An important property of the translation is that it is the identity on expressions that do not use polymorphic equality. Thus, one pays for polymorphic equality only when it is used. In particular, the translation is the identity on the map function.

In the next section, we give an overview of related work. The language that we consider is described in the sections to follow. We then proceed to present a translation for eliminating polymorphic equality. In Sect. 7 and Sect. 8, we demonstrate type correctness and semantic soundness of the translation. In Sect. 9 and Sect. 10, we show how the approach is extended to full ML and how it is implemented in the Kit. We then proceed to present experimental results. Finally, we conclude.

## 2   Related Work

A type based dictionary transformation similar to equality elimination allows type classes in Haskell to be eliminated at compile time [25, 13, 16]. However, the motivation for equality elimination is different from the motivation behind the dictionary transformation, which is to separate dictionary operations from values at runtime. In lazy languages such as Haskell, tagging cannot be eliminated even if tag-free garbage collection is used. A more aggressive elimination of dictionaries is possible by generating specialised versions of overloaded functions [8]. This technique does not work well with separate compilation and may lead to unnecessary code duplication. No work on dictionary transformations demonstrates semantic soundness.

Harper and Stone present an alternative semantics to Standard ML in terms of a translation into an intermediate typed language [6]. Similar to the translation we present here, polymorphic equality is eliminated during the translation. However, because the semantics of their source language is given by the translation, they cannot show correctness of the translation.

Ohori demonstrates how Standard ML may be extended with polymorphic record operations in such a way that these operations can be translated into efficient indexing operations [14]. His translation is much similar to equality elimination in that record indices are passed to instantiations of functions that use record operations polymorphically; Ohori demonstrates both type correctness and semantic soundness for the approach.

The TIL compiler, developed at Carnegie Mellon University, uses intensional polymorphism and nearly tag-free garbage collection to allow tag-free representations of values at runtime [20]. An intermediate language of TIL allows a function to take types as arguments, which can then be inspected by the function. This means that polymorphic equality can be encoded in the intermediate language, thus, eliminating the primitive notion of polymorphic equality. However, for nearly tag-free garbage collection, records and other objects stored in the heap are still tagged in order for the garbage collector to trace pointers. It has been reported, however, that the nearly tag-free scheme can be extended to an entirely tag-free scheme [21].

## 3   Language and Types

We consider a typed lambda calculus extended with pairs, conditionals, a polymorphic equality primitive, and a let-construct to allow polymorphic bindings. First, we introduce some terminology. A *finite map* is a map with finite domain and if $f$ and $g$ are such maps we denote by $\text{Dom}(f)$ the domain of $f$ and by $\text{Ran}(f)$ the range of $f$. Further, we write $f + g$ to mean the *modification* of $f$ by $g$ with domain $\text{Dom}(f) \cup \text{Dom}(g)$ and values $(f + g)(x) =$ if $x \in \text{Dom}(g)$ then $g(x)$ else $f(x)$.

We assume a denumerably infinite set of *equality type variables*, ranged over by $\varepsilon$, and a denumerably infinite set of *ordinary type variables*, ranged over by

$\alpha$. Types, ranged over by $\tau$, and type schemes, ranged over by $\sigma$, are defined as follows:

$$\tau ::= \varepsilon \mid \alpha \mid \tau_1 \to \tau_2 \mid \tau_1 \times \tau_2 \mid bool$$
$$\sigma ::= \forall \vec{\varepsilon}\vec{\alpha}.\tau$$

A type $\tau$ *admits equality* if either $\tau = bool$ or $\tau = \varepsilon$ or $\tau = \tau_1 \times \tau_2$ and $\tau_1$ and $\tau_2$ admit equality.

## 3.1 Substitutions

A *substitution* $S$ is a pair $(S^\varepsilon, S^\alpha)$, where $S^\varepsilon$ is a finite map from equality type variables to types such that, for all $\tau \in \mathrm{Ran}(S^\varepsilon)$, $\tau$ admits equality and $S^\alpha$ is a finite map from ordinary type variables to types. When $A$ is any object and $S = (S^\varepsilon, S^\alpha)$ is a substitution, we write $S(A)$ to mean simultaneous capture free substitution of $S^\varepsilon$ and $S^\alpha$ on $A$.

For any type scheme $\sigma = \forall \varepsilon_1 \cdots \varepsilon_n \alpha_1 \cdots \alpha_m.\tau$ and type $\tau'$, we say that $\tau'$ is an *instance of* $\sigma$ *(via $S$)*, written $\sigma \geq \tau'$, if there exists a substitution $S = (\{\varepsilon_1 \mapsto \tau_1, \ldots, \varepsilon_n \mapsto \tau_n\}, \{\alpha_1 \mapsto \tau_1', \ldots, \alpha_m \mapsto \tau_m'\})$ such that $S(\tau) = \tau'$. The *instance list of* $S$, written $il(S)$, is the pair $([\tau_1, \ldots, \tau_n], [\tau_1', \ldots, \tau_m'])$. Pairs of the above form are referred to as instance lists and we use $il$ to range over them.

When $A$ is any object, we denote by $\mathrm{ftv}(A)$ a pair of a set of equality type variables free in $A$ and a set of ordinary type variables free in $A$. Further, we denote by $\mathrm{fetv}(A)$ the set of equality type variables that occur free in $A$.

## 3.2 Typed Expressions

In the following, we use $x$ and $y$ to range over a denumerably infinite set of *lambda variables*. The grammar for typed expressions is as follows:

$$e ::= \lambda x : \tau.e \mid e_1 e_2 \mid (e_1, e_2) \mid \pi_i e \mid x_{il}$$
$$\mid \text{let } x : \sigma = e_1 \text{ in } e_2 \mid \text{true} \mid \text{false}$$
$$\mid \text{if } e \text{ then } e_1 \text{ else } e_2 \mid \text{eq}_\tau$$

We sometimes abbreviate $x_{([],[])}$ with $x$.

# 4 Static Semantics

The static semantics for the language is described by a set of inference rules. Each of the rules allows inferences among sentences of the form $\Delta, TE \vdash e : \tau$, where, $\Delta$ is a set of equality type variables, $TE$ is a *type environment*, mapping lambda variables to type schemes, $e$ is a typed lambda expression, and $\tau$ is a type. Sentences of this form are read "under assumption $(\Delta, TE)$, the expression $e$ has type $\tau$."

A type $\tau$ is *well-formed* with respect to a set of equality type variables $\Delta$, written $\Delta \vdash \tau$, if $\Delta \supseteq \mathrm{fetv}(\tau)$. Moreover, an instance list $il = ([\tau_1, \ldots, \tau_n], [\tau_1', \ldots, \tau_m'])$ is *well-formed* with respect to a set of equality type variables $\Delta$, written $\Delta \vdash il$, if $\Delta \vdash \tau_i$, $i = 1..n$ and $\Delta \vdash \tau_i'$, $i = 1..m$.

**Expressions**  $\boxed{\Delta, TE \vdash e : \tau}$

$$\frac{\Delta, TE + \{x \mapsto \tau\} \vdash e : \tau'}{\Delta, TE \vdash \lambda x : \tau.e : \tau \to \tau'} \quad (1)$$

$$\frac{\begin{array}{c} \Delta, TE \vdash e_1 : \tau_1 \to \tau_2 \\ \Delta, TE \vdash e_2 : \tau_1 \end{array}}{\Delta, TE \vdash e_1 \ e_2 : \tau_2} \quad (2)$$

$$\frac{\begin{array}{c} \Delta, TE \vdash e_1 : \tau_1 \\ \Delta, TE \vdash e_2 : \tau_2 \end{array}}{\Delta, TE \vdash (e_1, e_2) : \tau_1 \times \tau_2} \quad (3)$$

$$\frac{i \in \{1,2\} \quad \Delta, TE \vdash e : \tau_1 \times \tau_2}{\Delta, TE \vdash \pi_i \ e : \tau_i} \quad (4)$$

$$\frac{\begin{array}{c} TE(x) \geq \tau \text{ via } S \\ \Delta \vdash il(S) \end{array}}{\Delta, TE \vdash x_{il(S)} : \tau} \quad (5)$$

$$\frac{\begin{array}{c} \sigma = \forall \vec{\varepsilon}\vec{\alpha}.\tau \quad \mathrm{ftv}(\vec{\varepsilon}\vec{\alpha}) \cap \mathrm{ftv}(\Delta, TE) = \emptyset \\ \Delta \cup \mathrm{fetv}(\vec{\varepsilon}), TE \vdash e_1 : \tau \\ \Delta, TE + \{x \mapsto \sigma\} \vdash e_2 : \tau' \end{array}}{\Delta, TE \vdash \mathtt{let} \ x : \sigma = e_1 \ \mathtt{in} \ e_2 : \tau'} \quad (6)$$

$$\frac{}{\Delta, TE \vdash \mathtt{true} : bool} \quad (7)$$

$$\frac{\begin{array}{c} \Delta, TE \vdash e : bool \\ \Delta, TE \vdash e_1 : \tau \quad \Delta, TE \vdash e_2 : \tau \end{array}}{\Delta, TE \vdash \mathtt{if} \ e \ \mathtt{then} \ e_1 \ \mathtt{else} \ e_2 : \tau} \quad (8)$$

$$\frac{}{\Delta, TE \vdash \mathtt{false} : bool} \quad (9)$$

$$\frac{\Delta \vdash \tau \quad \tau \text{ admits equality}}{\Delta, TE \vdash \mathtt{eq}_\tau : \tau \times \tau \to bool} \quad (10)$$

There are only a few comments to note about the rules. In the rule for applying the equality primitive to values of a particular type, we require the type to be well-formed with respect to quantified equality type variables. Similarly, in the variable rule, we require the instance list be well-formed with respect to quantified equality type variables.

For simplifying the type system in languages with imperative updates and polymorphism, there is a tendency to restrict polymorphism to bindings of non-side-effecting terminating expressions. This tendency is known as the *value restriction*, which is enforced by both the Objective Caml system [10] and the Standard ML language [11]. To simplify the presentation, we do not enforce the value restriction in rule 6. We return to this issue later, in Sect. 8.

## 5  Dynamic Semantics

The dynamic semantics for the language is, as the static semantics, described by a set of inference rules.

An *untyped expression* may be obtained from a typed expression by eliminating all type information. In the rest of this section, we use $e$ to range over untyped expressions.

A *dynamic environment*, $\mathcal{E}$, maps lambda variables to values, which again are defined by the grammar:

$$v ::= \text{clos}(\lambda x.e, \mathcal{E}) \mid \text{true} \mid \text{false} \mid (v_1, v_2) \mid \text{eq}$$

The rules of the dynamic semantics allow inferences among sentences of the forms $\mathcal{E} \vdash e \Downarrow v$ and $\vdash_{\text{eq}} (v_1, v_2) \Downarrow v$, where $\mathcal{E}$ is a dynamic environment, $e$ is an untyped expression, and $v$, $v_1$, and $v_2$ are values. Sentences of the former form are read "under assumptions $\mathcal{E}$, the expression $e$ evaluates to $v$." Sentences of the latter form are read "equality of values $v_1$ and $v_2$ is $v$."

**Expressions** $\boxed{\mathcal{E} \vdash e \Downarrow v}$

$$\frac{\mathcal{E}(x) = v}{\mathcal{E} \vdash x \Downarrow v} \quad (11) \qquad \frac{}{\mathcal{E} \vdash \lambda x.e \Downarrow \text{clos}(\lambda x.e, \mathcal{E})} \quad (12)$$

$$\frac{\begin{array}{c} \mathcal{E} \vdash e_1 \Downarrow \text{clos}(\lambda x.e, \mathcal{E}_0) \\ \mathcal{E} \vdash e_2 \Downarrow v \\ \mathcal{E}_0 + \{x \mapsto v\} \vdash e \Downarrow v' \end{array}}{\mathcal{E} \vdash e_1 \, e_2 \Downarrow v'} \quad (13) \qquad \frac{\begin{array}{c} \mathcal{E} \vdash e_1 \Downarrow \text{eq} \\ \mathcal{E} \vdash e_2 \Downarrow v \qquad \vdash_{\text{eq}} v \Downarrow v' \end{array}}{\mathcal{E} \vdash e_1 \, e_2 \Downarrow v'} \quad (14)$$

$$\frac{}{\mathcal{E} \vdash \text{true} \Downarrow \text{true}} \quad (15) \qquad \frac{}{\mathcal{E} \vdash \text{false} \Downarrow \text{false}} \quad (16)$$

$$\frac{}{\mathcal{E} \vdash \text{eq} \Downarrow \text{eq}} \quad (17) \qquad \frac{\mathcal{E} \vdash e_1 \Downarrow v_1 \qquad \mathcal{E} \vdash e_2 \Downarrow v_2}{\mathcal{E} \vdash (e_1, e_2) \Downarrow (v_1, v_2)} \quad (18)$$

$$\frac{i \in \{1, 2\} \qquad \mathcal{E} \vdash e \Downarrow (v_1, v_2)}{\mathcal{E} \vdash \pi_i \, e \Downarrow v_i} \quad (19) \qquad \frac{\mathcal{E} \vdash e \Downarrow \text{true} \qquad \mathcal{E} \vdash e_1 \Downarrow v}{\mathcal{E} \vdash \text{if } e \text{ then } e_1 \text{ else } e_2 \Downarrow v} \quad (20)$$

$$\frac{\mathcal{E} \vdash e \Downarrow \text{false} \qquad \mathcal{E} \vdash e_2 \Downarrow v}{\mathcal{E} \vdash \text{if } e \text{ then } e_1 \text{ else } e_2 \Downarrow v} \quad (21) \qquad \frac{\begin{array}{c} \mathcal{E} \vdash e_1 \Downarrow v_1 \\ \mathcal{E} + \{x \mapsto v_1\} \vdash e_2 \Downarrow v_2 \end{array}}{\mathcal{E} \vdash \text{let } x = e_1 \text{ in } e_2 \Downarrow v_2} \quad (22)$$

**Equality of Values** $\boxed{\vdash_{eq} (v_1, v_2) \Downarrow v}$

$$\frac{\begin{array}{c} v_1 = v_2 \\ v_1, v_2 \in \{\mathbf{true, false}\} \end{array}}{\vdash_{eq} (v_1, v_2) \Downarrow \mathbf{true}} \ (23)$$

$$\frac{\vdash_{eq} (v_{11}, v_{21}) \Downarrow \mathbf{false}}{\vdash_{eq} ((v_{11}, v_{12}), (v_{21}, v_{22})) \Downarrow \mathbf{false}} \ (24)$$

$$\frac{\begin{array}{c} v_1 \neq v_2 \\ v_1, v_2 \in \{\mathbf{true, false}\} \end{array}}{\vdash_{eq} (v_1, v_2) \Downarrow \mathbf{false}} \ (25)$$

$$\frac{\begin{array}{c} \vdash_{eq} (v_{11}, v_{21}) \Downarrow \mathbf{true} \\ \vdash_{eq} (v_{12}, v_{22}) \Downarrow v \end{array}}{\vdash_{eq} ((v_{11}, v_{12}), (v_{21}, v_{22})) \Downarrow v} \ (26)$$

The dynamic semantics includes rules for the polymorphic equality primitive (rules 23 through 26). If the equality primitive is only ever applied to values of type *bool* (if rules 24 and 26 are not used), the primitive need not distinguish booleans from values of pair type and no runtime tagging is required.

## 6 Equality Elimination

In this section, we present inference rules for translating typable expressions into typable expressions for which the equality primitive is used only with instance *bool*. The translation is the identity for typable expressions that do not use polymorphic equality.

A *translation environment*, $E$, is a finite map from equality type variables to lambda variables. We occasionally need to construct a function for checking structural equality on a pair of values of the same type. We define a relation that allows inferences among sentences of the form $E \vdash_{eq} \tau \Rightarrow e$, where $E$ is a translation environment, $\tau$ is a type, and $e$ is an expression. Sentences of this form are read "under the assumptions $E$, $e$ is an equality function for values of type $\tau$."

**Equality Function Construction** $\boxed{E \vdash_{eq} \tau \Rightarrow e}$

$$\frac{E(\varepsilon) = x}{E \vdash_{eq} \varepsilon \Rightarrow x} \ (27)$$

$$\frac{}{E \vdash_{eq} bool \Rightarrow \mathbf{eq_{bool}}} \ (28)$$

$$\frac{\begin{array}{c} E \vdash_{eq} \tau_1 \Rightarrow e_1 \quad E \vdash_{eq} \tau_2 \Rightarrow e_2 \quad x \text{ fresh} \\ e = e_2 \ (\pi_2 \ (\pi_1 \ x), \pi_2 \ (\pi_2 \ x)) \\ e' = \mathbf{if} \ e_1 \ (\pi_1 \ (\pi_1 \ x), \pi_1 \ (\pi_2 \ x)) \ \mathbf{then} \ e \ \mathbf{else} \ \mathbf{false} \end{array}}{E \vdash_{eq} \tau_1 \times \tau_2 \Rightarrow \lambda x : (\tau_1 \times \tau_2) \times (\tau_1 \times \tau_2).e'} \ (29)$$

Each rule for the translation of expressions allows inferences among sentences of the form $E \vdash e \Rightarrow e'$, where $e$ and $e'$ are expressions and $E$ is a translation environment. Sentences of this form are read "under the assumptions $E$, $e$ translates to $e'$."

**Expressions** $\boxed{E \vdash e \Rightarrow e'}$

$$\frac{E \vdash e \Rightarrow e'}{E \vdash \lambda x : \tau.e \Rightarrow \lambda x : \tau.e'} \ (30) \qquad \frac{E \vdash e_1 \Rightarrow e_1' \quad E \vdash e_2 \Rightarrow e_2'}{E \vdash e_1 \ e_2 \Rightarrow e_1' \ e_2'} (31)$$

$$\frac{E \vdash e_1 \Rightarrow e_1' \quad E \vdash e_2 \Rightarrow e_2'}{E \vdash (e_1, e_2) \Rightarrow (e_1', e_2')}(32) \qquad \frac{E \vdash e \Rightarrow e'}{E \vdash \pi_i \ e \Rightarrow \pi_i \ e'} \ (33)$$

$$\frac{\begin{array}{c} il = ([\tau_1, \ldots, \tau_n], [\ldots]) \quad n \geq 0 \\ E \vdash_{eq} \tau_i \Rightarrow e_i \quad i = 1..n \end{array}}{E \vdash x_{il} \Rightarrow (\cdots (x_{il} \ e_1) \cdots e_n)} \ (34) \qquad \frac{E \vdash_{eq} \tau \Rightarrow e}{E \vdash eq_\tau \Rightarrow e} \ (35)$$

$$\frac{\begin{array}{c} \sigma = \forall \varepsilon_1 \cdots \varepsilon_n \vec{\alpha}.\tau \quad y_1 \cdots y_n \text{ fresh} \quad n \geq 0 \\ E + \{\varepsilon_1 \mapsto y_1, \ldots, \varepsilon_n \mapsto y_n\} \vdash e_1 \Rightarrow e_1' \\ \tau_i = \varepsilon_i \times \varepsilon_i \to bool \quad i = 1..n \\ e_1'' = \lambda y_1 : \tau_1 . \cdots . \lambda y_n : \tau_n.e_1' \quad E \vdash e_2 \Rightarrow e_2' \\ \sigma' = \forall \varepsilon_1 \cdots \varepsilon_n \vec{\alpha}.\tau_1 \to \cdots \to \tau_n \to \tau \end{array}}{E \vdash \text{let } x : \sigma = e_1 \text{ in } e_2 \Rightarrow \text{let } x : \sigma' = e_1'' \text{ in } e_2'} \ (36)$$

$$\frac{}{E \vdash \text{true} \Rightarrow \text{true}} \ (37) \qquad \frac{}{E \vdash \text{false} \Rightarrow \text{false}} \ (38)$$

$$\frac{E \vdash e \Rightarrow e' \quad E \vdash e_1 \Rightarrow e_1' \quad E \vdash e_2 \Rightarrow e_2'}{E \vdash \text{if } e \text{ then } e_1 \text{ else } e_2 \Rightarrow \text{if } e' \text{ then } e_1' \text{ else } e_2'} \ (39)$$

In the translation rule for the let-construct, we generate abstractions for equality functions for each bound equality type variable in the type scheme for the let-bound variable. Accordingly, in the rule for variable occurrences, appropriate equality functions are applied according to type instances for abstracted equality type variables. In rule 35, we generate a function for checking equality of values of type $\tau$.

# 7 Type Correctness

In this section, we demonstrate that the translation preserves types and that all typable expressions may be translated.

## 7.1 Type Preservation

We first give a few definitions for relating type environments and translation environments.

**Definition 1. (Extension)** *A type scheme* $\sigma = \forall \varepsilon_1 \cdots \varepsilon_n \vec{\alpha}.\tau$ *extends another type scheme* $\sigma' = \forall \varepsilon_1' \cdots \varepsilon_m' \vec{\alpha}'.\tau'$, *written* $\sigma \succ \sigma'$, *if* $n = m$ *and* $\varepsilon_i = \varepsilon_i'$, $i = 1..n$ *and* $\vec{\alpha} = \vec{\alpha}'$ *and* $\tau = (\varepsilon_1 \times \varepsilon_1 \to bool) \to \cdots \to (\varepsilon_n \times \varepsilon_n \to bool) \to \tau'$.

*A type environment* $TE'$ *extends another type environment* $TE$, *written* $TE' \succ TE$, *if* $\mathrm{Dom}(TE') \supseteq \mathrm{Dom}(TE)$ *and* $TE'(x) \succ TE(x)$ *for all* $x \in \mathrm{Dom}(TE)$.

**Definition 2. (Environment Matching)** *A translation environment* $E$ *matches a type environment* $TE$, *written* $E \sqsubseteq TE$, *if* $TE(E(\varepsilon)) = \varepsilon \times \varepsilon \to bool$ *for all* $\varepsilon \in \mathrm{Dom}(E)$.

The following proposition states that the equality function generated for a specific type that admits equality has the expected type.

**Proposition 1.** *If* $E \vdash_{eq} \tau \Rightarrow e$ *and* $E \sqsubseteq TE$ *and* $\Delta \vdash \tau$ *then* $\Delta, TE \vdash e : \tau \times \tau \to bool$.

*Proof.* By induction over the structure of $\tau$. $\quad\square$

We can now state a proposition saying that the translation preserves types.

**Proposition 2. (Type Preservation)** *If* $\Delta, TE \vdash e : \tau$ *and* $E \vdash e \Rightarrow e'$ *and* $E \sqsubseteq TE' \succ TE$ *then* $\Delta, TE' \vdash e' : \tau$.

*Proof.* By induction over the structure of $e$. We show the three interesting cases.

$\boxed{\text{CASE } e = x_{il}}$ From (5), we have $TE(x) = \sigma$ and $\sigma = \forall \varepsilon_1 \cdots \varepsilon_n \vec{\alpha}.\tau'$ and $\sigma \geq \tau$ via $S$ and $\Delta \vdash il$ and $\Delta, TE \vdash x_{il} : \tau$, where $il = il(S)$. From (34), we have that $il = ([\tau_1, \ldots, \tau_n], [\ldots])$ and $E \vdash_{eq} \tau_i \Rightarrow e_i$, $i = 1..n$ and $E \vdash x_{il} \Rightarrow (\cdots (x_{il} \ e_1) \cdots e_n)$.

Because $\Delta \vdash il$, we have $\Delta \vdash \tau_i$, $i = 1..n$ and because $E \sqsubseteq TE'$ follows from assumptions, we have by Proposition 1 that $\Delta, TE' \vdash e_i : \tau_i \times \tau_i \to bool$, $i = 1..n$.

Because $TE' \succ TE$ follows from assumptions, we have $TE'(x) = \sigma'$, where $\sigma' = \forall \varepsilon_1 \cdots \varepsilon_n \vec{\alpha}.(\varepsilon_1 \times \varepsilon_1 \to bool) \to \cdots \to (\varepsilon_n \times \varepsilon_n \to bool).\tau'$, and because $\sigma \geq \tau$ via $S$ and $S(\varepsilon_i) = \tau_i$, $i = 1..n$ follows from $il(S) = ([\tau_1, \ldots, \tau_n], [\ldots])$, we have $\sigma' \geq \tau''$ via $S$, where $\tau'' = (\tau_1 \times \tau_1 \to bool) \to \cdots \to (\tau_n \times \tau_n \to bool) \to \tau$. Because $\Delta \vdash il$, we can now apply (5) to get $\Delta, TE' \vdash x_{il} : \tau''$.

Now, because $\Delta, TE' \vdash e_i : \tau_i \times \tau_i \to bool$, $i = 1..n$, we can apply (2) $n$ times to get $\Delta, TE' \vdash (\cdots (x_{il} \; e_1) \cdots e_n) : \tau$, as required.

$\boxed{\text{CASE } e = \texttt{let } x : \sigma = e_1 \texttt{ in } e_2}$ From (6), we have $\sigma = \forall \varepsilon_1 \cdots \varepsilon_n \vec{\alpha}.\tau$ and $ftv(\varepsilon_1 \cdots \varepsilon_n \vec{\alpha}) \cap ftv(\Delta, TE) = \emptyset$ and $\Delta \cup \{\varepsilon_1, \ldots, \varepsilon_n\}, TE \vdash e_1 : \tau$ and $\Delta, TE + \{x \mapsto \sigma\} \vdash e_2 : \tau'$ and $\Delta, TE \vdash e : \tau'$.

Further, from (36), we have $y_1 \cdots y_n$ fresh and $E + \{\varepsilon_1 \mapsto y_1, \ldots, \varepsilon_n \mapsto y_n\} \vdash e_1 \Rightarrow e_1'$ and $\tau_i = \varepsilon_i \times \varepsilon_i \to bool$, $i = 1..n$ and $e_1'' = \lambda y_1 : \tau_1. \cdots . \lambda y_n : \tau_n.e_1'$ and $E \vdash e_2 \Rightarrow e_2'$ and $\sigma' = \forall \varepsilon_1 \cdots \varepsilon_n \vec{\alpha}.\tau_1 \to \cdots \to \tau_n \to \tau$ and $E \vdash e \Rightarrow \texttt{let } x : \sigma' = e_1'' \texttt{ in } e_2'$.

It now follows from assumptions and from the definitions of extension and matching that $E + \{\varepsilon_1 \mapsto y_1, \ldots, \varepsilon_n \mapsto y_n\} \sqsubseteq TE'' \succ TE$, where $TE'' = TE' + \{y_1 \mapsto \tau_1, \ldots, y_n \mapsto \tau_n\}$, because $Dom(TE') \cap \{y_1, \ldots y_n\} = \emptyset$ and $Dom(E) \cap \{\varepsilon_1, \ldots, \varepsilon_n\} = \emptyset$ can be assumed by appropriate renaming of bound type variables of $\sigma$. We can now apply induction to get $\Delta \cup \{\varepsilon_1, \ldots, \varepsilon_n\}, TE'' \vdash e_1' : \tau$. By applying (1) $n$ times, we get $\Delta \cup \{\varepsilon_1, \ldots, \varepsilon_n\}, TE' \vdash e_1'' : \tau_1 \to \cdots \to \tau_n \to \tau$.

To apply induction the second time, we observe that $E \sqsubseteq TE' + \{x \mapsto \sigma'\} \succ TE + \{x \mapsto \sigma\}$ by assumptions and definitions of matching and extension and because $Dom(TE') \cap \{x\} = \emptyset$ can be assumed by appropriate renaming of $x$ in $e$. By induction, we have $\Delta, TE' + \{x \mapsto \sigma'\} \vdash e_2' : \tau'$.

Because we can assume $ftv(\varepsilon_1 \cdots \varepsilon_n \vec{\alpha}) \cap ftv(TE') = \emptyset$ by appropriate renaming of bound equality type variables and type variables in $\sigma$, we can apply (6) to get $\Delta, TE' \vdash \texttt{let } x : \sigma' = e_1'' \texttt{ in } e_2' : \tau'$, as required.

$\boxed{\text{CASE } e = \texttt{eq}_\tau}$ From (10), we have $\Delta \vdash \tau$ and $\tau$ admits equality and $\Delta, TE \vdash \texttt{eq}_\tau : \tau \times \tau \to bool$. From (35), we have $E \vdash_{eq} \tau \Rightarrow e'$ and $E \vdash \texttt{eq}_\tau \Rightarrow e'$.

By assumptions, we have $E \sqsubseteq TE'$ and because $\Delta \vdash \tau$, we can apply Proposition 1 to get $\Delta, TE' \vdash e' : \tau \times \tau \to bool$, as required. $\qquad \square$

## 7.2 Typable Expressions are Translatable

We now demonstrate that all typable expressions may indeed be translated by the translation rules. The following proposition states that for a type that admits equality it is possible to construct a function that checks for equality on pairs of values of this type.

**Proposition 3.** *If $\tau$ admits equality and $fetv(\tau) \subseteq Dom(E)$ then there exists an expression $e$ such that $E \vdash_{eq} \tau \Rightarrow e$.*

*Proof.* By induction over the structure of $\tau$. $\qquad \square$

The following proposition states that all typable expressions may be translated.

**Proposition 4. (Typable Expressions are Translatable)** *If $\Delta, TE \vdash e : \tau$ and $\Delta = Dom(E)$ and $Dom(TE) \cap Ran(E) = \emptyset$ then there exists $e'$ such that $E \vdash e \Rightarrow e'$.*

*Proof.* By induction over the structure of $e$. We show the three interesting cases.

CASE $e = x_{il}$ From (5), we have $TE(x) = \sigma$ and $\sigma \geq \tau$ via $S$ and $\Delta \vdash il(S)$ and $\Delta, TE \vdash x_{il(S)} : \tau$.

Let $il(S)$ be written as $([\tau_1, \ldots, \tau_n], [\ldots])$. Because $\Delta \vdash il(S)$, we have $\Delta \vdash \tau_i$, $i = 1..n$, hence, $\text{fetv}(\tau_i) \subseteq \text{Dom}(E)$, $i = 1..n$. Further, from the definition of substitution, we have $\tau_i$ admits equality, $i = 1..n$. We can now apply Proposition 3 to get, there exists an expression $e_i$ such that $E \vdash_{\text{eq}} \tau_i \Rightarrow e_i$, $i = 1..n$. By applying (34), we have $E \vdash x_{il(S)} \Rightarrow (\cdots (x_{il(S)} \; e_1) \cdots e_n)$, as required.

CASE $e = \text{let } x : \sigma = e_1 \text{ in } e_2$ From (6), we have $\sigma = \forall \vec{\varepsilon}\vec{\alpha}.\tau$ and $\text{ftv}(\vec{\varepsilon}\vec{\alpha}) \cap \text{ftv}(\Delta, TE) = \emptyset$ and $\Delta \cup \text{fetv}(\vec{\varepsilon}), TE \vdash e_1 : \tau$ and $\Delta, TE + \{x \mapsto \sigma\} \vdash e_2 : \tau'$ and $\Delta, TE \vdash e : \tau'$.

Write $\vec{\varepsilon}$ as $\varepsilon_1 \cdots \varepsilon_n$ and let $y_1 \cdots y_n$ be fresh. Further, let $E' = E + \{\varepsilon_1 \mapsto y_1, \ldots, \varepsilon_n \mapsto y_n\}$. By assumptions, we have $\Delta \cup \text{fetv}(\vec{\varepsilon}) = \text{Dom}(E')$ and $\text{Dom}(TE) \cap \text{Ran}(E') = \emptyset$. We can now apply induction to get, there exists an expression $e_1'$ such that $E' \vdash e_1 \Rightarrow e_1'$. Also, let $e_1'' = \lambda y_1 : \tau_1. \cdots . \lambda y_n : \tau_n . e_1'$, where $\tau_i = \varepsilon_i \times \varepsilon_i \to bool$, $i = 1..n$.

By assumptions and by appropriate renaming of $x$ in $e$, we have $\text{Dom}(TE + \{x \mapsto \sigma\}) \cap \text{Ran}(E) = \emptyset$, hence, we can apply induction to get, there exists $e_2'$ such that $E \vdash e_2 \Rightarrow e_2'$. Letting $\sigma' = \forall \vec{\varepsilon}\vec{\alpha}.\tau_1 \to \cdots \to \tau_n \to \tau$, we can apply (36) to get $E \vdash e \Rightarrow \text{let } x : \sigma' = e_1'' \text{ in } e_2'$, as required.

CASE $e = \text{eq}_\tau$ From (10), we have $\Delta \vdash \tau$ and $\tau$ admits equality and $\Delta, TE \vdash \text{eq}_\tau : \tau \times \tau \to bool$. Because $\Delta = \text{Dom}(E)$ follows from assumptions and $\Delta \vdash \tau$, we have $\text{fetv}(\tau) \subseteq \text{Dom}(E)$, hence, from Proposition 3, we have, there exists an expression $e'$ such that $E \vdash_{\text{eq}} \tau \Rightarrow e'$. From (35), we now have $E \vdash e \Rightarrow e'$, as required. $\square$

# 8 Semantic Soundness

In this section, we demonstrate semantic soundness of the translation inspired by other proofs of semantic soundness of type systems [9, 22].

Because equality functions are represented differently in the original program and the translated program, the operational semantics may assign different values to them. For this reason, we define a notion of *semantic equivalence* between values corresponding to the original program and values corresponding to the translated program. We write it $\Gamma \models v : \tau \approx v'$. The type is needed to correctly interpret the values and to ensure well-foundedness of the definition. The environment $\Gamma$ is formally a pair $(\Gamma^\varepsilon, \Gamma^\alpha)$ providing interpretations of equality type variables and ordinary type variables in $\tau$. Interpretations are non-empty sets $\mathcal{V}$ of pairs $(v_1, v_2)$ of values. We often abbreviate projections from $\Gamma$ and injections in $\Gamma$. For instance, when $\Gamma = (\Gamma^\varepsilon, \Gamma^\alpha)$, we write $\Gamma(\varepsilon)$ to mean $\Gamma^\varepsilon(\varepsilon)$ and $\Gamma + \{\alpha \mapsto \mathcal{V}\}$ to mean $(\Gamma^\varepsilon, \Gamma^\alpha + \{\alpha \mapsto \mathcal{V}\})$, for any $\varepsilon$, $\alpha$, and $\mathcal{V}$.

- $\Gamma \models \text{true} : bool \approx \text{true}$

- $\Gamma \models \mathtt{false} : bool \approx \mathtt{false}$
- $\Gamma \models (v_1, v_2) : \tau_1 \times \tau_2 \approx (v_1', v_2')$ iff $\Gamma \models v_1 : \tau_1 \approx v_1'$ and $\Gamma \models v_2 : \tau_2 \approx v_2'$
- $\Gamma \models \mathtt{eq} : bool \times bool \to bool \approx \mathtt{eq}$
- $\Gamma \models \mathtt{eq} : \tau \times \tau \to bool \approx \mathtt{clos}(\lambda x.e, \mathcal{E})$ iff for all values $v_1$, $v_2$, $v_1'$ such that $\Gamma \models v_1 : \tau \times \tau \approx v_1'$ and $\vdash_{\mathtt{eq}} v_1 \Downarrow v_2$, we have $\mathcal{E} + \{x \mapsto v_1'\} \vdash e \Downarrow v_2$
- $\Gamma \models \mathtt{clos}(\lambda x.e, \mathcal{E}) : \tau_1 \to \tau_2 \approx \mathtt{clos}(\lambda x.e', \mathcal{E}')$ iff for all values $v_1$, $v_2$, $v_1'$ such that $\Gamma \models v_1 : \tau_1 \approx v_1'$ and $\mathcal{E} + \{x \mapsto v_1\} \vdash e \Downarrow v_2$, there exists a value $v_2'$ such that $\mathcal{E}' + \{x \mapsto v_1'\} \vdash e' \Downarrow v_2'$ and $\Gamma \models v_2 : \tau_2 \approx v_2'$
- $\Gamma \models v : \alpha \approx v'$ iff $(v, v') \in \Gamma(\alpha)$
- $\Gamma \models v : \varepsilon \approx v'$ iff $(v, v') \in \Gamma(\varepsilon)$

The semantic equivalence relation extends to type schemes and environments:

- $\Gamma \models v : \forall \alpha_1 \cdots \alpha_n.\tau \approx v'$ iff for all interpretations $\mathcal{V}_1^\alpha \cdots \mathcal{V}_m^\alpha$, we have $\Gamma + \{\alpha_1 \mapsto \mathcal{V}_1^\alpha, \cdots, \alpha_n \mapsto \mathcal{V}_n^\alpha\} \models v : \tau \approx v'$
- $\Gamma \models v : \forall \varepsilon_1 \cdots \varepsilon_n \alpha_1 \cdots \alpha_m.\tau \approx \mathtt{clos}(\lambda y_1.\cdots.\lambda y_n.e, \mathcal{E})$ iff for all interpretations $\mathcal{V}_1^\varepsilon \cdots \mathcal{V}_n^\varepsilon \mathcal{V}_1^\alpha \cdots \mathcal{V}_m^\alpha$, values $v_1 \cdots v_n$ and semantic environments $\Gamma'$, such that $\Gamma' \models \mathtt{eq} : \varepsilon_i \times \varepsilon_i \to bool \approx v_i$, $i = 1..n$ and $\Gamma' = \Gamma + \{\varepsilon_1 \mapsto \mathcal{V}_1^\varepsilon, \cdots, \varepsilon_n \mapsto \mathcal{V}_n^\varepsilon, \alpha_1 \mapsto \mathcal{V}_1^\alpha, \cdots, \alpha_m \mapsto \mathcal{V}_m^\alpha\}$, we have there exists a value $v'$ such that $\Gamma' \models v : \tau \approx v'$ and $\mathcal{E} + \{y_1 \mapsto v_1, \cdots, y_n \mapsto v_n\} \vdash e \Downarrow v'$
- $\Gamma \models \mathcal{E} : TE \approx_E \mathcal{E}'$ iff $\mathrm{Dom}(\mathcal{E}) = \mathrm{Dom}(TE)$ and $\mathrm{Dom}(\mathcal{E}) \subseteq \mathrm{Dom}(\mathcal{E}')$ and for all $x \in \mathrm{Dom}(\mathcal{E})$ we have $\Gamma \models \mathcal{E}(x) : TE(x) \approx \mathcal{E}'(x)$. Further, for all $\varepsilon \in \mathrm{Dom}(E)$ we have $\Gamma \models \mathtt{eq} : \varepsilon \times \varepsilon \to bool \approx \mathcal{E}'(E(\varepsilon))$

The following proposition states that a generated equality function for a given type has the expected semantics. We leave elimination of type information from typed expressions implicit.

**Proposition 5.** *If* $E \vdash_{eq} \tau \Rightarrow e$ *and for all* $\varepsilon \in \mathrm{Dom}(E)$ *we have* $\Gamma \models \mathtt{eq} : \varepsilon \times \varepsilon \to bool \approx \mathcal{E}(E(\varepsilon))$ *then there exists a value* $v$ *such that* $\mathcal{E} \vdash e \Downarrow v$ *and* $\Gamma \models \mathtt{eq} : \tau \times \tau \to bool \approx v$.

*Proof.* By induction over the structure of $\tau$. $\square$

The semantic equivalence relation is closed with respect to substitution.

**Proposition 6.** *Let* $S$ *be a substitution* $(\{\varepsilon_1 \mapsto \tau_1, \cdots, \varepsilon_n \mapsto \tau_n\}, \{\alpha_1 \mapsto \tau_1', \cdots, \alpha_m \mapsto \tau_m'\})$. *Define* $\mathcal{V}_i^\varepsilon = \{(v, v') \mid \Gamma \models v : \tau_i \approx v'\}$, $i = 1..n$ *and* $\mathcal{V}_i^\alpha = \{(v, v') \mid \Gamma \models v : \tau_i' \approx v'\}$, $i = 1..m$.
*Then* $\Gamma + \{\varepsilon_1 \mapsto \mathcal{V}_1^\varepsilon, \cdots \varepsilon_n \mapsto \mathcal{V}_n^\varepsilon, \alpha_1 \mapsto \mathcal{V}_1^\alpha, \cdots, \alpha_m \mapsto \mathcal{V}_m^\alpha\} \models v : \tau \approx v'$ *iff* $\Gamma \models v : S(\tau) \approx v'$.

*Proof.* By induction over the structure of $\tau$. $\square$

We can now state a semantic soundness proposition for the translation.

**Proposition 7. (Semantic Soundness)** *If* $\Delta, TE \vdash e : \tau$ *and* $E \vdash e \Rightarrow e'$ *and* $\Gamma \models \mathcal{E} : TE \approx_E \mathcal{E}'$ *and* $\mathcal{E} \vdash e \Downarrow v$ *then there exists a value* $v'$ *such that* $\mathcal{E}' \vdash e' \Downarrow v'$ *and* $\Gamma \models v : \tau \approx v'$.

*Proof.* By induction over the structure of $e$. We show the three interesting cases.

$\boxed{\text{CASE } e = x_{il}, \; il = ([\tau_1, \cdots, \tau_n], [\tau'_1, \cdots, \tau'_m]), \, n \geq 1}$ From assumptions, (11), (5), the definition of semantic equivalence, and the definition of instantiation, we have $\Gamma \models v : \sigma \approx v''$ and $v'' = \mathcal{E}'(x)$ and $\sigma = \forall \varepsilon_1 \cdots \varepsilon_n \alpha_1 \cdots \alpha_m . \tau'$ and $TE(x) = \sigma$ and $S = (\{\varepsilon_1 \mapsto \tau_1, \cdots, \varepsilon_n \mapsto \tau_n\}, \{\alpha_1 \mapsto \tau'_1, \cdots, \alpha_m \mapsto \tau'_m\})$. Because $n \geq 1$, we have $v'' = \texttt{clos}(\lambda y_1. \cdots . \lambda y_n.e', \mathcal{E}'')$, for some lambda variables $y_1 \cdots y_n$, expression $e'$, and dynamic environment $\mathcal{E}''$.

From assumptions and (34), we have $\Gamma \models \mathcal{E} : TE \approx_E \mathcal{E}'$ and $E \vdash_{eq} \tau_i \Rightarrow e_i$, $i = 1..n$, hence, we can apply Proposition 5 $n$ times to get, there exist values $v_i$, $i = 1..n$ such that $\Gamma \models \texttt{eq} : \tau_i \times \tau_i \to bool \approx v_i$ and $\mathcal{E}' \vdash e_i \Downarrow v_i$, $i = 1..n$.

Letting $\mathcal{V}_i^\varepsilon = \{(v, v') | \Gamma \models v : \tau_i \approx v'\}$, $i = 1..n$ and $\mathcal{V}_i^\alpha = \{(v, v') | \Gamma \models v : \tau'_i \approx v'\}$, $i = 1..m$ and $\Gamma' = \Gamma + \{\varepsilon_1 \mapsto \mathcal{V}_1^\varepsilon, \cdots, \varepsilon_n \mapsto \mathcal{V}_n^\varepsilon, \alpha_1 \mapsto \mathcal{V}_1^\alpha, \cdots, \alpha_m \mapsto \mathcal{V}_m^\alpha\}$, we can apply Proposition 6 to get $\Gamma' \models \texttt{eq} : \varepsilon_i \times \varepsilon_i \to bool \approx v_i$, $i = 1..n$.

From the definition of semantic equivalence, we now have, there exists a value $v'$ such that $\Gamma' \models v : \tau' \approx v'$ and $\mathcal{E}'' + \{y_1 \mapsto v_1, \cdots, y_n \mapsto v_n\} \vdash e' \Downarrow v'$. Now, because $v'' = \mathcal{E}'(x)$ and $\mathcal{E}' \vdash e_i \Downarrow v_i$, $i = 1..n$, we can derive $\mathcal{E}' \vdash (\cdots (x \; e_1) \cdots e_n) \Downarrow v'$ from (13), (11), and (12). By applying Proposition 6 again, we get $\Gamma \models v : \tau \approx v'$, as required.

$\boxed{\text{CASE } e = \texttt{eq}_{\tau'}}$ From assumptions, (17), (35), and the definition of semantic equivalence, we have from Proposition 5 that there exists a value $v'$ such that $\mathcal{E}' \vdash e' \Downarrow v'$ and $\Gamma \models \texttt{eq} : \tau' \times \tau' \to bool \approx v'$, as required.

$\boxed{\text{CASE } e = \texttt{let } x : \sigma = e_1 \text{ in } e_2, \, \sigma = \forall \varepsilon_1 \cdots \varepsilon_n \vec{\alpha}.\tau, \, n \geq 1}$ Write $\vec{\alpha}$ in the form $\alpha_1 \cdots \alpha_m$. Let $\mathcal{V}_1^\varepsilon \cdots \mathcal{V}_n^\varepsilon \mathcal{V}_1^\alpha \cdots \mathcal{V}_m^\alpha$ be interpretations, let $v_1^{eq} \cdots v_n^{eq}$ be values, and let $\Gamma'$ be a semantic environment such that $\Gamma' = \Gamma + \{\varepsilon_1 \mapsto \mathcal{V}_1^\varepsilon, \cdots, \varepsilon_n \mapsto \mathcal{V}_n^\varepsilon, \alpha_1 \mapsto \mathcal{V}_1^\alpha, \cdots, \alpha_m \mapsto \mathcal{V}_m^\alpha\}$ and $\Gamma' \models \texttt{eq} : \varepsilon_i \times \varepsilon_i \to bool \approx v_i^{eq}$, $i = 1..n$.

From assumptions and from (36), we have $y_1 \cdots y_n$ are chosen fresh and $E' \vdash e_1 \Rightarrow e'_1$ and $e''_1 = \lambda y_1 : \tau_1. \cdots . \lambda y_n : \tau_n.e'_1$, where $\tau_i = \varepsilon_i \times \varepsilon_i \to bool$, $i = 1..n$ and $E' = E + \{\varepsilon_1 \mapsto y_1, \cdots, \varepsilon_n \mapsto y_n\}$. From the definition of semantic equivalence, we can now establish $\Gamma' \models \texttt{eq} : \varepsilon \times \varepsilon \to bool \approx \mathcal{E}''(E'(\varepsilon))$, for all $\varepsilon \in \text{Dom}(E')$, where $\mathcal{E}'' = \mathcal{E}' + \{y_1 \mapsto v_1^{eq}, \cdots, y_n \mapsto v_n^{eq}\}$, and hence $\Gamma' \models \mathcal{E} : TE \approx_{E'} \mathcal{E}''$. From assumptions, (6), and (22), we have $\Delta \cup \text{fetv}(\varepsilon_1 \cdots \varepsilon_n)$, $TE \vdash e_1 : \tau$ and $\mathcal{E} \vdash e_1 \Downarrow v_1$ and because we have $E' \vdash e_1 \Rightarrow e'_1$, we can apply induction to get, there exists a value $v'_1$ such that $\mathcal{E}'' \vdash e'_1 \Downarrow v'_1$ and $\Gamma' \models v_1 : \tau \approx v'_1$.

Letting $v''_1 = \texttt{clos}(\lambda y_1. \cdots . \lambda y_n.e'_1, \mathcal{E})$, we have from the definition of semantic equivalence that $\Gamma \models v_1 : \sigma \approx v''_1$ and $\Gamma \models \mathcal{E} + \{x \mapsto v_1\} : TE + \{x \mapsto \sigma\} \approx_E \mathcal{E}' + \{x \mapsto v''_1\}$. From assumptions and from (22), (6), and (36), we have $\mathcal{E} + \{x \mapsto v_1\} \vdash e_2 \Downarrow v_2$ and $\Delta, TE + \{x \mapsto \sigma\} \vdash e_2 : \tau'$ and $\mathcal{E} \vdash e_2 \Rightarrow e'_2$, hence, we can apply induction a second time to get, there exists a value $v'_2$ such that $\mathcal{E}' + \{x \mapsto v''_1\} \vdash e'_2 \Downarrow v'_2$ and $\Gamma \models v_2 : \tau' \approx v'_2$.

We can now apply (12) to get $\mathcal{E}' \vdash e''_1 \Downarrow v''_1$, hence, we can apply (22) to get $\mathcal{E}' \vdash e' \Downarrow v'_2$, as required. $\qquad \square$

We now return to the value restriction issue. The translation rule for the let-construct does not preserve semantics unless (1) $e_1$ is known to terminate and not to have side effects or (2) no equality type variables are generalised. In the language we consider, (1) is always satisfied. For Standard ML, the value restriction always enforces either (1) or (2). However, the restriction is enforced by limiting generalisation to so called non-expansive expressions, which include function applications. Adding such a requirement to the typing rule for the let-construct makes too few programs typable; to demonstrate type correctness for the translation, applications of functions to generated equality functions must also be considered non-expansive.

# 9  Extension to Full ML

It is straightforward to extend equality elimination to allow imperative features and to allow a letrec-construct for declaration of recursive functions. We now demonstrate how the approach is extended to deal with parametric datatypes and modules.

## 9.1  Datatype Declarations

In Standard ML, lists may be implemented by a datatype declaration

$$\textbf{datatype } \alpha \ list = :: \textbf{ of } \alpha \times \alpha \ list \mid nil$$

Because lists are declared to be parametric in the type of the elements, it is possible to write polymorphic functions to manipulate the elements of any list. In general datatype declarations may be parametric in any number of type variables and they may even be declared mutually recursive with other datatype declarations. The datatype declaration for lists elaborates to the type environment

$$\{list \mapsto (t, \ \{:: \ \mapsto \forall \alpha.\alpha \times \alpha \ t \to \alpha \ t, \ nil \mapsto \forall \alpha.\alpha \ t\})\}$$

where $t$ is a fresh type name [11]. Every type name $t$ possess a boolean attribute that denotes whether $t$ admits equality. In the example, $t$ will indeed be inferred to admit equality. This property of the type name $t$ allows values of type $\tau \ t$ to be checked for equality if $\tau$ admits equality.

When a datatype declaration elaborates to a type environment, an equality function is generated for every fresh type name $t$ in the type environment such that $t$ admits equality. For a parametric datatype declaration, such as the *list* datatype declaration, the generated equality function is parametric in equality functions for parameters of the datatype.

The Kit does not allow all valid ML programs to be compiled using equality elimination. Consider the datatype declaration

$$\textbf{datatype } \alpha \ t = A \textbf{ of } (\alpha \times \alpha) \ t \mid B \textbf{ of } \alpha$$

Datatypes of the above form are called *non-uniform* datatypes [15, page 86]. It is possible to declare non-uniform datatypes in ML, but they are of limited use, because ML does not support polymorphic recursive functions. In particular, it is not possible to declare a function in ML that checks values of non-uniform datatypes for structural equality. However, the problem is not inherent to equality elimination. Adding support for polymorphic recursion in the intermediate language would solve the problem. Other compilation techniques also have troubles dealing with non-uniform datatypes. The TIL compiler developed at Carnegie Mellon University does not support non-uniform datatypes due to problems with compiling constructors of such datatypes in the framework of intensional polymorphism [12, page 166].

## 9.2 Modules

The translation extends to Standard ML Modules [11]. However, to compile functors separately, structures must contain equality functions for each type name that admits equality and that occurs free in the structure. Moreover, when constraining a structure to a signature, it is necessary to enforce the implementation of a function to follow its type by generating appropriate stub code. The body of a functor may then uniformly extract equality functions from the formal argument structure.

# 10 Implementation

The Kit compiles the Standard ML Core language by first elaborating and translating programs into an intermediate typed lambda language. At this point, polymorphic equality is eliminated. Then, a simple optimiser performs various optimisations inspired by [1] and small recursive functions are specialised as suggested in [17].

The remaining phases of the compiler are based on region inference [24]. Each value generated by the program resides in a region and region inference is the task of determining when to allocate and deallocate regions. Various analyses determine how to represent different regions at runtime [3]. Some regions can be determined to only ever contain word-sized unboxed values, such as integers and booleans. Such regions need never be allocated. Other regions can be determined to only ever hold one value at runtime. Such regions may be implemented on the stack. Other regions are implemented using a stack of linked pages.

The backend of the Kit implements a simple graph coloring technique for register allocation and emits code for the HP PA-RISC architecture [5].

## 10.1 Datatype Representation

The Kit supports different schemes for representing datatypes at runtime. The simplest scheme implements all constructed values (except integers and booleans) as boxed objects at runtime. Using this scheme, the list [1, 2], for instance, is represented as shown in Fig. 1.

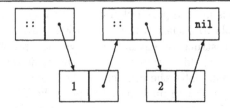

**Fig. 1.** Boxed representation of the list [1, 2] with untagged integers.

The Standard ML of New Jersey compiler version 110 (SML/NJ) implements lists as shown in Fig. 2, using the observation that pointers are four-aligned on most modern architectures [1]. In this way, the two least significant bits of pointers to constructed values may be used to represent the constructor. However, because SML/NJ implements polymorphic equality and garbage collection by following pointers, only one bit remains to distinguish constructed values.

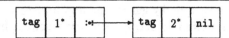

**Fig. 2.** Unboxed representation of the list [1, 2] with tagged tuples and tagged integers.

Utilising the two least significant bits of pointers to constructed values, we say that a type name associated with a datatype declaration is *unboxed* if the datatype binding declares at-most three unary constructors (and any number of nullary constructors) and for all argument types $\tau$ for a unary constructor, $\tau$ is not a type variable and $\tau$ is not unboxed (for recursion, we initially assume that the declared type names of the declaration are unboxed.) A type $\tau$ is *unboxed* if it is on the form $(\tau_1, \ldots, \tau_n)$ $t$ and $t$ is unboxed.

The Kit treats all values of unboxed types as word-sized unboxed objects. Using this scheme, lists are represented uniformly at runtime as shown in Fig. 3. Efficient unboxed representations of many tree structures are also obtained using this scheme.

In the context of separate compilation of functors, as implemented in Standard ML of New Jersey, version 0.93, problems arise when a unique representation of datatypes is not used [2]. If instead functors are specialised for each application, no restrictions are enforced on datatype representations and no representation overhead is introduced by programming with Modules. Current research addresses this idea.

## 11 Experimental Results

In this section, we present some experimental results obtained with the Kit and the Standard ML of New Jersey compiler version 110 (SML/NJ). The purpose of the experiments are (1) to assess the feasibility of eliminating polymorphic

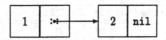

**Fig. 3.** Unboxed representation of the list [1, 2] with untagged tuples and untagged integers.

equality, (2) to assess the importance of efficient datatype representations, and (3) to compare the code generated by the Kit with that generated by SML/NJ.

All tests are run on a HP PA-RISC 9000s700 computer. For SML/NJ, executables are generated using the `exportFn` built-in function. We use KitT to mean the Kit with a tagging approach to implement polymorphic equality. Further, KitE is the Kit with equality elimination enabled. In KitE, tagging of values is disabled as no operations need tags at runtime. Finally, KitEE is KitE with efficient representation of datatypes enabled. All versions of the Kit generate efficient equality checks for values that are known to be of base type (e.g., int or real).

Measurements are shown for eight benchmark programs. Four of these are non-trivial programs based on the SML/NJ distribution benchmarks (`life`, `mandelbrot`, `knuth-bendix` and `simple`). The program `fib35` is the simple Fibonacci program and `mergesort` is a program for sorting 200,000 pseudo-random integers. The programs `life` and `knuth-bendix` use polymorphic equality extensively. The program `lifem` is a monomorphic version of `life` for which polymorphic functions are made monomorphic by insertion of type constraints. The program `sieve` computes all prime numbers in the range from 1 to 2000, using the Sieve of Eratosthenes.

Running times for all benchmarks are shown in Fig. 4. Equality elimination, and thus, elimination of tags, appears to have a positive effect on the running time for most programs. In particular, the `life` benchmark runs 48 percent faster under KitE than under KitT. However, programs do exist for which equality elimination has a negative effect on the running time of the program. There are potentially two reasons for a slowdown. First, extra function parameters to equality polymorphic functions may lead to less efficient programs. Second, functions generated by KitE and KitEE for checking two structural values for equality do not check if the values are located on the same address. This check is performed by the polymorphic equality primitive of KitT. In principle, such a check could also be performed by equality functions generated by KitE and KitEE. The `knuth-bendix` benchmark runs slightly slower under KitE than under KitT.

Not surprisingly, efficient representation of datatypes improves the running time of most programs – with up to 40 percent for the `sieve` benchmark.

The Kit does not implement the minimum typing derivation technique for decreasing the degree of polymorphism [4]. Decreasing the degree of polymorphism has been reported to have a great effect on performance; it makes it possible to transform slow polymorphic equality tests into fast monomorphic ones [19, 18]. Due to the decrease in polymorphism, the `lifem` benchmark is 12 percent faster than the `life` benchmark (under KitEE).

| Running time | KitT | KitE | KitEE | SML/NJ |
|---|---|---|---|---|
| fib35 | 10.9 | 10.2 | 10.1 | 18.5 |
| sieve | 9.01 | 6.18 | 3.71 | 9.24 |
| life | 35.4 | 18.5 | 18.1 | 5.28 |
| lifem | 35.2 | 16.2 | 16.0 | 5.25 |
| mergesort | 12.9 | 11.9 | 9.25 | 15.9 |
| mandelbrot | 35.4 | 32.3 | 31.9 | 7.17 |
| knuth-bendix | 26.4 | 26.7 | 23.3 | 17.7 |
| simple | 47.1 | 40.7 | 40.6 | 15.5 |

**Fig. 4.** Running times in seconds for code generated by three versions of the Kit and SML/NJ, measured using the UNIX `time` program.

Space usage for the different benchmarks is shown in Fig. 5. No benchmark program uses more space due to elimination of equality. For programs allocating a large amount of memory, equality elimination, and thus, elimination of tags, reduces memory significantly – with up to 31 percent for the `simple` program. Efficient datatype representation reduces space usage further up to 33 percent for the `mergesort` program.

| Space usage | KitT | KitE | KitEE | SML/NJ |
|---|---|---|---|---|
| fib35 | 108 | 108 | 108 | 1,380 |
| sieve | 1,248 | 1,052 | 736 | 6,180 |
| life | 428 | 376 | 272 | 1,408 |
| lifem | 428 | 376 | 272 | 1,420 |
| mergesort | 16,000 | 13,000 | 8,728 | 18,000 |
| mandelbrot | 304 | 296 | 296 | 712 |
| knuth-bendix | 4,280 | 3,620 | 2,568 | 2,724 |
| simple | 1,388 | 960 | 748 | 2,396 |

**Fig. 5.** Space used for code generated by the three versions of the Kit and SML/NJ. All numbers are in kilobytes and indicate maximum resident memory used, measured using the UNIX `top` program.

Sizes of executables for all benchmarks are shown in Fig. 6. Equality elimination does not seem to have a dramatic effect on the sizes of the executables. Efficient datatype representation reduces sizes of executables with up to 22 percent for the `life` benchmark.

The Kit and SML/NJ are two very different compilers. There can be dramatic differences between using region inference and reference tracing garbage collection, thus, the numbers presented here should be read with caution. The Kit currently only allows an argument to a function to be passed in one register. Moreover, the Kit does not allocate floating point numbers in registers. Instead, floating point numbers are always boxed. The benchmark programs `mandelbrot` and `simple` use floating point operations extensively. No doubt, efficient calling

| Program size | KitT | KitE | KitEE | SML/NJ |
|---|---|---|---|---|
| fib35 | 0 | 0 | 0 | 0 |
| sieve | 16 | 20 | 16 | 29 |
| life | 92 | 92 | 72 | 17 |
| lifem | 92 | 92 | 72 | 17 |
| mergesort | 20 | 24 | 20 | 40 |
| mandelbrot | 8 | 12 | 12 | 37 |
| knuth-bendix | 160 | 168 | 140 | 71 |
| simple | 356 | 352 | 328 | 199 |

**Fig. 6.** Sizes of executables (with the size of the empty program subtracted) for code generated by three versions of the Kit and SML/NJ. All numbers are in kilobytes.

conventions and register allocation of floating point numbers will improve the quality of the code generated by the Kit.

## 12  Conclusion

The translation suggested in this paper makes it possible to eliminate polymorphic equality completely in the front-end of a compiler. Experimental results show that equality elimination can lead to important space and time savings even for programs that use polymorphic equality.

Although tags may be needed at runtime to implement reference tracing garbage collection, it is attractive to eliminate polymorphic equality at an early stage during compilation. Various optimisations, such as boxing analysis [9, 7], must otherwise treat polymorphic equality distinct from other primitive operations. Checking two arbitrary values for equality may cause both values to be traversed to any depth. This is in contrast to how other polymorphic functions behave. Further, no special demands are placed on the implementor of the runtime system and the backend of the compiler. For instance, there is no need to flush all values represented in registers into the heap prior to testing two values for equality.

*Acknowledgements.* I would like to thank Lars Birkedal, Niels Hallenberg, Fritz Henglein, Tommy Højfeld Olesen, Peter Sestoft, and Mads Tofte for valuable comments and suggestions.

## References

1. Andrew Appel. *Compiling With Continuations.* Cambridge University Press, 1992.
2. Andrew Appel. A critique of Standard ML. In *Journal of Functional Programming*, pages 3(4):391–429, October 1993.
3. Lars Birkedal, Mads Tofte, and Magnus Vejlstrup. From region inference to von Neumann machines via region representation inference. In *23st ACM Symposium on Principles of Programming Languages*, January 1996.

4. Nikolaj Bjørner. Minimal typing derivations. In *ACM Workshop on Standard ML and its Applications*, June 1994.
5. Martin Elsman and Niels Hallenberg. An optimizing backend for the ML Kit using a stack of regions. Student Project, July 1995.
6. Robert Harper and Chris Stone. An interpretation of Standard ML in type theory. Technical report, Carnegie Mellon University, June 1997. CMU-CS-97-147.
7. Fritz Henglein and Jesper Jørgensen. Formally optimal boxing. In *21st ACM Symposium on Principles of Programming Languages*, pages 213–226, January 1994.
8. Mark Jones. Dictionary-free overloading by partial evaluation. In *ACM Workshop on Partial Evaluation and Semantics-Based Program Manipulation, Orlando, Florida*, June 1994.
9. Xavier Leroy. Unboxed objects and polymorphic typing. In *19th ACM Symposium on Principles of Programming Languages*, pages 177–188, 1992.
10. Xavier Leroy. The Objective Caml system. Software and documentation available on the Web, 1996.
11. Robin Milner, Mads Tofte, Robert Harper, and David MacQueen. *The Definition of Standard ML (Revised)*. MIT Press, 1997.
12. Greg Morrisett. *Compiling with Types*. PhD thesis, School of Computer Science, Carnegie Mellon University, Pittsburgh, PA 15213, December 1995.
13. Martin Odersky, Philip Wadler, and Martin Wehr. A second look at overloading. In *7'th International Conference on Functional Programming and Computer Architecture*, June 1995.
14. Atsushi Ohori. A Polymorphic Record Calculus and its Compilation. *ACM Transactions on Programming Languages and Systems*, 17(6), November 1995.
15. Chris Okasaki. *Purely Functional Data Structures*. PhD thesis, School of Computer Science, Carnegie Mellon University, Pittsburgh, PA 15213, September 1996.
16. John Peterson and Mark Jones. Implementing type classes. In *ACM Symposium on Programming Language Design and Implementation*, June 1993.
17. Manuel Serrano and Pierre Weis. Bigloo: a portable and optimizing compiler for strict functional languages. In *Second International Symposium on Static Analysis*, pages 366–381, September 1995.
18. Zhong Shao. Typed common intermediate format. In *1997 USENIX Conference on Domain-Specific Languages*, Santa Barbara, CA, Oct 1997.
19. Zhong Shao and Andrew Appel. A type-based compiler for Standard ML. Technical report, Yale University and Princeton University, November 1994.
20. David Tarditi, Greg Morrisett, Perry Cheng, Chris Stone, Robert Harper, and Peter Lee. TIL: A type-directed optimizing compiler for ML. In *ACM Symposium on Programming Language Design and Implementation*, 1996.
21. David Tarditi, Greg Morrisett, Perry Cheng, Chris Stone, Robert Harper, and Peter Lee. The TIL/ML compiler: Performance and safety through types. In *Workshop on Compiler Support for Systems Software*, 1996.
22. Mads Tofte. Type inference for polymorphic references. *Information and Computation*, 89(1), November 1990.
23. Mads Tofte, Lars Birkedal, Martin Elsman, Niels Hallenberg, Tommy Højfeld Olesen, Peter Sestoft, and Peter Bertelsen. Programming with regions in the ML Kit. Technical report, Department of Computer Science, University of Copenhagen, April 1997.
24. Mads Tofte and Jean-Pierre Talpin. Region-based memory management. *Information and Computation*, 132(2):109–176, 1997.
25. Philip Wadler and Stephen Blott. How to make ad-hoc polymorphism less ad hoc. In *16th ACM Symposium on Principles of Programming Languages*, January 1989.

# Optimal Type Lifting*

Bratin Saha and Zhong Shao

Dept. of Computer Science
Yale University
New Haven, CT 06520-8285
{saha,shao}@cs.yale.edu

**Abstract.** Modern compilers for ML-like polymorphic languages have used explicit run-time type passing to support advanced optimizations such as intensional type analysis, representation analysis and tagless garbage collection. Unfortunately, maintaining type information at run time can incur a large overhead to the time and space usage of a program. In this paper, we present an optimal type-lifting algorithm that lifts all type applications in a program to the *top* level. Our algorithm eliminates all run-time type constructions within any core-language functions. In fact, it guarantees that the number of types built at run time is strictly a static constant. We present our algorithm as a type-preserving source-to-source transformation and show how to extend it to handle the entire SML'97 with higher-order modules.

## 1 Introduction

Modern compilers for ML-like polymorphic languages [16, 17] usually use variants of the Girard-Reynolds polymorphic λ-calculus [5, 26] as their intermediate language (IL). Implementation of these ILs often involves passing types explicitly as parameters [32, 31, 28] at runtime: each polymorphic type variable gets instantiated to the actual type through run-time type application. Maintaining type information in this manner helps to ensure the correctness of a compiler. More importantly, it also enables many interesting optimizations and applications. For example, both pretty-printing and debugging on polymorphic values require complete type information at runtime. Intensional type analysis [7, 31, 27], which is used by some compilers [31, 28] to support efficient data representation, also requires the propagation of type information into the target code. Run-time type information is also crucial to the implementation of tag-less garbage collection [32], pickling, and type dynamic [15].

---

* This research was sponsored in part by the DARPA ITO under the title "Software Evolution using HOT Language Technology", DARPA Order No. D888, issued under Contract No. F30602-96-2-0232, and in part by an NSF CAREER Award CCR-9501624, and NSF Grant CCR-9633390. The views and conclusions contained in this document are those of the authors and should not be interpreted as representing the official policies, either expressed or implied, of the Defense Advanced Research Projects Agency or the U.S. Government.

However, the advantages of runtime type passing do not come for free. Depending on the sophistication of the type representation, run-time type passing can add a significant overhead to the time and space usage of a program. For example, Tolmach [32] implemented a tag-free garbage collector via explicit type passing; he reported that the memory allocated for type information sometimes exceeded the memory saved by the tag-free approach. Clearly, it is desirable to optimize the run-time type passing in polymorphic code [18]. In fact, a better goal would be to guarantee that explicit type passing never blows up the execution cost of a program.

Consider the sample code below – we took some liberties with the syntax by using an explicitly typed variant of the Core-ML. Here $\Lambda$ denotes type abstraction, $\lambda$ denotes value abstraction, $x[\alpha]$ denotes type application and $x(e)$ denotes term application.

```
pair = Λs.λx:s*s.
  let f = Λt.λy:t. ... (x , y)
  in  ... f[s*s](x) ...


......


main = Λα.λa:α.
  let doit = λi:Int.
        let elem = Array.sub[α*α](a,i)
        in  ... pair[α](elem) ...

      loop = λn₁:Int.λn₂:Int.λg:Int→Unit.
                if n₁ <= n₂
                  (g(n₁);
                   loop(n₁+1,n₂,g))
                else ()
  in loop(1,n,doit)
```

Here, f is a polymorphic function defined inside function pair; it refers to the parameter x of pair so f cannot be easily lifted outside pair. Function main executes a loop: in each iteration, it selects an element elem of the array a and then performs some computation (i.e, pair) on it. Executing the function doit results in three type applications arising from the Array.sub function, pair, and f. In each iteration, sub and pair are applied to types $\alpha * \alpha$ and $\alpha$ respectively. A clever compiler may do a *loop-invariant removal* [1] to avoid the repeated type construction (e.g., $\alpha * \alpha$) and application (e.g., pair[$\alpha$]). But optimizing type applications such as f[s*s] is less obvious; f is nested inside pair, and its repeated type applications are not apparent in the doit function. We may type-specialize f to get rid of the type application but in general this may lead to substantial code duplication. Every time doit is called, pair[$\alpha$] gets executed and then every time pair is called, f[s*s] will be executed. Since loop calls doit repeatedly and each such call generates type applications of pair and f, we are forced to incur the overhead of repeated type construction and application. If the type representation is complicated, this is clearly expensive.

In this paper, we present an algorithm that minimizes the cost of run-time type passing. More specifically, the optimization eliminates all type application inside any core-language function - it guarantees that the amount of type information constructed at runtime is a static constant. This guarantee is important because it allows us to use more sophisticated representations for run-time types without having to worry about the run-time cost of doing so.

The basic idea is as follows. We lift all polymorphic function definitions and type applications in a program to the "top" level. By top level, we mean "outside any core-language function." Intuitively, no type application is nested inside any function abstraction ($\lambda$); they are nested only inside type abstractions ($\Lambda$). All type applications are now performed once and for all at the beginning of execution of each compilation unit. In essence, the code after our type lifting would perform all of its type applications at "link" time.[1] In fact, the number of type applications performed and the amount of type information constructed can be determined statically.

This leads us to a natural question. Why do we restrict the transformation to type applications alone? Obviously the transformation could be carried out on value computations as well but what makes type computations more amenable to this transformation is the guarantee that all type applications can be lifted to the top level. Moreover, while the transformation is also intended to increase the runtime efficiency, a more important goal is to ensure that type passing in itself is not costly. This in turn will allow us to use a more sophisticated runtime type representation and make greater use of type information at runtime.

We describe the algorithm in later sections and also prove that it is both type-preserving and semantically sound. We have implemented it in the FLINT/ML compiler [28] and tested it on a few benchmarks. We provide the implementation results at the end of this paper.

## 2 The Lifting Algorithm for Core-ML

This section presents our optimal type lifting algorithm. We use an explicitly typed variant of the Core-ML calculus [6] (Figure 1) as the source and target languages. The type lifting algorithm (Figure. 2) is expressed as a type-directed program transformation that lifts all type applications to the top-level.

### 2.1 The language

We use an explicitly typed variant of the Core-ML calculus [6] as our source and target languages. The syntax is shown in Figure 1. The static and dynamic semantics are standard, and are given in the Appendix (Section 7).

Here, terms $e$ consist of identifiers ($x$), integer constants ($i$), function abstractions, function applications, and let expressions. We differentiate between

---

[1] We are not referring to "link time" in the traditional sense. Rather, we are referring to the run time spent on module initialization and module linkage (e.g., functor application) in a ML-style module language.

$$
\begin{array}{lll}
(con's) & \mu & ::= t \mid \text{Int} \mid \mu_1 \rightarrow \mu_2 \\
(types) & \sigma & ::= \mu \mid \forall \overline{t_i}.\,\mu \\
(terms) & e & ::= i \mid x \mid \lambda x{:}\mu.e \mid @x_1 x_2 \mid \text{let } x = e \text{ in } e' \mid \text{let } x = \Lambda\overline{t_i}.\,e_v \text{ in } e \mid x[\overline{\mu_i}] \\
(vterms) & e_v & ::= i \mid x \mid \lambda x{:}\mu.e \mid \text{let } x = e_v \text{ in } e'_v \mid \text{let } x = \Lambda\overline{t_i}.\,e_v \text{ in } e'_v \mid x[\overline{\mu_i}]
\end{array}
$$

**Fig. 1.** An explicit Core-ML calculus

monomorphic and polymorphic let expressions in our language. We use $\overline{t_i}$ (and $\overline{\mu_i}$) to denote a sequence of type variables $t_1, ..., t_n$ (and types) so $\forall \overline{t_i}.\,\mu$ is equivalent to $\forall t_1 \ldots \forall t_n.\mu$. The *vterms* ($e_v$) denote values – terms that are free of side-effects.

There are several aspects of this calculus that are worth noting. First, we restrict polymorphic definitions to value expressions ($e_v$) only, so that moving type applications and polymorphic definitions is semantically sound [33]. Variables introduced by normal $\lambda$-abstraction are always monomorphic, and polymorphic functions are introduced only by the **let** construct. In our calculus, type applications of polymorphic functions are never curried and therefore in the algorithm in Figure 2, the *exp* rule assumes that the variable is monomorphic. The *tapp* rule also assumes that the type application is not curried and therefore the newly introduced variable v (bound to the lifted type application) is monomorphic and is not applied further to types. Finally, following SML [17, 16], polymorphic functions are not recursive. [2] *This restriction is crucial to proving that all type applications can be lifted to the top level.*

Throughout the paper we take a few liberties with the syntax: we allow ourselves infix operators, multiple definitions in a single **let** expression to abbreviate a sequence of nested **let** expressions, and term applications that are at times not in A-Normal form [4]. We also use indentation to indicate the nesting.

## 2.2 Informal description

Before we move on to the formal description of the algorithm, we will present the basic ideas informally.

Define the depth of a term in a program as the number of $\lambda$(value) abstractions within which it is nested. Consider the terms outside all value abstractions to be at depth zero. Obviously, terms at depth zero occur outside all loops in the program. In a strict language like ML, all these terms are evaluated once and for all at the beginning of program execution. To avoid repeated type applications, the algorithm therefore tries to lift all of them to depth zero. But since we want to lift type applications, we must also lift the polymorphic functions to depth zero. The algorithm scans the input program and collects all the type applications and polymorphic functions occuring at depths greater than zero and adds them to a list H. (In the algorithm given in Figure 2, the depth is implicitly

---

[2] Our current calculus does not support recursive functions but they can be easily added. As in SML, recursive functions are always monomorphic.

assumed to be greater than zero). When the algorithm returns to the top level of the program, it dumps the expressions contained in the list.

We will illustrate the algorithm on the sample code given in Section 1. In the example code, $f[s*s]$ is at depth 1 since it occurs inside the $\lambda x$, $Array.sub[\alpha*\alpha]$ and $pair[\alpha]$ are at depth 2 since they occur inside the $\lambda a$ and $\lambda i$. We want to lift all of these type applications to depth zero. Translating main first, the resulting code becomes –

```
pair = Λs.λx:s*s.
         let f = Λt.λy:t. ... (x , y)
         in  ... f[s*s](x) ...
......
main = Λα.
         let v₁ = Array.sub[α*α]
             v₂ = pair[α]
         in  λa:α.
                let
                    doit = λi:Int.
                            let elem = v₁(a,i)
                            in ... v₂(elem) ...
                    loop = λn₁:Int.λn₂:Int.λg:Int→Unit.
                            if n₁ <= n₂
                              (g(n₁);
                               loop(n₁+1,n₂,g))
                            else ()
                in loop(1,n,doit)
```

We then lift the type application of f (inside pair). This requires us to lift f's definition by abstracting over its free variables. In the resulting code, all type applications occur at depth zero. Therefore when main is called at the beginning of execution, $v_1$, $v_2$ and $v_3$ get evaluated. During execution, when the function loop runs through the array and repeatedly calls function doit, none of the type applications need to be performed – the type specialised functions $v_1$, $v_2$ and $v_3$ can be used instead.

```
pair = Λs.
        let f = Λt.λx:s*s.λy:t. ... (x , y)
            v₃ = f[s*s]
        in  λx:s*s. ... (v₃(x))(x) ...
......
main = Λα.
        let v₁ = Array.sub[α*α]
            v₂ = pair[α]
        in  λa:α.
                let doit =
                        λi:Int.
                            let elem = v₁(a,i)
                            in  ... v₂(elem) ...
                    loop =
                        λn₁:Int.λn₂:Int.λg:Int→Unit.
                            if n₁ <= n₂
                                (g(n₁);
                                loop(n₁+1,n₂,g))
                            else ()
                in loop(1,n,doit)
```

## 2.3  Formalization

Figure 2 shows the type-directed lifting algorithm. The translation is defined as a relation of the form $\Gamma \vdash e : \mu \Rightarrow e'; H; F$, that carries the meaning that $\Gamma \vdash e : \mu$ is a derivable typing in the input program, the translation of the input term $e$ is the term $e'$, and $F$ is the set of free variables of $e'$. (The set $F$ is restricted to the monomorphically typed free variables of $e'$) The *header* $H$ contains the polymorphic functions and type applications occuring in $e$ at depths greater than zero. The final result of lifting a closed term $e$ of type $\mu$ is $LET(H, e')$ where the algorithm infers $\emptyset \vdash e : \mu \Rightarrow e'; H; \emptyset$. The function $LET(H, e)$ expands a list of bindings $H = [\langle x_1, e_1 \rangle, \ldots, \langle x_n, e_n \rangle]$ and a term $e$ into the resulting term let $x_1 = e_1$ in $\ldots$ in let $x_n = e_n$ in $e$.

The environment $\Gamma$ maps a variable to its type and to a list of the free variables in its definition. In the algorithm, we use standard notation for lists and operations on lists; in addition, the functions $List$ and $Set$ convert between lists and sets of variables using a canonical ordering. The functions $\lambda^*$ and $@^*$ are defined so that $\lambda^* L. e$ and $@^* v L$ reduce to $\lambda x_1 : \mu_1 \ldots \lambda x_n : \mu_n . e$ and $@(\ldots (@v x_1) \ldots) x_n$, respectively, where $L = [x_1 : \mu_1, \ldots, x_n : \mu_n]$.

Rules (*exp*) and (*app*) are just the identity transformations. Rule (*fn*) deals with abstractions. We translate the body of the abstraction and return a header $H$ containing all the type applications and type functions in the term $e$.

The translation of monomorphic let expressions is similar. We translate each of the subexpressions replacing the old terms with the translated terms and return this as the result of the translation. The header $H$ of the translation is the concatenation of the headers $H_1$ and $H_2$ from the translation of the subexpressions.

$(exp)$  
$$\frac{\Gamma(x) = (\mu, \_)}{\Gamma \vdash x : \mu \Rightarrow x; \emptyset; \{x : \mu\}} \qquad\qquad \Gamma \vdash i : \text{Int} \Rightarrow i; \emptyset; \emptyset$$

$(app)$  
$$\frac{\Gamma(x_1) = \langle \mu_1 \to \mu_2, \_\rangle \qquad \Gamma(x_2) = \langle \mu_1, \_\rangle}{\Gamma \vdash @x_1 x_2 : \mu_2 \Rightarrow @x_1 x_2; \emptyset; \{x_1 : \mu_1 \to \mu_2, x_2 : \mu_1\}}$$

$(fn)$  
$$\frac{\Gamma[x \mapsto \langle \mu, \_\rangle] \vdash e : \mu' \Rightarrow e'; H; F}{\Gamma \vdash \lambda x : \mu.e : \mu \to \mu' \Rightarrow \lambda x : \mu.e'; H; F \setminus \{x : \mu\}}$$

$(let)$  
$$\frac{\Gamma \vdash e_1 : \mu_1 \Rightarrow e_1'; H_1; F_1 \quad \Gamma[x \mapsto \langle \mu_1, \_\rangle] \vdash e_2 : \mu_2 \Rightarrow e_2'; H_2; F_2}{\Gamma \vdash \text{let } x = e_1 \text{ in } e_2 : \mu_2 \Rightarrow \text{let } x = e_1' \text{ in } e_2'; H_1 \| H_2; F_1 \cup (F_2 \setminus \{x : \mu_1\})}$$

$(tfn)$  
$$\frac{\begin{array}{c}\Gamma \vdash e_1 : \mu_1 \Rightarrow e_1'; H_1; F_1 \qquad L = List(F_1) \\ \Gamma[x \mapsto \langle \forall\overline{t_i}.\mu_1, L\rangle] \vdash e_2 : \mu_2 \Rightarrow e_2'; H_2; F_2\end{array}}{\Gamma \vdash \text{let } x = \Lambda\overline{t_i}.e_1 \text{ in } e_2 : \mu_2 \Rightarrow e_2'; \underbrace{\langle x, \Lambda\overline{t_i}. LET(H_1, \lambda^* L.e_1')\rangle}_{H_r} :: H_2; F_2}$$

$(tapp)$  
$$\frac{\Gamma(x) = \langle \forall\overline{t_i}.\mu, L\rangle \qquad v \text{ a fresh variable}}{\Gamma \vdash x[\overline{\mu_i}] : [\mu_i/t_i]\mu \Rightarrow @^* vL; \underbrace{[\langle v, x[\overline{\mu_i}]\rangle]}_{H_r}; Set(L)}$$

**Fig. 2.** The Lifting Translation

The real work is done in the last two rules which deal with type expressions. In rule $(tfn)$, we first translate the body of the polymorphic function definition. $H_1$ now contains all the type expressions that were in $e_1$ and $F_1$ is the free variables of $e_1'$. We then translate the body of the let expression($e_2$). The result of the translation is only $e_2'$; the polymorphic function introduced by the let is added to the result header $H_r$ so that it is lifted to the top level. The polymorphic function body (in $H_r$) is closed by abstracting over its free variables $F_1$ while the header $H_1$ is dumped right after the type abstractions. Note that since $H_r$ will be lifted to the top level, the expressions in $H_1$ will also get lifted to the top level.

The $(tapp)$ rule replaces the type application by an application of the newly introduced variable ($v$) to the free variables($L$) of the corresponding function definition. The type application is added to the header and lifted to the top level where it gets bound to $v$. Note that the free variables of the translated term do not include the newly introduced variable $v$. This is because when the header is written out at the top level, the translated expression remains in the scope of the dumped header.

**Proposition 1.** *Suppose $\Gamma \vdash e : \mu \Rightarrow e'; H; F$. Then in the expression LET(H,e'), the term e' does not contain any type application and H does not contain any type application nested inside a value($\lambda$) abstraction.*

This propostion can be proved by a simple structural induction on the structure of the source term $e$.

**Theorem 1 (Full Lifting).** *Suppose $\Gamma \vdash e : \mu \Rightarrow e'; H; F$. Then the expression LET(H,e'), does not have any type application nested inside a value abstraction.*

The theorem follows from Proposition 1.

In the Appendix, we prove the type preservation and the semantic soundness theorems.

## 2.4 A closer look

There are two transformations taking place simultaneously. One is the lifting of type applications and the other is the lifting of polymorphic function definitions. At first glance, the lifting of function definitions may seem similar to lambda lifting [10]. However the lifting in the two cases is different. Lambda lifting converts a program with local function definitions into a program with global function definitions whereas the lifting shown here preserves the nesting structure of the program.

The lifting of type applications is similar in spirit to the hoisting of loop invariant expressions outside a loop. It could be considered as a special case of a *fully lazy transformation* [9, 24] with the maximal free subexpressions restricted to be type applications. However, the fully-lazy transformation as described in Peyton Jones [24] will not lift all type applications to the top level. Specifically, type applications of a polymorphic function that is defined inside other functions will not be lifted to the top level.

Minamide [18] uses a different approach to solve this problem. He lifts the construction of type parameters from within a polymorphic function to the call sites of the function. This lifting is recursively propagated to the call sites at the top level. At runtime, type construction is replaced by projection from type parameters.

His method eliminates the runtime construction of types and replaces it by projection from type records. The transformation also does not rely on the value restriction for polymorphic definitions. However, he requires a more sophisticated type system to type-check his transformation; he uses a type system based on the qualified type system of Jones [12] and the implementation calculus for the compilation of polymorphic records of Ohori [21]. Our algorithm on the other hand is a source-to-source transformation. Moreover, Minamide's algorithm deals only with the Core-ML calculus whereas we have implemented our algorithm on the entire SML'97 language with higher-order modules.

Jones [11] has also worked on a similar problem related to dictionary passing in Haskell and Gofer. Type classes in these languages are implemented by passing dictionaries at runtime. Dictionaries are tuples of functions that implement the methods defined in a type class.

Consider the following Haskell [8] example

```
f :: Eq a => a -> a -> Bool
f x y = ([x] == [y]) && ([y] == [x])
```

The actual type of f is $Eq[a] \Rightarrow a \rightarrow a \rightarrow Bool$. Context reduction leads to the type specified in the example. Here [a] means a list of elements of type a. $Eq\ a$ means that the type a must be an instance of the equality class. In a naive implementation, this function would be passed a dictionary for $Eq\ a$ and the dictionary for $Eq\ [a]$ would be constructed inside the function. Jones optimises this by constructing a dictionary for $Eq\ [a]$ at the call site of f and passing it in as a parameter. This is repeated for all overloaded functions so that all dictionaries are constructed statically. But this approach does not work with separately compiled modules since f's type in other modules does not specify the dictionaries that are constructed inside it.

In Gofer [11], instance declarations are not used to simplify the context. Therefore the type of f in the above example would be $Eq[a] \Rightarrow a \rightarrow a \rightarrow Bool$. Jones' optimisation of dictionary passing can now be performed in the presence of separately compiled modules. However, we now require a more complicated type system to typecheck the code. Assume two functions f and g have the same type $(\mu \rightarrow \mu')$. Both f and g can be passed as a parameter to h in $(h = \lambda x : \mu \rightarrow \mu'.e)$. However, f and g could, in general, be using different dictionaries $(d_f$ and $d_g)$. This implies that after the transformation, the two functions will have different types – $d_f \Rightarrow \mu \rightarrow \mu'$ and $d_g \Rightarrow \mu \rightarrow \mu'$. Therefore, we can no longer use f and g interchangeably.

## 3   The Lifting Algorithm for FLINT

Till now, we have considered only the Core-ML calculus while discussing the algorithm. But what happens when we take into account the module language as well?

To handle the Full-ML langauge, we compile the source code into the FLINT intermediate language. The details of the translation are given in [29]. FLINT is based upon a predicative variant of the Girard-Reynolds polymorphic $\lambda$-calculus [5, 26], with the term language written in A-normal form [4]. It contains the following four syntactic classes: kinds $(\kappa)$, constructors $(\mu)$, types $(\sigma)$ and terms $(e)$, as shown in Figure 3. Here, kinds classify constructors, and types classify terms. Constructors of kind $\Omega$ name monotypes. The monotypes are generated from variables, from Int, and through the $\rightarrow$ constructor. The application and abstraction constructors correspond to the function kind $\kappa_1 \rightarrow \kappa_2$. Types in Core-FLINT include the monotypes, and are closed under function spaces and polymorphic quantification. We use $T(\mu)$ to denote the type corresponding to the constructor $\mu$ (when $\mu$ is of kind $\Omega$). The terms are an explicitly typed $\lambda$-calculus (but in A-normal form) with explicit constructor abstraction and application.

$$
\begin{array}{lll}
(kinds) & \kappa & ::= \Omega \mid \kappa_1 \to \kappa_2 \\
(cons) & \mu & ::= t \mid \text{Int} \mid \mu_1 \to \mu_2 \mid \lambda t :: \kappa.\mu \mid \mu_1[\mu_2] \\
(types) & \sigma & ::= T(\mu) \mid \sigma_1 \to \sigma_2 \mid \forall t :: \kappa.\sigma \\
(terms) & e & ::= i \mid x \mid \text{let } x = e_1 \text{ in } e_2 \mid @x_1 x_2 \\
& & \quad \mid \lambda^c x : T(\mu).e \mid \lambda^m x : \sigma.e \\
& & \quad \mid \text{let } x = \Lambda \overline{t_i} :: k_i.e_v \text{ in } e_2 \mid x[\mu_i] \\
(values) & e_v & ::= i \mid x \mid \text{let } x = e_v \text{ in } e_v' \mid \lambda^c x : T(\mu).e \mid \lambda^m x : \sigma.e \\
& & \quad \text{let } x = \Lambda \overline{t_i} :: k_i.e_v \text{ in } e_v' \mid x[\mu_i]
\end{array}
$$

**Fig. 3.** Syntax of the Core-FLINT calculus

In ML, structures are the basic module unit and functors abstract over structures. Polymorphic functions may now escape as part of structures and get initialized later at a functor application site. In the FLINT translation [29], functors are represented as a polymorphic definition combined with a polymorphic abstraction ($\text{fct} = \Lambda \overline{t_i} :: \overline{k_i}.\lambda^m x : \sigma.e$). The variable $x$ in the functor definition is polymorphic since the parameterised structure may contain polymorphic components. In the functor body $e$, the polymorphic components of $x$ are instantiated by type application. Functor applications are a combination of a type application and a term application. with the type application instantiating the type parameters ($t_i's$). Though abstractions model both functors and functions, the translation allows us to distinguish between them. In the FLINT calculus, $\lambda^c x : T(\mu).e$ denotes functions, whereas $\lambda^m x : \sigma.e$ denotes functors. The rest of the term calculus is standard.

This calculus complicates the lifting since type applications arising from an abstracted variable (the variable $x$ in $\text{fct}$ above) can not be lifted to the top level. This also differs from the Core-ML calculus in that type applications may now be curried to model escaping polymorphic functions.

However, the module calculus obeys some nice properties. Functors in a program always occur outside any Core-ML functions. Type applications arising out of functor parameters (when the input structure contains a polymorphic component) can therefore be lifted outside all functions. Escaping polymorphic functions occur outside Core-ML functions. Therefore the corresponding curried type application is not nested inside Core-ML functions.

Therefore a FLINT source program can be converted into a *well-formed* program satisfying the following constraints –

– All functor abstractions ($\lambda^m$) occur outside function abstractions ($\lambda^c$).
– No partial type application occurs inside a function abstraction.

We now redefine the depth of a term in a program as the number of function abstractions within which it is nested with *depth 0 terms occuring outside all function abstractions only.* Note that depth 0 terms may not occur outside all abstractions since they may be nested inside functor abstractions. We then perform type lifting as in Figure 2 for terms at depth greater than zero and lift the polymorphic definitions and type applications to depth 0. For terms already at depth zero, the translation is just the identity function and the header returned is empty.

We illustrate the algorithm on the example code in Figure 4. The syntax is not totally faithful to the FLINT syntax in Figure 3 but it makes the code easier to understand. In the code in Figure 4, $F$ is a functor which takes the structure

```
F = Λt₀.λᵐX:S.
      f = λᶜv.
            let id = Λt₁.λᶜx₂.x₂
                .....
                v₁ = ... id[Int](3) ....
            in  v₁
      v₂ = (#1(X))[t₀]
      ....
```

**Fig. 4.** Example FLINT code

$X$ as a parameter. The type $S$ denotes a structure type. Assume the first component of $X$ ($\#1(X)$) is a polymorphic function which gets instantiated in the functor body($v_2$). $f$ is a locally defined function in the functor body. According to the definition of depth above, $f$ and $v_2$ are at depth 0 even though they are nested inside the functor abstraction($\lambda X$). Moreover, the type application $(\#1(X))[t_0]$ is also at depth 0 and will therefore not be lifted. It is only inside the function $f$ that the depth increases which implies that the type application $id[Int]$ occurs at $d > 0$. The algorithm will lift the type application to just outside the function abstraction ($\lambda v$), it is not lifted outside the functor abstraction ($\lambda X$). The resulting code is shown in Figure 5.

Is the reformulation merely an artifice to get around the problems posed by FLINT ? No, the main aim of the type lifting transformation is to perform all the type applications during "link" time—when the top level code is being executed—and eliminate runtime type construction inside functions. Functors are top level code and are applied at "link" time. Moreover they are non-recursive. Therefore having type applications nested only inside functors results in the type applications being performed once and for all at the beginning of program execution. As a result, we still eliminate runtime type passing inside functions.

To summarize, we note that depth 0 in Core-ML (according to the definition above) coincides with the top level of the program since Core-ML does not

```
F = Λt₀.λᵐX:S.
    f = let
            id = Λt₁.λᶜx₂.x₂
            z₁ = id[Int]
            .. (Other type expressions in f's body)..
        in  λᶜv.
                let  ..... (type lifted body of f)
                        v₁ = ... z₁(3) ....
                    in   v₁
    v₂ = (#1(X))[t₀]
    ....
```

**Fig. 5.** FLINT code after type lifting

have functors; therefore the Core-ML translation is merely a special case of the translation for FLINT.

## 4 Implementation

We have implemented the type-lifting algorithm in the FLINT/ML compiler version 1.0 and the experimental version of SML/NJ v109.32. All the tests were performed on a Pentium Pro 200 Linux workstation with 64M physical RAM. Figure 6 shows CPU times for executing the Standard ML benchmark suite with type lifting turned on and turned off. The third column (New Time) indicates the execution time with lifting turned on and the next column (Old Time) indicates the execution time with lifting turned off. The last column gives the ratio of the new time to the old time.

| Benchmark | Description | New Time | Old Time | Ratio |
|-----------|-------------|----------|----------|-------|
| Simple | A fluid-dynamics program | 7.04 | 9.78 | 0.72 |
| Vliw | A VLIW instruction scheduler | 4.22 | 4.31 | 0.98 |
| lexgen | lexical-analyzer generator | 2.38 | 2.36 | 1.01 |
| ML-Yacc | The ML-yacc | 1.05 | 1.11 | 0.95 |
| Mandelbrot | Mandelbrot curve construction | 4.62 | 4.62 | 1.0 |
| Kb-comp | Knuth-Bendix Algorithm | 2.98 | 3.11 | 0.96 |
| Ray | A ray-tracer | 10.68 | 10.66 | 1.01 |
| Life | The Life Simulation | 2.80 | 2.80 | 1.0 |
| Boyer | A simple theorem prover | 0.49 | 0.52 | 0.96 |

**Fig. 6.** Type Lifting Results

The current FLINT/ML and SML/NJ compilers maintain a very minimal set of type information. Types are represented by integers since the compiler only needs to distinguish primitive types (e.g., int, real) and special record types. As a result, runtime type construction and type application are not expensive. The test results therefore yield a moderate speedup for most of the benchmarks and a good speedup for one benchmark—an average of about 5% for the polymorphic benchmarks. Simple has a lot of polymorphic function calls occuring inside loops and therefore benefits greatly from lifting. Boyer and mandelbrot are monomorphic benchmarks (involving large lists) and predictably do not benefit from the optimization.

Our algorithm makes the simultaneous uncurrying of both value and type applications difficult. Therefore at runtime, a type application will result in the formation of a closure. However, these closures are created only once at linktime and do not represent a significant penalty.

We also need to consider the closure size of the lifted functions. The (tapp) rule in Figure 2 introduces new variables (the set L) which may increase the number of free variables of a function. Moreover after type applications are lifted, the type specialised functions become free variables of the function body. On the other hand, since all type applications are lifted, we no longer need to include the free type variables in the closure which decreases the closure size. We believe therefore that the increase in closure size, if any, does not incur a significant penalty. This is borne out by the results on the benchmark suite – none of the benchmarks slows down significantly.

The creation of closures makes function application more expensive since it involves the extraction of the environment and the code. However, in most cases, the selection of the code and the environment will be a loop invariant and can therefore be optimised.

The algorithm is implemented in a single pass by a bottom up traversal of the syntax tree. The (tfn) rule shown in Figure 2 simplifies the implementation considerably by reducing the type information to be adjusted. In the given rule, all the expressions in $H_1$ are dumped right in front of the type abstraction. Note however that we require to dump only those terms (in $H_1$) which contain any of the $t_i's$ as free type variables. The advantage of dumping all the expressions is that the *de Bruijn* depth of the terms in $H_1$ remains the same even after lifting. The algorithm needs to adjust the type information only while abstracting the free variables of a polymorphic definition. (The types of the abstracted variables have to be adjusted.) The implementation also optimises the number of variables abstracted while lifting a definition – it remembers the depth at which a variable is defined so that variables that will still remain in scope after the lifting are not abstracted.

# 5 Related Work and Conclusions

Tolmach [32] has worked on a similar problem and proposed a method based on the lazy substitution on types. He used the method in the implementation of the tag-free garbage collector. Minamide [18] proposes a refinement of Tolmach's method to eliminate runtime construction of type parameters. The speedups obtained in our method are comparable to the ones reported in his paper. Mark P. Jones [11] has worked on the related problem of optimising dictionary passing in the implementation of type classes.

In their study of the type theory of Standard ML, Harper and Mitchell [6] argued that an explicitly typed interpretation of ML polymorphism has better semantic properties and scales more easily to cover the full language. The idea of passing types to polymorphic functions is exploited by Morrison *et al.* [19] in the implementation of Napier. The work of Ohori on compiling record operations [21] is similarly based on a type passing interpretation of polymorphism. Jones [12] has proposed *evidence passing*—a general framework for passing data derived from types to "qualified" polymorphic operations. Harper and Morisett [7] proposed an alternative approach for compiling polymorphism where types are passed as arguments to polymorphic routines in order to determine the representation of an object. The boxing interpretation of polymorphism which applies the appropriate coercions based on the type of an object was studied by Leroy [14] and Shao [27]. Many modern compilers like the FLINT/ML compiler [28], TIL [31] and the Glasgow Haskell compiler [22] use an explicitly typed language as the intermediate language for the compilation.

Lambda lifting and full laziness are part of the folklore of functional programming. Hughes [9] showed that by doing lambda lifting in a particular way, full laziness can be preserved. Johnsson [10] describes different forms of lambda lifting and the pros and cons of each. Peyton Jones [25, 23, 24] also described a number of optimizations which are similar in spirit but have totally different aims. Appel [2] describes let hoisting in the context of ML. In general, using correctness preserving transformations as a compiler optimization [1, 2] is a well established technique and has received quite a bit of attention in the functional programming area.

We have proposed a method for minimizing the cost of runtime type passing. Our algorithm lifts all type applications out of functions and therefore eliminates the runtime construction of types inside functions. The amount of type information constructed at run time is a static constant. We can guarantee that in Core-ML programs, all type applications will be lifted to the top level. We are now working on making the type representation in FLINT more comprehensive so that we can maintain complete type information at runtime.

## 6 Acknowledgements

We would like to thank Valery Trifonov, Chris League and Stefan Monnier for many useful discussions and comments about earlier drafts of this paper. We also thank the annonymous referees who suggested various ways of improving the presentation.

## References

1. A. V. Aho, R. Sethi, and J. D. Ullman. *Compilers: Principles, Techniques, and Tools.* Addison-Wesley, Reading, MA, 1986.

2. A. W. Appel. *Compiling with Continuations*. Cambridge University Press, 1992.

3. N. de Bruijn. A survey of the project AUTOMATH. In *To H. B. Curry: Essays on Combinatory Logic, Lambda Calculus and Formalism*, pages 579–606. Edited by J. P. Seldin and J. R. Hindley, Academic Press, 1980.

4. C. Flanagan, A. Sabry, B. F. Duba, and M. Felleisen. The essence of compiling with continuations. In *Proc. ACM SIGPLAN '93 Conf. on Prog. Lang. Design and Implementation*, pages 237–247, New York, June 1993. ACM Press.

5. J. Y. Girard. *Interpretation Fonctionnelle et Elimination des Coupures dans l'Arithmetique d'Ordre Superieur*. PhD thesis, University of Paris VII, 1972.

6. R. Harper and J. C. Mitchell. On the type structure of Standard ML. *ACM Trans. Prog. Lang. Syst.*, 15(2):211–252, April 1993.

7. R. Harper and G. Morrisett. Compiling polymorphism using intensional type analysis. In *Twenty-second Annual ACM Symp. on Principles of Prog. Languages*, pages 130–141, New York, Jan 1995. ACM Press.

8. P. Hudak, S. P. Jones, and P. W. *et al.* Report on the programming language Haskell, a non-strict, purely functional language version 1.2. *SIGPLAN Notices*, 21(5), May 1992.

9. R. Hughes. *The design and implementation of programming languages*. PhD thesis, Programming Research Group, Oxford University, Oxford, UK, 1983.

10. T. Johnsson. Lambda Lifting: Transforming Programs to Recursive Equations. In *The Second International Conference on Functional Programming Languages and Computer Architecture*, pages 190–203, New York, September 1985. Springer-Verlag.

11. M. P. Jones. *Qualified Types: Theory and Practice*. PhD thesis, Oxford University Computing Laboratory, Oxford, july 1992. Technical Monograph PRG-106.

12. M. P. Jones. A theory of qualified types. In *The 4th European Symposium on Programming*, pages 287–306, Berlin, February 1992. Spinger-Verlag.

13. M. P. Jones. Dictionary-free overloading by partial evaluation. In *Proceedings of the ACM SIGPLAN Workshop on Partial Evaluation and Semantics-Based Program Manipulation*, pages 107–117. University of Melbourne TR 94/9, June 1994.

14. X. Leroy. Unboxed objects and polymorphic typing. In *Nineteenth Annual ACM Symp. on Principles of Prog. Languages*, pages 177–188, New York, Jan 1992. ACM Press. Longer version available as INRIA Tech Report.

15. X. Leroy and M. Mauny. Dynamics in ML. In *The Fifth International Conference on Functional Programming Languages and Computer Architecture*, pages 406–426, New York, August 1991. Springer-Verlag.

16. R. Milner, M. Tofte, and R. Harper. *The Definition of Standard ML*. MIT Press, Cambridge, Massachusetts, 1990.

17. R. Milner, M. Tofte, R. Harper, and D. MacQueen. *The Definition of Standard ML (Revised)*. MIT Press, Cambridge, Massachusetts, 1997.

18. Y. Minamide. Full lifting of type parameters. Technical report, RIMS, Kyoto University, 1997.

19. R. Morrison, A. Dearle, R. C. H. Connor, and A. L. Brown. An ad hoc approach to the implementation of polymorphism. *ACM Trans. Prog. Lang. Syst.*, 13(3), July 1991.

20. G. Nadathur. A notation for lambda terms II: Refinements and applications. Technical Report CS-1994-01, Duke University, Durham, NC, January 1994.

21. A. Ohori. A compilation method for ML-style polymorphic record calculi. In *Nineteenth Annual ACM Symp. on Principles of Prog. Languages*, New York, Jan 1992. ACM Press.

22. S. Peyton Jones. Implementing lazy functional languages on stock hardware: the Spineless Tagless G-machine. *Journal of Functional Programming*, 2(2):127–202, April 1992.

23. S. Peyton Jones. Compiling haskell by program transformation: a report from trenches. In *Proceedings of the European Symposium on Programming*, Linkoping, April 1996.

24. S. Peyton Jones and D. Lester. A modular fully-lazy lambda lifter in haskell. *Software – Practice and Experience*, 21:479–506, 1991.

25. S. Peyton Jones, W. Partain, and A. Santos. Let-floating: moving bindings to give faster programs. In *Proc. International Conference on Functional Programming (ICFP'96)*, New York, June 1996. ACM Press.

26. J. C. Reynolds. Towards a theory of type structure. In *Proceedings, Colloque sur la Programmation, Lecture Notes in Computer Science, volume 19*, pages 408–425. Springer-Verlag, Berlin, 1974.

27. Z. Shao. Flexible representation analysis. In *Proc. 1997 ACM SIGPLAN International Conference on Functional Programming (ICFP'97)*, pages 85–98. ACM Press, June 1997.

28. Z. Shao. An overview of the FLINT/ML compiler. In *Proc. 1997 ACM SIGPLAN Workshop on Types in Compilation*, June 1997.

29. Z. Shao. Typed cross-module compilation. Technical Report YALEU/DCS/RR-1126, Dept. of Computer Science, Yale University, New Haven, CT, November 1997.

30. Z. Shao and A. W. Appel. A type-based compiler for Standard ML. In *Proc. ACM SIGPLAN '95 Conf. on Prog. Lang. Design and Implementation*, pages 116–129. ACM Press, 1995.

31. D. Tarditi, G. Morrisett, P. Cheng, C. Stone, R. Harper, and P. Lee. TIL: A type-directed optimizing compiler for ML. In *Proc. ACM SIGPLAN '96 Conf. on Prog. Lang. Design and Implementation*, pages 181–192. ACM Press, 1996.

32. A. Tolmach. Tag-free garbage collection using explicit type parameters. In *Proc. 1994 ACM Conf. on Lisp and Functional Programming*, pages 1–11, New York, June 1994. ACM Press.

33. A. K. Wright. Polymorphism for imperative languages without imperative types. Technical Report Tech Report TR 93-200, Dept. of Computer Science, Rice University, Houston, Texas, February 1993.

# 7 Appendix

In this section, we give the proofs of the type preservation theorem and the semantic-soundness theorem. Figure 7 gives the typing rules. Figure 8 gives a slightly modified version of the translation algorithm. The type environment $\Gamma_m$ binds monomorphic variables while the environment $\Gamma_p$ binds polymorphic variables.

**Notation 1** ($\lambda^* F.e$ **and** $@^* zF$) *We use* $\lambda^* F.e$ *and* $@^* zF$ *to denote repeated abstractions and applications respectively. If* $F = \{x_1, ..., x_n\}$, *then* $\lambda^* F.e$ *reduces to* $\lambda x_1 : \mu_1.(...(\lambda x_n : \mu_n.e)..)$ *where* $\mu_1, ...\mu_n$ *are the types of* $x_1, ..., x_n$ *in* $\Gamma_m$. *Similarly* $@^* zF$ *reduces to* $@(..(@zx_1)..)x_n$.

| $(const/var)$ | $\Gamma \vdash i : \text{Int}$ $\qquad$ $\Gamma \vdash x : \Gamma(x)$ |
|---|---|

$$(fn) \qquad \frac{\Gamma \uplus \{x : \mu_1\} \vdash e : \mu_2}{\Gamma \vdash \lambda x : \mu_1.e : \mu_1 \to \mu_2}$$

$$(app) \qquad \frac{\Gamma \vdash x_1 : \mu' \to \mu \quad \Gamma \vdash x_2 : \mu'}{\Gamma \vdash @x_1x_2 : \mu}$$

$$(tfn) \qquad \frac{\Gamma \vdash e_v : \mu_1 \quad \Gamma \uplus \{x : \forall \overline{t_i}.\mu_1\} \vdash e : \mu_2}{\Gamma \vdash \text{let } x = \Lambda \overline{t_i}.e_v \text{ in } e : \mu_2}$$

$$(tapp) \qquad \frac{\Gamma \vdash x : \forall \overline{t_i}.\mu}{\Gamma \vdash x[\overline{\mu_i}] : [\mu_i/t_i]\mu}$$

$$(let) \qquad \frac{\Gamma \vdash e_1 : \mu_1 \quad \Gamma \uplus \{x : \mu_1\} \vdash e_2 : \mu_2}{\Gamma \vdash \text{let } x = e_1 \text{ in } e_2 : \mu_2}$$

**Fig. 7.** Static Semantics

**Notation 2 ($T(L)$)** *If $L$ is a set of variables, then $T(L)$ refers to the types of the variables in $L$ in the environment $\Gamma_m$. If $L = \{x_1, x_2, ..., x_n\}$ and the types of the variables are respectively $\mu_1, ..., \mu_n$, then $T(L) \to \tau$ is shorthand for $\mu_1 \to (... \to (\mu_n \to \tau)..)$.*

Throughout this section, we assume unique variable bindings – variables are never redefined in the program.

### 7.1 Type preservation

Before we prove the type soundness of the translation, we will define a couple of predicates on the header — $\Gamma_H$ and well-typedness of $H$. Intuitively, $\Gamma_H$ denotes the type that we annotate with each expression in $H$ during the translation and well-typedness ensures that the type we annotate is the correct type. Together these two ensure that the header formed is well typed.

**Definition 1 (The header type environment – $\Gamma_H$).**

If $H = (h_0 \ldots h_n)$, then $\Gamma_H = \Gamma_{h_0} \ldots \Gamma_{h_n}$. If $h_i ::= (x = e, \tau)$, then $\Gamma_{h_i} := x \mapsto \tau$.

**Definition 2 (Let H in e).**

If $H = h_0 \ldots h_n$, then **Let H in e** is shorthand for *let $h_0$ in $\ldots$ let $h_n$ in e*. The typing rule is as follows — $\Gamma_m \vdash \text{Let } H \text{ in } e : \mu$ iff $\Gamma_m; \Gamma_H \vdash e : \mu$.

$$(exp) \quad \frac{\Gamma_m(x) = \mu}{\Gamma_m; \Gamma_p; H \vdash x : \mu \Rightarrow x; \emptyset; \{x\}} \qquad \Gamma_m; \Gamma_p; H \vdash i : \mathrm{Int} \Rightarrow i; \emptyset; \emptyset$$

$$(app) \quad \frac{\Gamma_m(x_1) = \mu_1 \to \mu_2 \qquad \Gamma_m(x_2) = \mu_1}{\Gamma_m; \Gamma_p; H \vdash @x_1x_2 : \mu_2 \Rightarrow @x_1x_2; \emptyset; \{x_1, x_2\}}$$

$$(fn) \quad \frac{\Gamma_m[x \mapsto \mu]; \Gamma_p; H \vdash e : \mu' \Rightarrow e'; H_1; F}{\Gamma_m; \Gamma_p; H \vdash \lambda x : \mu.e : \mu \to \mu' \Rightarrow \lambda x : \mu.e'; H_1; F \backslash \{x : \mu\}}$$

$$(let) \quad \frac{\Gamma_m; \Gamma_p; H \vdash e_1 : \mu_1 \Rightarrow e_1'; H_1; F_1 \quad \Gamma_m[x \mapsto \mu_1]; \Gamma_p; H \vdash e_2 : \mu_2 \Rightarrow e_2'; H_2; F_2}{\Gamma_m; \Gamma_p; H \vdash \mathrm{let}\ x = e_1\ \mathrm{in}\ e_2 : \mu_2 \Rightarrow \mathrm{let}\ x = e_1'\ \mathrm{in}\ e_2'; H_1 + H_2; F_1 \cup (F_2 \backslash \{x\})}$$

$$(tfn) \quad \frac{\begin{array}{c} \Gamma_m; \Gamma_p; H \vdash e_1 : \mu_1 \Rightarrow e_1'; H_1'; F_1 \\ H_1 = \langle x = \Lambda \overline{t_i}.\mathrm{Let}\ H_1'\ \mathrm{in}\ \lambda^* F_1.e_1', \forall \overline{t_i}.T(F_1) \to \mu_1 \rangle \\ \Gamma_m; \Gamma_p[x \mapsto \langle \forall \overline{t_i}.\mu_1, F_1 \rangle]; H + H_1 \vdash e_2 : \mu_2 \Rightarrow e_2'; H_2; F_2 \end{array}}{\Gamma_m; \Gamma_p; H \vdash \mathrm{let}\ x = \Lambda \overline{t_i}.e_1\ \mathrm{in}\ e_2 : \mu_2 \Rightarrow e_2'; H_1 + H_2; F_2}$$

$$(tapp) \quad \frac{\Gamma_p(x) = \langle \forall \overline{t_i}.\mu, F \rangle \quad \Gamma_H(x) = \forall \overline{t_i}.T(F) \to \mu \quad z\ \text{a fresh variable}}{\Gamma_m; \Gamma_p; H \vdash x[\overline{\mu_i}] : [\mu_i/t_i]\mu \Rightarrow @^* zF; \underbrace{\langle z = x[\overline{\mu_i}], T(F) \to [\mu_i/t_i]\mu \rangle}_{H_1}; F}$$

**Fig. 8.** The Lifting Translation

**Definition 3 (H is well typed).**

$H$ is well typed if $h_0...h_n$ are well typed. $h_i$ is well typed if $h_0...h_{i-1}$ are well typed and —

- $h_i ::= (x = \Lambda \overline{t_i}.\mathrm{Let}\ H_1\ \mathrm{in}\ e, \forall \overline{t_i}.\mu)$, then $\Gamma_{h_0..h_{i-1}} \vdash \mathrm{Let}\ H_1\ \mathrm{in}\ e : \mu$.

- $h_i ::= (z = x[\overline{\mu_i}], [\mu_i/t_i]\mu)$, then $\Gamma_{h_0...h_i} \vdash z : [\mu_i/t_i]\mu$

**Lemma 1.** *Suppose* $\Gamma_m; \Gamma_p; H \vdash e \Rightarrow e'; H'; F$. *If* $x \in \Gamma_m$ *and* $x$ *does not occur free in* $H$, *then* $x$ *does not occur free in* $H + H'$.

**Proof.** This is proved by induction on the structure of $e$.

**Theorem 2 (Type Preservation).** *Suppose* $\Gamma_m; \Gamma_p; H \vdash e : \mu \Rightarrow e'; H_1; F$. *If* $H$ *is well typed then* $H + H_1$ *is well typed and if* $\Gamma_m; \Gamma_p \vdash e : \mu$ *then* $\Gamma_m; \Gamma_H \vdash \mathrm{Let}\ H_1\ \mathrm{in}\ e' : \mu$

**Proof.** The proof is by induction on the structure of $e$. We will consider only *tfn* and *tapp*.

**Case tapp.** To prove that if $H$ is well-typed, $H + \overbrace{(z = x[\overline{\mu_i}], T(F) \to [\mu_i/t_i]\mu)}^{H'}$ is also well-typed and $\Gamma_m; \Gamma_H \vdash Let\ H'\ in\ @^*zF : [\mu_i/t_i]\mu$

Since we assume $H$ is well typed, we need to prove $H'$ is well typed. By the precondition on the translation $\Gamma_H \vdash x : \forall \overline{t_i}.T(F) \to \mu$. Since $F$ consists of the free variables of $x$, $T(F)$ cannot have any of the $t_i's$ as a free type variable. Therefore $\Gamma_{H+H'} \vdash z : T(F) \to [\mu_i/t_i]\mu$ which proves that $H'$ is well-typed. This also leads to $\Gamma_m; \Gamma_{H+H'} \vdash @^*zF : [\mu_i/t_i]\mu$.

**Case tfn =** To prove - given $H$ is well-typed, $H + H_1 + H_2$ is also well-typed and $\Gamma_m; \Gamma_H \vdash Let\ H_1 + H_2\ in\ e_2' : \mu_2$.

By the inductive assumption on the translation of $e_1$, $H + H_1'$ is well-typed and $\Gamma_m; \Gamma_H \vdash Let\ H_1'\ in\ e_1' : \mu_1$. Since the variables in $F_1$ are bound in $\Gamma_m$ (and not in $H_1'$), this implies that $\Gamma_m; \Gamma_H \vdash Let\ H_1'\ in\ \lambda^* F_1.e_1' : T(F_1) \to \mu_1$. Since $\lambda^* F_1.e_1'$ is closed with respect to monomorphic variables, we no longer require the environment $\Gamma_m$. Therefore $\Gamma_H \vdash Let\ H_1'\ in\ \lambda^* F_1.e_1' : T(F_1) \to \mu_1$. This implies $H_1$ is well-typed.

Again by induction, if $H + H_1$ is well-typed, then $H + H_1 + H_2$ is well-typed and $\Gamma_m; \Gamma_{H+H_1} \vdash Let\ H_2\ in\ e_2' : \mu_2$. This implies that $\Gamma_m; \Gamma_{H+H_1+H_2} \vdash e_2' : \mu_2$ which leads to the type preservation theorem. $\qquad\square$

## 7.2  Semantic soundness

The operational semantics is shown in Figure 9.

There are only three kinds of values - integers, function closures and type function closures.

$$(values)\ v ::= i\ |\ Clos\langle x^\mu, e, a\rangle\ |\ Clos^t\langle\overline{t_i}, e, a\rangle$$

**Definition 4 (Type of a Value).**

- $\Gamma \vdash i : int$
- if $\Gamma \vdash \lambda x : \mu.e : \mu \to \mu'$, then $\Gamma \vdash Clos\langle x^\mu, e, a\rangle : \mu \to \mu'$
- if $\Gamma \vdash \Lambda\overline{t_i}.e_v : \forall\overline{t_i}.\mu$, then $\Gamma \vdash Clos^t\langle\overline{t_i}, e_v, a\rangle : \forall\overline{t_i}.\mu$

**Notation 3** *The notation $a : \Gamma \vdash e \to v$ means that in a value environment $a$ respecting $\Gamma$, $e$ evaluates to $v$. If $a$ respects $\Gamma$, then $a(x) = v$ and $\Gamma(x) = \mu$ implies $\Gamma \vdash v : \mu$.*

**Notation 4** *The notation $a(x \mapsto v)$ means that in the environment $a$, $x$ has the value $v$. Whereas $a[x \mapsto v]$ means that the environment $a$ is augmented with the given binding.*

| | |
|---|---|
| (*const/var*) | $a \vdash i \to i \qquad a \vdash x \to a(x)$ |
| (*fn*) | $a \vdash \lambda x : \mu.e \to Clos\langle x^\mu, e, a\rangle$ |

$$(\textit{app}) \qquad \frac{a \vdash x_1 \to Clos\langle x^\mu, e, a'\rangle \quad a \vdash x_2 \to v' \quad a' + x \mapsto v' \vdash e \to v}{a \vdash @x_1 x_2 \to v}$$

$$(\textit{tfn}) \qquad \frac{}{a \vdash \Lambda \overline{t_i}.e_v \mapsto Clos^t\langle \overline{t_i}, e_v, a\rangle}$$

$$(\textit{let}) \qquad \frac{a \vdash e_1 \to v_1 \quad a + x \mapsto v_1 \vdash e_2 \to v}{a \vdash \text{let } x = e_1 \text{ in } e_2 \to v}$$

$$(\textit{tapp}) \qquad \frac{a \vdash x \mapsto Clos^t\langle \overline{t_i}, e_v, a'\rangle \quad a' \vdash e_v[\mu_i/t_i] \to v}{a \vdash x[\overline{\mu_i}] \mapsto v}$$

**Fig. 9.** Operational Semantics

We need to define the notion of equivalence of values before we can prove that two terms are semantically equivalent.

**Definition 5 (Equivalence of Values).**

- **Equivalence of Int** $i \approx i'$ iff
  - $\Gamma \vdash i : int$ and $\Gamma' \vdash i' : int$ and $i = i'$.
- **Equivalence of Closures** $Clos\langle x^\mu, e, a\rangle \approx Clos\langle x^\mu, e', a'\rangle$ iff
  - $\Gamma \vdash Clos\langle x^\mu, e, a\rangle : \mu \to \mu'$ and $\Gamma' \vdash Clos\langle x^\mu, e', a'\rangle : \mu \to \mu'$.
  - $\forall v_1, v_1'$ such that $\Gamma \vdash v_1 : \mu$ and $\Gamma' \vdash v_1' : \mu$ and $v_1 \approx v_1'$.
  - $a : \Gamma + x \mapsto v_1 \vdash e \to v$ and $a' : \Gamma' + x \mapsto v_1' \vdash e' \to v'$ and $v \approx v'$
- **Equivalence of Type Closures** $Clos^t\langle \overline{t_i}, e_v, a\rangle \approx Clos^t\langle \overline{t_i}, e_v', a'\rangle$ iff
  - $\Gamma \vdash Clos^t\langle \overline{t_i}, e_v, a\rangle : \forall t_i.\mu$ and $\Gamma' \vdash Clos^t\langle \overline{t_i}, e_v', a'\rangle : \forall t_i.\mu$ and
  - $a : \Gamma \vdash e_v[\mu_i/t_i] \to v$ and $a' : \Gamma' \vdash e_v'[\mu_i/t_i] \to v'$ and $v \approx v'$.

**Definition 6 (Equivalence of terms).**
*Suppose $a : \Gamma \vdash e \to v$ and $a' : \Gamma' \vdash e' \to v'$. Then the terms $e$ and $e'$ are semantically equivalent iff $v \approx v'$. We denote this as $a : \Gamma \vdash e \approx a' : \Gamma' \vdash e'$.*

Before we get into the proof, we want to define a couple of predicates on the header - $a_H$ and well-formedness of $H$. Intuitively $a_H$ represents the addition of new bindings in the environment as the header gets evaluated. Well-formedness of the header ensures that the lifting of polymorphic functions and type applications is semantically sound.

**Definition 7 (The header value environment – $a_H$).**

$a_H$ is equal to $a_{h_0} \ldots a_{h_n}$ and $a_{h_j}$ is –

- if $h_j ::= (x = \Lambda \overline{t_i}.e, \tau)$ then $a_{h_j} := x \mapsto Clos^t \langle \overline{t_i}, e, a_{h_0 \ldots h_{j-1}} \rangle$
- if $h_k ::= (z = x[\overline{\mu_i}], \tau)$ then $a_{h_k} := z \mapsto v$ where
  $h_j ::= x \mapsto Clos^t \langle \overline{t_i}, e, a_h \rangle$ for some $j < k$ and $a_h : \Gamma_h \vdash e[\mu_i/t_i] \to v$

**Definition 8 (Let H in e).**

Suppose $H = h_1 \ldots h_n$. Then **Let H in e** is shorthand for $let\ h_1 \ldots in\ let\ h_n\ in\ e$. If $h_j ::= (x = e, \tau)$, then $let\ h_j$ is shorthand for $let\ x = e$. From the operational semantics we get $a_m : \Gamma_m \vdash Let\ H\ in\ e \approx a_m : \Gamma_m; a_H : \Gamma_H \vdash e$.

**Definition 9 (H is well-formed w.r.t $a_m : \Gamma_m; a_p : \Gamma_p$).**

$H$ is well-formed w.r.t. $a_m : \Gamma_m; a_p : \Gamma_p$, if $h_0, \ldots, h_n$ are well-formed. A header entry $h_j$ is well-formed if all its predecessors $h_0, \ldots, h_{j-1}$ are well-formed and –

- If $h_j ::= (x = \Lambda \overline{t_i}.e, \tau)$, and $\Gamma_p(x) = (\forall \overline{t_i}.\mu, F)$ then
  $a_m : \Gamma_m; a_p : \Gamma_p \vdash x[\overline{\mu_i}] \approx a_m : \Gamma_m; a_{h_0 \ldots h_j} : \Gamma_{h_0 \ldots h_j} \vdash let\ z = x[\overline{\mu_i}]\ in\ @^* z F$
- If $h_j ::= (z = x[\overline{\mu_i}], \tau)$, then $h_j$ is well-formed.

$H$ is well-formed w.r.t. $a_m : \Gamma_m; a_p : \Gamma_p$ will be abbreviated in this section to $H$ is well-formed.

**Theorem 3 (Semantic Soundness).** *Suppose* $\Gamma_m; \Gamma_p; H \vdash e : \mu \Rightarrow e'; H_1; F$. *If* $a_m : \Gamma_m; a_p : \Gamma_p \vdash e \to v$ *and* $H$ *is well-formed w.r.t* $a_m : \Gamma_m; a_p : \Gamma_p$ *then* $a_m : \Gamma_m; a_H : \Gamma_H \vdash Let\ H_1\ in\ e' \to v'$ *and* $v \approx v'$.

**Proof.** The proof is by induction on the structure of $e$. We will consider the *tapp* and *tfn* cases here.

**Case tapp =** To prove – If $H$ is well-formed then
$a_m : \Gamma_m; a_p : \Gamma_p \vdash x[\overline{\mu_i}] \approx a_m : \Gamma_m; a_H : \Gamma_H \vdash Let\ H_1\ in\ @^* z F$

Substituting $Let\ H_1$ in the above equation leads to
$a_m : \Gamma_m; a_p : \Gamma_p \vdash x[\overline{\mu_i}] \approx a_m : \Gamma_m; a_H : \Gamma_H \vdash let\ z = x[\overline{\mu_i}]\ in\ @^* z F$

By the precondition on the translation rule $\Gamma_p(x) = (\forall \overline{t_i}.\mu, F)$ and there exists some $h_j \in H$ such that $h_j ::= (x = \Lambda \overline{t_i}.e, \tau)$. Since $H$ is well-formed, $h_j$ is well-formed as well and therefore by definition

$a_m : \Gamma_m; a_p : \Gamma_p \vdash x[\overline{\mu_i}] \approx a_m : \Gamma_m; a_{h_0 \ldots h_j} : \Gamma_{h_0 \ldots h_j} \vdash let\ z = x[\overline{\mu_i}]\ in\ @^* z F$

But since we assume unique variable bindings, no $h_k$ for $k > j$ rebinds $x$. This leads to –

$a_m : \Gamma_m; a_p : \Gamma_p \vdash x[\overline{\mu_i}] \approx a_m : \Gamma_m; a_H : \Gamma_H \vdash let\ z = x[\overline{\mu_i}]\ in\ @^* z F$

which is what we want to prove.

**Case tfn =** To prove - given $H$ is well-formed

$$a_m:\Gamma_m; a_p:\Gamma_p \vdash \text{let } x = \Lambda \overline{t_i}.e_1 \text{ in } e_2 \approx a_m:\Gamma_m; a_H:\Gamma_H \vdash Let\ H_1 + H_2\ in\ e_2'$$

which means we must prove that if

$$a_m:\Gamma_m; a_p[x \mapsto Clos^t\langle \overline{t_i}, e_1, a_m + a_p\rangle]:\Gamma_p[x \mapsto \langle \forall \overline{t_i}.\mu_1, F\rangle] \vdash e_2 \to v$$

and $\quad a_m:\Gamma_m; a_{H+H_1}:\Gamma_{H+H_1} \vdash Let\ H_2\ in\ e_2' \to v'$

then $\quad v \approx v'$ .

Assume for the time being that $H + H_1$ is well-formed. Then the inductive hypothesis on the translation of $e_2$ leads to the above condition.

We are therefore left with proving that $H + H_1$ is well-formed. By assumption, $H$ is well-formed, therefore we must prove that $H_1$ is well-formed. According to the definition we need to prove that

$$a_m':\Gamma_m'; a_p':\Gamma_p' \vdash x[\overline{\mu_i}] \approx a_m':\Gamma_m'; a_{H+H_1}:\Gamma_{H+H_1} \vdash let\ z = x[\overline{\mu_i}]\ in\ @^*zF$$

In the above equation $a_{H_1} := x \mapsto Clos^t\langle \overline{t_i}, Let\ H_1'\ in\ \lambda^* F.e_1', a_H\rangle$, therefore the operational semantics leads to $z \mapsto Clos\langle F^{T(F)}, e_1'[\mu_i/t_i], a_H + a_{H_1'[\mu_i/t_i]}\rangle$

This implies that we must prove –

$$a_m':\Gamma_m'; a_p':\Gamma_p' \vdash x[\overline{\mu_i}] \approx a_m'(F):\Gamma_m'; a_H:\Gamma_H + a_{H_1'[\mu_i/t_i]}:\Gamma_{H_1'[\mu_i/t_i]} \vdash e_1'[\mu_i/t_i]$$

In the source term $x \mapsto Clos^t\langle \overline{t_i}, e_1, a_m + a_p\rangle$ which implies that

$$a_m':\Gamma_m'; a_p':\Gamma_p' \vdash x[\overline{\mu_i}] \approx a_m:\Gamma_m; a_p:\Gamma_p \vdash e_1[\mu_i/t_i]$$

Therefore we need to prove that –

$$a_m:\Gamma_m; a_p:\Gamma_p \vdash e_1[\mu_i/t_i] \approx a_m'(F):\Gamma_m'; a_H:\Gamma_H + a_{H_1'[\mu_i/t_i]}:\Gamma_{H_1'[\mu_i/t_i]} \vdash e_1'[\mu_i/t_i] \tag{1}$$

But $a_m'(F) = a_m(F)$ since variables are bound only once. $F$ consists of all the free variables of $e_1'$ that are bound in $a_m'$ and therefore in $a_m$. Hence evaluating $e_1'$ in $a_m(F)$ is equivalent to evaluating it in $a_m$ . So proving Eqn 1 reduces to proving

$$a_m:\Gamma_m; a_p:\Gamma_p \vdash e_1[\mu_i/t_i] \approx a_m:\Gamma_m; a_H:\Gamma_H + a_{H_1'[\mu_i/t_i]}:\Gamma_{H_1'[\mu_i/t_i]} \vdash e_1'[\mu_i/t_i]$$

which follows from the inductive assumption on the translation of $e_1$.

$\square$

# Formalizing Resource Allocation in a Compiler

Peter Thiemann

Department of Computer Science
University of Nottingham
Nottingham NG7 2RD, England
pjt@cs.nott.ac.uk

**Abstract.** On the basis of an A-normal form intermediate language we formally specify resource allocation in a compiler for a strict functional language. Here, resource is to be understood in the most general sense: registers, temporaries, data representations, etc. All these should be (and can be, but have never been) specified formally. Our approach employs a non-standard annotated type system for the formalization. Although A-normal form turns out not to be the ideal vehicle for this investigation, we can prove some basic properties using the formalization.

## 1 Resource Allocation

Resource allocation in the back end of a compiler is often poorly specified. More often than not register allocation, administration of temporaries, and representation conversions are only specified procedurally [1, 6]. Code generators based on such algorithmic specifications can be hard to maintain or prove correct. Even the authors of such code generators are sometimes not aware of all the invariants that must be preserved.

Therefore, we investigate a declarative approach to resource allocation in the back end of a compiler. The approach is based on an annotated type system of *implementation types* that makes resource allocation and conversion explicit. The use of type conversion rules enables us to defer memory and register allocation until the context of use forces an allocation. For example, a constant initially leads to an annotation of the type of the variable holding the constant without generating any code. The annotation holds the "immediate value" of the constant. There are type conversion rules that change the annotation from "immediate value" to "value in register $k$" and generate a corresponding piece of code if the context of use requires the value of the variable in a register. Further conversion rules create or remove indirection. The indirection rules move a value to memory and change the annotation to "value in memory at address $R[k] + i$", where $R[k]$ is an address in register $k$ and $i$ is an offset. The indirection removing rules work the other way round. The indirection rules usually apply to the arguments of function calls or to values that are put into data structures. Spilling the contents of registers is another application of the last kind of conversion rules. Other rules may make direct use of immediate values, for example when generating instructions with immediate operands.

The resulting high degree of flexibility allows for arbitrary intra-module calling conventions. Since the calling convention is part of every function's type, each function "negotiates" its convention with all its call sites. Contrast this with the algorithm used in the SML/NJ compiler [2] where the first call encountered by the code generator determines the calling convention for a procedure. Obviously, this is one pragmatic way of negotiating, but surely not a declarative one (nor a democratic one). External functions can have arbitrary calling conventions, too, as long as their implementation type is known. If the external functions are unknown, any standard calling convention (including caller saves/callee saves registers) can be enforced just by imposing a suitable implementation type. The same holds for exported functions, where the only requirement is that their implementation type is also exported, for example, in an interface file.

Implementation types can also model some other worthwhile optimizations. For example, a *lightweight closure* does not contain all free variables of a function. It can only be used correctly if all variables that it is not closed over are available at all call sites. Implementation types can guarantee the correctness of a variant of lightweight closure conversion (cf. [20]). In our case, this conversion does not take place at the level of the source language, it rather happens while translating to actual machine code. The translation ensures that the values that are not put into the closure are available at all call sites.

## 1.1 Overview

In the next section, we define the source language, its operational semantics, the implementation type language, and the target language. The introduction and discussion of the typing rules is subject of Section 3. Section 4 documents some properties of the system. Finally, we discuss related work (Sec. 5) and draw conclusions (Sec. 6).

## 2 Language

We have chosen a simply typed lambda calculus in A-normal form, a typical intermediate language used in compilers, as the starting point of our investigation. Compiling with A-normal forms [5] is said to yield the principal benefits of compiling with continuations (explicit control flow, naming of intermediate results, making continuations explicit) without incurring the overhead of actually transforming the program to continuation-passing style and without complicating the types in the intermediate language.

### 2.1 Terms

We strengthen our requirements somewhat with respect to the usual definition of A-normal form. Figure 1 defines the terms of *restricted A-normal form*. There are computation terms $a$ and value terms $v$. Value terms are integer constants

$$a ::= \text{let } x = v \text{ in } a \mid \text{let } x = x \; @ \; x \text{ in } a \mid \text{let } x = x + x \text{ in } a \mid$$
$$x \mid x \; @ \; x$$
$$v ::= n \mid x \mid \lambda x.a$$

**Fig. 1.** Restricted A-normal form: terms

$n$, variables $x$, or lambda abstractions $\lambda x.a$. Computation terms either sequentialize computations let $x = \ldots$ in $a$ or they return a result, which can either be the value of a variable or it can take the form of a tail call to some function. Usually, A-normal form [5] only requires the arguments of applications and primitives to be values $v$. Restricted A-normal form requires variables $x$ in all these places. With this restriction, no resource allocation occurs "inside" of a term and resource conversions can be restricted to occur between some let and its body, without lack of generality.

## 2.2 Operational semantics

The semantics is defined by a fairly conventional CEK machine (see Fig. 2). A machine state is a triple $(a, \rho, \kappa)$ where

- $a \in$ Term is a term in A-normal form,
- $\rho \in$ Env $=$ Var$- \to$ Val is an environment, and
- $\kappa \in$ K is a continuation where K $=$ Void $+$ Env $\times$ Var $\times$ Term $\times$ K.

Here, partial functions are denoted by $- \to$, $\rho|_F$ restricts the domain of $\rho$ to $F$, Void is a one-element set, and $+$ denotes disjoint union of sets. A value $\in$ Val is either Num ($n$) or Fun ($\rho, \lambda y.a$) where $\rho \in$ Env and $\lambda y.a \in$ Term.

Inspection of the last rule reveals that the semantics enforces proper tail recursion, because the function call in tail position does not create a new continuation. The transitions that state additional constraints are undefined if the constraints are not met.

## 2.3 Types

Figure 3 defines implementation types, which form an extension of simple types. In an implementation type, each type constructor carries a location $l$. If the location is $\varepsilon$ ("not allocated") then the information corresponding to the type constructor is only present in the type. For example, (going beyond the fragment considered in this paper) if the product type constructor $\times$ carries the annotation $\varepsilon$ then only its components are allocated as prescribed by their locations; the pair itself is not physically represented.

If the location is imm $n$ ("immediate value $n$") then the value corresponding to the type carrying this location is know to be the integer $n$. The name comes from the immediate addressing mode that is present in many architectures, and

$$(\text{let } x = n \text{ in } a, \rho, \kappa) \quad \mapsto (a, \rho[x \mapsto \mathsf{Num}\ (n)], \kappa)$$
$$(\text{let } x = y \text{ in } a, \rho, \kappa) \quad \mapsto (a, \rho[x \mapsto \rho(y)], \kappa)$$
$$(\text{let } x = \lambda y.a' \text{ in } a, \rho, \kappa) \quad \mapsto (a, \rho[x \mapsto \mathsf{Fun}\ (\rho|_{FV(\lambda y.a')}, \lambda y.a')], \kappa)$$
$$(\text{let } x = w \ @\ z \text{ in } a, \rho, \kappa) \mapsto (a', \rho'[y \mapsto \rho(z)], \langle \rho|_{FV(\text{let } x = w \ @\ z \text{ in } a)}, x, a, \kappa\rangle)$$
$$\text{if } \rho(w) = \mathsf{Fun}\ (\rho', \lambda y.a')$$
$$(\text{let } x = w + z \text{ in } a, \rho, \kappa) \mapsto (a, \rho[x \mapsto \mathsf{Num}\ (m + n)], \kappa)$$
$$\text{if } \rho(w) = \mathsf{Num}\ (m) \text{ and } \rho(z) = \mathsf{Num}\ (n)$$
$$(z, \rho', \langle \rho, x, a, \kappa\rangle) \quad \mapsto (a, \rho[x \mapsto \rho'(z)], \kappa)$$
$$(w + z, \rho', \langle \rho, x, a, \kappa\rangle) \quad \mapsto (a, \rho[x \mapsto \mathsf{Num}\ (m + n)], \kappa)$$
$$\text{if } \rho(w) = \mathsf{Num}\ (m) \text{ and } \rho(z) = \mathsf{Num}\ (n)$$
$$(w \ @\ z, \rho, \kappa) \quad \mapsto (a', \rho'[y \mapsto \rho(z)], \kappa)$$
$$\text{if } \rho(w) = \mathsf{Fun}\ (\rho', \lambda y.a')$$

**Fig. 2.** Operational semantics

$$\tau ::= (\sigma; l)$$
$$\sigma ::= \mathsf{int} \mid \tau \xrightarrow{F, P, M, F', k} \mathsf{cont}\ l\ \tau \mid \mathsf{cont}\ F$$
$$l ::= \varepsilon \mid \mathsf{imm}\ n \mid A[\mathsf{reg}\ n]$$
$$A ::= [\ ] \mid \mathsf{mem}\langle i, A\rangle$$

**Fig. 3.** Syntax of implementation types

immediate values are expected to take part in generating instructions using immediate addressing.

If the location is reg $k$ then the value of that type is resident in register $k$. In addition, the register might hold an indirection, i.e., the address of a block of memory where the value is stored at some offset $i$: $\mathsf{mem}\langle i, \mathsf{reg}\ k\rangle$. In general, this indirection step may be repeated an arbitrary number of times, which is expressed by $\mathsf{mem}\langle i, A[\mathsf{reg}\ k]\rangle$.

There are two syntactic categories for types. $\tau$ ranges over implementation types, i.e., $\tau$ is a pair of a "stripped" implementation type $\sigma$ and the location of its top-level type constructor. For this paper, $\sigma$ ranges over int, the type of integers, and $\tau_2 \xrightarrow{F, P, M, F', k} \mathsf{cont}\ l\ \tau_1$, the type of functions that map objects of type $\tau_2$ to objects of type $\tau_1$ involving a continuation closure at location $l$, and cont $F$, the type of a continuation. The annotation $F, P, M, F', k$ on the function arrow is reminiscent to effect systems [7, 11]. It determines the latent resource usage of the function, which becomes effective when the function is called. It is explained in the next section 3 together with the judgements of implementation typing. The last alternative, $\sigma \equiv \mathsf{cont}\ F$ is the type of a continuation identifier. This type carries the location information of the current continuation, which would otherwise be lost (see Sec. 3).

## 2.4  Additional conventions

The architecture of a real processor places certain limits on the use of registers. For example, processors may have

- dedicated floating-point registers;
- special address registers ("pointers" to closures and tuples);
- special register(s) for continuations;
- special register(s) for condition codes.

In addition, the number of such registers is limited. These restrictions are modeled by a function Regs

$$\text{Regs} : \text{TypeConstructor} \rightarrow \mathcal{P}(\text{RegisterNames})$$

that maps a type constructor to a set of register names (which might be represented by integers). Occasionally, we apply Regs to a stripped implementation type $\sigma$ when it should be applied to the top-level type constructor of $\sigma$. We do not define Regs here since it depends on the particular architecture that we want to generate code for.

## 2.5  Target code

The target code of the translation is an assembly language for an abstract RISC processor. It has the following commands, expressed in a rather suggestive way with $R[k]$ denoting register reference and $M[a]$ denoting a memory reference. Here, $k, j \in$ RegisterNames, $a, i$ are memory addresses for data, $t$ is a symbolic label for a code address, and $n$ is an integer.

| | | |
|---|---|---|
| $t$ : | | label declaration |
| $R[k]$ | $:= n$ | load numeric constant |
| $R[k]$ | $:= t$ | load address constant |
| $R[k]$ | $:= R[i] + R[j]$ | arithmetic operation |
| $R[k]$ | $:= n + R[j]$ | arithmetic operation |
| $R[k]$ | $:= M[i + R[j]]$ | load indirect with offset |
| $M[i + R[j]]$ | $:= R[k]$ | store indirect with offset |
| $R[k]$ | $:= \text{Allocate}(n)$ | memory allocation |
| Goto $t$ | | unconditional jump |
| Goto $R[i]$ | | unconditional indirect jump |

The infix operator ";" performs concatenation of code sequences. We identify singleton code sequences with single instructions. For simplicity, we assume that all data objects have a standard representation of the same size (which might be a pointer).

The state of the abstract processor is a triple $\langle C, \overline{R}, \overline{M} \rangle$ where $C$ is a code sequence, $\overline{R}$ is the register bank (a mapping from a finite set of register names to data), and $\overline{M}$ is the memory (a mapping from an infinite set of addresses to data). The program store, which maps labels (code addresses) to code sequences, is left implicit. The instruction Allocate($n$) returns the address of a contiguous block of memory of size $n$. It guarantees that there is no overlap with previously allocated blocks, i.e., it never returns the same address twice. Some of our proofs exploit this guarantee by relying on the uniqueness of data addresses for identification. In practice there will be a garbage collector that maps the infinite address space into a finite one, which removes old unreachable addresses from the system.

## 3 Typing

The typing judgement is reminiscent to that of an effect system [7, 11]. The typing process determines a translation to abstract assembly code as defined above. Therefore, we use a translation judgement $\Gamma, P, F, S \vdash a : \tau; M, F', C$ to describe both together. In every judgement,

- $\Gamma$ is a type assumption, i.e., a list of pairs $x : \tau$. By convention, type assumptions are extended by appending a new pair on the right as in $\Gamma, x : \tau$. The same notation $\Gamma, x : \tau$ also serves to extract the rightmost pair from a type assumption.
- $P$ is a set of *preserved registers*. The translation guarantees that all registers $k \in P$ hold the same value after evaluation of $a$ as before, but during evaluation of $a$ these values may be spilled and register $k$ may hold different values temporarily. Members of $P$ correspond to callee-saves registers.
- $F, F'$ are sets of *fixed registers*. The translation guarantees that a register $k \in F$ is not used as long as there is some reference to it in the type assumption or in the context modeled by $F'$. Furthermore, it expects that the context of $a$ handles the registers mentioned in $F'$ in the same way. Members of $F$ must not be spilled. However, if there is no reference remaining to some $k \in F$ then $k$ may be removed from $F$.
  The main use of $F$ and $F'$ is lightweight closure conversion and avoiding the allocation of closures altogether. In both cases, the type assumption contains a variable $w$ of type $\tau_2 \xrightarrow{F_1, P_1, M_1, F_1', k_1} \text{cont } l \ \tau_1$ where $F_1$ describes the components of the closure that have not been allocated (i.e., they reside in registers drawn from $F_1$). Consequently, $F_1 \subseteq F$ must hold at a call site $a \equiv \text{let } x = w @ z \text{ in } a'$ so that all registers in $F_1$ contain the correct values.
- $S$ is a list of reloads of the form $\langle k, i_1 \ldots i_p \rangle \ldots$ where register $k$ points to a spill area and $i_1$ through $i_p$ are the spilled registers. The notation $\varepsilon$ is used for the empty list of reloads, i.e., when all values are either implicit or reside in registers: $S = \varepsilon$ means that nothing is currently spilled.
- $M$ is a set of registers that are possibly modified while evaluating $a$.
- $C$ is code of the target machine (see Sec. 2.5).

Before we start discussing the typing rules proper, we need to define the set of registers referenced from a type assumption.

**Definition 1.** *The reference set of a location, type, or type assumption is the set of registers that the location, type, or type assumption refers to.*

- Refer $\varepsilon = \emptyset$, Refer (imm $n$) = $\emptyset$, Refer ($A$[reg $n$]) = $\{n\}$;
- Refer (int; $l$) = Refer $l$;
- Refer $(\tau_2 \xrightarrow{F,P,M,F',k}$ cont $l'$ $\tau_1$; $l$) = Refer $l \cup F$;
- Refer (cont $F$ ; $l$) = Refer $l \cup F$;
- Refer $\Gamma = \bigcup_{x:\tau \in \Gamma}$ Refer $\tau$.

## 3.1 Typing rules

The typing rules are organized into context rules that manipulate type assumptions, value rules that provide typings for variables and constants, representation conversion rules, computation rules that deal with let expressions, and return rules that describe returning values from function invocations. Of these rules, the context rules and the conversion rules are nondeterministic, the remaining rules are tied to specific syntactic constructs, i.e., syntax-directed.

**Context rules** Each use of a variable consumes an element of the type assumption. This convention saves us from spilling dead variables since a "good" derivation only duplicates variables that are still live. Hence there is a rule to duplicate assumptions $x : \tau$.

$$(dup) \frac{(\Gamma, x : \tau, x : \tau), P, F, S \vdash a : \tau', M, F', C}{(\Gamma, x : \tau), P, F, S \vdash a : \tau', M, F', C}$$

There is a dual weakening rule that drops a variable assumption. The set of fixed registers is updated accordingly. Dropping of variable assumptions starts on the left side of a type assumption to avoid problems with shadowed assumptions.

$$(weak) \frac{\Gamma, P, F \cap \text{Refer } \Gamma, S \vdash a : \tau', M, F', C}{(x : \tau, \Gamma), P, F, S \vdash a : \tau', M, F', C}$$

Finally, there is a rule to organize access to the type assumptions. It exchanges adjacent elements of the type assumption *provided that they bind different variables.*

$$(exch) \frac{\Gamma, y : \tau_2, x : \tau_1, \Gamma', P, F, S \vdash a : \tau', M, F', C}{\Gamma, x : \tau_1, y : \tau_2, \Gamma', P, F, S \vdash a : \tau', M, F', C} \quad x \not\equiv y$$

The explicit presence of these rules is reminiscent of linear type systems [8, 23].

**Value rules** And here is a simple rule that consumes a variable assumption for $y : \tau$ at the price of producing one for $x : \tau$.

$$(let\text{-}var) \frac{(\Gamma, x : \tau), P, F, S \vdash a : \tau'; M, F', C}{(\Gamma, y : \tau), P, F, S \vdash \text{let } x = y \text{ in } a : \tau'; M, F', C}$$

Application of the *(let-var)* rule does not imply a change in the actual location of the value. The variable $x$ becomes an alias for $y$ in the expression $a$. The rule can be eliminated in favor of a reduction rule for expressions in restricted A-normal form: let $x = y$ in $a \mapsto a[x := y]$ (capture-avoiding substitution of $y$ for $x$ in $a$). There is no penalty for this reduction, because the system allows the conversion of each occurrence of a variable individually. So former occurrences of $x$ can still be treated differently than former occurrences of $y$.

A constant starts its life as an immediate value which is only present in the implementation type. The typing derivation propagates this type and value to the point where it either selects an instruction with an immediate operand or where the context forces allocation into a register.

$$(\textit{let-const}) \quad \frac{(\Gamma, x : (\text{int}; \text{imm } n)), P, F, S \vdash a : \tau'; M, F', C}{\Gamma, P, F, S \vdash \text{let } x = n \text{ in } a : \tau'; M, F', C}$$

**Conversion rules** Some primitives expect their arguments allocated in registers. As we have seen, values are usually not born into registers. So, how do they get there? The solution lies in conversion rules that transform the type assumption. These rules generate code and allocate registers.

A register $k$ is deemed available if it is neither referred to by $\Gamma$ nor mentioned in $P \cup F$: $k \notin \text{Refer } \Gamma \cup P \cup F$.

Immediate integer values generate a simple load instruction. In this case, the register selected must be suitable for an integer ($k \in \text{RegisterNames}\text{int}$) besides being available for allocation.

$$(\textit{conv-imm}) \quad \frac{(\Gamma, x : (\text{int}; \text{reg } k)), P, F, S \vdash a : \tau; M, F', C}{(\Gamma, x : (\text{int}; \text{imm } n)), P, F, S \vdash a : \tau; M \cup \{k\}, F', C'}$$

$$\text{where } k \in \text{Regs}(\text{int}) \setminus (\text{Refer } \Gamma \cup P \cup F)$$
$$C' = (R[k] := n; C)$$

The resolution of an indirection $\text{mem}\langle i, \text{reg } n \rangle$ generates a memory load with index register $R[n]$ and offset $i$.

$$(\textit{conv-mem}) \quad \frac{(\Gamma, x : (\sigma; A[\text{reg } k])), P, F, S \vdash a : \tau; M, F', C}{(\Gamma, x : (\sigma; A[\text{mem}\langle i, \text{reg } n \rangle])), P, F, S \vdash a : \tau; M \cup \{k\}, F', C'}$$

$$\text{where } k \in \text{Regs}(\sigma) \setminus (\text{Refer } \Gamma \cup P \cup F)$$
$$C' = (R[k] := M[R[n] + i]; C)$$

There is also an operation that generates indirections by spilling a group of registers to memory. The register $k$ must be suitable to hold the standard representation of a tuple (a pointer to a contiguous area of memory) as indicated by $k \in \text{RegisterNames}\times$. The *(spill)* rule is not applicable if there is no such register $k$. The rule chooses nondeterministically a set $X$ of registers to spill which does not interfere with the fixed registers $F$. If preserved registers are spilled the corresponding reloads are scheduled in the $S$ component.

$$(spill) \quad \frac{\tilde{\Gamma},(P \setminus X) \cup \{k\}, F, \langle k, i_1 \ldots i_p \rangle S \vdash a : \tau; M, F', C}{\Gamma, P, F, S \vdash a : \tau; (M \setminus X) \cup \{k\}, F', C'}$$

where $\tilde{\Gamma} = \Gamma[\text{reg } i_j := \text{mem}\langle j, \text{reg } k \rangle \mid 1 \leq j \leq n]$
$\quad X = \{i_1, \ldots i_n\}$
$\quad X \cap F = \emptyset$
$\quad X \cap P = \{i_1, \ldots, i_p\}, 0 \leq p \leq n$
$\quad k \in \text{Regs}(\times) \setminus (\text{Refer } \Gamma \cup P \cup F)$
$\quad C' = (R[k] := \text{Allocate}(|X|);$
$\qquad M[R[k] + 0] := R[i_1]; \ldots; M[R[k] + n - 1] := R[i_n]; C)$

The notation $\Gamma[\text{reg } i_j := \text{mem}\langle j, \text{reg } k \rangle \mid 1 \leq j \leq n]$ denotes the textual replacement of all occurrences of reg $i_j$ in implementation types mentioned in $\Gamma$ by $\text{mem}\langle j, \text{reg } k \rangle$ for $1 \leq j \leq n$.

The corresponding inverse rule *(reload)* pops one reload entry from $S$.

$$(reload) \quad \frac{\Gamma, (P \setminus \{k\}) \cup \{i_1, \ldots, i_p\}, F, S \vdash a : \tau; M, F', C}{\tilde{\Gamma}, P, F, \langle k, i_1 \ldots i_p \rangle S \vdash a : \tau; M, F', C'}$$

where $\tilde{\Gamma} = \Gamma[\text{reg } i_j := \text{mem}\langle j, \text{reg } k \rangle \mid 1 \leq j \leq p]$
$\quad C' = (R[i_1] := M[R[k] + 0]; \ldots; R[i_p] := M[R[k] + p - 1]; C)$

**Computation rules** The first computation rule deals with lambda abstraction. The type assumptions are divided in those for the free variables of the function $\Gamma$ and those for the continuation $\Delta$. The function's body $a_1$ is processed with $\tilde{\Gamma}$ where some free variables are relocated into the closure, a set $P'$ of preserved registers as determined by the call sites of the function, and a set of fixed variables $F'$ that contains those fixed registers that are referred to from the assumption $\Gamma$. Also, the register $m$ on the function arrow must match the register which is assumed to hold the closure while translating the body of the abstraction. It is not necessary that $m = k$, where $k$ is the register where the closure is allocated. Finally, the let's body $a_2$ is processed with $\Delta$.

$$(let\text{-}abs) \quad \frac{(\tilde{\Gamma}, x_2 : \tau_2, c : (\text{cont } F'' ; l)), P', F', \varepsilon \vdash a_1 : \tau_1; M', F'', C_1}{(\Delta, x_1 : (\tau_2 \xrightarrow{F',P',M',F'',m} \text{cont } l \; \tau_1; \text{reg } k)), P, F, S \vdash a_2 : \tau_0; M, F', C_2}{(\Gamma, \Delta), P, F, S \vdash \text{let } x_1 = \lambda x_2.a_1 \text{ in } a_2 : \tau_0; M \cup \{k\}, F', C'}$$

where $F \cap \text{Refer } \Gamma \subseteq F' \subseteq \text{Refer } \Gamma$
$\quad k \in \text{Regs}(\rightarrow) \setminus (\text{Refer }(\Gamma, \Delta) \cup P \cup F)$
$\quad m \in \text{Regs}(\rightarrow) \setminus (\text{Refer } \Gamma \cup P' \cup F')$
$\quad \tilde{\Gamma} = \Gamma[\text{reg } i_j := \text{mem}\langle j, \text{reg } m \rangle \mid 1 \leq j \leq n]$
$\quad \{i_j\} = \text{Refer } \Gamma \setminus F', |\{i_j\}| = n$
$\quad C' = (\text{Goto } t_2; t_1 : C_1; t_2 : R[k] = \text{Allocate}(n + 1);$
$\qquad M[R[k]] := t_1; M[R[k] + 1] := R[i_1]; \ldots; M[R[k] + n] := R[i_n]; C_2)$

All registers that do not become fixed in the function must be evacuated into the closure for the function which is composed in $R[k]$. Since the continuation (which is located in $l$) can be handled like any other value, we invent a continuation identifier $c$ and bind it to the continuation. This is a drawback of A-normal form in comparison to continuation-passing style where continuation identifiers are explicit.

Next, we consider a typical primitive operation.

$$\text{(let-add)} \quad \frac{(\Gamma, x_1 : (\text{int}; \text{reg } k)), P, F, S \vdash a : \tau, M, F', C}{(\Gamma, x_2 : (\text{int}; \text{reg } i), x_3 : (\text{int}; \text{reg } j)), P, F, S \vdash a' : \tau, M \cup \{k\}, F', C'}$$

where $k \in \text{Regs}(\text{int}) \setminus (\text{Refer } \Gamma \cup P \cup F)$
$C' = (R[k] := R[i] + R[j]; C)$
$a' = \text{let } x_1 = x_2 + x_3 \text{ in } a$

In addition, we could include a rule for constant propagation (in the case where the arguments are imm $n_1$ and imm $n_2$) and also rules to exploit immediate addressing modes if the processor provides for these.

Next, we consider the application of a function.

$$\text{(let-app)} \quad \frac{(\Gamma, x_1 : \tau_1), P, F'', S \vdash a : \tau, M, F', C}{\Gamma', P, F, S \vdash a' : \tau, M \cup M' \cup \{j, k\}, F', C'}$$

where $P \cup \{i_1, \ldots, i_p\} \subseteq P', F' \subseteq F$
$\{i_1, \ldots, i_n\} = \text{Refer } \Gamma \setminus F', |\{i_j\}| = n$
$\{j, k\} \subseteq \text{Regs}(\to) \setminus (\text{Refer } \Gamma, x_1 : \tau_1 \cup P \cup F), j \neq k$
$\Gamma' = (\Gamma, x_2 : (\tau_2 \xrightarrow{F', P', M', F'', i} \text{cont } (\text{reg } j) \ \tau_1; \text{reg } i), x_3 : \tau_2)$
$a' = \text{let } x_1 = x_2 @ x_3 \text{ in } a$
$C' = (R[j] := \text{Allocate}(n - p + 1); M[R[j] + 0] := t;$
  $M[R[j] + 1] := R[i_{p+1}]; \ldots; M[R[j] + n - p] := R[i_n];$
  $R[k] := M[R[i] + 0]; \text{Goto } R[k];$
  $t : R[i_{p+1}] := M[R[j] + 1]; \ldots; R[i_n] := M[R[j] + n - p]; C)$

The memory allocation in this rule saves values that are accessed by the continuation $a$. The preservation of the remaining registers is left to the callee by placing them $\{i_1, \ldots, i_p\}$ in the set of preserved registers $P'$. $R[j]$ points to the continuation closure. The sole purpose of the cont $(\text{reg } j)$ $\tau_1$ construction lies in the transmission of the location of the continuation. The set of currently preserved registers must be a subset of the set of registers preserved by the function. Conversely, the set of currently fixed registers must contain the set of fixed registers demanded by the function. The continuation has to fix registers as indicated by the annotation $F''$ of the function type.

The $i$ on the function arrow indicates the register where the function body expects its closure. It must coincide with the register in which the closure actually is.

**Return rules** Finally, we need to consider rules that pass a value to the continuation. The most simple rule just returns the value of a variable. Due to the conversion rules, we can rely on $x : \tau$ already being placed in the location where the continuation expects it. All return rules expect that their reload list is empty.

$$(ret\text{-}var) \quad \frac{k \in \mathsf{Regs}(\to) \setminus (\mathsf{Refer}\ x : \tau, c : (\mathsf{cont}\ F\ ; \mathsf{reg}\ i) \cup P \cup F)}{(x : \tau, c : (\mathsf{cont}\ F\ ; \mathsf{reg}\ i)), P, F, \varepsilon \vdash x : \tau, \{k\}, F, C}$$

$$\text{where}\quad C = (R[k] := M[R[i] + 0]; \mathsf{Goto}\ R[k])$$

In this rule, the current continuation identifier $c$ indicates that register $i$ contains the continuation closure. As with any closure, its zero-th component contains the code address.

The final rule specifies a tail call to another function.

$$(ret\text{-}app) \quad \frac{P \subseteq P', F' \subseteq F, k \in \mathsf{Regs}(\to) \setminus (\{j, i\} \cup \mathsf{Refer}\ \tau_2 \cup P \cup F)}{\Gamma, P, F, \varepsilon \vdash x_1 @ x_2 : \tau_1, \{k\}, F, (R[k] := M[R[i] + 0]; \mathsf{Goto}\ R[k])}$$

$$\text{where}\quad \Gamma = (x_1 : (\tau_2 \xrightarrow{F', P', M', F''} \mathsf{cont}\ (\mathsf{reg}\ j)\ \tau_1; \mathsf{reg}\ i),$$
$$x_2 : \tau_2, c : (\mathsf{cont}\ F\ ; (\mathsf{reg}\ j)))$$

There is neither a return term nor a return rule for addition, because the allocation properties of let $x = y + z$ in $x$ are identical to those of $y + z$, if the latter was a legal return term.

# 4 Properties

In this section, we formalize some of the intuitive notions introduced in the preceding sections. First, we show that preserved registers really deserve their name.

**Theorem 1.** *Suppose* $\Gamma, P, F, S \vdash a : \tau; M, F_1, C$ *and the processor is in state* $\langle C, \overline{R}, \overline{M} \rangle$. *For each register* $r \in P$:

*Suppose* $c : (\mathsf{cont}\ F''\ ; \mathsf{reg}\ w) \in \Gamma$, $y = R[r]$, $c = R[w]$, *and* $\langle C, \overline{R}, \overline{M} \rangle \xmapsto{*} \langle C', \overline{R}', \overline{M}' \rangle$. *If* $R'[w] = c$ *and* $C'$ *is a suffix of* $C$ *such that* $\Gamma', P', F', S' \vdash a' : \tau; M', F_1', C'$ *and in the derivation steps between* $a$ *and* $a'$ *the reload component always has* $S$ *as a suffix then* $R'[r] = y$.

The reference to the continuation $c$ ensures that both machine states belong to the same procedure activation, by the uniqueness of addresses returned by $\mathsf{Allocate}(n)$. It provides the only link between the two machine states. If we dropped this requirement we would end up comparing machine states from different invocations of the same function and we could not prove anything. The condition on the reload component means that arbitrary spills are allowed between $p$ and $p'$, but reloads are restricted not to remove the reload record that was top-level at $p$. In other words, $S$ serves as a low-water mark. Our main interest will be in the case where $S = S' = \varepsilon$, $a$ is the body of a function, and $a'$ is a return term. In this case, the theorem says that registers mentioned in $P$ are preserved across function calls.

This theorem can be proved by induction on the number of control transfers in $\langle C, \overline{R}, \overline{M} \rangle \overset{*}{\hookrightarrow} \langle C', \overline{R}', \overline{M}' \rangle$ and then by induction on the derivation.

Next, we want to formalize a property for $F$. A value stored in $f \in F$ will remain there unchanged as long as the variable binding that $f$ belongs to is in effect or reachable through closures or the continuation.

As a first step, we define a correspondence between an environment $\Gamma$ and a state of the CEK machine (cf. Sec. 2.2).

**Definition 2.** $\Gamma \vdash (a, \rho, \kappa)$ *if*

1. *there exist* $P, F, S, M, F_1, C$ *such that* $\Gamma, P, F, S \vdash a : \tau; M, F_1, C;$
2. $x : \tau$ *in* $\Gamma$ *implies* $x \in \text{dom}(\rho)$ *and* $\rho(x) \in \text{TSem } \tau;$
3. *if* $c :$ (cont $F''$ ; reg $w$) *in* $\Gamma$ *then there are* $\rho$, $x$, *and* $a$ *such that* $\kappa = \langle \rho, x, a, \kappa' \rangle$. *Otherwise* $\kappa = \langle \rangle$.

Unfortunately the connection between $c$ and $\kappa$ is not very deep. We cannot properly relate $c$ to $\kappa$ since the "type" of $c$ does not refer to an environment. In fact, $c$ and its type cannot refer to a specific environment $\Gamma'$ because $a$ may be called from several places with different environments. Therefore, the type of the return environment of the continuation must be polymorphic. The function TSem $\tau$ maps an implementation type to a subset of Val.

$$\text{TSem } (\text{int}; l) = \{\text{Num } (n) \mid n \text{ is an integer}\}$$
$$\text{TSem } (\tau_2 \xrightarrow{F, P, M, F'} \text{cont } l' \ \tau_1; l) =$$
$$\{\text{Fun } (\rho', \lambda y.a) \mid$$
$$\forall z \in \text{TSem } \tau_2.$$
$$(a, \rho'[y \mapsto z], \langle \rangle) \overset{*}{\hookrightarrow} (x, \rho'', \langle \rangle) \text{ such that } \rho''(x) \in \text{TSem } \tau_1 \text{ or}$$
$$(a, \rho'[y \mapsto z], \langle \rangle) \overset{*}{\hookrightarrow} (x + w, \rho'', \langle \rangle) \text{ and } \tau_1 = (\text{int}; l')\}$$

However, to formalize reachability through closures and continuations and link this concept with the environment, we need a stronger notion than $\Gamma \vdash (a, \rho, \kappa)$.

What we can actually prove by inspection of the rules is a much weaker theorem.

**Theorem 2.** *Suppose* $\Gamma, P, F, S \vdash a : \tau; M, F_1, C$ *and the processor is in state* $\langle C, \overline{R}, \overline{M} \rangle$. *For each* $r \in F$:

*Suppose* $y = R[r]$ *and* $\langle C, \overline{R}, \overline{M} \rangle \overset{*}{\hookrightarrow} \langle C', \overline{R}', \overline{M}' \rangle$ *such that* $\Gamma', P', F', S' \vdash a' : \tau; M', F_1', C'$ *and there is no intermediate state with a corresponding derivation step. If furthermore* $r \in F'$ *then* $R'[r] = y$.

Finally, we establish a formal correspondence between steps of the CEK machine and steps of the translated machine program. To this end, we need a notion of compatibility between a CEK state and a machine state, $\Gamma \vdash (a, \rho, \kappa) \cong \langle C, \overline{R}, \overline{M} \rangle$.

**Definition 3.** *Suppose* $\Gamma, P, F, S \vdash a : \tau; M, F_1, C$.
$\Gamma \vdash (a, \rho, \kappa) \cong (C, \overline{R}, \overline{M})$ *if for all* $x : \tau$ *in* $\Gamma$:

- *if* $\tau = (\text{int}; \text{imm } n)$ *then* $\rho(x) = \text{Num } (n)$ *(the value is not represented in the machine state);*
- *if* $\tau = (\text{int}; \text{reg } r)$ *then there exists an integer* $n$ *s.t.* $\rho(x) = \text{Num } (n)$ *and* $R[r] = n$;
- *if* $\tau = (\text{int}; \text{mem}\langle j, \text{reg } r\rangle)$ *then there exists* $n$ *s.t.* $\rho(x) = \text{Num } (n)$ *and* $M[R[r] + j] = n$;
- *if* $\tau = (\text{int}; \text{mem}\langle j_k, \ldots \text{mem}\langle j_0, \text{reg } r\rangle\rangle)$ *then there exist* $n, i_0, \ldots, i_k$ *s.t.* $\rho(x) = \text{Num } (n)$ *and* $i_k = n$, $i_\nu = M[i_{\nu-1} + j_\nu]$ *for* $1 \leq \nu \leq k$, *and* $i_0 = R[r]$;
- *if* $\tau = (\tau_2 \xrightarrow{F', P', M', F_1'} \text{cont } (\text{reg } s) \ \tau_1; \text{reg } r)$ *then there exists* $\rho', y, a'$ *s.t.* $\rho(x) = \text{Fun } (\rho', \lambda y.a')$ *and for all* $z \in \text{TSem } \tau_2$ $(a', \rho'[y \mapsto z], \langle\rangle) \xrightarrow{*} (x', \rho'', \langle\rangle)$ *where* $\rho''(x') \in \text{TSem } \tau_1$, $M[R[r]]$ *holds the address of* $C'$ *such that*

$$(\Gamma', y : \tau_2, c : (\text{cont } F_2 \ ; \text{reg } s)), P', F', S' \vdash a' : \tau_1; M', F_1', C'$$

  *which starts with*

$$\Gamma'', P'', F'', S'' \vdash x' : \tau_1; M', F_1', C''$$

  *and for each CEK state* $(C', \overline{R'}, \overline{M'}) \xrightarrow{*} (C'', \overline{R''}, \overline{M''})$ *where* $R'[s] = R''[s]$ *we have that* $(\Gamma', y : \tau_2, c : (\text{cont } F_2 \ ; l)) \vdash (a', \rho'[y \mapsto z], \kappa') \cong (C', \overline{R'}, \overline{M'})$ *and* $\Gamma'' \vdash (x', \rho'', \kappa') \cong (C'', \overline{R''}, \overline{M''})$;
- *if* $\tau = (\text{cont } F_2 \ ; \text{reg } r)$ *then* $\kappa = \langle \rho', x', a', \kappa'\rangle$ *such that* $\Gamma', P', F', S' \vdash a' : \tau'; M', F_1', C'$ *and* $M[R[r]]$ *holds the address of* $C'$.

**Theorem 3.** *Suppose* $\Gamma, P, F, S \vdash a : \tau; M, F_1, C$.
*If* $\Gamma \vdash (a, \rho, \kappa) \cong (C, \overline{R}, \overline{M})$ *and* $(a, \rho, \kappa) \xrightarrow{*} (a', \rho', \kappa')$ *where* $\kappa$ *is a suffix of* $\kappa'$ *then* $(C, \overline{R}, \overline{M}) \xrightarrow{*} (C', \overline{R'}, \overline{M'})$ *and there exist* $\Gamma', P', F', S', \tau', M',$ *and* $F_1'$ *such that* $\Gamma', P', F', S' \vdash a' : \tau', M', F_1', C'$ *and* $\Gamma' \vdash (a', \rho', \kappa') \cong (C', \overline{R'}, \overline{M'})$.

## 5 Related Work

Compiling with continuations has already a long history. Steele's Rabbit compiler [21] has pioneered compilation by first transforming source programs to continuation-passing style and then transforming it until the assembly code can be read of directly. Also the Orbit compiler [13] and other successful systems [2, 3, 12] follow this strategy.

Recently, there has been some interest in approaches which do not quite transform the programs to continuation-passing style. The resulting intermediate language has been called nqCPS[1], A-normal form [5], monadic normal form [9], etc. These languages are still direct style languages, but have the following special features

---

[1] This term has been coined by Peter Lee [14] but it has never appeared in a published paper.

1. the evaluation order (and hence the control flow) is made explicit;
2. all intermediate results are named;
3. the structure of an expression makes the places obvious where serious computations are performed (i.e., where a continuation is required in the implementation).

Another related line of work is boxing analysis (e.g., [10, 18, 19, 22]). Here the idea is to try to avoid using the inefficient boxed representation of values in polymorphic languages. We believe that our system is powerful enough so that (an polymorphic extension of) it can also express the necessary properties.

Representation analysis [4] which is used in conjunction with region inference has one phase (their section 5 "Unboxed Values") whose concerns overlap with the goals of our system. Otherwise, their system is concerned with finding the number of times a value is put into a region, the storage mode of a value which determines whether a previous version may be overwritten, or the physical size of a region.

Typed assembly language [15] is an approach to propagate polymorphic type information throughout all phases of compilation. This work defines a fully typed translation from the source language (a subset of core ML) down to assembly language in four stages: CPS conversion, closure conversion, allocation, and code generation. As it is documented, the allocation phase takes the conventional fully boxed approach to allocating closures and tuples. It remains to investigate whether the allocation phase operates on the right level of abstraction to take the decisions that we are interested in controlling with our approach.

# 6 Conclusion

We have investigated an approach to specify decisions taken in the code generation phase of a compiler using a non-standard type system. The system builds on simple typing and uses a restricted version of A-normal form as its source language. We have defined a translation that maps the source language into abstract assembly language and have verified some properties of the translation. One goal of the approach is the verification and specification of code generators by adding constraints to our system that make the typing judgements deterministic.

In the course of the work on this system, we have learned a number of lessons on intermediate languages for compilers that want to apply advanced optimization techniques (like unboxing, lightweight closure conversion, and so on):

It is essential to start from an intermediate language that clearly distinguishes serious computations (that need a continuation) from trivial ones (that yield values directly). Otherwise, rules like the *(spill)* rule could not be applied immediately before generating the machine code for the actual function call.

It is also essential that A-normal form sequentializes the computation. For unrestricted direct-style expressions the control flow is sufficiently different from the propagation of information in typing judgements to make such a formulation awkward, at best. For example, it would be necessary to thread the typing assumptions through the derivation according to the evaluation order.

Also, in an unrestricted direct-style term it is sometimes necessary to perform a resource operation (for example, spilling or representation conversion) on return from the evaluation of an expression. This leads to a duplication of typing rules, one set determining the operations on control transfer into the expression and another set for the operations on return from the expression. In A-normal form, returning from one expression is always entering the next expression, so there is no restriction in having only the first set of these rules.

On the negative side, we found that A-normal form does not supply sufficient information when it comes to naming continuations. In contrast to continuation-passing style, our translation has to invent continuation variables in order to make the continuation visible to the resource allocation machinery. It would be interesting to investigate a similar system of implementation types for an intermediate language in continuation-passing style and to establish a formal connection between the two.

Another point in favor of continuation-passing style is the allocation of continuation closures. Presently this allocation clutters the rule for function application *(let-app)*. A system based on continuation-passing style might be able to decompose the different tasks present in *(let-app)* into several rules.

Finally, in places the rules are rather unwieldy so that it is debatable whether the intermediate language that we have chosen is the right level of abstraction to take the decisions that we are interested in. Imposing the system, for example, on the allocation phase of a system like that of Morrisett et al. [15] might in the end lead to a simpler system and one where the interesting properties can be proved more easily.

Beyond the work reported in this paper, we have already extended the framework to conditionals, and to sum and product types. The current formulation does not allow for unboxed function closures. This drawback can be addressed at the price of a plethora of additional rules. Future work will address the incorporation of polymorphic types and investigate the possibilities of integrating our work with typed assembly language.

**Acknowledgment** Many thanks to the reviewers. Their detailed comments helped to clean up the presentation substantially.

# References

1. Alfred V. Aho, Ravi Sethi, and Jeffrey D. Ullman. *Compilers Principles, Techniques, and Tools*. Addison-Wesley, 1986.
2. Andrew W. Appel. *Compiling with Continuations*. Cambridge University Press, 1992.
3. Andrew W. Appel and Trevor Jim. Continuation-passing, closure-passing style. In POPL1989 [16], pages 293–302.
4. Lars Birkedal, Mads Tofte, and Magnus Vejlstrup. From region inference to von Neumann machines via region representation inference. In *Proc. 23rd Annual ACM Symposium on Principles of Programming Languages*, pages 171–183, St. Petersburg, Fla., January 1996. ACM Press.

5. Cormac Flanagan, Amr Sabry, Bruce F. Duba, and Matthias Felleisen. The essence of compiling with continuations. In *Proc. of the ACM SIGPLAN '93 Conference on Programming Language Design and Implementation*, pages 237–247, Albuquerque, New Mexico, June 1993.

6. Christopher W. Fraser and David R. Hanson. *A Retargetable C Compiler: Design and Implementation*. Benjamin/Cummings, 1995.

7. David K. Gifford and John M. Lucassen. Integrating functional and imperative programming. In *Proceedings of the 1986 ACM conference on Lisp and Functional Programming*, pages 28–38, 1986.

8. Jean-Yves Girard. Linear logic. *Theoretical Computer Science*, 50:1–102, 1987.

9. John Hatcliff and Olivier Danvy. A generic account of continuation-passing styles. In POPL1994 [17], pages 458–471.

10. Fritz Henglein and Jesper Jørgensen. Formally optimal boxing. In POPL1994 [17], pages 213–226.

11. Pierre Jouvelot and David K. Gifford. Algebraic reconstruction of types and effects. In *Proc. 18th Annual ACM Symposium on Principles of Programming Languages*, pages 303–310, Orlando, Florida, January 1991. ACM Press.

12. Richard Kelsey and Paul Hudak. Realistic compilation by program transformation. In POPL1989 [16], pages 281–292.

13. D. Kranz, R. Kelsey, J. Rees, P. Hudak, J. Philbin, and N. Adams. ORBIT: An optimizing compiler for Scheme. *SIGPLAN Notices*, 21(7):219–233, July 1986. Proc. Sigplan '86 Symp. on Compiler Construction.

14. Peter Lee. The origin of nqCPS. Email message, March 1998.

15. Greg Morrisett, David Walker, Karl Crary, and Neal Glew. From system F to typed assembly language. In Luca Cardelli, editor, *Proc. 25th Annual ACM Symposium on Principles of Programming Languages*, San Diego, CA, USA, January 1998. ACM Press.

16. *16th Annual ACM Symposium on Principles of Programming Languages*, Austin, Texas, January 1989. ACM Press.

17. *Proc. 21st Annual ACM Symposium on Principles of Programming Languages*, Portland, OG, January 1994. ACM Press.

18. Zhong Shao. Flexible representation analysis. In Mads Tofte, editor, *Proc. International Conference on Functional Programming 1997*, pages 85–98, Amsterdam, The Netherlands, June 1997. ACM Press, New York.

19. Zhong Shao and Andrew W. Appel. A type-based compiler for Standard ML. In *Proc. of the ACM SIGPLAN '95 Conference on Programming Language Design and Implementation*, La Jolla, CA, USA, June 1995. ACM Press.

20. Paul Steckler and Mitchell Wand. Lightweight closure conversion. *ACM Transactions on Programming Languages and Systems*, 19(1):48–86, January 1997.

21. Guy L. Steele. Rabbit: a compiler for Scheme. Technical Report AI-TR-474, MIT, Cambridge, MA, 1978.

22. Peter Thiemann. Polymorphic typing and unboxed values revisited. In Simon Peyton Jones, editor, *Proc. Functional Programming Languages and Computer Architecture 1995*, pages 24–35, La Jolla, CA, June 1995. ACM Press, New York.

23. Philip Wadler. Is there a use for linear logic? In Paul Hudak and Neil D. Jones, editors, *Proc. ACM SIGPLAN Symposium on Partial Evaluation and Semantics-Based Program Manipulation PEPM '91*, pages 255–273, New Haven, CT, June 1991. ACM. SIGPLAN Notices 26(9).

# An Approach to Improve Locality Using Sandwich Types

Daniela Genius, Martin Trapp, and Wolf Zimmermann

Institut für Programmstrukturen
und Datenorganisation
University of Karlsruhe
76128 Karlsruhe
Germany
E-Mail: { genius | trapp | zimmer }@ipd.info.uni-karlsruhe.de

**Abstract.** We show how to increase locality of object-oriented programs using several heaps. We introduce the notion of sandwich types which allow a coarser view on objects. Our idea for increasing locality is to use one heap per object of sandwich types. Performance measurements demonstrate that the running time is improved by upto a factor 5 using this strategy. The paper shows how to derive sandwich types from classes. Thus, it is possible to control the allocation of the different heaps using compile-time information.

## 1 Introduction

In object-oriented programs, the notion of an object is rather fine-grained. The objects are usually allocated on a heap and the size of these objects is small. Thus, a single heap may destroy locality. Improving locality may improve execution time due to caching and paging effects. Often, a coarser view on objects is possible. For example, a list may be considered as a collection of small objects linked in an adequate way, but it may also be considered as one object. We introduce the notion of *sandwich types* in order to characterize this situation. Our goal is to maintain objects of sandwich types (called *sandwich objects*) in one single heap (i.e. consecutive fragment of memory) in order to increase locality. We maintain these heaps for a sandwich object by the doubling strategy well-known from the theory of algorithms and data structures (see e.g. [3]).

This work was initiated by observations during experiments where lists, trees, sets etc. were implemented with flexible arrays using the doubling strategy. These implementations improved the performance considerably compared to linked implementations.

Increasing locality of reference by partitioning the heap is a well known technique. The language EUCLID [7] introduced special *collections* which can be viewed as independent heaps. Dynamically allocated data structures could be assigned to a single collection. The same idea is exploited by the Gnu *obstack* structure [4]. This package gives the programmer control over an arbitrary number of heaps that require stack discipline for allocation and deallocation. However, the responsibility for mapping objects to heaps remains totally with the programmer, both in using EUCLID as well as *obstacks*.

Approaches in automatically finding such mappings have been developed in the context of SMALLTALK. The Object-Oriented Zoned Environment (OOZE) locates all instances of a type in one contiguous interval of virtual addresses [8]. This increases locality of reference for objects of the same type, but is unable to deal with structures built from objects of various types. STAMOS [12] presents also additional algorithms for grouping related objects with the intention of increasing locality of reference. This technique requires complete knowledge of the dynamic object graph and are used for restructuring the memory image during garbage collection. Thus, the mapping cannot be found at compile time. In [6], Hayes suggested the use of key objects as representatives for clusters. Death of a key object triggers garbage collection of the structure it represents. Again, key object candidates and the clusters they represent are identified during collection at runtime and can not be statically determined. To the authors' knowledge, there is no work on automatic a priori mapping of dynamically allocated objects to multiple heaps for sequential object-oriented programs.

Section 2 introduces the notion of sandwich types and gives some examples. Section 3 shows the performance improvements obtained by object heaps. Finally, Section 4 shows a conservative analysis for identifying sandwich types. Section 5 concludes the paper. Appendix A defines syntax, static and dynamic semantics of a basic object-oriented language BOOL. Every object-oriented language has at least the features of BOOL.

## 2  Sandwich Types

The notion of *sandwich types* is a generalization of balloon types [2]. All objects in a balloon can be accesses only via a distinguished balloon object. However, this excludes container types such as e.g. lists or sets. These types usually contain methods to return their elements and to insert elements. Thus, these elements can be accessed from outside, destroying the balloon type property. However, there is often an internal structure which cannot be accessed from outside. This is the reason for the term *sandwich object*: its internal structure can be accessed only via the sandwich object, but parts of its structure are known externally. It is the sandwich object which decides what is external. Figure 1 visualizes this idea.

Based on the definition of memory states in Appendix A, a *state*[1] of a program is a triple $(OBJ, REF, ROOTS)$ where $OBJ$ is a set of objects, $STATE = (OBJ, REF)$ is a directed graph where $o_1 \overset{a}{\to} o_2 \in REF$ iff there is an attribute $a$ of object $o_1$ that refers to object $o_2$, and $ROOTS \subseteq OBJ$ is the set of objects

---

[1] We speak of states instead of memory states because the instruction pointer and current method plays no role in our discussion.

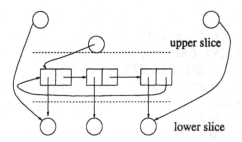

**Fig. 1.** A Sandwich

refered by the environment *env*. In particular, *obj* ∈ *ROOTS* iff there is a frame $f \in env$ such that $obj = f \downarrow_2$ or there is a variable $x$ such that $(x, obj) \in f \downarrow_1$.

$PRED_{obj}$ and $outdeg_{obj}$ denote the direct predecessors and the number of outgoing edges of *obj* in the graph *STATE*, respectively. $obj_1 \overset{*}{\to} obj_2$ denotes[2] that there is a path from $obj_1$ to $obj_2$ in $(OBJ, REF)$. An object *o* is *reachable* iff there is an object $o' \in ROOTS$ such that $o' \overset{*}{\to} o$. Otherwise it is unreachable. [10, 11] defines an operational semantics based on this definition of states. Suppose that there is a state transition such that objects become unreachable in a state. Then, they will be unreachable forever. Therefore, we can assume w.l.o.g. that unreachable objects are removed, i.e. no state contains unreachable objects. The paper does not require any further knowledge of state transitions.

**Definition 1 (Sandwich Objects and Types).** *Let A be a class whose attributes are all private. Let $s = (OBJ, REF, ROOTS)$ be a state and x be an object of class A. The set $INTERNAL_x^{(s)}$ of objects* internal *to x is the smallest set satisfying*

$$INTERNAL_x^{(s)} = \{y : x \overset{+}{\to} y \land PRED_y \subseteq INTERNAL_x^{(s)} \cup \{x\}\}$$

*x is a* sandwich object *or* upper slice *iff $INTERNAL_x^{(s)} \neq \emptyset$ or $outdeg_x = 0$. All objects $z \in OBJ \setminus (\{x\} \cup INTERNAL_x^{(s)})$ are* external *to x. If $outdeg_x \neq 0$, the* lower slice *of x is the set of all external objects that have a predecessor $y \in INTERNAL_x^{(s)}$. A* sandwich *is a sandwich object x together with the set of its internal objects. A is a* sandwich type *iff for all states s every object x of type A in s is a sandwich object.*

*Remark 1.* If there is no lower slice, a sandwich object is also a balloon object according to [2]. Observe that the attributes of internal objects need not be private.

*Example 1.* Consider the following implementation of a doubly-linked list (*next* and *previous* are used to navigate in the list):

---

[2] $\overset{+}{\to}$ denotes that there is at least one edge in the path.

```
class LIST(T) is
    private head : LIST_CELL(T);
    private end : LIST_CELL(T);
    private current : LIST_CELL(T);
    previous() is ··· end;
    next() is ··· end;
    insert(T) is ··· end;
    delete() is ··· end;
    elem() : T is ··· end;
    is_empty() : BOOL is ··· end;
    at_head() : BOOL is ··· end;
    at_end() : BOOL is ··· end;
end

class LIST_CELL(T) is
    elem : T;
    previous : LIST_CELL(T);
    next : LIST_CELL(T);
end
```

For every type $T$, $LIST(T)$ is a sandwich type.

Let $x : LIST(T)$. Then $x$ is a sandwich object. Examples of internal objects are the head and the end of $x$. The elements of the list are the lower slice of the sandwich. For every type $T$, $LIST(T)$ is a sandwich type.

Container types are typical examples of sandwich types. Internal objects can be reached only via the upper slice, i.e.

**Lemma 1.** *Let $s = (OBJ, REF, ROOTS)$ be a state and $x \in OBJ$ a sandwich object of type $A$. Then for every $y \in OBJ$: $y \in INTERNAL_x^{(s)}$ iff for every $z \in OBJ$ satisfying $z \xrightarrow{*} y$ one of the following conditions hold:*

*(i) $z \in INTERNAL_x^{(s)}$.*
*(ii) Each path from $z$ to $y$ contains $x$.*

*Proof.* "$\Rightarrow$": Suppose this would not be the case, i.e. there is a $z \notin INTERNAL_x^{(s)}$ and a path $\pi$ from $z$ to $y$ not containing $x$. Since $y \in INTERNAL_x^{(s)}$ there must be $u, v \in \pi$ such that $u \notin INTERNAL_x^{(s)}$, $v \in INTERNAL_x^{(s)}$, and $u \to v \in REF$. The definition of $INTERNAL_x^{(s)}$ implies that $u = x$ contradicting our assumption that $\pi$ does not contain $x$.
"$\Leftarrow$": Suppose (i) and (ii) holds, but $y \notin INTERNAL_x^{(s)}$. Then either, $x \not\xrightarrow{*} y$ or there is a $z \in PRED_y$ such that $z \notin INTERNAL_x^{(s)} \cup \{x\}$. The latter contradicts (ii). Thus $x \not\xrightarrow{*} y$. Consider a $z \in OBJ$ such that $z \xrightarrow{+} y$. Then (i) must hold since (ii) is excluded by $x \not\xrightarrow{*} y$. (i) implies $x \xrightarrow{+} z$, contradicting $x \not\xrightarrow{*} y$. Thus, there is no path to $y$, i.e. $y$ cannot be reached. This is what we excluded from the definition of states.

198

The next Lemma states that sandwiches are either disjoint or nested (i.e. non-overlapping):

**Lemma 2.** *Let $s = (OBJ, REF, ROOTS)$ be a state, $x \in OBJ$ be any sandwich object of type A and $y \in OBJ$ be a sandwich object of type B. If $y$ is internal to $x$, then every object of the lower slice of $x$ is external to $y$.*

*Proof.* Suppose there is a state $s$ such that $y \in INTERNAL_x^{(s)}$ and there is an object $u \in INTERNAL_y^{(s)}$ of the lower slice of $x$. Figure 2 visualizes this situation. Since $u$ is in the lower slice of $x$, it is external to $x$, i.e., there is a path from an object $w$ external to $x$ which does not contain $x$. Since $u \in INTERNAL_y^{(s)}$, by Lemma 1, every path from an object external to $y$ must contain $u$. Thus, $w$ must be internal to $y$.

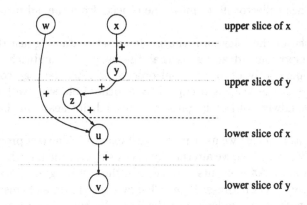

**Fig. 2.** Contrary of Lemma 2

Let $v$ be an arbitrary object external to $x$. Since $y$ is internal in $x$, every path from $v$ to $y$ must contain $x$ (by Lemma 1). Since $w$ is internal to $y$, every path from $x$ to $w$ must contain $y$ (by Lemma 1). Hence, every path from $v$ to $w$ must contain $x$. This contradicts the fact that $w$ is external to $x$.

*Example 2.* Consider the class $HASHTAB(T)$ with collision resolution by chain lists:

```
class HASHTAB(T) is
      private tab : ARR[n](LIST(T));
      insert(x : T) is ··· end;
      delete is ··· end;
      member(T) is ··· end;
end
```

Objects of class $HASHTAB(T)$ are sandwich objects. The collision lists in the array *tab* are also sandwich objects. Each lower slice of a collision list is contained in the lower slice of hash tables.

# 3   Performance Improvement Using Object Heaps

In general, the number of objects that will be allocated in a sandwich's heap is unknown at compile time. Thus, the heap must be able to grow (and shrink) at runtime. To achieve locality of reference for the objects in a heap, the latter must extend over a minimal number of physical memory pages. I.e. all but at most one page used must be used completely or not at all for object allocation. We guarantee this by allocating a contiguous[3] area of virtual memory for a heap and doubling the size whenever the heap would overflow. Since it is not possible to grow a heap in place, we copy its data to a new memory area. This works in amortized constant time, see [3].

Note that all references pointing at objects in a sandwich's heap come from inside that heap or from its upper slice. We exploit this fact by using a compacting copy garbage collector [9] to move the objects from the old memory area to the new one.

The root set for the collector is the singleton set containing just the sandwich object. The important advantage is that the heap of a sandwich can be copy collected independently of all external objects. If after garbage collection less than a quarter of the heap is occupied by allocated objects, we halve its size. Whenever a sandwich object is garbage collected, its heap can be deleted at once.

For our measurements we use the small list example. The test program creates first two empty lists. Then, we alternately insert single elements in both lists until they both contain MAX elements. Afterwards, the test program iterates through each list separately ITER times. Figure 3 shows the runtime of this iterated list traversals depending on the length of the lists. We have chosen the values of of MAX and ITER so that their product is constant ($10^7$). In the first part of the plot, runtime decreases with the length of the list because the iteration overhead becomes less significant.

Both axes of the plot are logarithmically scaled. The x-axis shows the number of elements in the list, while the y-axis shows the total runtime in seconds. The values are measured on a 200 MHz i586 Linux system. Each program is run 10 times and the smallest elapsed time is shown in Figure 3.

The curve labeled single shows run times for the usual implementation (i.e. one heap for all objects created by the program). The multi curve denotes the result of our method: As noted above, LIST(T) is a sandwich type. Both list objects are sandwich objects by themselves. Thus, they have their own heaps for their internal LIST_CELL(T) objects. There is a third heap for all other objects created by the program.

As long as all list elements fit into the data cache, both variants have approximatly the same running time ($< 0.3$ seconds). If the lists contain more than approximately 100 elements, cache misses occur in the single heap implementation. With the multi heap implementation this effect is postponed to lists

---

[3] If it is guaranteed that the sizes of all internal objects evenly divide the physical page size, it would not matter whether the pages are contiguous in virtual memory.

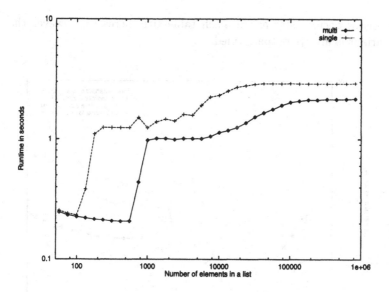

**Fig. 3.** Measurements: Lists

of approximately 500 elements because of the better locality. For 500 elements, the multi heap variant is almost 5 times faster than the single heap variant. Also after the sharp increase in run time of the multi heap variant due to cache misses and page faults the multi heap variant still clearly outperforms the single heap version. Less memory pages have to be accessed to traverse the lists. For very long lists results for classical allocation stay below 3 seconds, while using multiple heaps never greatly exceed 2 seconds. An overall improvement by our method of about 25 per cent emerges in this case. In general the improvement is even larger: For lists of around 10000 elements the multi heap variant is twice as fast.

Although the test program on lists is artificial, it reflects a situation which occurs in practice. Consider for example hash-tables with collision resolution by chaining. Each insertion or look-up in the hash-table traverses a collision list. Furthermore, it is unlikely that the collision lists are stored in contiguous memory cells. This is precisely the situation covered by our experiment. Figure 4 demonstrates this argument. The implementation with collision lists reuses the single and multiple heap implementations for LIST. A simple modulo hashing equally distributes elements over the lists modulo table size. Once the hash value is computed, searching for a key that is *not* present in the hash table means that one entire collision list has to be traversed once the hash value is computed. The collision lists are treated analogously to the LIST example. MAX elements are distributed over a hash table. Again, MAX and ITER are chosen such that their product is $10^7$. Figure 4 shows for hash table sizes 23 and 501 that the relative behaviour is similar to the list example. The sharp increase in run time due to cache misses occurs later as the hash table size increases, however the single heap variant is always outperformed.

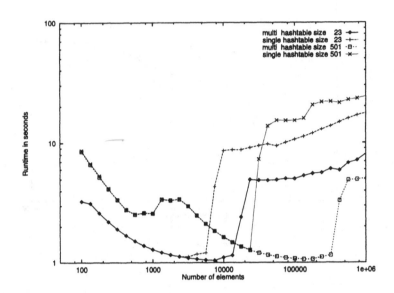

**Fig. 4.** Measurements: Hashtables

# 4 Recognition of Sandwich Types

This section shows how sandwich types can be recognized in a program. We first derive a sufficient condition for sandwich types. This sufficient condition abstracts from the state by considering the types of the objects. In particular, we consider the *type graph* of an object-oriented program, i.e. a graph $TG = (CLASSES, USE)$ where $CLASSES$ are the classes of a program and $(A, B) \in USE$ iff $A$ has an attribute of type $B$ or has a method with parameter type $B$ or return type $B$. $\overset{*}{\Rightarrow}$ denotes the reachability relation in type graphs. A class $A$ is *recursive* iff $A \overset{*}{\Rightarrow} A$. Now, we lift Definition 1 to types.

**Definition 2.** *Let $TG = (CLASSES, USE)$ and $A \in CLASSES$ be a nonrecursive class whose attributes are private. Classes which are parameter types or return types of methods of $A$ are called the* accessible types *of $A$. $ACCESSIBLE_A$ denotes the set of accessible types of class $A$. The set $INTERNAL_A$ of classes that are* internal *to $A$ is the smallest set satisfying*

$$INTERNAL_A = \{B : A \overset{*}{\Rightarrow} B \wedge B \notin ACCESSIBLE_A \cup \{A\} \wedge \\ PRED_B \subseteq INTERNAL_A \cup \{A\}\}$$

*All classes $B \in CLASSES \setminus INTERNAL_A$ are* external *to $A$.*

The following lemma relates type graphs and states.

**Lemma 3.** *Let $TG = (CLASSES, USE)$ be a type graph of a program and $s = (OBJ, REF, ROOTS)$ an arbitrary state. Then $x \overset{*}{\to} y$ implies $type(x) \overset{*}{\Rightarrow} type(y)$ for every two objects $x, y \in OBJ$.*

*Proof.* From Corollary 1 follows that $x \to y \in REF$ implies $(type(x), type(y)) \in USE$. The claim follows by induction.

A class $B$ internal to a class $A$ can be reached only via $A$:

**Lemma 4.** *Let $TG = (CLASSES, USE)$ be a type graph of a program and $A$ be a non-recursive class whose attributes are private, and $INTERNAL_A \neq \emptyset$. Then, for any class $C \in INTERNAL_A$ and every class $B$ such that $B \overset{*}{\Rightarrow} C$, one of the following properties hold*

*(i) $B \in INTERNAL_A$*
*(ii) $B$ is external to $A$ and every path from $B$ to $C$ contains $A$.*

*Proof.* Analogous to Lemma 1.

Every object $y$ whose type is internal to a class $A$ is either reachable from an object $z$ on the stack whose type is internal to $A$ or an object internal to a sandwich object of class $A$:

**Lemma 5.** *Let $TG = (CLASSES, USE)$ be the type graph of a program and $A$ be a non-recursive class whose attributes are private and $INTERNAL_A \neq \emptyset$. For every state $s = (OBJ, REF, ROOTS)$ and for every object $y$ with $type(y) \in INTERNAL_A$ there is an object $x$ of type $A$ such that $y \in INTERNAL_x^{(s)}$ or an object $z \in ROOTS$ of type internal to $A$ such that $z \overset{*}{\to} y$.*

*Proof.* Suppose there is a $C \in INTERNAL_A$ and an object $y$ of type $C$ such that it is not internal to an object $x$ of type $A$. Suppose there is an object $z$ with a path $\pi$ from $z$ to $y$ where $type(z) \notin INTERNAL(A)$ and the type of every $u \in \pi$ is different from $A$. By Lemma 3 there is path $\pi'$ from $type(z)$ to $type(y)$ not containing $A$. This contradicts Lemma 4(ii). Thus, $type(z) \in INTERNAL_A$ for all objects $z$ such that $z \overset{*}{\to} y$. Since $A \notin INTERNAL_A$, by Lemma 3 there is no object of type which is external to $A$ that can reach $z$ or $x$. Since $s$ does not contain unreachable objects, there must be an object $w \in ROOTS$ of type internal to $A$ such that $w \overset{*}{\to} y$.

There is a nesting property analogous to nesting of sandwiches (cf. Lemma 2):

**Lemma 6.** *Let $TG = (CLASSES, USE)$ be a type graph of a program, $A$ be a non-recursive class whose attributes are private, and $INTERNAL_A \neq \emptyset$, and $B$ be a non-recursive class whose attributes are private and $INTERNAL_B \neq \emptyset$. If there is a $C \in ACCESSIBLE_B \cap INTERNAL_A$, then $ACCESSIBLE_A \cap INTERNAL_B = \emptyset$.*

*Proof.* Analogous to Lemma 2.

If a class $B$ is recursive and reachable from a class $A$, all classes in the strongly connected component of $TG$ are either external or internal to $A$.

**Lemma 7.** *Let $TG = (CLASSES, USE)$ be the type graph of a program, $A$ be a non-recursive class where all attributes are private and $INTERNAL_A \neq \emptyset$, and $B$ be a type reachable from $A$, i.e. $A \stackrel{+}{\Rightarrow} B$. If $B$ is recursive, then either all $C \in \mathfrak{B}$ are external to $A$ or all $C \in \mathfrak{B}$ are internal to $A$ where $\mathfrak{B}$ is the strongly connected component of $TG$ containing $B$.*

*Proof.* Suppose there is a class $C \in \mathfrak{B}$ internal to $A$ and a class $C' \in \mathfrak{B}$ external to $A$. Since $\mathfrak{B}$ is a strongly connected component and $\mathfrak{A}$ is non-recursive, there is a path from $C'$ to $C$ in $TG$ not containing $A$. Then, by Lemma 4, $A$ cannot be a non-recursive class satisfying $INTERNAL_A \neq \emptyset$ whose attributes are private, i.e. the assumptions of Lemma 7 are violated. ∎

Finally, we show that all objects of classes which have internal classes are sandwich objects:

**Theorem 1.** *Let $TG = (CLASSES, USE)$ and $A$ be a non-recursive class with accessible types whose attributes are private with unaccessible types. Then, for every state $s = (OBJ, REF, ROOTS)$, all objects $x \in OBJ$ of type $A$ are either sandwich objects or none of the attributes of $x$ refer to objects.*

*Proof.* Suppose that there is a state $s = (OBJ, REF, ROOTS)$ which contains an $x \in OBJ$ of type $A$ that is not a sandwich object and one of the attributes refers to an object $y$. Since the type of this attribute is not accessible this attribute refers to an object $y$ with $type(y) \in INTERNAL_A$. Since $x$ is not a sandwich type, there must be an object $w$ with a path $\pi$ from $w$ to $y$ not containing $x$. By Lemma 5 there is a sandwich object $z$ of type $A$ in path $\pi$ such that $y$ is internal to $z$. But then there cannot be a reference to $y$ from $x$ contradicting our assumption. ∎

Algorithm *sandwich_types* (defined below) identifies the types satisfying the sufficient condition of Theorem 1. The algorithm computes these types by maintaining a set of candidates. The invariant is that all classes which are not candidates do not satisfy the sufficient condition of Theorem 1. After the last step, every candidate satisfies the sufficient condition of Theorem 1, i.e. they are sandwich types. Furthermore, for every sandwich type $A$, the set of its internal types is computed. Objects of these types are allocated in the heap associated with sandwich objects of type $A$.

The algorithm *sandwich_types* performs the following steps:

1. Compute the the type graph $TG = (CLASSES, USE)$ of $\pi$. Define the set *Candidates* of candidates to be the set of all classes that have only private attributes.
2. Compute the strongly connected components $SCC$ of $TG$ and the reduced graph, i.e. $RUSE = (SCC, RE)$ where $(\mathfrak{A}, \mathfrak{B}) \in RE$ iff there are $A \in \mathfrak{A}$ and $B \in \mathfrak{B}$ such that $(A, B) \in USE$.

3. Let *Candidates* := $\{A \in Candidates : A \in \mathfrak{A}$ for an $\mathfrak{A} \in SCC$ with $|\mathfrak{A}| = 1 \wedge$ $(A, A) \notin USE\}$.

4. For every $A \in Candidates$ compute its accessible types $ACCESSIBLE_A$. Remove all classes $A$ from candidates which contain an attribute whose type is accessible.

5. For every $A \in Candidates$ define and perform the following step (starting with $\mathbb{I}_A = \emptyset$) until $I_A$ does not change:

$$\mathbb{I}_A := \mathbb{I}_A \cup \{B \in CLASSES : B \notin ACCESSIBLE_A \wedge$$
$$\forall C \in PRED_B : B \in \mathbb{I}_A \cup \{A\}\}.$$

6. Remove every $A$ from *Candidates* where $\mathbb{I}_A = \emptyset$,

7. Declare every $A \in Candidates$ to be a sandwich type and define $INTERNAL_A = \mathbb{I}_A$.

*Remark 2.* Algorithm *sandwich_types* recognizes all examples of Section 2.

The following lemmas explain algorithm *sandwich_types*:

**Lemma 8 (Step 1).** *After Step 1, all classes $A \in OBJ \setminus Candidates$ violate the assumption of Theorem 1.*

*Proof.* The assumption of Theorem 1 requires that all attributes of a class are private.

**Lemma 9 (Step 3).** *After Step 3, all classes $A \in OBJ \setminus Candidates$ violate the assumption of Theorem 1.*

*Proof.* Suppose $(A, A) \in USE$ or there is a strongly connected component $\mathfrak{A} \in SCC$ such that $A \in \mathfrak{A}$. In both cases $A \stackrel{*}{\Rightarrow} A$, i.e. $A$ is recursive. Hence, the assumptions of Theorem 1 are violated.

**Lemma 10 (Step 4).** *After Step 4, all classes $A \in OBJ \setminus Candidates$ violate the assumption of Theorem 1.*

*Proof.* Let $A$ be a class not in *Candidates* after Step 4. Suppose, it is not eliminated by Steps 1 and 3. Then, it is eliminated by Step 4, i.e. it contains an attribute whose type is accessible. Thus, the assumption of Theorem 1 is violated.

**Lemma 11 (Step 5).** *After Step 5, for all classes $A \in Candidates$, $\mathbb{I}_A$ contains the set of all classes internal to $A$.*

*Proof.* Step 5 is a closure algorithm in the lattice of sets (ordered by the subset relation) starting with the smallest element. Each step increases the set. Thus, by the fix-point theorem of Tarski [13], the smallest set satisfying

$$\mathbb{I}_A = \mathbb{I}_A \cup \{B \in CLASSES : B \notin ACCESSIBLE_A \wedge$$
$$\forall C \in PRED_B : B \in \mathbb{I}_A \cup \{A\}\}$$

is computed. It is not hard to see that $\mathbb{I}_A$ is also the smallest set satisfying

$$\mathbb{I}_A = \{B \in CLASSES : A \overset{+}{\Rightarrow} B \wedge B \notin ACCESSIBLE_A$$
$$\wedge \forall C \in PRED_B : B \in \mathbb{I}_A \cup \{A\}\}.$$

Thus, the claim follows by Definition 2.

**Lemma 12 (Step 6).** *After Step 6, for every class $A \in CLASSES$: $A \in Candidates$ iff $A$ is non-recursive and contains only private attributes with types internal to $A$.*

*Proof.* Before Step 6, $A \in Candidates$ iff $A$ is non-recursive and contains only private attributes whose types are not accessible (Lemmas 8, 9, and 10). Thus, after Step 6, $A \in Candidates$ iff $A$ is non-recursive, contains only private attributes, and $\mathbb{I}_A$. The claim follows from Lemma 11 since it implies $INTERNAL_A = \mathbb{I}_A$.

**Theorem 2 (Correctness of Algorithm** *sandwich_type***).** *Let $\pi$ be a program. Every class $A$ declared by Algorithm sandwich_type to be a sandwich type is a sandwich type and $INTERNAL_A$ is the set of its internal classes.*

*Proof.* Follows directly from Step 7, Lemmas 11 and 12, and Theorem 1

It remains to prove the time complexity of Algorithm *sandwich_type*:

**Theorem 3.** *Algorithm sandwich_type terminates for every program $\pi$ in time $O(m \cdot n)$ where $n$ is the size of program $\pi$ (i.e. number of nodes in the abstract syntax tree of $\pi$) and $m$ is the number of classes in the program.*

*Proof.* Obviously, the type graph $TG$ can be constructed in time $O(n)$ by a traversal through the abstract syntax tree of $\pi$. Hence, it is $|USE| = O(n)$. Step 2 can be performed in $O(|CLASSES| + |USE|) = O(m + n)$ (see e.g. [1, Section 6.7]). While computing the strongly connected components of $TG$ it is possible to mark the classes $A$ such that $(A, A) \notin USE$ and $\{A\} \in SCC$. Thus, Step 3 can be executed in time $O(|Candidates|) = O(m)$. The accessible types of a class $A$ can be computed by a traversal through the abstract syntax tree of class $A$. Thus, Step 4 can be executed in time $O(n)$. If the sets $\mathbb{I}_A$ are implemented by Bit vectors over the classes, it is sufficient to set the Bit for the classes $B$ to true in one iteration iff $B \notin ACCESSIBLE_A \wedge \forall C \in PRED_B : C \in \mathbb{I}_A$. The initialization costs time $O(m)$ and the test costs time $O(|USE|)$ amortized over all classes. The maximum number of iterations is $O(m)$. Hence, Step 5 can be executed in time $O(m \cdot n)$. The implementation of Step 5 can be extended with additional $O(m)$ execution time such that every class $A$ with $\mathbb{I}_A = \emptyset$ is marked. Thus, the execution time of Step 5 remains $O(m \cdot n)$ and the execution time of Step 6 is $O(m)$. It is not hard to see that the execution time of Step 7 is $O(m^2) = O(m \cdot n)$, because $m \leq n$.

## 5 Conclusions

We introduced the notions of sandwich types and sandwich object and showed that using object heaps (i.e. one heap per sandwich object) can improve the execution time of object-oriented programs. Theorem 1 gives a sufficient condition for sandwich types. This is used to recognize sandwich types in object-oriented programs. Upon creation of a sandwich object, its heap is created and maintained independently of other heaps.

Further work focuses on extending the assumptions in Theorem 1. In particular, the requirement that all attributes are private may be relaxed by defining the type of non-private attributes to be accessible. Another candidate for generalization is the notion of internal classes: Lemma 4 implies that every class can be internal to at most one class except a nesting property is satisfied (Lemma 6). This excludes, e.g. that the type $LIST\_CELL$ in our example is used for more than one sandwich type. Hence, the next step is to relax Definition 2 allowing for some classes to be internal to more than one class without nesting. If it would be allowed in general that a class $B$ is internal to more than one class, the condition $INTERNAL_A \neq \emptyset$ would not be sufficient to imply that $A$ is a sandwich type: it is not excluded that an object is internal to two different sandwich objects (cf. Figure 5). The key question is: What is the restriction such that $INTERNAL_A \neq \emptyset$ implies that $A$ is a sandwich type? Our further work will address this question.

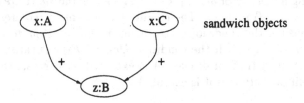

**Fig. 5.** Situation if a class $B$ is internal to different classes

An alias and pointer analysis may lead to additional improvements for the implementation of object heaps. For example, stacks, heaps, and lists may be implemented even more efficiently than sketched in this paper. For example, there is no necessity to have a general garbage collection on stacks, queues, and double-ended queues. Since the elements are inserted and deleted at their ends, it is is sufficient to maintain pointers that mark the beginning and the end of the allocated part of the heap. When copying a heap of a list object, it can be linearized. This leads to an additional improvement of locality.

Another issue that should be investigated the influence of sandwich types in object-oriented design. It seems natural to use sandwich types when designing object-oriented programs, because it is a way of information hiding. Furthermore, aliasing and sharing of objects can be controlled.

# A  BOOL – A Basic Object-Oriented Language

We define a language which is a prototype of intermediate languages of many object-oriented languages. It is based on [10, 11]. We do not consider inheritance and basic types such as integers or booleans since these notions are not important in the discussion of sandwich types. Instead introducion parameterized classes, we assume that in a program the parameters of every parameterized class are instantiated with types. We further focus on the basic features of object-oriented languages (calling methods, accessing attributes, creating objects) and add a few statements required for making BOOL Turing-complete (assignments, conditional statements, method returns). For simplicity, we consider only methods with return types (functions). Method without return types (procedures) can be defined similarly as functions. We define the abstract syntax, the static semantics (in particular typing rules), and the dynamic semantics by abstract state machines.

## A.1  Abstract Syntax

A *program* is a collection of classes together with a designated class MAIN containing a procedure main. main is called when starting the program. Fig. 6 shows the EBNF defining the abstract syntax of BOOL. Attributes of a class $A$ may be *private*. Private attributes of every object $obj$ of class $A$ can only be accessed when executing a method of $obj$. $T_1 \times \cdots \times T_k \to T$ is the *signature* of a method $m(x_1 : T_1, \ldots, x_k : T_k) : T \ldots$. The conditional statement requires further explanation. Consider the conditional statement if $Des\ '='\ Expr$ then $n$ occuring in a method $m$ of class $A$. If the condition $Des\ '='\ Expr$ is satisfied, then the $n$-th statement of method $m$ of class $A$ is executed. Otherwise, the statement after the conditional statement is executed.

## A.2  Static Semantics

A BOOL-program must satisfy the following properties on classes, attributes, methods, variable names, and jump targets:

- All class names are pairwise disjoint.
- For every class, the attribute names and method names are pairwise disjoint.
- For every method, the parameter names and the names of local variables are pairwise disjoint.
- For every method $m$, the jump targets of the conditional statements of $m$ must be smaller than the number of statements of $m$.

Furthermore, we assume for simplicity[4]:

- All attribute names and all methods names are different from class names.

---

[4] This can be viewed as a result after name analysis.

$$
\begin{aligned}
Prog &::= Class^* \\
Class &::= \text{class } Name \text{ is } Attr^* Method^* \text{end } ';' \\
Attr &::= [\text{private}] \; Var \; ':' \; Type \; ';' \\
Method &::= Id \; '(' \; [(Par';')^* Par] \; ')' \; ':' \; Type \text{ is } (Par \; ';')^* (Stat \; ';')^* \text{end } ';' \\
Par &::= Var \; ':' \; Type \\
Type &::= Name \\
Stat &::= Assign|Return|If \\
Assign &::= Des \; ':=' \; Expr \\
Return &::= \text{return } Expr \\
If &::= \text{if } Des \; '=' \; Expr \text{ then } n \\
Des &::= (Var \; '.')^* \; Var \\
Expr &::= Des|Call|\text{void}|New \\
Call &::= [Des \; '.']Id \; '(' \; [(Des \; ',')^* Des] \; ')' \\
New &::= '\#' \; Type
\end{aligned}
$$

where *Var* is any variable name, *Id* is any procedure identifier, *Name* is any class name, and $n$ is a natural number.

**Fig. 6.** Abstract Syntax of BOOL

- Within every class $A$, for every method $m$ the names of parameters and local variables are different from the attribute names of $A$, method names of $A$, and from the class names.

It remains to define types. In our case, it is sufficient to assume that classes are types (identified by class names). For defining typing rules, the following context information is required:

- $\Gamma$ contains all classes with their names, attributes, and method signatures.
- A class $A$ where the attribute, method, statement, designator, or expression to be typed occurs.
- A method $m$ where the statement, designator, or expression to be typed occurs.

**Notations:** $\Gamma, A, m \vdash e : T$ denotes that within a given context, it can be derived that designator or expression $e$ is of type $T$. $\Gamma, A, m \vdash s\sqrt{}$ denotes that statement $s$ is correctly typed within a given context. A program is *statically correct* iff every statement is correctly typed within the context it occurs. $\Gamma, A \vdash x : T$ denotes that class $A$ has an attribute $x$ of type $T$ or method of signature $T$. ■

Fig. 7 shows the typing rules of BOOL using the above notations.

Axioms :

$\Gamma, A, m \vdash \text{void} : T$      for all types $T$

$\Gamma, A, m \vdash \#T : T$

Rules :

$$\frac{\Gamma, A \vdash x : T}{\Gamma, A, m \vdash x : T} \quad \text{for all methods } m \text{ of } A$$

$$\frac{\Gamma, A, m \vdash des : B \qquad \Gamma, B \vdash x : C}{\Gamma, A, m \vdash des.x : C} \quad \text{if } x \text{ is not private in } B$$

$$\frac{\Gamma, A \vdash m : T_1 \times \cdots \times T_k \to T \qquad \Gamma, A, \bar{m} \vdash d_1 : T_1 \ \cdots \ \Gamma, A, \bar{m} \vdash d_k : T_k}{\Gamma, A, \bar{m} \vdash m(d_1, \ldots, d_k) : T}$$

$$\frac{\Gamma, B \vdash m : T_1 \times \cdots \times T_k \to T \qquad \Gamma, A, \bar{m} \vdash des : B \qquad \Gamma, A, \bar{m} \vdash d_1 : T_1 \ \cdots \ \Gamma, A, \bar{m} \vdash d_k : T_k}{\Gamma, A, \bar{m} \vdash des.m(d_1, \ldots, d_k) : T}$$

$$\frac{\Gamma, A, m \vdash des : T \qquad \Gamma, A, m \vdash expr : T}{\Gamma, A, m \vdash des := expr \sqrt{}}$$

$$\frac{\Gamma, A \vdash m : T_1 \times \cdots \times T_k \to T \qquad \Gamma, A, m \vdash expr : T}{\Gamma, A, m \vdash \text{return } expr \sqrt{}}$$

$$\frac{\Gamma, A, m \vdash des : T \qquad \Gamma, A, m \vdash expr : T}{\Gamma, A, m \vdash \text{if } des = exr \text{ then } n \sqrt{}}$$

**Fig. 7.** Typing Rules for BOOL

## A.3 Abstract State Machines

We define the operational semantics by *abstract state machines* (ASMs). In this subsection we introduce ASMs as it is required for the operational semantics of BOOL. For the generalization, we refer the reader to [5]. An ASM consists of a signature $\Delta$ of the *state space*, an interpretation of $\Delta$ (the *initial state*), and set of transition rules (used for changing the interpretation of $\Delta$). A *state* is an interpretation of $\Delta$. It is convenient to assume that interpretations are algebras. In our examples, a *transition rule* has the form

**if** *Condition* **then** *Updates*

where *Condition* is a term and *Updates* is a set of updates. An *update* has one of the following forms:

1. $f(t_1, \ldots, t_n) := t$ for $f \in \Delta$ and terms $t, t_1, \ldots, t_n$.
2. **extend** $M$ **by** $o$ *Updates* **end** where $M \in \Delta$ is interpreted by sets, $o$ is a new symbol, and *Updates* is a set of updates (here: only of form (1))

*Execution of update (1)* means that $t_1, \ldots, t_n$, and $t$ are interpreted in the current state, and the interpretation of $f$ is changed to $t$ at point $(t_1, \ldots, t_n)$ and unchanged otherwise. *Execution of update (2)* means that the set $M$ is extended by a new element[5] $o$, and after this, the updates in *Updates* are executed. A transition rule *fires* if its condition evaluates to *true* in the current state. In this case, its updates are executed. In our example, there is at most one transition rule that fires in a given state. A state is *final* iff no transition rule fires. It is easy to see that the transition rules define a state transition relation.

**Notation:** Upper case letters denote sets, lower case letters other elements of $\Delta$. Sets are denoted as usual. $X_1 \times \cdots \times X_n$ denotes the cartesian product of sets $X_1, \ldots, X_n$. Tuples are denoted as usual, $x \downarrow_i$ denotes the projection to the $i$-th component of tuple $x$. $X \to Y$ denotes the set of relations $R \subset X \times Y$ which are functions. $R(x)$ denotes the unique element $y$ such that $(x, y) \in R$. $X^*$ denotes lists with element type $X$. $[x|X]$ denotes the list obtained from list $X$ by adding element $x$, $[]$ denotes the empty list, and $[x_1, \ldots, x_k]$ denotes the list of elements $x_1, \ldots, x_k$. As usual $hd$ and $tl$ denote the head and tail of a list, respectively. ∎

## A.4 Operational Semantics

We assume that only static correct programs are executed. The state space of BOOL consists of the symbols defined in Table 1. A *frame* consists of a set of bindings of local variables and parameters of the method being executed, an object where the method belongs to, and return point (specified by a method and instruction pointer). The *memory state space* is the set $M = \Delta \setminus \{curmethod, ip\}$. A *memory state* is an interpretation of the memory state space $M$.

| | |
|---|---|
| $OBJ$ | set of objects |
| $type \in OBJ \to Name$ | dynamic type of an object |
| $REF \subseteq OBJ \times OBJ \times Name$ | references between objects (via attributes) |
| $ac \in OBJ$ | the accumulator. |
| $env \in FRAME^*$ | the environment. |
| $curmethod \in Id$ | the method currently be executed |
| $ip \in \mathbb{N}$ | the instruction pointer |

$$\text{where} \quad FRAME = SET(BINDING) \times OBJ \times Id \times \mathbb{N}$$
$$BINDING = Id \times (OBJ \uplus \{\text{void}\})$$

**Table 1.** State Space of BOOL

---

[5] This new element is taken from an infinite universe, called *Reserve*.

The initial state is defined by the updates

$$OBJ := \{\text{system}\}$$
$$type := \{(\text{system}, \text{MAIN})\}$$
$$REF := \emptyset$$
$$ac := \text{system}$$
$$env := [(\{(y_1, \text{void}), \dots, (y_1, \text{void})\}, \text{system}, \textit{undef}, \textit{undef})]$$
$$curmethod := \text{main}$$
$$ip := 0$$

where main contains the local variables $y_1, \dots, y_k$.

For the definition of the operational semantics, it is convenient to assume that assignments, conditionalte statements, and return statements are decomposed into the statement sequences shown in Table 2. load *expr* loads the object computed by *expr* into the accumulator, store *des* stores the object contained in the accumulator to the object designated by *des*, and beq *des n* compares the object in the accumulator with the object designated by *des* and jumps to the *n*-th statement of the current procedure. The return instruction returns the object contained in the accumulator.

| statement | instructions |
|---|---|
| *des*:=*expr* | load *expr*; store *des* |
| if *des*=*expr* then *n* | load *expr*; beq *des n* |
| return *e* | load *e*; return |

**Table 2.** Decomposition of Statements into Instructions

**Notations:** The operational semantics uses the following abbreviations and notations. Each of these can be formally defined. Sometimes we leave the formal definition to the reader. $self = hd(env) \downarrow_3$ denotes the object where the current method is executed. *Cmd* is *instr* denotes the instruction to be executed, i.e. if $ip = i$ and $curmethod = m$, then *instr* is the $i$-th instruction of method $m$ in $type(self)$. $binding = hd(env) \downarrow_1$ denotes the bindings of the method currently being executed. $is\_local(x)$ is *true* iff $x$ is a local variable or parameter of the method currently being executed. $is\_attribute(x)$ is *true* iff $x$ is an attribute of $type(self)$. We write $o_1 \overset{x}{\to} o_2 \in REF$ instead of $(o_1, o_2, x) \in REF$. $o_1 \to o_2 \in REF$ denotes that there is an attribute $x$ such that $o_1 \overset{x}{\to} o_2 \in REF$. $succ(x, obj)$ denotes the object referenced by object $obj$ via attribute $x$, i.e., it denotes the unique element $o$ such that $obj \overset{x}{\to} o \in REF$ if it exists (otherwise it is void). In this case $ref(obj, x)$ denotes this reference. $bind(x)$ denotes the object bound by *binding* to local variable or parameter $x$ of the current procedure. $object(des)$

denotes the object designated by designator *des*, i.e.

$$object(des) = \begin{cases} \text{void} & \text{if } des = \text{void} \\ succ(self, x) & \text{if } is\_attribute(x) \\ bind(x) & \text{if } is\_local(x) \\ succ(object(des'), x) & \text{if } des = des'.x \text{ for a designator } des' \end{cases}$$

For a method $m(x_1 : T_1; \ldots ; x_n : T_n) : T \ldots$ with local variables $y_1, \ldots, y_k$,

$$bindto(m, obj_1, \ldots, obj_n) =$$
$$\{(x_1, obj_1), \ldots, (x_n, obj_n), (y_1, \text{void}), \ldots, (y_k, \text{void})\}$$

denotes the binding that binds $obj_i$ to $x_i$, $i = 1, \ldots, n$. $update\_binding(x, o)$ updates the binding for $x$, i.e. binds $o$ to $x$, i.e.,

$$update\_binding(x, o) = binding := binding \setminus \{(x, bind(x))\} \cup \{(x, o)\}$$

$update(o, x, d)$ updates the object referenced by object $o$ via attribute $x$ to the object designated by desigator $d$, i.e.

$$update(o_1, x, o_2) =$$
$$\begin{cases} undefined & \text{if } o_1 = \text{void} \\ REF := REF \setminus \{ref(o_1, x)\} & \text{if } o_1 \neq \text{void and } o_2 = \text{void} \\ REF := REF \setminus \{ref(o_1, x)\} \cup \{o_2 \xrightarrow{x} o_2\} & \text{otherwise} \end{cases}$$

Figure 8 shows the transition rules for loading objects into accumulators using the above notations. Figure 9 shows the other transition rules. A transition rule is not applicable if it would access an attribute or call a method of void.

The following theorem relates typing rules to the dynamic type of objects. The proof is a induction on the number of state transitions and left to the reader.

**Theorem 4.** *Let $\pi \in$ BOOL be any program, $q$ be any state of $\pi$ reachable from an initial state, $A = type(self)$ and $m = curmethod$ in state $q$. Then, the following properties hold:*

**(a)** *If $\Gamma, A, m \vdash des : T$, then $type(object(des)) = T$ or $object(des) = \text{void}$ in state $q$.*

**(b)** *If $\Gamma, A, m \vdash expr : T$ and the command to be executed in state $q$ is a store-instruction (resulting from an assignment $des := expr$), a return (resulting from return $expr$), or a conditional statement (resulting from if $des = expr$ then $n$), then $type(ac) = T$ or $ac = \text{void}$ in state $q$.*

This theorem implies directly the

**Corollary 1.** *Let $\pi \in$ BOOL be any program and $q$ be any state of $\pi$ reachable from an initial state. Then, for every objects $obj, obj' \in$ OBJ and $obj \xrightarrow{a} obj'$ in state $q$, the following properties are satisfied:*

**(a)** *$T = type(obj)$ contains an attribute $a$.*
**(b)** *If $\Gamma, A \vdash a : T'$, then $type(obj') = T'$.*

```
if Cmd is load des
then ac := object(des)
     ip := ip + 1

if Cmd is load #T
then extend OBJ by o
              ac := obj
              type(obj) := T
     end
     ip := ip + 1

if Cmd is load m(d_1, ... , d_n)
then env := [(bindto(m, object(d_1), ... , object(d_n)), self, curmethod, ip + 1)|env]
     curmethod := m
     ip := 0

if Cmd is load des.m(d_1, ... , d_n) ∧ object(des) ≠ void
then env :=
     [(bindto(m, object(d_1), ... , object(d_n)), object(des), curmethod, ip + 1)|env]
     curmethod := m
     ip := 0
```

**Fig. 8.** Transition Rules for loading the Accumulator

```
if Cmd is store des ∧ object(des) ≠ void
then store(des, ac)
     ip := ip + 1

where
```

$$store(des, ac) = \begin{cases} update\_bindings(des, ac) & \text{if } is\_local(des) \\ update(self, des, ac) & \text{if } is\_attribute(des) \\ update(object(des'), x, ac) & \text{if } des = des'.x \end{cases}$$

```
if Cmd is return ∧ curmethod ≠ main
then env := tl(env)
     curmethod := hd(env) ↓_3
     ip := hd(env) ↓_4

if Cmd is beq des n ∧ object(des) = ac
then ip := n

if Cmd is beq des n ∧ object(des) ≠ ac
then ip := pc + 1
```

**Fig. 9.** Other Transition Rules

# References

1. A. V. Aho, J. E. Hopcroft, and J. D. Ullman. *Data Structures and Algorithms*. Addison-Wesley, 1983.
2. P. S. Almeida. Balloon types: Controlling sharing of state in data types. In *ECOOP' 97 - Object-Oriented Programming*, volume 1241 of *Lecture Notes in Computer Science*, pages 32–59, 1997.
3. T. H. Cormen, C. E. Leiserson, and R. L. Rivest. *Introduction to Algorithms*. McGraw Hill, 1991.
4. Free Software Foundation. The GNU C library. URL: http://www.gnu.ai.mit.edu/software/libc/libc.html.
5. Y. Gurevich. Evolving Algebras: Lipari Guide. In E. Börger, editor, *Specification and Validation Methods*. Oxford University Press, 1995.
6. Barry Hayes. Using Key Object Opportunism to Collect Old Objects. In *Proceedings of the OOPSLA '91 Conference on Object-oriented Programming Systems, Languages and Applications*, pages 33–46, nov 1991. Published as ACM SIGPLAN Notices, volume 26, number 11.
7. J. J. Horning. A case study in language design: Euclid. In F. L. Bauer and M. Broy, editors, *Proceedings of the International Summer School on Program Construction*, volume 69 of *LNCS*, pages 125–132, Marktoberdorf, FRG, July-August 1978. Springer.
8. Daniel H. H. Ingalls. The smalltalk-76 programming system design and implementation. In *Conference Record of the Fifth Annual ACM Symposium on Principles of Programming Languages, Tucson, Arizona*, pages 9–16. ACM, January 1978.
9. Richard E. Jones. *Garbage Collection: Algorithms for Automatic Dynamic Memory Management*. Wiley, July 1996. With a chapter on Distributed Garbage Collection by R. Lins. Reprinted February 1997.
10. H. W. Schmidt and W. Zimmermann. A complexity calculus for object-oriented programs. *Journal of Object-Oriented Systems*, 1(2):117–147, 1994.
11. H. W. Schmidt and W. Zimmermann. Reasoning about complexity of object-oriented programs. In E.-R. Olderog, editor, *Programming Concepts, Methods and Calculi*, volume A-56 of *IFIP Transactions*, pages 553–572, 1994.
12. James W. Stamos. Static grouping of small objects to enhance performance of a paged virtual memory. *ACM Transactions on Computer Systems*, 2(2):155–180, May 1984.
13. A. Tarski. A lattice-theoretical fixpoint theorem and its application. *Pacific J.Math.*, 5:285–309, 1955.

# Garbage Collection via Dynamic Type Inference
# — A Formal Treatment —

Haruo Hosoya and Akinori Yonezawa

Department of Information Science, The University of Tokyo, Hongo 7-3-1,
Bunkyo-ku, Tokyo 113-0033, Japan
{haruo, yonezawa}@is.s.u-tokyo.ac.jp

**Abstract.** A garbage collection (GC) scheme — what we call *type infer-ence GC* — that dynamically performs type inference is studied. In con-trast to conventional garbage collection that can collect only unreachable objects, this scheme can collect objects that are reachable yet semanti-cally garbage. The idea is to exploit ML-like polymorphic types that can tell whether or not each object may be used in the rest of computation. There has been some work studying algorithms of the GC scheme. How-ever, their descriptions had some obscurity in details of their methods, and did not give any formal correctness proof that captures the details. These facts, we believe, make their descriptions still unconvincing for implementors.

This paper aims to present a trustworthy specification of the GC scheme. In this specification, we first consider an underlying language that suit-ably reflects implementation details, on top of which we then formulate an algorithm of type inference GC, and formally prove its correctness. A significant point in our formulation is that we specify how to deal with Hindley-Milner polymorphism. Furthermore, showing our experimental results, we discuss in what cases this GC scheme is beneficial.

## 1 Introduction

In a program, some objects (i.e., heap-allocated values) are never accessed after a given point of execution. We call such objects *semantic garbage* at that point. These include not only *unreachable* objects with no pointers from the live part of the heap, but also some reachable objects whose values are not needed in the rest of the computation. For example, consider the following functional program:

```
let l = [[1], [2], [3]]
    g = λf.(f l)
in g length
end
```

Suppose that a garbage collection (GC) is invoked just before the application $(f\ l)$ is evaluated. Since the elements of the list $l$ are reachable, these elements are retained by conventional trace-based GC schemes, such as mark & sweep and copying. However, they will never be accessed from then on. We could enable conventional GCs to collect such semantic garbage by inserting assignments that "nullify" variables or fields of data structures holding the garbage. However, clearly it would impose a heavy burden on programmers and considerably decrease readability of programs.

In order to collect such reachable garbage, recent work has suggested a sophisticated GC scheme — what we call *type inference GC* — that exploits ML-like polymorphic type systems [5, 4]. Basically, the GC scheme traces objects, using their types that indicate their structures. These types are recovered partly from static types. However, due to ML-polymorphism, some static types contain *type variables* whose actual types are determined dynamically. The GC scheme infers such types at GC time. Not all actual types for type variables can be recovered. Surprisingly, however, objects whose types are not recovered, i.e., remain to be type variables, can safely be collected. In the above example, the global state just before $(f\ l)$ is evaluated can be represented as

$$
\begin{aligned}
\textsf{letrec } l_1 &= [1] \\
l_2 &= [2] \\
l_3 &= [3] \\
l &= [l_1, l_2, l_3] \\
f &= \textsf{length} \\
\textsf{in } f\ l
\end{aligned}
$$

where the bindings represent the heap, and the body expression represents the remaining computation, which is only the application of $f$ to $l$. In other words, the body expression represents the stack. Let the pointers $f$ and $l$ in the stack be given static types $t_1 \rightarrow t_2$ and $t_1$, respectively. Suppose that the GC is triggered at this point. The GC first traces the stack, which contains two pointers $f$ and $l$. Since the static type $t_1$ of $l$ does not tell what type of object it refers to, the GC suspends to trace $l$. The GC then traces $f$ with static type $t_1 \rightarrow t_2$, and performs unification between this type and the type $\forall t.(t\ \textsf{list}) \rightarrow \textsf{int}$ of the object length. Since this will instantiate the static type $t_1$ of $l$ to be $t$ list, the GC traces $l$, resulting in giving type $t$ to the pointers $l_1$, $l_2$, and $l_3$ to list elements. Finally, these elements are collected as semantic garbage. It is correct intuitively because the pointers $l_1$, $l_2$, and $l_3$ can be assumed to refer to objects of *any* type (nil, for example) for correctly performing the rest of computation.

Closely viewing the algorithm, notice that we had to remember the pointer $l$ that was given type variable, because the type variable might be instantiated in the rest of tracing. Goldberg and Gloger uses a mechanism called "defer-list" for this purpose [5]. The GC keeps an association of addresses with types. When the GC finds pointer, it associates the pointed address with the static type given to the pointer. The GC traces an address only when it is associated with a concrete type (a type other than a type variable, such as a function type and a list type). If there are multiple pointers to an address, the GC may trace the same address more than once. When such sharing occurs, the GC unifies the types given to the pointers. For example, if the GC encounters another pointer to the list that is given type (int list) list, then it unifies $t$ list and (int list) list.

From the above presentation, we can see that type inference GC is a rather complicated scheme and raises several non-trivial questions. First, it is not obvious that GC-time unifications always succeed, especially those for shared addresses. Second, it is subtle how to unify polymorphic types that are not trivially related (e.g., $t_1 \to t_2$ and $\forall t.(t \text{ list}) \to \text{int}$). Third, we may not easily understand that the collected objects are actually garbage. Previous papers on the topic have not addressed these questions rigorously.

Therefore we aim in this paper to give a trustworthy specification of type inference GC, in the sense that it specifies a GC algorithm reasonably in detail, and that it is given a robust trust by a formal proof of its correctness. For this goal, we first define an underlying language that suitably treats sharing and embeds static type information. On top of it, we construct an algorithm of type inference GC that uses information contained in the language. We then prove correctness of the algorithm. The correctness consists of termination which includes success of each GC-time unification, and soundness with respect to an operational semantics of the underlying language, which tells that collected objects are actually garbage. A significant point in our formulation is that we use Hindley-Milner polymorphism, and specify how to deal with polymorphic types in the GC.

Although our framework uses a strict functional language, we believe that it can be applied to languages in other evaluation orders such as a lazy functional language. In addition, our framework can be extended to include other popular features such as tuples, variants, and ML references. It should be remarked, however, that this scheme does not work for languages with operations that may inspect types of their actual arguments. The operations include polymorphic equalities, typecase constructs, and dynamic type checks.

Among many questions on practicality, we are especially interested in how much semantic garbage can be collected by the type inference GC scheme in comparison with conventional GCs. We examined it by a preliminary experiment using a prototype interpreter and a type inference GC that we implemented in Standard ML. From the results, though we cannot claim that this scheme benefits for every application, we expect that it benefits particularly for programs with a program structure that we call the *phase structure*.

The rest of this paper is organized as follows. After defining basic notation in Section 3, we present our language in Section 4. On top of this, we describe an algorithm of the GC scheme in Section 5 with its correctness. We formally proved all theorems in this paper. In Section 6, we show results of our experiment and give a discussion on them. In Section 7, we remark on cost of this scheme. Section 8 reviews related work. In Section 9, we conclude this paper as well as touch upon future directions.

## 2 Underlying Idea

When discussing algorithms of GC, we often consider a notion of *accessibility*, with which we may give a GC algorithm in such a way that it repeatedly finds

218

an accessible object and traces it. Particularly in traced-based GC schemes, all objects referred from a (live) object are accessible. For example, an object $\lambda x.(f\ l)$ has two free variables $f$ and $l$ and the objects referred by these variables are accessible.

In the type inference GC scheme, we use a type-based accessibility. The above object will have the following type judgment:

$$\{f : t_1 \to t_2, l : t_1\} \vdash \lambda x.(f\ l) : t_3 \to t_2$$

Usually, we would read this as "under the type environment $\{f : t_1 \to t_2, l : t_1\}$, the object $\lambda x.(f\ l)$ has type $t_3 \to t_2$." However, the type judgment tells more interesting information:

The type environment $\{f : t_1 \to t_2, l : t_1\}$ tells how the object $\lambda x.(f\ l)$ accesses the free variables. Specifically, the object accesses the variable $f$ at most as a function of type $t_1 \to t_2$, and does not access the variable $l$.

In our formulation, we refer to such a pair of a type environment and a type as a *typing*. For a given typing for an object, if it gives to a free variable $x$ a type other than a type variable, then we say that the object referred by $x$ is accessible.

The idea of this accessibility will be understood as follows. As in usual ML-like type systems, well-typedness property of an object is preserved by any instantiation of type variables. Moreover, the well-typedness property ensures that evaluation will never get stuck as far as any subexpression of the object is the redex of the evaluation. Therefore free variables that are assigned type variables can be assumed to refer to arbitrary objects. This intuitively means that the objects referred by the free variables will never be accessed.[1]

## 3 Basic Definitions

Let $TVar$ be a set of *type variables* ranged over by $s, t, \ldots$. Define *monotypes* and *polytypes* as usual:

$$\begin{aligned}\text{(monotypes)} \ &\tau ::= t \mid \text{int} \mid \tau_1 \to \tau_2 \\ \text{(polytypes)} \ &\sigma ::= \tau \mid \forall t.\sigma\end{aligned}$$

Monotypes are either type variables, integer types, or function types. The type $\forall t_1 \ldots \forall t_n.\tau$ is abbreviated as $\forall t_1 \ldots t_n.\tau$ or $\forall \bar{t}.\tau$. Define $\text{Unq}(\forall \bar{t}.\tau) = \tau$. Let there be a set of (program) *variables*, ranged over by $w, x, y, \ldots$. Addresses are a subset of variables, which are ranged over by $a, b, \ldots$ and are assumed to contain a distinct address $\#$. The address $\#$ will be used to be temporarily assigned to

---

[1] Of course, this reasoning fails when we have some operations such as typecase that may *inspect* types of objects.

a variable. We define a *type environment* as a set of pairs of a variable (including #) and a polytype in the form of $x : \sigma$, with no variable $x$ occurring twice:

$$\text{(type environments) } \Gamma, \Delta ::= \{x_1 : \sigma_1, \ldots, x_n : \sigma_n\}$$

We regard a type environment $\Gamma$ as a finite function that maps $x$ into $\sigma$ for each $x : \sigma \in \Gamma$.

A *type substitution* $S$ is a substitution of monotypes for free type variables. $FTV(\tau)$ and $FTV(\Gamma)$ denote the sets of free type variables occurring in $\tau$ and $\Gamma$, respectively. $S\Gamma$ is defined by $(S\Gamma)(x) = S(\Gamma(x))$ for $x \in Dom(\Gamma)$. Pairs of type environments and monotypes, written $\langle \Gamma, \tau \rangle$, are called *typings*. The monotype $\tau$ of a typing $\langle \Gamma, \tau \rangle$ is called *result type*. A type $\tau'$ is a *substitution instance* or simply an instance of $\tau$ via $S$, written $\tau \prec_S \tau'$, iff $S\tau = \tau'$. A typing $\langle \Gamma, \tau \rangle$ is *less instantiated* than $\langle \Gamma', \tau' \rangle$, written $\langle \Gamma, \tau \rangle \prec_S \langle \Gamma', \tau' \rangle$, iff $S\Gamma \subseteq \Gamma'$ and $\tau \prec_S \tau'$. We omit the subscript $S$ if it is not important.

A monotype $\tau$ is a *generic instance* of a polytype $\sigma = \forall t_1 \ldots t_n.\tau'$, written $\sigma \geq \tau$, iff there is a type substitution $S$ for $t_1, \ldots, t_n$ such that $S\tau' = \tau$. As for polytypes, we write $\sigma \geq \sigma'$ iff there is an $\alpha$-variant $\forall s_1 \ldots s_m.\tau'$ of $\sigma'$ such that no $s_i$ $(1 \leq i \leq m)$ occurs free in $\sigma$ and $\sigma \geq \tau'$. When $Dom(\Gamma) = Dom(\Gamma')$, we write $\Gamma \geq \Gamma'$ iff $\Gamma(x) \geq \Gamma'(x)$ for any $x \in Dom(\Gamma)$.

Let $f$ and $g$ be finite mappings. $Dom(f)$ and $Rng(f)$ are the domain and the range of $f$, respectively. The function composition $f \circ g$ is a function defined by $(f \circ g)(d) = f(g(d))$ for $d \in Dom(g)$. When the domains of $f$ and $g$ are disjoint, the disjoint sum $f \uplus g$ is a function defined by

$$(f \uplus g)(d) = \begin{cases} f(d) & (d \in Dom(f)) \\ g(d) & (d \in Dom(g)). \end{cases}$$

We write $f|_A$ for the restriction of $f$ to the domain $A$.

# 4 Language

As mentioned in Introduction, we consider an underlying language in which sharing and static type information are embodied. In the language, adopting ideas in [12, 11], we use explicit temporary variables, environments, stacks, and heaps.

## 4.1 Source Language

Before giving how to embed static type information in our language, we explain what static type information to use. Instead of type information obtained by a usual static type inference, we use finer type information, which was proposed by Fradet [4]. In this method, we use the principal typing for each continuation. The motivation is as following. The usual type information monolithically gives each variable a single type. However, for a continuation when the GC is invoked, such type information may be too instantiated. For example, consider the following program:

```
let x = hd (hd l)
in length l
```

Because of the first line, $l$ is given type $(t'$ list) list. Suppose that the GC is invoked just before length $l$. Even though the elements of $l$ will not be used, the GC cannot collect them because they are given a concrete type $t'$ list. We can (partly) overcome this problem by providing "minimal" type information individually for each continuation. Specifically, we may give $l$ type $(t'$ list) list for let $x = $ hd (hd$l$) in length $l$, and give $l$ type $t$ list for length $l$.

In our formulation, to express this static type information, as a source language, we use the form of expressions that each intermediate result is explicitly bound to a "temporary" variable (also known as A-normal form), and annotate each expression with static type information. The annotation has the form $^{\langle \Gamma,\tau \rangle}e$, where $\langle \Gamma, \tau \rangle$ gives a typing for $e$. That is, intuitively, $\Gamma$ tells how $e$ accesses its free variables, and $\tau$ tells at least what type $e$ has, as explained in Section 2. We can easily see that this form is suitable for computing type information for each continuation at compile time. In the above example, we may give annotation typings as

$$^{\langle \Gamma_1,\tau_1 \rangle} \text{let } x = \text{hd } l$$
$$\text{in } ^{\langle \Gamma_2,\tau_2 \rangle} \text{let } y = \text{hd } x$$
$$\text{in } ^{\langle \Gamma_3,\tau_3 \rangle}(\text{length } l)$$

where $\Gamma_1(l) = (t'$ list) list and $\Gamma_3(l) = t$ list.

Formally, the syntax of our source language is summarized as follows:

(values) $v ::= \,^{\langle \Gamma,\tau \rangle}i \mid \,^{\langle \Gamma,\tau \rangle}\lambda x.c$
(codes) $\bar{c} ::= \,^{\langle \Gamma,\tau \rangle}\text{let } x : \sigma = v \text{ in } c \mid \,^{\langle \Gamma,\tau \rangle}\text{let } w : \sigma = x\, y \text{ in } c \mid \,^{\langle \Gamma,\tau \rangle}x$

Values are either integers[2], ranged over by $i$, or functions. A code is a sequence of let expressions that terminates with a variable for result of the code. The let expression binds the result of either a value or an application to a variable. Each value or code is added an annotation typing.


## 4.2 Evaluation

In real implementation, of course, the GC uses the static type information as it is given at compile time. Therefore we want the description never to operate on the annotation typing at run time. For this purpose, it is not appropriate to use substitutions in our operational semantics. If we used substitutions, we might have to somehow define "$\Gamma[y/x]$" for considering $(^{\langle \Gamma,\tau \rangle}e)[y/x]$ where $[y/x]$ is substitution of $y$ for the variable $x$. This would involve modification of a mapping from $x$ to a mapping from $y$, and even unification between the type of $x$ and the type of $y$ if mappings from both variables already exist. (Actually, such manipulations should be postponed until GC time.)

---

[2] To simplify the arguments, we allocate integers to heaps, which are usually represented in actual implementation as unboxed values.

Instead of substitutions, we use explicit environments and stacks. An environment is a finite function from variables into addresses, as defined by:

$$\text{(environments) } V ::= \{x_1 = a_1, \ldots, x_n = a_n\}$$

We define frames as pairs of environments and codes, and objects as pairs of environments and values:[3]

$$\text{(frames) } F ::= \langle\!\langle V, c \rangle\!\rangle$$
$$\text{(objects) } h ::= \langle\!\langle V, v \rangle\!\rangle$$

An environment attached to a code or value maps variables in the code or value into addresses in heaps. Thus environments represent local variables in frames of stacks or closure records of function objects. A stack is a semicolon-separated sequence of frames where the right-most frame is "top":

$$\text{(stacks) } C ::= F \mid F^{[\sigma]}; C$$

A stack is extended at a function call and is shrunk at a result. We assume that the environment of each frame in a stack maps some variable $x$ into # except for the top frame.

Moreover, to treat sharing, we use explicit heaps. A heap is a finite function from addresses into objects:

$$\text{(heaps) } H ::= \{a_1 = h_1^{[\sigma_1]}, \ldots, a_n = h_n^{[\sigma_n]}\}$$

When a value is evaluated, an object for the value is allocated in a heap. When an application is evaluated, the variable referring to a function is automatically dereferenced. Heaps can treat cycle. However, it will make sense only when our source language includes some feature to create cycles in heaps. A global state is represented as a program in the letrec form that consists of a heap and a stack. An answer is a program that has only one frame whose code is just a variable:

$$\text{(programs) } P ::= \text{letrec } H \text{ in } C$$
$$\text{(answers) } A ::= \text{letrec } H \text{ in } \langle\!\langle V, {}^{\langle \Gamma, \tau \rangle} x \rangle\!\rangle$$

Above, we have another type annotation $\sigma$ in $h^{[\sigma]}$ and $\sigma$ in $F^{[\sigma]}$. We call these types "declaration types" and will explain them later.

Before giving our operational semantics, we show an example of evaluation in our language in Figure 1. At the beginning, the program has the empty heap and a stack with one frame that has the empty environment and the code $c_1$. In the first step, we evaluate the value $v_1$. It results in allocation of an object at a new address $a$ in the heap. The object is formed by coupling the current environment and the value as $\langle\!\langle \{\}, v_1 \rangle\!\rangle$. The address $a$ is assigned to the temporary variable $x$ in the environment, and the code is now set as $c_2$. In the second step, we

---

[3] We can include tuples in the same way by expressing a tuple object as $\langle\!\langle V, \langle x_1, x_2 \rangle \rangle\!\rangle$, though it should be represented in actual implementation as $\langle V(x_1), V(x_2) \rangle$.

$$\text{letrec} \qquad \{\} \qquad \text{in } \langle\!\langle \{\}, c_1 \rangle\!\rangle$$
$$\xrightarrow{\text{alloc}} \text{letrec } \{a = \langle\!\langle \{\}, v_1 \rangle\!\rangle\} \text{ in } \langle\!\langle \{x = a\}, c_2 \rangle\!\rangle$$
$$\xrightarrow{\text{app}} \text{letrec } \{a = \langle\!\langle \{\}, v_1 \rangle\!\rangle\} \text{ in } \langle\!\langle \{x = a, y = \#\}, c_3 \rangle\!\rangle; \langle\!\langle \{z = 1\}, c_4 \rangle\!\rangle$$
$$\xrightarrow{\text{ret}} \text{letrec } \{a = \langle\!\langle \{\}, v_1 \rangle\!\rangle\} \text{ in } \langle\!\langle \{x = a, y = 1\}, c_3 \rangle\!\rangle$$

$$\text{where} \quad \begin{aligned} c_1 &= {}^{\langle \Gamma_1, \tau_1 \rangle} \text{let } x = v_1 \text{ in } c_2 & v_1 &= {}^{\langle \Gamma_5, \tau_5 \rangle} \lambda z. c_4 \\ c_2 &= {}^{\langle \Gamma_2, \tau_2 \rangle} \text{let } y = (x\ 1) \text{ in } c_3 & c_4 &= {}^{\langle \Gamma_4, \tau_4 \rangle} z \\ c_3 &= {}^{\langle \Gamma_3, \tau_3 \rangle} y \end{aligned}$$

**Fig. 1.** Example of evaluation

evaluate the application $(x\ 1)$. It dereferences the variable $x$, which refers to the function object $\langle\!\langle \{\}, v_1 \rangle\!\rangle$ that has just been allocated in the heap. The stack is extended with a new "callee" frame that is constructed from the object, with the parameter $z$ being assigned the actual argument 1, and the code being set as the body code $c_4$. In the "caller" frame, $\#$ is temporarily assigned to the variable $y$ until the callee returns. In the third step, the callee returns the value 1 that was assigned to $z$. We shrink the stack and reassign 1 to the variable $y$ in the caller frame that has been assigned $\#$. Notice that all the annotation typings on the codes and the values are never manipulated in the evaluation. Thus the static type information is available whenever GC is invoked.

Our operational semantics is given by an evaluation relation $\longrightarrow$ over programs, defined in Figure 2.[4] The (stack) rule says that if a program can be reduced, then a program obtained by adding a frame at the bottom to the program can also be reduced. The other three rules are as explained above.

The GC will use declaration types, which have two kinds. One is on objects. When a let expression let $x : \sigma = v$ in $c$ of allocation is evaluated, the declared type $\sigma$ is attached to the allocated object, as $h^{[\sigma]}$. The other is on frames. When a let expression let $w : \sigma = (x\ y)$ in $c$ of application is evaluated, the declared type $\sigma$ is attached to the caller frame, as $F^{[\sigma]}$. While the declaration type on an object is relevant to the type of the object, the declaration type on a frame is relevant to the type of $\#$ in the frame. Therefore declaration types are attached to every frame except for the top one. Declaration types are used only at GC time and are not essential for deriving type judgments.

We formally define accessing of an address, and semantic garbage.

**Definition 4.1.** *We say $P$ accesses $a$ iff $V(x) = a$, $a \in Dom(H)$ and either*

*1. $P = \text{letrec } H \text{ in } \langle\!\langle V, {}^{\langle \Gamma, \tau \rangle} x \rangle\!\rangle$; or*

---

[4] In this formulation, an environment may contain variables not free in a code or value. This may not only make closures uselessly large but also cause unnecessary unification at GC time. It would be more close to implementation if we restricted the environment as $\langle\!\langle V|_{FV(e)}, e \rangle\!\rangle$. Our experiment shown in Section 6 is based on it. Our formulation, however, does not adopt it for simplicity. Instead, we avoid unnecessary unification on the side of GC formulation. (See Section 5.)

$$\frac{\text{letrec } H \text{ in } C \longrightarrow \text{letrec } H' \text{ in } C'}{\text{(stack) letrec } H \text{ in } F^{[\sigma]}; C \longrightarrow \text{letrec } H' \text{ in } F^{[\sigma]}; C'}$$

(alloc) letrec $H$ in $\langle\!\langle V, {}^{\langle \Gamma, \tau \rangle} \text{let } x : \sigma = v \text{ in } c \rangle\!\rangle$
$\longrightarrow$ letrec $H \uplus \{a = \langle\!\langle V, v \rangle\!\rangle^{[\sigma]}\}$ in $\langle\!\langle V \uplus \{x = a\}, c \rangle\!\rangle$     $(a \notin Dom(H))$

(app) letrec $H$ in $\langle\!\langle V, {}^{\langle \Gamma, \tau \rangle} \text{let } w : \sigma = (x\ y) \text{ in } c \rangle\!\rangle$
$$(H(V(x)) = \langle\!\langle V', {}^{\langle \Gamma', \tau' \rangle} \lambda z.c' \rangle\!\rangle^{[\sigma']})$$
$\longrightarrow$ letrec $H$ in $\langle\!\langle V \uplus \{w = \#\}, c \rangle\!\rangle^{[\sigma]}; \langle\!\langle V' \uplus \{z = V(y)\}, c' \rangle\!\rangle$

(ret) letrec $H$ in $\langle\!\langle V \uplus \{w = \#\}, c \rangle\!\rangle^{[\sigma]}; \langle\!\langle V', {}^{\langle \Gamma, \tau \rangle} x \rangle\!\rangle$
$\longrightarrow$ letrec $H$ in $\langle\!\langle V \uplus \{w = V'(x)\}, c \rangle\!\rangle$

**Fig. 2.** Operational semantics

2. $P = \text{letrec } H \text{ in } F^{[\sigma]}; \ldots; \langle\!\langle V, {}^{\langle \Gamma, \tau \rangle} \text{let } w = (x\ y) \text{ in } c \rangle\!\rangle$.

$H_1$ *is semantic garbage for* $P = \text{letrec } H_1 \uplus H_2 \text{ in } C$ *iff there is no* $P'$ *s.t.* $P \longrightarrow^*$
$P'$ *and* $P'$ *accesses some* $a \in Dom(H_1)$.

## 4.3 Type System

We give the typing rules for our language in Figure 3. To make the set of typing rules compact, we define *expressions* as a super set of both the set of values and the set of codes:

(expressions) $e ::= x \mid i \mid \lambda x.e \mid e_1\ e_2 \mid \text{let } x : \sigma = e_1 \text{ in } e_2 \mid {}^{\langle \Gamma, \tau \rangle} e$

The typing rules derive the following judgments:

$\Gamma \vdash e : \tau$      well-typed code or value
$\Gamma \vdash \langle\!\langle V, e \rangle\!\rangle : \tau$ well-typed frame or object
$\Gamma \vdash C : \tau$      well-typed stack
$\Gamma \vdash H : \Gamma'$      well-typed heap
$\vdash P : \tau$         well-typed program

Although these type judgments carry almost the same information as usual Hindley-Milner type systems, we can read these, as mentioned in Section 2, that the type environment indicates how the syntactic object accesses its free variables and what type the syntactic object itself has.

The first five rules are the same as in usual type systems. The (annot) rule gives conditions for static type information by two premises. The first premise ensures that any typing for an enclosing context must be more instantiated than the annotation typing. The second premise ensures that the expression must be well-typed under the annotation typing. In Section 4.1, we mentioned that annotation typings were intended to express the principal typings for expressions.

*Expressions:*

$$\frac{}{\Gamma \vdash i : \mathsf{int}} \; (int) \qquad \frac{\Gamma(x) \geq \tau}{\Gamma \vdash x : \tau} \; (var) \qquad \frac{\Gamma \uplus \{x : \tau_1\} \vdash e : \tau_2}{\Gamma \vdash \lambda x.e : \tau_1 \to \tau_2} \; (abs)$$

$$\frac{\Gamma \vdash e_1 : \tau' \quad \sigma = \forall \bar{t}.\tau' \quad \bar{t} \cap FTV(\Gamma) = \emptyset \quad \Gamma \uplus \{x : \sigma\} \vdash e_2 : \tau}{\Gamma \vdash \mathsf{let}\; x : \sigma = e_1 \; \mathsf{in}\; e_2 : \tau} \; (let)$$

$$\frac{\Gamma \vdash e_1 : \tau_1 \to \tau_2 \quad \Gamma \vdash e_2 : \tau_1}{\Gamma \vdash e_1\, e_2 : \tau_2} \; (app) \qquad \frac{\langle \Gamma', \tau' \rangle \prec \langle \Gamma, \tau \rangle \quad \Gamma' \vdash e : \tau'}{\Gamma \vdash {}^{\langle \Gamma', \tau' \rangle}e : \tau} \; (annot)$$

*Environments, stacks, heaps, and programs:*

$$\frac{\Gamma \circ V \geq \Gamma' \quad \Gamma' \vdash e : \tau}{\Gamma \vdash \langle\!\langle V, e \rangle\!\rangle : \tau} \; (env) \qquad \frac{\emptyset \vdash H : \Gamma \quad \Gamma \vdash C : \tau}{\vdash \mathsf{letrec}\; H \;\mathsf{in}\; C : \tau} \; (prog)$$

$$\frac{\Gamma \vdash C : \tau' \quad \sigma' = \forall \bar{t}.\tau' \quad \bar{t} \cap FTV(\Gamma) = \emptyset \quad \Gamma \uplus \{\# : \sigma'\} \vdash F : \tau \quad \sigma \asymp \sigma'}{\Gamma \vdash F^{[\sigma]}; C : \tau} \; (stack)$$

$$\frac{\forall a \in Dom(\Gamma') = Dom(H).\, \big(H(a) = h^{[\sigma]} \quad \Gamma \uplus \Gamma' \vdash h : \mathsf{Unq}(\Gamma'(a)) \quad \sigma \asymp \Gamma'(a)\big)}{\Gamma \vdash H : \Gamma'} \; (heap)$$

**Fig. 3.** Typing rules

However, we do not incorporate the principality in our formulation because it is not relevant to soundness of the GC.

The (env) rule has two premises. Assuming a type environment $\Gamma'$ for local variables, the second premise ensures that the expression must be well-typed under $\langle \Gamma', \tau \rangle$. The first premise then relates by generic instance between types of addresses given in $\Gamma$ and types of the local variables given in $\Gamma'$. This premise would intuitively be understood by regarding the environment-attached expression $\langle\!\langle \{x_1 = a_1, \ldots\}, e \rangle\!\rangle$ as a let expression $\mathsf{let}\; \{x_1 = a_1, \ldots\}$ in $e$. In order to give a typing for this expression, we would require $\Gamma(a_1) \geq \Gamma'(x_1), \ldots$. Note that this typing rule ensures that $x \in Dom(V)$ and $V(x) \in Dom(\Gamma)$, for any $x \in FV(e)$. Combining the (annot) rule and the (env) rule, we can relate the type of an address $a$ in $\Gamma$ and the type of a variable $x$ in $\Gamma'$ that refers to $a$, as $\Gamma(a) \geq \Gamma''(x)$ and $\Gamma'(x) \prec \Gamma''(x)$ for some $\Gamma''$. Since this relation is often used in the next section, we abbreviate it as $\Gamma(a) \lessdot \Gamma'(x)$. Formally, we write $\sigma \lessdot_S \sigma'$ iff $\sigma' \geq \sigma''$ and $\sigma \prec \sigma''$ for some $\sigma''$. Similarly, we write $\langle \Gamma, \tau \rangle \lessdot_S \langle \Gamma', \tau' \rangle$ iff $\Gamma' \geq \Gamma''$ and $\langle \Gamma, \tau \rangle \prec \langle \Gamma'', \tau' \rangle$ for some $\Gamma''$.

The (stack) rule is analogous to the (let) rule. The (heap) rule deals with potential cycles in heaps. The (stack) rule and the (heap) rule additionally require "compatibility" between declaration types and types that are inferred by the rules. Polytypes $\sigma_1$ and $\sigma_2$ are *compatible*, written $\sigma_1 \asymp \sigma_2$, iff $\sigma_3 \prec \sigma_1$ and $\sigma_3 \prec \sigma_2$, for some polytype $\sigma_3$. In the (stack) rule, the declaration type $\sigma$ on

$F$ must be compatible with the inferred type $\sigma'$ of $\#$. In the (heap) rule, the declaration type $\sigma$ on $h$ must be compatible with the inferred type $\Gamma'(a)$.

Although we do not describe in this paper, we can infer annotation typings from source programs using a standard algorithm of polymorphic type reconstruction [10] with a small modification.

We can show type soundness of our language as the following theorem that a well-typed program terminates or proceeds without a type error.

**Theorem 4.1 (Type Soundness).** *If* $\vdash P : \tau$, *then either* $P$ *is an answer or else there exists* $P'$ *s.t.* $P \longrightarrow P'$ *and* $\vdash P' : \tau$.

## 5  Garbage Collection

### 5.1  Overview

Let us begin with viewing the type inference GC scheme on the analogy of the trace-based GC scheme. Both schemes maintain a *live set*, which is memory regarded as live during the GC, A live set consists of the current stack, and a part of the current heap, called "to-heap". Then these schemes can be seen as a fixpoint algorithm to find a live set that satisfies the following conditions: the live set contains the stack and all objects *accessible* from the live set. Concretely, the algorithm begins with a live set consisting of the stack; it then repeatedly finds an object that is accessible from the live set and that is not yet in the live set, and adds the object to the live set; the algorithm terminates when it cannot find such an object.

While the trace-based GC uses "refer-to" accessibility, the type inference GC uses a type-based accessibility, as mentioned in Section 2. To obtain an accessible object, we maintain a *GC typing* during GC. A GC typing gives a "typing for a live set", that is, it tells the following information:

- how the stack accesses addresses
- how each object in the to-heap accesses addresses

An accessible object can be obtained by picking up an object whose address is given a concrete type in the GC typing.

When finding an accessible object, the GC adds it to the live set. At this point, the GC typing must be updated so that it also tells how the added object accesses addresses. It is precisely for this purpose that we perform GC-time unification. In the unification, we extract the annotation typing given in the object, and unify the GC typing with the annotation typing. We call this action "tracing", which is a reminiscence of the trace-based GC. An interesting point is that the GC typing precisely corresponds to the types of pointers kept at addresses that are mentioned in Introduction.

The rest of this section formally describes the above algorithm of type inference GC and proves its correctness. Section 5.2 describes our treatment of polytypes in the GC-time unification. In Section 5.3, we give a function for tracing an object or a stack, which involves unification between a GC typing and an annotation typing. Section 5.4 presents the main loop of the fixpoint algorithm.

## 5.2 Polytype Unification

It seems inevitable that the GC-time unification encounters polytypes that are
not trivially related. For example, consider the program

$$\text{let } g : \forall t_1 t_2.t_2 \to (t_2 \to t_1) \to t_1 = \lambda x.\lambda y.^{\langle \Gamma_2, \tau_2 \rangle}(y\ x)$$
$$\text{in let } z = (g\ l\ \text{length})$$
$$\text{in } ^{\langle \Gamma_1, \tau_1 \rangle}\text{length}$$

where $\Gamma_1(\text{length}) = \forall t_3.t_3$ list $\to$ int and $\Gamma_2(y) = t_2 \to t_1$. After the application
$(g\ l\ \text{length})$, the program will be

$$\text{letrec}\ \left\{ a_{\text{length}} = \langle\!\langle \{\}, \ldots \rangle\!\rangle^{[\forall t_3.t_3\ \text{list} \to \text{int}]} \right\}$$
$$\ldots$$
$$\text{in } \langle\!\langle \{\ldots, \text{length} = a_{\text{length}}, z = \# \}, ^{\langle \Gamma_1, \tau_1 \rangle}\text{length} \rangle\!\rangle;$$
$$\langle\!\langle \{\ldots, y = a_{\text{length}} \}, ^{\langle \Gamma_2, \tau_2 \rangle}(y\ x) \rangle\!\rangle$$

where $a_{\text{length}}$ is the address where the function length allocated. Because the
variable length in the first frame and the variable $y$ in the second frame share the
same address $a_{\text{length}}$, GC would have to somehow unify their types $\Gamma_1(\text{length}) =$
$\forall t_3.t_3$ list $\to$ int and $\Gamma_2(y) = t_2 \to t_1$.

Since considering unification between arbitrary two polytypes seems difficult,
we develop a unification method that works specially in our framework. First of
all, the goal of unification is to obtain a GC typing $\langle \Delta, \tau \rangle$ under which a newly
added object or frame is well-typed. In the above case, when we trace the first
frame, the GC typing should satisfy $\Delta(a_{\text{length}}) \twoheadleftarrow \Gamma_1(\text{length})$, and when we trace
the second frame, the GC typing should satisfy $\Delta(a_{\text{length}}) \twoheadleftarrow \Gamma_2(y)$.

It turns out technically convenient to initially give a GC typing that maps
every address into the *least instantiated type* of the declaration type on it. In the
above case, since the declaration on $a_{\text{length}}$ is $\forall t_3.t_3$ list $\to$ int, we initially give
$\Delta(a_{\text{length}}) = \forall t_3.t_3$ list $\to t_4$, where $t_4$ is a fresh type variable.

Our unification method is rather simple. Suppose we have as inputs a type
$\Delta(a) = \sigma_1$ and a type $\Gamma(x) = \sigma_2$. We first instantiate all quantified type variables in the types $\sigma_1$ and $\sigma_2$ with fresh type variables, and then unify the obtained monotypes. As a result, we obtain a type substitution $S$ and update
the GC typing as $S\Delta(a) = S\sigma_1$. In the above example, we will obtain for the
first frame a type substitution $S_1 = \{t_4 \mapsto \text{int}\}$, and update the GC typing
as $S_1\Delta(a_{\text{length}}) = \forall t_3.t_3$ list $\to$ int. For the second frame, we will obtain a
type substitution $S_2 = \{t_1 \mapsto t_3'\ \text{list}, t_2 \mapsto \text{int}\}$, and update the GC typing
as $S_2 S_1 \Delta(a_{\text{length}}) = \forall t_3.t_3$ list $\to$ int (actually unchanged).

To roughly explain why this method works, we have the following invariant
at any time in the GC. For any address $a$, we have its "actual type" $\Gamma_0(a)$ that
satisfies $\Delta(a) \prec \Gamma_0(a)$, and $\Gamma_1(x) \twoheadleftarrow \Gamma_0(a)$ for all annotation typings $\langle \Gamma_1, \tau_1 \rangle$.
The first condition is ensured by our initial GC typing and unification method
given above, and the second condition is ensured by our type system. From these
conditions, our unification can be shown to succeed with $S\Delta(a) \geq S\Gamma_1(x)$, which
implies the goal condition of unification: $S\Delta(a) \twoheadleftarrow \Gamma_1(x)$.

The following function PolyUni formally specifies our unification method where we generalize the above method to take typings as inputs:

$$\mathsf{PolyUni}(\langle \Gamma_1, \tau_1\rangle, \langle \Gamma_2, \tau_2\rangle) =$$
$$\quad \mathsf{let}\ E = \{\mathsf{Unique}(\Gamma_1(x)) = \mathsf{Unique}(\Gamma_2(x)) \mid x \in Dom(\Gamma_1)\} \cup \{\tau_1 = \tau_2\}$$
$$\quad \mathsf{in}\ \ S = \mathsf{Unify}(E)$$

The function Unify is the well-known unification algorithm to compute the most general unifier of a set $E$ of unifiable equations of monotypes [14]. Unique instantiates all quantified type variables in a polytype as fresh type variables, defined as $\mathsf{Unique}(\forall \bar{t}.\tau) = S\tau$ where $S(t) = t'$ ($t \in \bar{t}$, and $t'$ is a fresh type variable). The following lemma summarizes the above-mentioned properties for PolyUni.

**Lemma 5.1.** *Suppose* $FTV(\Gamma_1, \tau_1) \cap FTV(\Gamma_2, \tau_2) = \emptyset$ *and* $Dom(\Gamma_1) = Dom(\Gamma_2)$. *If* $\langle \Gamma_1, \tau_1\rangle \prec_{S_1} \langle \Gamma_0, \tau_0\rangle$, $\langle \Gamma_2, \tau_2\rangle \prec_{S_2} \langle \Gamma_0, \tau_0\rangle$, *then* $\mathsf{PolyUni}(\langle \Gamma_1, \tau_1\rangle, \langle \Gamma_2, \tau_2\rangle)$ *succeeds to produce* $S$ *such that* $S\Gamma_1 \geq S\Gamma_2$, $S\tau_1 = S\tau_2$, *and* $S_1 = S' \circ (S|_{FTV(\Gamma_1, \tau_1)})$ *for some* $S'$.

## 5.3 Trace Function

When tracing an object or stack, we use the function Trace defined below. Trace takes a GC typing $\langle \Delta, \tau\rangle$ and an object, frame or stack, and unifies the GC typing and the annotation typing in the object, frame or stack, computing a type substitution $S$. As a result, the object, frame or stack will be well-typed under the new GC typing $\langle S\Delta, S\tau\rangle$:

$$\mathsf{Trace}(\langle \Delta, \tau\rangle, \langle\!\langle V, {}^{\langle \Gamma, \tau'\rangle}e\rangle\!\rangle) = \mathsf{let}\ S = \mathsf{PolyUni}(\langle \Delta \circ V|_{FV(e)}, \tau\rangle, \langle \Gamma|_{FV(e)}, \tau'\rangle)$$
$$\qquad \qquad \mathsf{where}\ FTV(\Delta, \tau) \cap FTV(\Gamma, \tau') = \emptyset$$
$$\qquad \mathsf{in}\ S|_{FTV(\Delta, \tau)}$$
$$\mathsf{Trace}(\langle \Delta, \tau\rangle, F^{[\sigma]}; C) = \mathsf{let}\ \sigma' = \mathsf{LIT}(\sigma)$$
$$\qquad \qquad S = \mathsf{Trace}(\langle \Delta \uplus \{\# : \sigma'\}, \tau\rangle, F)$$
$$\qquad \qquad S' = \mathsf{Trace}(\langle S\Delta, \mathsf{Unq}(S\sigma')\rangle, C)$$
$$\qquad \mathsf{in}\ S' \circ S$$

The function LIT computes the least instantiated type of a polytype, as defined by $\mathsf{LIT}(\forall \bar{t}.\tau) = \forall \bar{t}.\mathsf{LIT}'(\bar{t}, \tau)$ where

$$\mathsf{LIT}'(\bar{t}, \tau) = \begin{cases} t' & (\bar{t} \cap FTV(\tau) = \emptyset, t'\ \text{is fresh}) \\ \mathsf{LIT}'(\bar{t}, \tau_1) \to \mathsf{LIT}'(\bar{t}, \tau_2) & (\tau = \tau_1 \to \tau_2) \\ \tau & (\text{otherwise}). \end{cases}$$

LIT replaces every subterm in a polytype that contains only unquantified type variables with a fresh type variable. For example, $\mathsf{LIT}(\forall t.(\mathsf{int} \to \mathsf{int}) \to (t \to t)) = \forall t.t' \to (t \to t)$ where $t'$ is a fresh type variable. In particular, if $\sigma$ is a monotype, $\mathsf{LIT}(\sigma)$ is simply a fresh type variable.

For an object or frame, Trace computes a type substitution that unifies the GC typing $\langle \Delta, \tau\rangle$ and the annotation typing $\langle \Gamma, \tau'\rangle$ given to the value or code $e$. To explain more specifically,

- for each (local or free) variable $x$ in the environment $V$ (that is free in $e$,) Trace unifies the type of $x$ given in the annotation typing ($\Gamma(x)$) and the type of the address assigned to $x$ that is given in the GC typing ($\Delta(V(x))$);
- Trace unifies the result type of the annotation typing ($\tau'$) and the result type of the GC typing ($\tau$).

For a stack, Trace scans the frames in the stack in a bottom-up manner, unifying the GC typing and the annotation typing of each frame. A technical note is that when tracing a frame $F$, we pass a GC typing that gives # a type $\sigma'$, which is LIT of the declaration type $\sigma$ attached to $F$. In the tracing of $F$, $\sigma'$ is expected to be unified as $S\sigma'$ with the type given to a variable assigned # in the annotation typing of $F$. When tracing the rest stack $C$, we pass a GC typing that has result type $\mathsf{Unq}(S\sigma')$. This type is expected to be unified with the result type of the annotation typing of the next frame.

We can prove the following lemma about the Trace function.

**Lemma 5.2.** *If* $\Gamma_0 \vdash C : \tau_0$ *and* $\langle \Delta, \tau \rangle \prec \langle \Gamma_0, \tau_0 \rangle$, *then* $S = \mathsf{Trace}(\langle \Delta, \tau \rangle, C)$ *and* $S\Delta \vdash C : S\tau$ *and* $S_0 = S_1 \circ S$ *for some* $S_1$.

## 5.4 Main Loop

We describe the main part of our GC algorithm. Suppose that the GC is triggered just when a program is evaluated to $P = \mathsf{letrec}\ H_0\ \mathsf{in}\ C$ with $\vdash P : \tau_0$. For simplifying discussion, we consider only the case $\tau_0 = \mathsf{int}$. For initialization of the GC, we first set the GC typing as $\langle \Delta_0, \tau_0 \rangle$ where[5]

$$\Delta_0(a) = \mathsf{LIT}(\sigma)\ (\forall (a = h^{[\sigma]}) \in H).$$

We then trace the stack $C$ using the function Trace and update the GC typing by the resulting type substitution $S$:

$$\langle \Delta_{init}, \tau_{init} \rangle = \langle S\Delta_0, S\tau_0 \rangle \text{ where } S = \mathsf{Trace}(\langle \Delta_0, \tau_0 \rangle, C)$$

The rest part of our algorithm is described in terms of *GC states* in the form $\langle H_f, H_t, \langle \Delta, \tau \rangle \rangle$ where $H_f$ and $H_t$ are heaps respectively called "from-heap" and "to-heap", and $\langle \Delta, \tau \rangle$ is a GC typing. In the terminology used in Section 5.1, a live set corresponds to the to-heap $H_t$ plus the stack $C$. We initialize the GC state as $\langle H_0, \emptyset, \langle \Delta_{init}, \tau_{init} \rangle \rangle$. At this point, the live set contains only the stack $C$. Then the GC iterates steps described by a rewriting relation $\Longrightarrow$ over GC states, given by the following rule:

$$\langle H_f \uplus \{a = h^{[\sigma]}\}, H_t, \langle \Delta, \tau \rangle \rangle \Longrightarrow \langle H_f, H_t \uplus \{a = h^{[\sigma]}\}, \langle S\Delta, S\tau \rangle \rangle$$
$$\text{where } \Delta(a) \notin TVar$$
$$\text{and } S = \mathsf{Trace}(\langle \Delta, \mathsf{Unq}(\Delta(a)) \rangle, h)$$

---

[5] In our formulation, polymorphic objects can never be reclaimed even if they are unreachable. An easy way to resolve this problem is to keep track of the set of free addresses in a to-heap and to trace only addresses in the set. However, reachable yet inaccessible polymorphic objects still cannot be reclaimed. It is left in our future work.

The GC first finds an object $h$ that is allocated at an address $a$ in the from-heap $H_f$, i.e., not yet in the live set, and that is not given a type variable in $\Delta$, i.e., accessible from the live set. The GC then moves the object $h$ to the to-heap $H_t$, i.e., adds the object to the live set. Next, the GC traces the object $h$ using the Trace function and updates the GC typing $\langle \Delta, \tau \rangle$ by the resulting type substitution $S$ as $\langle S\Delta, S\tau \rangle$. The GC proceeds until all addresses in $H_f$ are given type variables in the GC typing. The final $H_t$ will be used as a heap for the remaining computation. We can prove correctness of the GC algorithm as the following theorem that the algorithm terminates and finds semantic garbage.

**Theorem 5.1 (GC Correctness).** *Let* $\emptyset \vdash H_0 : \Gamma_0$, $\Gamma_0 \vdash C : \text{int}$ *and* $\Delta_{init}$ *be as defined above. Then,*

1. $\langle H_0, \emptyset, \langle \Delta_{init}, \text{int} \rangle \rangle \Longrightarrow^* \langle H_f, H_t, \langle \Delta, \text{int} \rangle \rangle$, *for some* $H_f$, $H_t$, $\Delta$; *and*
2. $H_f$ *is semantic garbage for* letrec $H_0$ *in* $C$.

# 6 Preliminary Experiment

This section presents results of our preliminary experiment and gives a discussion on them. In this experiment, we focus on how much garbage the type inference GC scheme can collect in comparison with conventional trace-based GCs. We did not experiment on costs of the type inference GC scheme. We will remark on it in Section 7.

Our prototype system consists of an interpreter of our language and both a type inference GC and a trace-based GC. All of these are implemented in Standard ML. We use as applications a recursive fibonacci function of 10 (fib10), a quick sort program for a list of length 10 (qs10), a merge sort program for a list of length 10 (ms10), a 4-queens program (queen4), a program of the next permutation problem for a list of length 4 (nextperm4), and a simple register allocation program for a series of instructions of length 15. For each application, we measure the live memory size by each GC (i.e., the total size of objects that the GC retains as live) every several steps. The size of each object is calculated as follows: 0 for an integer (since it is usually unboxed[6]); 2 for a cons cell (a tag and a pointer to a pair); the number of elements for a tuple; and the number of the free variables plus one for code pointer for a closure.

The first graph in Figure 4 indicates the number of steps where the type inference GC has gain more than zero. Gain means difference of live memory size by the type inference GC and by the trace-based GC. We have no gain for fib10 and qs10, and very little for queen4 and ms10, while we have some gain for nextperm4 and reg15. The second graph in the figure compares the progresses of live memory size by the two GCs during the execution of nextperm4. The third graph shows a similar comparison for reg15. In the second graph, the type

---

[6] To be more precise, our interpreter allocates integers in heaps. However, since integers are usually represented as unboxed values in real implementations, we consider that these should be treated as zero-size objects when we measure live memory size.

inference GC collects some objects earlier than the trace-based GC does. In the third graph, the type inference GC collects dramatically (42% at the best) in the last quarter period.

We observe two kinds of program structure in the applications that gained some. In one structure, a function takes a tuple as its multiple arguments and dereferences the tuple every time one of the arguments is necessary. Since the tuple is reachable, the trace-based GC cannot collect unnecessary elements of the tuple, but the type inference GC can. Another structure was observed particularly in the register allocation program. This program consists of three phases. It first computes live variables at each instruction and keeps this information in a data structure representing the instruction. Next, the program obtains register assignments for variables, and it finally generates instructions using this information. In the final phase, the information of live variables is never used but kept in reachable data structures. Therefore the trace-based GC cannot collect this data, but the type inference GC can.

Generalizing the observation, we expect that the type inference GC scheme is beneficial particularly for programs that possess what we call *phase structure*. A program possessing this structure has multiple phases and maintains some data structures during the phases. On some phase, the program keeps temporary data in specific fields of the data structures, and it never uses the data after another phase. The two benefiting programs in our experiment are typical examples. To give another example, a compiler program may keep inferred type information in specific fields of data structures representing nodes of parse tree, and never uses the information after some phase.

It is interesting how these results are sensitive to other factors. If we increase the size of input, we expect that gain will become large because the size of the useless temporary data tends to depend on the input size. For another factor, if we test the live memory size much less frequently (with intervals larger than one phase), we will see in the graph gain around the average gain over the whole execution.

## 7 Remark on Cost

Despite that the type inference GC aims to save memory, this scheme itself requires extra memory. First, we will need one pointer field per object for implementing defer-list, that is, a linked-list to keep objects whose traversal are suspended.

Second, extra memory is necessary for the GC-time unification.[7] Not all of this memory can be allocated at compile time. The unification assumes that the given GC typing and the given annotation typing have no type variables in common (see Section 5.3). Therefore we should copy the annotation typing for each object where the contained type variables are renamed as fresh type

---

[7] The unification may be implemented in a destructive way. That is, we may represent type variables as pointers (initially null), and when the type variables are instantiated to be some types, the pointers are assigned the types.

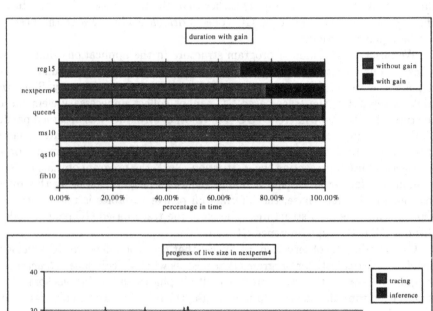

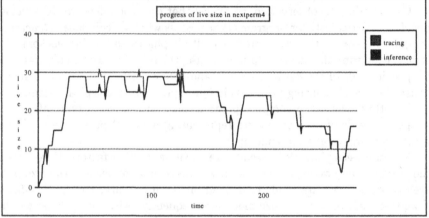

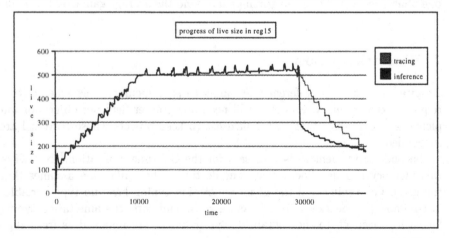

**Fig. 4.** Experimental results

variables. This allocation can be done either at run time or at GC time. Another allocation that cannot be done at compile time occurs in generating fresh type variables in the polytype unification described in Section 5.2. It seems inevitable to be done at GC time.

Although it is usually said that no memory should be allocated at GC time, we believe that this scheme should allocate the extra memory (especially the second one) at GC time rather than at run time. It is because the extra memory seems to be so large that if it is allocated at run time, it would exceed the memory saving by this GC scheme. On the other hand, if the extra memory is allocated at GC time, allocated space may be momentarily high, but it is completely useless after the GC finishes and therefore can be released. It would be acceptable if the GC is rather infrequent. We can even use the conventional GC for the most time and the type inference GC very infrequently. We believe that allocating at GC time is not prohibitive in most platforms, because even if the run-time system decides to trigger GC, free memory can be expected available from the underlying operating system. (If it turned out that free memory is actually unavailable, we could safely switch to the conventional GC.)

We may theoretically estimate space cost of type inference GC. In the worst case, as in the ML type inference, the size of type expression is exponential on the program size (more precisely, the number of nesting of let expressions), so is the space requirement of the GC. However, in practice, type expressions in the program will be within a reasonable size. Then, the space requirement is reasonably linear on the number of live objects.

# 8 Related Work

Some efforts have been made to resolve some memory leaks in ways specific to their target languages. Wadler [17] proposed a GC technique that makes use of an execution scheme of a lazy functional language. The GC detects the run time representation of the form fst $\langle x, y \rangle$ and reduces it as $x$; thus collecting unused tuple elements. We believe that the type inference GC can collect such objects in most cases.

Type inference GC originates in researches of tag-free GC for polymorphic-typed languages. The most important motivation in this area is to eliminate tags indicating pointer or non-pointer, which incur overheads either at every arithmetic or at every pointer operation. In our description, this kind of tags is not necessary. Annotation typings attached to values of objects do not correspond to them and do not involve run time overheads.

Several researchers have studied type inference GC. Goldberg and Gloger [5] discovered that semantic garbage can be detected by dynamic type inference in their research of tag-free GC. (Strictly speaking, we may not regard their scheme as type inference GC because their original goal was to traverse all reachable objects. Because of the goal, they use more unification than necessary.) Because their description and correctness argument of the GC algorithm was informal, its soundness was not clear. Fradet [4] also presented a formulation of type inference GC and proof of its correctness using Reynolds' abstraction/parametricity theorem [13]. However, his framework was so abstract that there still remains a gap between models and implementation. Specifically, his formulation did not treat sharing, did not specify precise conditions of static type information, and did not prove that GC-time unification succeeds. Morrisett et al. [12] gave an argument on type inference GC. However, they specified conditions of a heap that a GC should find, but did not give an algorithm. Neither Fradet [4] nor Morrisett et al. [12] have dealt with polymorphism.

Several papers have proposed another scheme to realize a tag-free GC in a polymorphically typed language [1, 16, 11]. In this scheme, a program is transformed into a second-order program where polymorphic functions are passed as extra arguments actual types for type variables in polytypes. Using these types, GC reconstructs types of all reachable objects and traverses all these objects. While this scheme does not collect any reachable garbage, these papers reported that it can be implemented in reasonably low cost. Therefore there would be trade-off between memory saving and speed, possibly depending on applications. This should be investigated through experiments in the future.

Many techniques have been proposed to statically estimate life times of objects [2, 8, 6, 15, 3]. Techniques using sharing analysis [2, 8, 6] cannot collect more garbage than type inference GCs can since they use reachability-based liveness of objects. Techniques using region inference [15, 3] can collect some semantic garbage. Since we have not studied to the extent to make a precise comparison between their scheme and our scheme, we will below just give examples and show that objects collected by one scheme may not be collected by the other. In an expression fst $\langle e_1, e_2 \rangle$, our scheme can collect the second element of the tuple just after the tuple is allocated, while their scheme cannot. On the other hand, in an expression

( let $y = \langle 1, 2 \rangle$
  in $\lambda x.$(fst $\langle x, \lambda w.$(fst $y$)))
  end) $e$

their scheme can collect $\langle 1, 2 \rangle$ just after the evaluation of the let expression, while our scheme cannot.

## 9 Conclusion and Future Work

This paper has given a formal description of type inference GC with fully proved correctness. Our framework is sufficiently detailed yet reasonably abstract. Therefore it will serve as a specification for implementing a type inference GC and as a foundation for discussing and extending the GC scheme. We conjecture, in addition to soundness, optimality in the sense that the described algorithm collects more garbage than any other algorithm using the same type system does. We have already proved the optimality for a monomorphic type system by requiring principality of annotation typings. We could do it for polymorphic type systems, but it may be more complicated.

From our experimental results, we expect that type inference GC benefits particularly for programs with the phase structure. In order to claim more, we need to implementation the GC scheme in more low-level language, on some existing ML system. Then we should measure space and time cost of the GC scheme. We should also investigate larger applications for which the GC scheme is effective. We expect that one such application would be a compiler program that would contain many phase structures. Even for non-benefiting applications, the GC should be at least not worse. Optimization techniques to reduce extra memory at GC-time by using statically available information as much as possible would be effective. We could even use a conventional GC or a type-passing tag-free GC for the most time, and the type inference GC very infrequently.

## Acknowledgments

We express our warmest thanks to Kenjiro Taura for encouraging us in this research and for giving us a precious advice for clarifying the motivation of our work. Comments from Benjamin Pierce, Naoki Kobayashi, Atsushi Igarashi and the TIC referees were very helpful in improving the presentation of the paper. We also give thanks for many discussions to members of Yonezawa's Group and members of Programming Language Seminor in Indiana University.

## References

1. S. Aditya, C. Flood, and J. Hicks. Garbage collection for strongly-typed languages using run-time type reconstruction. In *Proceedings of Conference on LISP and Functional Programming*, pages 12–23, 1994.
2. H. G. Baker. Unify and conquer (garbage, updating, aliasing, ...) in functional languages. In *Proceedings of Conference on LISP and Functional Programming*, pages 218–226, 1990.
3. L. Birkedal, M. Tofte, and M. Vejlstrup. From Region Inferrence to von Neumann Machines via Region Representation. In *Conference record of Symposium on Principles of Programming Languages*, pages 171–183, 1996.
4. P. Fradet. Collecting more garbage. In *Proceedings of Conference on LISP and Functional Programming*, pages 24–33, 1994.
5. B. Goldberg and M. Glogar. Polymorphic type reconstruction for garbage collection without tags. In *Proceedings of Conference on LISP and Functional Programming*, pages 53–65, 1992.
6. K. Inoue, H. Seki, and H. Yagi. Analysis of functional programs to detect run-time garbage cells. *ACM Transactions on Programming, Languages and Systems*, 10(4):555–579, 1988.
7. R. Jones. Tail recursion without space leaks. *Journal of Functional Programming*, 2(1):73–79, 1992.
8. S. B. Jones and D. L. Métayer. Compile-time garbage collection by sharing analysis. In *Conference Proceedings of Functional Programming Languages and Computer Architecture*, pages 54–74, Imperial College, London, September 1989.
9. S. L. P. Jones. *The Implementation of Functional Programming Languages*. Prentice-Hall, 1987.

10. R. Milner. A theory of type polymorphism in programming. *Journal of Computer and System Sciences*, 17:348–185, 1978.

11. G. Morrisett. *Compiling with Types*. PhD thesis, School of Computer Science Carnegie Mellon University, 1995.

12. G. Morrisett, M. Felleisen, and R. Harper. Abstract models of memory management. In *Proceedings of Functional Programming Languages and Computer Architecture*, pages 66–76, 1995.

13. J. Reynolds. Types, abstraction, and parametric polymorphism. In *Information Processing*, volume 83, pages 513–523, 1983.

14. J. A. Robinson. A machine-oriented logic based on the resolution principle. *Journal of ACM*, 12, 1965.

15. M. Tofte and J.-P. Talpin. Implementation of the Typed Call-by-Value $\lambda$-calculus using a Stack of Regions. In *Conference record of Symposium on Principles of Programming Languages*, pages 188–201, 1994.

16. A. Tolmach. Tag-free garbage collection using explicit type parameters. In *Proceedings of Conference on LISP and Functional Programming*, pages 1–11, 1994.

17. P. Wadler. Fixing some space leaks with a garbage collector. *Software Practice and Experience*, 17(9):595–608, September 1987.

# Appendix

## A  Proof of Theorem 4.1

**Lemma A.1.** *If* $\langle \Gamma, \tau \rangle \prec\!\!\!\prec \langle \Gamma', \tau' \rangle$ *and* $\Gamma \vdash^{\langle \Gamma'', \tau'' \rangle} e : \tau$, *then* $\Gamma' \vdash^{\langle \Gamma'', \tau'' \rangle} e : \tau'$.

*Proof.* Trivial.

**Lemma A.2 (Type Preservation).** *If* $\vdash P : \tau$ *and* $P \longrightarrow P'$, *then* $\vdash P' : \tau$.

*Proof.* By induction on the derivation of $P \longrightarrow P'$. We have the following four cases.

**(stack)** $P$ = letrec $H$ in $F^{[\sigma]}; C \longrightarrow$ letrec $H'$ in $F^{[\sigma]}; C' = P'$ with $P_1 =$ letrec $H$ in $C \longrightarrow$ letrec $H'$ in $C' = P_1'$. From $\vdash P : \tau, \vdash P_1 : \tau'$. By the induction hypothesis, $\vdash P_1' : \tau'$, which implies $\emptyset \vdash H' : \Gamma'$ and $\Gamma' \vdash C' : \tau$ with $\Gamma' \supseteq \Gamma$. Using Lemma A.1, we can derive $\vdash P' : \tau'$.

**(alloc)** $P =$ letrec $H$ in $\langle\!\langle V, c \rangle\!\rangle$ with $c = {}^{\langle \Gamma', \tau' \rangle}$let $x : \sigma = v$ in $c'$. Let $\sigma = \forall \bar{t}.\tau''$. From $\vdash P : \tau$, $\Gamma_0 \vdash \langle\!\langle V, c \rangle\!\rangle : \tau$, which implies for some $\Gamma_0$,

$$\Gamma_0 \circ V \geq \Gamma \tag{1}$$

$$\langle \Gamma', \tau' \rangle \prec_S \langle \Gamma, \tau \rangle \tag{2}$$

$$\Gamma' \vdash (\text{let } x : \sigma = v \text{ in } c') : \tau' \tag{3}$$

We can assume that $Dom(S) \cap \bar{t} = \emptyset$ by an appropriate renaming of $\bar{t}$ in $\sigma$. Therefore $\text{Unq}(S\sigma) = S\tau''$. From (2), $\langle \Gamma', \tau' \rangle \prec_S \langle \Gamma, S\tau'' \rangle$ and from (3), $\Gamma' \vdash v : \tau''$. Applying Lemma A.1 to these, we conclude that $\Gamma \vdash v : S\tau''$, which implies $\Gamma_0 \vdash \langle\!\langle V, v \rangle\!\rangle : S\tau''$ together with (1). We also know $\emptyset \vdash H^{[\Delta]}$ :

$\Gamma_0$ from $\vdash P : \tau$. Easily, $\emptyset \vdash H \uplus \{a = \langle\!\langle V, v\rangle\!\rangle^{[\sigma]}\} : \Gamma_0 \uplus \{a : S\sigma\}$. Therefore it is sufficient to show $\Gamma_0 \uplus \{a : S\sigma\} \vdash \langle\!\langle V \uplus \{x = a\}, c'\rangle\!\rangle : \tau$. It follows from Lemma A.1 applied to $\Gamma' \uplus \{x : \sigma\} \vdash c' : \tau'$ by (3), $(\Gamma_0 \uplus \{a : S\sigma\}) \circ (V \uplus \{x = a\}) \geq \Gamma \uplus \{x : S\sigma\}$ by (1), and $\langle\Gamma' \uplus \{x : \sigma\}, \tau'\rangle \prec_S \langle\Gamma \uplus \{x : S\sigma\}, \tau\rangle$ by (2).

(app) $P =$ letrec $H^{[\Delta]}$ in $\langle\!\langle V, c\rangle\!\rangle$ with $c = {}^{\langle\Gamma', \tau'\rangle}$let $w : \sigma = (x\ y)$ in $c'$. Let $\sigma = \forall \bar{t}.\tau''$. From $\vdash P : \tau$, $\Gamma_0 \vdash \langle\!\langle V, c\rangle\!\rangle : \tau$, which implies for some $\Gamma_0$,

$$\Gamma_0 \circ V \geq \Gamma \tag{4}$$

$$\langle\Gamma', \tau'\rangle \prec_S \langle\Gamma, \tau\rangle \tag{5}$$

$$\Gamma' \vdash (\text{let } w : \sigma = (x\ y) \text{ in } c') : \tau' \tag{6}$$

We can assume that $Dom(S) \cap \bar{t} = \emptyset$ by an appropriate renaming of $\bar{t}$ in $\sigma$. Therefore $\text{Unq}(S\sigma) = S\tau''$. We obtain $(\Gamma_0 \uplus \{\# : S\sigma\}) \circ (V \uplus \{w = \#\}) \geq \Gamma \uplus \{w : S\sigma\}$ from (4), $\langle\Gamma' \uplus \{w : \sigma\}, \tau'\rangle \prec_S \langle\Gamma \uplus \{w : S\sigma\}, S\sigma\rangle$ from (5), and $\Gamma' \uplus \{w : \sigma\} \vdash c' : \tau'$ from (6). Applying Lemma A.1 to these, we conclude that $\Gamma_0 \uplus \{\# : S\sigma\} \circ (V \uplus \{w = \#\}) \vdash c' : \tau$, which implies $\Gamma_0 \uplus \{\# : S\sigma\} \vdash \langle\!\langle V \uplus \{w = \#\}, c'\rangle\!\rangle : \tau$.

Then it is sufficient to show $\Gamma_0 \vdash \langle\!\langle V'' \uplus \{z = V(y)\}, c''\rangle\!\rangle : S\tau''$. Let $H(V(x)) = \langle\!\langle V'', {}^{\langle\Gamma'', \tau_1 \to \tau_2\rangle}\lambda z.c''\rangle\!\rangle$, $\sigma_x = \Gamma_0(V(x))$ and $\sigma_y = \Gamma_0(V(y))$. Since $\emptyset \vdash H^{[\Delta]} : \Gamma_0$ from $\vdash P : \tau$, we have $\Gamma_0 \vdash H(V(x)) : \text{Unq}(\sigma_x)$, which implies

$$\Gamma_0 \circ V'' \geq \Gamma''' \tag{7}$$

$$\langle\Gamma'', \tau_1 \to \tau_2\rangle \prec_{S'} \langle\Gamma''', \text{Unq}(\sigma_x)\rangle \tag{8}$$

$$\Gamma'' \uplus \{z : \tau_1\} \vdash c'' : \tau_2 \tag{9}$$

From (6), we have $\Gamma'(x) \geq \tau_1'' \to \tau''$ and $\Gamma'(y) \geq \tau_1''$ for some $\tau''$. Therefore, together with (4) and (5), we obtain $\sigma_x = \Gamma_0(V(x)) \geq \Gamma(x) = S\Gamma'(x) \geq S(\tau_1'' \to \tau'')$ and $\sigma_y = \Gamma_0(V(y)) \geq \Gamma(y) = S\Gamma'(y) \geq S\tau_1''$. From $\sigma_x \geq S(\tau_1'' \to \tau'')$ and (8), we have $S''S'(\tau_1 \to \tau_2) = S(\tau_1'' \to \tau'')$ where $FTV(\Gamma''', \tau_1 \to \tau_2) \cap Dom(S'') = \emptyset$. Therefore $S''S'\tau_1 = S\tau_1''$, implying $\sigma_y \geq S''S'\tau_1$, and $S''S'\tau_2 = S\tau''$. Consequently, we have $(\Gamma_0 \circ V'') \uplus \{z : \sigma_y\} \geq \Gamma''' \uplus \{z : S''S'\tau_1\}$ and $\langle\Gamma'' \uplus \{z : \tau_1\}, \tau_2\rangle \prec_{S'} \langle\Gamma''' \uplus \{z : S'\tau_1\}, S'\tau_2\rangle \prec_{S''} \langle\Gamma''' \uplus \{z : S''S'\tau_1\}, S\tau''\rangle$. Applying Lemma A.1 to these and (9), we conclude that $\Gamma_0 \vdash \langle\!\langle V'' \uplus \{z = V(y)\}, c''\rangle\!\rangle : S\tau''$.

(ret) $P =$ letrec $H^{[\Delta]}$ in $F^{[\sigma]}; C$ with $F = \langle\!\langle V \uplus \{w = \#\}, c\rangle\!\rangle$ and $C = \langle\!\langle V', {}^{\langle\Gamma', \tau'\rangle}x\rangle\!\rangle$. From $\vdash P : \tau$, $\Gamma_0 \vdash F^{[\sigma]}; C : \tau$ for some $\Gamma_0$, which implies

$$\Gamma_0 \uplus \{\# : \sigma'\} \vdash F : \tau \tag{10}$$

$$\Gamma_0 \vdash C : \tau'' \tag{11}$$

$$\sigma' = \forall \bar{t}.\tau'' \text{ and } \bar{t} \cap FTV(\Gamma_0) = \emptyset \tag{12}$$

From (11), $\Gamma_0 \circ V' \geq \Gamma$ and $\langle\Gamma', \tau'\rangle \prec_S \langle\Gamma, \tau''\rangle$ and $\Gamma' \vdash x : \tau'$, for some $\Gamma$ and $S$. Therefore we can derive $\Gamma_0(V'(x)) \geq \Gamma(x) = S\Gamma'(x) \geq S\tau' = \tau''$.

From (12), $\Gamma_0(V'(x)) \geq \sigma'$. Then, from (10), we have $(\Gamma_0 \circ V) \uplus \{w : \sigma'\} \geq \Gamma'' \uplus \{w : \sigma''\}$ for some $\sigma''$. Thus $(\Gamma_0 \circ V) \uplus \{w : \Gamma_0(V'(x))\} \geq \Gamma'' \uplus \{w : \sigma''\}$. We also know from (10), $\Gamma'' \uplus \{w : \sigma''\} \vdash c : \tau$. Hence, we conclude $\Gamma_0 \vdash \langle\!\langle V \uplus \{w : V'(x)\}, c\rangle\!\rangle : \tau$.

**Theorem A.1 (Type Soundness).** *If $\vdash P : \tau$, then either $P$ is an answer or else there exists $P'$ s.t. $P \longrightarrow P'$ and $\vdash P' : \tau$.*

*Proof.* We can know that either $P$ is an answer or else there exists $P'$ s.t. $P \longrightarrow P'$ by induction on the structure of the stack of $P$ with case analysis on its top frame. Then Lemma A.2 is sufficient to prove this theorem.

# B    Proof of Theorem 5.1

**Lemma B.1 (Unification).** *There exists an algorithm Unify s.t. $\mathsf{Unify}(E)$ computes the most general unifier of $E$, for any set $E$ of unifiable equations of monotypes.*

**Lemma B.2.** *Suppose $FTV(\Gamma_1, \tau_1) \cap FTV(\Gamma_2, \tau_2) = \emptyset$ and $Dom(\Gamma_1) = Dom(\Gamma_2)$. If $\langle \Gamma_1, \tau_1 \rangle \prec_{S_1} \langle \Gamma_0, \tau_0 \rangle$, $\langle \Gamma_2, \tau_2 \rangle \prec\!\!\!\!\prec_{S_2} \langle \Gamma_0, \tau_0 \rangle$, then $\mathsf{PolyUni}(\langle \Gamma_1, \tau_1 \rangle, \langle \Gamma_2, \tau_2 \rangle)$ succeeds to produce $S$ such that $S\Gamma_1 \geq S\Gamma_2$, $S\tau_1 = S\tau_2$, and $S_1 = S' \circ (S|_{FTV(\Gamma_1, \tau_1)})$ for some $S'$.*

*Proof.* For $x \in Dom(\Gamma_1)$, let $\Gamma_i(x) = \forall \vec{t}_i^{(x)}.\tau_i^{(x)}$ $(i = 0, 1, 2)$ and $\mathsf{Unique}(\Gamma_i(x)) = S_i^{(x)}\tau_i^{(x)}$ where $Dom(S_i^{(x)}) = \vec{t}_i^{(x)}$ $(i = 1, 2)$. We assume $\vec{t}_0^{(x)} \cap \vec{t}_0^{(x')} = \emptyset$ if $x \neq x'$.

From $\langle \Gamma_2, \tau_2 \rangle \prec\!\!\!\!\prec_{S_2} \langle \Gamma_0, \tau_0 \rangle$, there is $S_3^{(x)}$ s.t. $Dom(S_3^{(x)}) = \vec{t}_0^{(x)}$ and $S_3^{(x)}\tau_0^{(x)} = S_2\tau_2^{(x)}$. From $\langle \Gamma_1, \tau_1 \rangle \prec_{S_1} \langle \Gamma_0, \tau_0 \rangle$, $\tau_0^{(x)} = S_1\tau_1^{(x)}$, implying $S_3^{(x)}\tau_0^{(x)} = S_3^{(x)}S_1\tau_1^{(x)}$. Therefore, defining $S_3 = \biguplus_{x \in Dom(\Gamma_1)} S_3^{(x)}S_1S_2$, we conclude that $S_3$ unifies $E$. Hence $\mathsf{Unify}(E)$ succeeds by Lemma B.1.

By Lemma B.1, we have $Dom(S) = FTV(S_1^{(x)}\tau_1^{(x)}, S_2^{(x)}\tau_2^{(x)}, \tau_1, \tau_2)$, $SS_1^{(x)}\tau_1^{(x)} = SS_2^{(x)}\tau_2^{(x)}$, $S\tau_1 = S\tau_2$. Since $S\Gamma_1(x) \geq SS_1^{(x)}\tau_1^{(x)}$ and $\vec{t}_2'^{(x)} \cap FTV(S\Gamma_1(x)) = \emptyset$ where $\vec{t}_2'^{(x)} = S_2^{(x)}\vec{t}_2^{(x)}$, we can derive $S\Gamma_1(x) \geq \forall \vec{t}_2'^{(x)}.SS_2^{(x)}\tau_2^{(x)} = S(\forall \vec{t}_2'^{(x)}.S_2^{(x)}\tau_2^{(x)}) = S\Gamma_2(x)$.

Since we already know $S_3S_1^{(x)}\tau_1^{(x)} = S_3S_2^{(x)}\tau_2^{(x)}$ and $S_3\tau_1 = S_3\tau_2$, by Lemma B.1, we conclude that there is $S''$ s.t. $S_3 = S'' \circ S$. From $S_3|_{FTV(\Gamma_1, \tau_1)} = S_1$, $S_1 = S'' \circ S|_{FTV(\Gamma_1, \tau_1)}$.

**Lemma B.3.** *If $\Gamma_0 \vdash C : \tau_0$, $\langle \Delta, \tau \rangle \prec_{S_0} \langle \Gamma_0, \tau_0 \rangle$ and $(Dom(S_0) \subseteq FTV(\Delta, \tau))$, then $S = \mathsf{Trace}(\langle \Delta, \tau \rangle, C)$, and $S\Delta \vdash C : S\tau$ and $S_0 = S_1 \circ S$ for some $S_1$.*

*Proof.* We first show that the lemma holds for $C = \langle\!\langle V, {}^{\langle \Gamma, \tau' \rangle}e \rangle\!\rangle$. From $\Gamma_0 \vdash C : \tau_0$, $\langle \Gamma, \tau' \rangle \prec\!\!\!\!\prec \langle \Gamma_0 \circ V, \tau_0 \rangle$. From the hypothesis, $\langle \Delta \circ V, \tau \rangle \prec_{S_0} \langle \Gamma_0 \circ V, \tau_0 \rangle$. By Lemma B.2, the $\mathsf{Unify}(E)$ in $\mathsf{Trace}$ succeeds with $\langle \Gamma, \tau' \rangle \prec\!\!\!\!\prec \langle S\Delta \circ V, S\tau \rangle$ and $S_0 = S_1 \circ (S|_{FTV(\Delta, \tau)})$ for some $S_1$. By Lemma A.1, $S\Delta \vdash C : S\tau$.

We then show the lemma by induction on the structure of $C$. $C$ is either $F$ or $F^{[\sigma]}; C'$. We have already shown the former case above. For the latter case, from $\Gamma_0 \vdash C : \tau_0$, $\Gamma_0 \uplus \{\# : \sigma'\} \vdash F : \tau_0$ with $\sigma \asymp \sigma'$. Let $\sigma'' = \mathsf{LIT}(\sigma)$. Then $\sigma'' \prec \sigma'$. By applying our first argument, we conclude $S(\Delta \uplus \{\# : \sigma''\}) \vdash F : S\tau$ and $S_0 = S_1 \circ S$ for some $S_1$. From $\Gamma_0 \vdash C : \tau_0$, $\Gamma_0 \vdash C' : \tau'$ with $\sigma' = \forall \bar{t}.\tau'$ and $\bar{t} \cap FTV(\Gamma_0) = \emptyset$. Since $\sigma'' \prec \sigma'$, we can let $\sigma'' = \forall \bar{t}.\tau''$. From $S_0 \bar{t} = \bar{t}$, $S\tau'' \prec_{S_1} \tau'$. Thus, we obtain $\langle S\Delta, S\tau'' \rangle \prec_{S_1} \langle S\Gamma_0, \tau' \rangle$ (with $Dom(S_1) \subseteq Dom(S_0) \cup FTV(Rng(S)) \subseteq FTV(S\Delta, S\tau''))$. Applying the induction hypothesis, we conclude $S''\Delta \vdash C' : S''\tau''$ with $S'' = S' \circ S$, and $S_1 = S_2 \circ S'$ for some $S_2$. Therefore $S_0 = S_1 \circ S = S_2 \circ S''$. Further, $S_2 S'' \bar{t} = S_0 \bar{t} = \bar{t}$. Let $\bar{t}' = S'' \bar{t}$. If there is $t \in \bar{t}' \cap FTV(S''\Delta)$, we obtain $S_2 t \in S_2 \bar{t}' = \bar{t}$ and $S_2 t \in FTV(S_2 S'' \Delta) = FTV(\Gamma_0)$, which contradicts with $\bar{t} \cap FTV(\Gamma_0) = \emptyset$. Therefore $\bar{t}' \cap FTV(S''\Delta) = \emptyset$. Consequently, since we have $S''\Delta \uplus \{\# : \forall \bar{t}'.S''\tau''\} \vdash F : S''\tau$ obtained from $S(\Delta \uplus \{\# : \sigma''\}) \vdash F : S\tau$, $S''\Delta \vdash C' : S''\tau''$, and $\sigma \asymp \forall \bar{t}'.S''\tau''$, we conclude that $S''\Delta \vdash F^{[\sigma]}; C' : S''\tau$.

The following well-formedness is a basic property of GC states.

**Definition B.1 (Well-formedness).** *Let* $\emptyset \vdash H_0 : \Gamma_0$ *and* $\Gamma_0 \vdash C : \tau_0$. $\langle H_f, H_t, \langle \Delta, \tau \rangle \rangle$ *is well-formed w.r.t.* letrec $H_0$ *in* $C$ *and* $\langle \Gamma_0, \tau_0 \rangle$ *iff*

1. $H_0 = H_f \uplus H_t$
2. $\Delta \vdash C : \tau$
3. $\Delta \vdash H_t(a) : \mathsf{Unq}(\Delta(a))$ *for* $x \in Dom(H_t)$.
4. $\langle \Delta, \tau \rangle \prec \langle \Gamma_0, \tau_0 \rangle$

A GC state always proceeds by $\Longrightarrow$ preserving the well-formedness as long as there remain live objects in the from-heap.

**Lemma B.4 (GC Progress).** *If* $\langle H_f, H_t, \langle \Delta, \tau \rangle \rangle$ *is well-formed w.r.t.* $P$ *and* $\langle \Gamma_0, \tau_0 \rangle$, *then*

1. $\Delta(a) \in TVar$ *for any* $a \in Dom(H_f)$; *or else*
2. $\langle H_f, H_t, \langle \Delta, \tau \rangle \rangle \Longrightarrow \langle H'_f, H'_t, \langle \Delta', \tau' \rangle \rangle$ *for some* $H'_f$, $H'_t$, $\Delta'$ *and* $\tau'$, *and* $\langle H'_f, H'_t, \langle \Delta', \tau' \rangle \rangle$ *is well-formed w.r.t.* $P$ *and* $\langle \Gamma_0, \tau_0 \rangle$.

*Proof.* Suppose (1) does not hold. Then, there is some $a \in Dom(H_f)$ s.t. $\Delta(a) \notin TVar$. Let $\tau'' = \mathsf{Unq}(\Delta(a))$, $H'_f = H_f \setminus \{a = h\}$ and $H'_t = H_t \uplus \{a = h\}$. From the well-formedness, we have $\Gamma_0 \vdash h : \tau_1$ where $\tau_1 = \mathsf{Unq}(\Gamma_0(a))$, and $\langle \Delta, \tau'' \rangle \prec_{S_0} \langle \Gamma_0, \tau_1 \rangle$ $(Dom(S_0) \subseteq FTV(\Delta, \tau))$. By Lemma B.3, we obtain $S\Delta \vdash h : S\tau''$ and $S_0 = S_1 \circ S$ for some $S_1$. Hence $\langle H_f, H_t, \langle \Delta, \tau \rangle \rangle \Longrightarrow \langle H'_f, H'_t, \langle S\Delta, S\tau \rangle \rangle$. We shall show each condition of the well-formedness of $\langle H'_f, H'_t, \langle S\Delta, S\tau \rangle \rangle$.

1. Trivial.
2. $S\Delta \vdash C : S\tau$ from $\Delta \vdash C : \tau$ in the well-formedness.
3. We have $\Delta \vdash H_t(a) : \mathsf{Unq}(\Delta(y))$ for $y \in Dom(H_t)$ from the well-formedness and we already know $S\Delta \vdash h : S\tau''$. Thus, noticing $Dom(S) \subseteq Dom(S_0) \subseteq FTV(\Delta, \tau)$, we conclude $S\Delta \vdash H'_t(a) : \mathsf{Unq}(S\Delta(y))$ for $y \in Dom(H'_t)$.
4. From $S_0 = S_1 \circ S$, we obtain $\langle S\Delta, S\tau \rangle \prec_{S_1} \langle \Gamma_0, \tau_0 \rangle$.

We then introduce a notion of *isolation*, which is defined as a well-formed GC state with the objects in $H_f$ having types of type variables. (We call $H_f$ the *isolated heap* of $H_0$.)

**Definition B.2 (Isolation).** $\langle H_f, H_t, \langle \Delta, \tau \rangle \rangle$ *is an isolation w.r.t.* $P$ *and* $\langle \Gamma_0, \tau_0 \rangle$ *iff*

1. $\langle H_f, H_t, \langle \Delta, \tau \rangle \rangle$ *is well-formed w.r.t.* $P$ *and* $\langle \Gamma_0, \tau_0 \rangle$
2. *For any* $a \in Dom(H_f)$, $\Delta(a) \in TVar$.

Once a heap is isolated for a program, its evaluation preserves the heap to be isolated.

**Lemma B.5 (Isolation Preservation).** *If* $\langle H_f, H_t, \langle \Delta, \tau \rangle \rangle$ *is an isolation w.r.t.* $P$ *and* $\langle \Gamma_0, \tau_0 \rangle$, *and* $P \longrightarrow P'$, *then there is an isolation* $\langle H_f, H_t', \langle \Delta', \tau \rangle \rangle$ *w.r.t.* $P'$ *and* $\langle \Gamma_0', \tau_0 \rangle$.

*Proof.* Analogous to the proof of Lemma A.2.

**Lemma B.6.** *If* $\langle H_f, H_t, \langle \Delta, \mathsf{int} \rangle \rangle$ *is an isolation w.r.t.* $P$ *and* $\langle \Gamma_0, \mathsf{int} \rangle$, *then* $P$ *does not accesses any* $x \in Dom(H_f)$.

*Proof.* Suppose that $P$ accesses $x$ and $x \in Dom(H_f)$. Then, $P$ is either letrec $H_0$ in $\langle V, {}^{\langle \Gamma, \tau \rangle} z \rangle$ or letrec $H_0$ in $F^{[\sigma]}; \ldots; \langle V, {}^{\langle \Gamma, \tau \rangle} \mathsf{let}\ w : \sigma = (z\ y)\ \mathsf{in}\ c \rangle$ where $V(z) = x$. In the former case, we have $\langle \Gamma, \tau \rangle \prec_S \langle \Delta \circ V, \mathsf{int} \rangle$. Since we know from $x \in Dom(H_f)$ that $\Delta(V(z))$ is a type variable $t$, $\Gamma(z)$ must also be a type variable $t'$ with $S(t') = t$. Since we can derive $\Gamma \vdash z : \tau$, we have $t' \geq \tau$, implying $t' = \tau$. However, it contradicts with $S(\tau) = \mathsf{int}$. In the latter case, we have $\langle \Gamma, \tau \rangle \prec_S \langle \Delta \circ V, S\tau \rangle$, $\Delta(V(z)) = t$ and $\Gamma(z) = t'$ s.t. $S(t') = t$. Since we can derive $\Gamma \vdash z : \tau_1 \to \tau_2$ for some $\tau_1, \tau_2$, we have $t' \geq \tau_1 \to \tau_2$ and it is impossible.

Using these lemmas, we can show that an isolated heap is semantic garbage.

**Theorem B.1 (Isolation Garbage).** *If* $\langle H_f, H_t, \langle \Delta, \mathsf{int} \rangle \rangle$ *is an isolation w.r.t.* $P$ *and* $\langle \Gamma_0, \mathsf{int} \rangle$, *then* $H_f$ *is semantic garbage for* $P$.

*Proof.* This follows from Lemma B.5 and Lemma B.6.

The proof of correctness of GC completes by the following theorem that our algorithm finds an isolation.

**Theorem B.2 (GC Correctness).** *Let* $\emptyset \vdash H_0 : \Gamma_0$, $\Gamma_0 \vdash C : \mathsf{int}$ *and* $\Delta_{init}$ *be as defined in Section 5.4. Then, there exists* $\langle H_f, H_t, \langle \Delta, \mathsf{int} \rangle \rangle$ *such that* $\langle H_0, \emptyset, \langle \Delta_{init}, \mathsf{int} \rangle \rangle \Longrightarrow^* \langle H_f, H_t, \langle \Delta, \mathsf{int} \rangle \rangle$ *and* $\langle H_f, H_t, \langle \Delta, \mathsf{int} \rangle \rangle$ *is an isolation w.r.t.* letrec $H_0$ in $C$ *and* $\langle \Gamma_0, \mathsf{int} \rangle$.

*Proof.* By Theorem B.4, it suffices to show that $\langle H_0, \emptyset, \langle \Delta_{init}, \mathsf{int} \rangle \rangle$ is well-formed w.r.t. letrec $H_0$ in $C$ and $\langle \Gamma_0, \mathsf{int} \rangle$. Let $\Delta_0'$ be as defined above. From $\emptyset \vdash H_0 : \Gamma_0$, we have $\langle \Delta_0', \mathsf{int} \rangle \prec \langle \Gamma_0, \mathsf{int} \rangle$. By Lemma B.3, we can obtain $S\Delta \vdash C : S\tau$ and $\langle \Delta_{init}, \mathsf{int} \rangle \prec \langle \Gamma_0, \mathsf{int} \rangle$, which are sufficient for the well-formedness.

# Strong Normalization
# by Type-Directed Partial Evaluation
# and Run-Time Code Generation

Vincent Balat[1] and Olivier Danvy[2]

[1] Département d'Informatique, École Normale Supérieure de Cachan
61, avenue du Président Wilson, F-94230 Cachan Cedex, France.
E-mail: balat@rip.ens-cachan.fr

[2] **BRICS**
Department of Computer Science, University of Aarhus
Building 540, Ny Munkegade, DK-8000 Aarhus C, Denmark
E-mail: danvy@brics.dk

**Abstract.** We investigate the synergy between type-directed partial evaluation and run-time code generation for the Caml dialect of ML. Type-directed partial evaluation maps simply typed, closed Caml values to a representation of their long $\beta\eta$-normal form. Caml uses a virtual machine and has the capability to load byte code at run time. Representing the long $\beta\eta$-normal forms as byte code gives us the ability to strongly normalize higher-order values (i.e., weak head normal forms in ML), to compile the resulting strong normal forms into byte code, and to load this byte code all in one go, at run time.
We conclude this note with a preview of our current work on scaling up strong normalization by run-time code generation to the Caml module language.

## 1 Introduction

### 1.1 Motivation

*Strong normalization:* Suppose one is given a strongly normalizable (closed) $\lambda$-term. How does one normalize this term? Typically one parses it into an abstract-syntax tree, one writes a strong normalizer over abstract-syntax trees, and one translates (unparses) the resulting normal form into whichever desired format (e.g., LaTeX).

*A solution in ML:* ML, like all functional languages, provides a convenient format for representing $\lambda$-terms: as an ML expression. Suppose thus that we are given a strongly normalizable ML expression. How do we normalize it? Type-directed partial evaluation [8] offers an efficient alternative to writing a parser to represent this ML expression as an ML data structure representing its abstract-syntax tree, writing a strong normalizer operating over this abstract-syntax tree, and unparsing the resulting normal form into an ML expression. Instead, the ML evaluator maps this ML expression into an ML value, and the type-directed partial evaluator maps this ML value into the abstract-syntax tree of its normal form. We can then either evaluate this abstract-syntax tree (for immediate use) or unparse it (for later use).

*Motivation:* Type-directed partial evaluation entrusts the underlying programming language with all the mechanisms of binding and substitution that are associated with normalization. Higher-order abstract syntax [24] shares the same motivation, albeit in a Logical Framework instead of in a functional setting.

*Goal:* Type-directed partial evaluation, as it is, maps an ML value into the text of its normal form. We want instead to map it into the corresponding ML value — and we want to do that in a lighter way than by invoking either an interpreter or the whole compiler, after normalization.

*An integrated solution in Objective Caml:* Objective Caml [22] is a byte-code implementation of a dialect of ML. This suggests us to represent normal forms as byte code, and to load this byte code at run time for both immediate and later use.

## 1.2 Contribution

We report our experiment of integrating type-directed partial evaluation within Caml, which in effect yields strong normalization by run-time code generation. We list below what we had to do to achieve this integration:

- we wrote several type-directed partial evaluators in Caml, in various styles and with various properties (listed below);
- we wrote a dedicated translator from normal forms to byte code;
- this required us to find the necessary (hidden) resources in the Caml implementation and recompile the system to make them available, in effect obtaining a more open implementation. These resources are mainly the representation of types, the representation of byte code, and the ability to load byte code at run time.

## 1.3 Non-contribution

Even though it is primarily inspired by theory, our work is experimental. Indeed, neither the OCaml compiler nor the OCaml virtual machine are formalized. We therefore have not formalized our byte-code translator either. As for type-directed partial evaluation, only its call-by-name version has been formalized so far [1, 2, 7].

In that sense our work is experimental: we want to investigate the synergy between type-directed partial evaluation and run-time code generation for OCaml.

```
     module ChurchNumbers
     = struct let cz s z = z
              let cs n s z = n s (s z)

              let rec n2cn n = if n=0 then cz else cs (n2cn (n-1))
              let cn2n n = n (fun i -> i+1) 0
         end
```
**Fig. 1.** Church numbers

## 1.4    An example: Church numbers

Let us illustrate strong normalization by run-time code generation to optimize a computation over Church numbers, which we define in Figure 1. The module ChurchNumbers defines zero (cz), the successor function (cs), and two conversion functions to and from ML numbers and Church numbers.

For example, we can convert the ML number 5 to a Church number, increment it, and convert the result back to ML as follows:

```
# ChurchNumbers.cn2n(ChurchNumbers.cs (ChurchNumbers.n2cn 5));;
- : int = 6
#
```

Thus equipped, let us define the function incrementing its argument with 1000:

```
# let cs1000 m = ChurchNumbers.n2cn 1000 ChurchNumbers.cs m;;
val cs1000 : (('a -> 'a) -> 'a -> 'b) -> ('a -> 'a) -> 'a -> 'b
           = <fun>
# ChurchNumbers.cn2n(cs1000 (ChurchNumbers.cz));;
- : int = 1000
#
```

If it were not for ML's weak-normalization strategy, 1000 $\beta$-reductions could be realized at definition time. We strongly normalize the value denoted by cs1000 by invoking our function nip (for "Normalize In Place") on the name of the identifier cs1000:

```
# nip "cs1000";;
- : unit = ()
#
```

Now cs1000 denotes the strongly normalized value, as reflected by its execution time: applying cs1000 to the Church number 0 is 4800 times faster now. Depending on the version of the type-directed partial evaluator, normalization takes between 0.1 and 18 seconds. In this example, cs1000 then needs to be applied between 5 and 1000 times to amortize the cost of normalization.

## 1.5 Overview

The rest of this article is organized as follows. We first review type-directed partial evaluation (Section 2), independently of run-time code generation, and with two simple examples: the Hilbert combinators and Church numbers. We then describe run-time code generation in OCaml (Section 3). Putting them together, we report the measures we have collected (Section 4) and we assess the overall system (Section 5). The Caml implementation of modules suggests a very simple extension of our system to handling both first-order and higher-order modules, and we describe this extension in Section 6. After reviewing related work (Section 7), we conclude.

## 2 Type-Directed Partial Evaluation

Type-directed partial evaluation strongly normalizes closed values of parametric type, by *two-level η-expansion* [8, 14]. Let us take two concrete examples, a simple one first, and a second one with Church numbers. We represent residual lambda-terms with the data type of Figure 2.

```
type exp = Var of string
         | Lam of string * exp
         | App of exp * exp
```

**Fig. 2.** Abstract syntax of the λ-calculus

```
module type SK_sig
= sig val cS : ('a -> 'b -> 'c) -> ('a -> 'b) -> 'a -> 'c
      val cK : 'a -> 'b -> 'a
  end

module SK : SK_sig
= struct let cS f g x = f x (g x)
         let cK a b = a
  end
```

**Fig. 3.** Hilbert's Combinatory Logic basis

## 2.1 The Hilbert combinators

As is well-known, the identity combinator $I$ can be defined with the Hilbert combinators $S$ and $K$. This is often illustrated in ML with the functions cS and cK defined in Figure 3:

```
# let cI x = SK.cS SK.cK SK.cK x;;
val cI : 'a -> 'a = <fun>
# cI 42;;
- : int = 42
```

It is the point of type-directed partial evaluation that one can visualize the text of cI by two-level $\eta$-expansion. In the present case, all we need is to $\eta$-expand cI with a dynamic introduction rule (the construction of a residual lambda-abstraction) and a static elimination rule (an ML application):

```
# let ee_id f = Lam("x", f (Var "x"));;
val ee_id : (exp -> exp) -> exp = <fun>
# ee_id (SK.cS SK.cK SK.cK);;
- : exp = Lam ("x", Var "x")
#
```

where in the definition of ee_id, x is fresh. The result of applying ee_id to the ML identity function is its text in normal form.

## 2.2 Church numbers

Let us play the same game with Church numbers. The type of a Church number is

$$('a \rightarrow 'a) \rightarrow 'a \rightarrow 'a$$

Since it is composed with three arrows, we need to $\eta$-expand it three times. Since the two outer arrows occur positively, we $\eta$-expand a Church number cn with two dynamic introduction rules and two static elimination rules:

```
Lam("s", Lam("z", cn (...(Var "s")...) (Var "z")))
```

where s and z are fresh.

Since the inner arrow occurs negatively, we $\eta$-expand the corresponding variable s with one static introduction rule (an ML abstraction) and one dynamic elimination rule (the construction of a residual application):

```
fun v -> App(Var "s", v)
```

The result reads as follows:

```
# let ee_cn cn
      = Lam("s", Lam("z", cn (fun v -> App(Var "s", v)) (Var "z")));;
val ee_cn : ((exp -> exp) -> exp -> exp) -> exp = <fun>
#
```

We are now equipped to visualize the normal form of a Church number, e.g., 2:

```
# ee_cn (ChurchNumbers.n2cn 2);;
- : exp = Lam("s", Lam("z", App(Var "s", App(Var "s", Var "z"))))
#
```

The result of applying ee_cn to the ML Church number 2 is the text of this Church number in normal form.

## 2.3 Summary and conclusion

We have illustrated type-directed partial evaluation in ML with two very simple examples: the Hilbert combinators and Church numbers. We have defined them in ML and we have constructed the text of their normal form, by two-level $\eta$-expansion.

Type-directed partial evaluation directly constructs two-level $\eta$-redices, given a representation of the type of the value to normalize. It also handles more types, such as base types (in restricted position), and can interpret function types as having a computational effect (in which case it inserts a residual let expression, using continuations). Figure 4 displays our grammar of admissible types.

```
            ⟨type⟩ ::= ⟨covariant-type⟩

   ⟨covariant-type⟩ ::= ⟨base-type⟩
                      | variable
                      | ⟨contravariant-type⟩ "->" ⟨covariant-type⟩
                      | ⟨covariant-type⟩ * ... * ⟨covariant-type⟩

 ⟨contravariant-type⟩ ::= bool
                      | variable
                      | ⟨covariant-type⟩ "->" ⟨contravariant-type⟩
                      | ⟨contravariant-type⟩ * ... * ⟨contravariant-type⟩

        ⟨base-type⟩ ::= unit | int | float | bool | string
```

**Fig. 4.** Abstract syntax of types

We therefore implemented several type-directed partial evaluators:

- inserting or not inserting let expressions; and
- in a purely functional way, i.e., implementing two-level eta-expansion directly in ML, using Andrzej Filinski and Zhe Yang's strategy,[1] or with an explicit representation of two-level terms as the abstract-syntax tree of an ML expression (which is then compiled).

---

[1] Personal communications to the second author, spring 1995 and spring 1996 [27].

In the following section, instead of constructing a normal form as an abstract-syntax tree, we construct byte code and load it in place, thereby obtaining the effect of strong normalization by type-directed partial evaluation and run-time code generation.

# 3 Run-Time Code Generation

We therefore have written a translator mapping a term in long $\beta\eta$-normal form into equivalent byte code for the OCaml virtual machine. And we load this byte code and update in place the value we have normalized.

## 3.1 Generating byte code

We do not generate byte code by calling the Caml compiler on the text of the normal forms. The language of normal forms is a tiny subset of ML, and therefore we represent it with a dedicated abstract syntax. Since normal forms are well typed, we also shortcut the type-checking phase of the compiler. Finally, we choose not to use the resident byte-code generator: instead, we use our own translator from normal forms to byte code.

## 3.2 Loading byte code

For this we need to access OCaml's byte-code loader, which required us to open its implementation. We have thus added more entry points in some of the modules that are available at the user level (i.e., Caml's toplevel). We have also made several interfaces available, by copying them in the OCaml libraries.

We essentially needed access to functions for loading byte code, and access to the current environment and its associated access functions. As a side benefit, our user does not need to specify the type of the value to optimize, since we can retrieve this information in the environment.

## 3.3 Updating in situ

Finally, being given the name of a variable holding a value to optimize, and being able to find its type in the environment, nothing prevents us to update the binding of this variable with the optimized value — which we do. We illustrated the whole process in Section 1.4, by

- defining a variable cs1000 denoting 1000 compositions of Church's successor function, and
- normalizing it in place with our function nip.

# 4 Applications

We have tested our system with traditional partial-evaluation examples, the biggest of which are definitional interpreters for programming languages. The results are consistent with the traditional results reported in the partial-evaluation literature [20]: the user's mileage may vary, depending (in the present case) on how much strong normalization is hindered by ML's weak-normalization strategy.

The definitional interpreters we have considered are traditional in partial evaluation: they range from a simple while language [5] to an Algol-like language with subtyping and recursion [16]. Our interpreters are written in Caml. Some use continuation-passing style (CPS), and the others direct style. In the definitional interpreters, iteration and recursion are handled with fixed-point operators.

All our examples clearly exhibit a speedup after normalization. The specialized version of an interpreter with respect to a program, for example, is typically 2.5 times faster after normalization. On some other examples (e.g., Section 1.4), the residual programs are several thousand times faster than the (unnormalized) source program.

The computational resources mobilized by type-directed partial evaluation vary wildly, depending on the source program. For example, specializing a direct-style interpreter with respect to a 10000-lines program takes 45 seconds and requires about 170 runs to be amortized. Specializing a CPS interpreter with respect to a 500-lines program, on the other hand, takes 20 minutes. We believe that this low performance is due to an inefficient handling of CPS in OCaml. Essentially the same implementation takes a handful of seconds in Chez Scheme for a 1000-lines program, with less than 0.5 seconds for type-directed partial evaluation proper, and with a fairly small difference if the interpreter is in direct style or in CPS.

We also experimented with the resident OCaml byte-code generator, which is slower by a factor of at least 3 than our dedicated byte-code generator. This difference demonstrates that using a special-purpose byte-code generator for normal forms is a worthwhile optimization.

# 5 Assessment

Although so far we are its only users, we believe that our system works reasonably well. In fact, we are in the process of writing a users's manual.

Our main problem at this point is the same as for any other partial evaluator: speedups are completely problem-dependent. In contrast with most other partial evaluators, however, we can quantify this statement: because (at least in its pure form) type-directed partial evaluation strongly normalizes its argument, we can state that it provides all the (strong) normalization steps that are hindered by ML's weak-normalization strategy.

Our secondary problem is efficiency: because OCaml is a byte-code implementation, it is inherently slower than a native code implementation such as

Chez Scheme [18], which is our reference implementation. Therefore our benchmarks in OCaml are typically measured in dozens of seconds whereas they are measured in very few seconds in Chez Scheme.[2] Efficiency becomes even more of a problem for the continuation-based version of the type-directed partial evaluator: whereas Chez Scheme represents continuations very efficiently [19], that is not the case at all for OCaml. On the other hand, the continuation-based partial evaluator yields perceptibly better residual programs (e.g., without code duplication because of let insertion).

*Caveat:* If our system is given a diverging source program, it diverges as well. In that it is resource-unbounded [13, 17].

## 6   Towards Modular Type-Directed Partial Evaluation

In a certain sense, ML's higher-order modules are essentially the simply typed lambda-calculus laid on top of first-order modules ("structures") [23]. Looking under the hood, that is precisely how they are implemented. This suggests us to extend our implementation to part of the Caml module language.

*Enabling technology:* After type-checking, first-order modules ("structures") are handled as tuples and higher-order modules ("functors") are handled as higher-order functions. Besides, enough typing information is held in the environment to be able to reconstruct their type. Put together, these two observations make it possible for us to reuse most of our existing implementation.

```
module type BCWK_sig
= sig val cB : ('a -> 'b) -> ('c -> 'a) -> 'c -> 'b
      val cC : ('a -> 'b -> 'c) -> 'b -> 'a -> 'c
      val cW : ('a -> 'a -> 'b) -> 'a -> 'b
      val cK : 'a -> 'b -> 'a
  end
module BCWK : BCWK_sig
= struct open SK
        let cB f g x = cS (cK cS) cK f g x
        let cC f x y = cS (cS (cK (cS (cK cS) cK)) cS) (cK cK) f x y
        let cW f x = cS cS (cK (cS cK cK)) f x
        let cK = cK
  end
```

**Fig. 5.** A Combinatory Logic basis of regular combinators

---

[2] For comparison, an interpreter-based and optimized implementation of type-directed partial evaluation in ML consistently performs between 1000 and 10000 times slower than the implementation in Chez Scheme [25]. The point here is not byte code vs. native code, but interpreted code vs. compiled code.

*Achievements and limitations:* We handle a subset of the Caml module language, excluding polymorphism and sharing constraints.

*An example: typed Combinatory Logic.* Let us build on the example of Section 2.1. We have located the definition of the Hilbert combinators in a module defining our standard Combinatory Logic basis (see Figure 3). We then define an alternative basis in another module, in terms of the first one (see Figure 5). Because of ML's weak-normalization strategy, using the alternative basis incurs an overhead. We can eliminate this overhead by normalizing in place the alternative basis:

```
# nip_module "BCWK";;
- : unit = ()
#
```

What happens here is that the identifier BCWK denotes a tuple with four entries, each of which we already know how to process. Given the name of this identifier, the implementation

1. locates it in the Caml environment;
2. accesses its type;
3. constructs the simple type of a tuple of four elements;
4. strongly normalizes it, using type-directed partial evaluation;
5. translates it into byte code, and loads it;
6. updates in place the environment to make the identifier BCWK denote the generated code.

## 7   Related Work

Partial evaluation is traditionally defined as a source-to-source program transformation [6, 20]. Type-directed partial evaluation departs from that tradition in that it is a compiled-to-source program transformation. Run-time code generation completes the picture by providing a source-to-compiled transformation at run time. It is thus a natural idea to compose both, and this has been done in two settings, using offline partial-evaluation techniques:

For imperative languages: the Compose research group at Rennes is doing run-time code generation for stock languages such as C, C++, and Java [3].

For functional languages: Sperber and Thiemann have paired a traditional, syntax-directed partial evaluator and a run-time code generator for a byte-code implementation of Scheme [26].

Both settings use binding-time analysis. Sperber and Thiemann's work is the most closely related to ours, even though their partial evaluator is syntax-directed instead of type-directed and though they consider an untyped and module-less language (Scheme) instead of a typed and modular one (ML). A remarkable aspect of their work, and one our implementation so far has failed to achieve, is that they deforest the intermediate representation of the specialized program, i.e., their partial evaluator directly generates byte code.

Alternative approaches to partial evaluation and run-time code generation include Leone and Lee's Fabius system [21], which only handles "staged" first-order ML programs but generates actual assembly code very efficiently.

# 8 Conclusion and Issues

We have obtained strong normalization in ML by pairing type-directed partial evaluation and run-time code generation. We have implemented a system in Objective Caml, whose byte code made it possible to remain portable. The system can be used in any situation where strong normalization could be of benefit. Besides the examples mentioned above, we have applied it to type specialization [9], lambda-lifting and lambda-dropping [10], formatting strings [11], higher-order abstract syntax [12], and deforestation [15]. We are also considering to apply it for cut elimination in formal proofs, in a proof assistant.

We are in the process of extending our implementation for a subset of the Caml module language. This extension relies on the run-time treatment of structures and of functors, which are represented as tuples and as higher-order functions. Therefore, in a pre-pass, we assemble type information about the module to normalize (be it first order or higher order), we coerce it into simply typed tuple and function constructions, and we then reuse our earlier implementation.

The practical limitations are the same as for offline type-directed partial evaluation, i.e., source programs must be explicitly factored prior to specialization. The module language, however, appears to be a pleasant support for expressing this factorization.

# Acknowledgements

This work is supported by BRICS (Basic Research in Computer Science, Centre of the Danish National Research Foundation; http://www.brics.dk). It was carried out at BRICS during the summer of 1997.

We are grateful to Xavier Leroy for supplying us with a version of call/cc for OCaml, and to the anonymous reviewers for comments.

# References

1. Ulrich Berger. Program extraction from normalization proofs. In M. Bezem and J. F. Groote, editors, *Typed Lambda Calculi and Applications*, number 664 in Lecture Notes in Computer Science, pages 91–106, Utrecht, The Netherlands, March 1993.
2. Ulrich Berger and Helmut Schwichtenberg. An inverse of the evaluation functional for typed λ-calculus. In *Proceedings of the Sixth Annual IEEE Symposium on Logic in Computer Science*, pages 203–211, Amsterdam, The Netherlands, July 1991. IEEE Computer Society Press.

3. The COMPOSE Project. Effective partial evaluation: Principles and applications. Technical report, IRISA (http://www.irisa.fr), Campus Universitaire de Beaulieu, Rennes, France, January 1996 – May 1998. A selection of representative publications.

4. Charles Consel, editor. *ACM SIGPLAN Symposium on Partial Evaluation and Semantics-Based Program Manipulation*, Amsterdam, The Netherlands, June 1997. ACM Press.

5. Charles Consel and Olivier Danvy. Static and dynamic semantics processing. In Robert (Corky) Cartwright, editor, *Proceedings of the Eighteenth Annual ACM Symposium on Principles of Programming Languages*, pages 14–24, Orlando, Florida, January 1991. ACM Press.

6. Charles Consel and Olivier Danvy. Tutorial notes on partial evaluation. In Susan L. Graham, editor, *Proceedings of the Twentieth Annual ACM Symposium on Principles of Programming Languages*, pages 493–501, Charleston, South Carolina, January 1993. ACM Press.

7. Catarina Coquand. From semantics to rules: A machine assisted analysis. In Egon Börger, Yuri Gurevich, and Karl Meinke, editors, *Proceedings of CSL'93*, number 832 in Lecture Notes in Computer Science. Springer-Verlag, 1993.

8. Olivier Danvy. Type-directed partial evaluation. In Guy L. Steele Jr., editor, *Proceedings of the Twenty-Third Annual ACM Symposium on Principles of Programming Languages*, pages 242–257, St. Petersburg Beach, Florida, January 1996. ACM Press.

9. Olivier Danvy. A simple solution to type specialization. Technical Report BRICS RS-98-1, Department of Computer Science, University of Aarhus, Aarhus, Denmark, January 1998. To appear in the proceedings of ICALP'98.

10. Olivier Danvy. An extensional characterization of lambda-lifting and lambda-dropping. Technical Report BRICS RS-98-2, Department of Computer Science, University of Aarhus, Aarhus, Denmark, January 1998.

11. Olivier Danvy. Formatting strings in ML (preliminary version). Technical Report BRICS RS-98-5, Department of Computer Science, University of Aarhus, Aarhus, Denmark, March 1998. To appear in the Journal of Functional Programming.

12. Olivier Danvy. The mechanical evaluation of higher-order expressions. In *Preliminary proceedings of the 14th Conference on Mathematical Foundations of Programming Semantics*, London, UK, May 1998.

13. Olivier Danvy, Nevin C. Heintze, and Karoline Malmkjær. Resource-bounded partial evaluation. *ACM Computing Surveys*, 28(2):329–332, June 1996.

14. Olivier Danvy, Karoline Malmkjær, and Jens Palsberg. The essence of eta-expansion in partial evaluation. *LISP and Symbolic Computation*, 8(3):209–227, 1995. An earlier version appeared in the proceedings of the 1994 ACM SIGPLAN Workshop on Partial Evaluation and Semantics-Based Program Manipulation.

15. Olivier Danvy and Kristoffer Høgsbro Rose. Deforestation by strong normalization. Technical report, BRICS, University of Aarhus and LIP, ENS Lyon, April 1998. To appear.

16. Olivier Danvy and René Vestergaard. Semantics-based compiling: A case study in type-directed partial evaluation. In Herbert Kuchen and Doaitse Swierstra, editors, *Eighth International Symposium on Programming Language Implementation and Logic Programming*, number 1140 in Lecture Notes in Computer Science, pages 182–197, Aachen, Germany, September 1996. Extended version available as the technical report BRICS-RS-96-13.

17. Saumya Debray. Resource-bounded partial evaluation. In Consel [4], pages 179–192.

18. R. Kent Dybvig. *The Scheme Programming Language*. Prentice-Hall, 1987.
19. Robert Hieb, R. Kent Dybvig, and Carl Bruggeman. Representing control in the presence of first-class continuations. In Bernard Lang, editor, *Proceedings of the ACM SIGPLAN'90 Conference on Programming Languages Design and Implementation*, SIGPLAN Notices, Vol. 25, No 6, pages 66–77, White Plains, New York, June 1990. ACM Press.
20. Neil D. Jones, Carsten K. Gomard, and Peter Sestoft. *Partial Evaluation and Automatic Program Generation*. Prentice Hall International Series in Computer Science. Prentice-Hall, 1993.
21. Mark Leone and Peter Lee. Lightweight run-time code generation. In Peter Sestoft and Harald Søndergaard, editors, *Proceedings of the ACM SIGPLAN Workshop on Partial Evaluation and Semantics-Based Program Manipulation*, Technical Report 94/9, University of Melbourne, Australia, pages 97–106, Orlando, Florida, June 1994.
22. Xavier Leroy. *The Objective Caml system, release 1.05*. INRIA, Rocquencourt, France, 1997.
23. David B. MacQueen. Modules for Standard ML. In Guy L. Steele Jr., editor, *Conference Record of the 1984 ACM Symposium on Lisp and Functional Programming*, pages 198–207, Austin, Texas, August 1984.
24. Frank Pfenning and Conal Elliott. Higher-order abstract syntax. In Mayer D. Schwartz, editor, *Proceedings of the ACM SIGPLAN'88 Conference on Programming Languages Design and Implementation*, SIGPLAN Notices, Vol. 23, No 7, pages 199–208, Atlanta, Georgia, June 1988. ACM Press.
25. Tim Sheard. A type-directed, on-line, partial evaluator for a polymorphic language. In Consel [4], pages 22–35.
26. Michael Sperber and Peter Thiemann. Two for the price of one: composing partial evaluation and compilation. In Ron K. Cytron, editor, *Proceedings of the ACM SIGPLAN'97 Conference on Programming Languages Design and Implementation*, SIGPLAN Notices, Vol. 32, No 5, pages 215–225, Las Vegas, Nevada, June 1997. ACM Press.
27. Zhe Yang. Encoding types in ML-like languages (preliminary version). Technical Report BRICS RS-98-9, Department of Computer Science, University of Aarhus, Aarhus, Denmark, April 1998.

# Determination of Dynamic Method Dispatches Using Run-Time Code Generation

Nobuhisa Fujinami

Sony Computer Science Laboratory Inc.

**Abstract.** Run-time code generation (RTCG) enables program optimizations specific to values that are unknown until run time and improves the performance. This paper shows that RTCG can be used to determine dynamic method dispatches. It can produce a better result than conventional method dispatch prediction mechanisms because other run-time optimizations help the determination. Further, the determined functions can be inlined, and this may lead to other optimizations. These optimizations are implemented in the author's RTCG system. The evaluation results showed good performance improvement.

## 1 Introduction

Run-time code generation (RTCG) is a partial evaluation [1] performed at run time. It generates machine code specific to values which are unknown until run time and enhances the speed of a program, while preserving its generality. RTCG itself is becoming a mature technique. Description languages and systems for run-time code generators have been proposed. Systems that automatically generate run-time code generators from source programs have also been proposed.

Also, much efforts has been made to improve the performance of object-oriented languages. Recent research papers have focused on using run-time type feedback or static type inference to optimize dynamic method dispatch.

This paper describes an RTCG system that can optimize dynamic method dispatches of an object-oriented language. This system can produce a better results than conventional method dispatch prediction mechanisms because other run-time optimizations, such as global constant propagation/folding and complete loop unrolling, help the determination. This paper focuses on these optimizations.

The basics of the RTCG system itself are described only briefly in this paper. Refer to [2], [3], and [4] for details. This system focuses on the instance variables of objects and uses the fact that objects can be regarded as closures [5]. If the values of some instance variables are run-time constants, the system generates specialized code generators for methods that use them. Machine code routines optimized to their values are generated at run time.

The rest of the paper is organized as follows: Section 2 overviews the RTCG system. The optimizations implemented in the system are described in Section 3. Section 4 evaluates the optimizations. Section 5 overviews related research. Finally, Section 6 provides a summary and future plans.

## 2 System Overview

This section describes briefly the RTCG system for an object-oriented language proposed by the author.

As stated in Section 1, RTCG improves the efficiency of programs by generating machine code optimized to values that are unknown until run time, e.g. intermediate results of computation and the user's inputs. If programs operating on these values are written in object-oriented languages, it is natural to define objects with instance variables that represent the values known at run time. For example, to program stream input/output functions, the programmer may assign descriptors of files, sockets, strings, etc., to instance variables of stream objects. Stream objects may have methods for reading or writing streams, which have the descriptors as their run-time constants. Another example is the generation and rendering of a three dimensional scene. The programmer may represent the scene, which is a run-time constant during rendering, as a scene object with instance variables representing a set of graphics objects, a viewing point, light sources, etc. The scene object's methods for rendering can be optimized through RTCG.

The benefits of focusing on instance variables of objects are as follows:

**Automation of the timing of code generation/invalidation:** Because of the encapsulation mechanism of object-oriented languages, all the assignments to non-public instance variables (e.g. private data members in C++) can be known, except for indirect accesses through pointers, from the definition of the class and its methods. Since the system knows when to generate/invalidate code, the programmer is freed from annotating programs and from providing suitable parameters to preserve consistency between the embedded values in the code and the actual values.

**Automation of the management of generated code:** Since generated machine code (a specialized method) can be viewed as a part of the instance, management of it can be left to the instance creation/destruction mechanism of a object-oriented language. Management of multiple machine code routines for the same method is trivial. The generated machine code can be automatically invoked instead of using the original method. The programmer is freed from managing memory for the code and from rewriting programs to invoke the code.

The system is implemented as a preprocessor of a C++ compiler. The current implementation is for Borland C++ compilers (Version 4.0 or higher) running on 80x86 based computers with a Win32 API. The executable file name is RPCC.EXE. The reasons for choosing C++ as the source language are as follows:

- Since C++ has static type declarations, it is easy to determine the types of values used in the run-time code generator.
- Since C++ is quite an efficient object-oriented language, the system can provide the best possible implementation of a program written in a high-level language.

The programmer directs the system to use RTCG by inserting the keyword
runtime before a declaration of a member function.[1] The system assumes all the
"known" data members (see the next paragraph) used but not changed in that
member function to be run-time constants. The programmer can direct not to
assume data members as run-time constants by putting the keyword dynamic
before the definitions of the members.

The "known" data members are detected as follows: In the first step of analyzing the source program, all private, protected, or const[2] data members
of the class without the keyword dynamic are marked "known". Then, if any of
the member functions of the class use the non-const member that satisfies the
following conditions, the mark for the member is cleared:

- The address of the member is taken, e.g. an operand of the unary & operator
  or a reference parameter.
- The address is passed directly or indirectly via casts or the binary + and −
  operators to a variable, as a function parameter, or as a return value.
- The type of the destination is not a pointer/reference to a const.

The values of the members still marked "known" are known in the sense that
only the functions that explicitly use or modify the members can use or modify
them.

Let F be a member function with the keyword runtime, and let X be any data
member marked "known". If X is used, but not changed in F, X is treated as a
run-time constant in the code generator for F. If X is a run-time constant in the
code generator for F and member function G changes X, the code to invalidate
the machine code for F is inserted into G. If such G's exist, and F calls other
functions, then X may be modified during the execution of the generated code.
In this case, a new data member is introduced to count the number of active
executions of F. Code to check the counter value is inserted into G. If the value
is not zero, the code warns the programmer that the insertion of the keyword
runtime is inappropriate.[3]

Figure 1 shows an overall organization of the system. The upper half illustrates the action at compile time, and the lower half illustrates the program
execution. At compile time, C++ preprocessor directives in a source program are
processed first (CPP32.EXE in Borland C++). Then RPCC.EXE analyzes the
program and generates, if necessary, run-time code generators in C++. The code
generators, the code for invoking them, and the code for invoking/invalidating
the generated code are embedded into the original source program. The output

---

[1] Automatic detection of the applicability is possible but not practical, because a too
aggressive application of RTCG increases the compilation time and the size of the
executable file.

[2] It may violate the assumption of the analysis to cast a pointer to const into a pointer
to non-const. Such an attempt is considered to be illegal because it is not safe to
modify an object through such a pointer.

[3] Using the exception handling of C++ may lead to false warnings because the counter
may not have been decreased correctly. In this case, catching exceptions in F will
solve the problem.

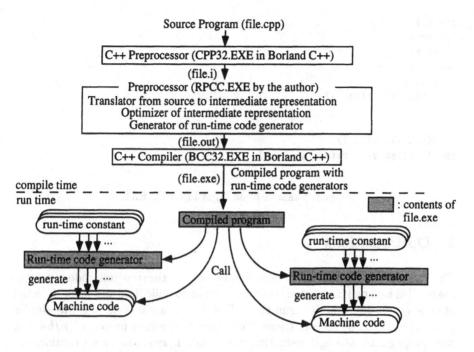

Source Program (file.cpp)

**Fig. 1.** Organization of the implemented system

is compiled into an executable file using a normal C++ compiler (BCC32.EXE in Borland C++). The source program and its intermediate representation are manipulated only at this compile time.

At run time, code generators are invoked with run-time constants as parameters. They generate member functions optimized to run-time constants in machine code format. Each code generator is specific to one member function. Since the code is directly written into memory, and since neither source program nor intermediate representation of it is used, code generation is efficient. One code generator may generate multiple machine code routines with different run-time constant values. The generated routines, which are expected to be more efficient than statically compiled ones, are invoked instead of the original member functions.

Figure 2 shows an example of an input to RPCC.EXE. Figure 3 shows the output (comments are added for readability). Preprocessor RPCC.EXE processes member functions with the keyword runtime and generates run-time code generators in C++. Pointers to generated machine code routines are added to the class as its data members; code generators are added as its member functions. The processed member functions are replaced with code fragments to check the validity of the generated code, to invoke the code generators if necessary, and to invoke the generated code. The preprocessor also inserts code for deleting generated machine code in the destructors and in the member functions that modifies the data members embedded in the generated machine code.

```
class A {
 private:
  int x;
 public:
  A(int i);
  runtime int f(int y);
};

A::A(int i): x(i) {}
int A::f(int y) { return y-x*x; }
```

**Fig. 2.** Example of an input to RPCC.EXE

# 3 Optimizations

The optimizations of the machine code generated by the run-time code generator are divided into two categories: those detected at compile time and those detected at code generation time (i.e. run time). The former are treated in a way similar to conventional code optimizations. They include constant propagation/folding, copy propagation, strength reduction, reassociation, redundant code elimination, algebraic simplification, jump optimization, delay slot filling, and loop invariant motion.

Since the latter is performed at run time, the efficiency is important. The system adopts a method to generate machine code directly. It does not manipulate any source program or its intermediate representation at run time. The output from RPCC.EXE contains optimization routines specialized to the target member functions. Optimizations performed at run time include local constant propagation/folding, strength reduction, redundant code elimination, and algebraic simplification. Because of the naive implementation of RPCC.EXE, redundant optimization code may be included in the code generator, but most of it is optimized away by the C++ compiler (Code generators are generated in C++. See Section 2.).

The rest of this section describes non-trivial optimizations performed at code generation time. These optimizations include global run-time constant propagation, complete loop unrolling, and virtual function inlining.

## 3.1 Intermediate Representation

This subsection describes intermediate representation used at compile time.

RPCC.EXE consists of three phases similar to conventional compilers (see Figure 1):

1. Translator from source to intermediate representation
2. Optimizer of intermediate representation
3. Generator of run-time code generator

```
#include <qqmacro.h>              // macros and functions for RTCG

class A {
 private:
  int x;
 public:
  A(int i);
  int f(int y);
  ~A()                           // destructor
  char *qq_f;                    // pointer to generated code
  void qq__f() const;            // code generator
  static char *qql_f;            // address of label "generate" in f
  static char *qql__f();         // function to initialize qql_f
};

A::~A() { if(qq_f!=qql_f) delete qq_f; }

A::A(int i): x(i) ,qq_f(qql_f){}

int A::f(int ) {
retry:
  asm MOV ECX,this;
  asm JMP DWORD PTR [ECX].qq_f; // jump to generated code
generate:
  qq__f();                       // invoke code generator
  goto retry;
}

char *A::qql_f=qql__f();

void A::qq__f() const {
  char *qqcode;                  // code address
  // prologue code generator (omitted)
  qqMOVdx(0,5,12);               // MOV EAX,[EBP+12] ; y
  qqSUB_I(0,(int)x*x);           // SUB EAX,x*x
  // epilogue code generator (omitted)
  *(char **)&qq_f=qqcode;        // set code address
}
```

**Fig. 3.** Example of an output from RPCC.EXE (Macro qqXX(YY) writes instruction XX with operand(s) YY into memory.)

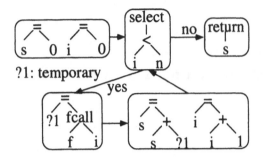

**Fig. 4.** Intermediate representation of { int i,s=0; for(i=0;i<n;i++) s+=f(i); return s; }

The intermediate representation format used in these phases is designed to be suitable for generating run-time code generators. Intermediate representation is a flow graph that represents the meaning of a function. It is generated for each function to be optimized or inlined. The nodes of the graph are basic blocks. They are represented as a sequence of statements. Figure 4 shows an example of intermediate representation.

A statement is one of assignment, function invocation, selection, switch, virtual, and return. A goto-statement is represented as an edge of the flow graph and has no special node. Some statements have expressions as their operands. Expressions are represented as directed acyclic graphs (DAGs) whose nodes are operators, identifiers, or constants. Expressions with side effects are divided into multiple statements. Conditional operators (&&, ||, and ?:) are expressed using separate basic blocks. Temporary variables may be introduced in this transformation.

The reasons for using DAGs instead of a conventional flat format such as a three-address code are as follows:

- It is easy to classify nodes into stages (see the next paragraph).
- It is easy to reconstruct C++ expressions to calculate run-time constants which will be embedded into run-time code generators.
- It is easy to replace variables with expressions. This operation is necessary in the optimization described in Subsection 3.2.

Leaf nodes of DAGs are identifiers or compile-time constants. Each identifier's entry in the symbol table has a flag that tells if the identifier is a data member treated as a run-time constant. RPCC.EXE classifies nodes into three stages: "compile time", "code generation time", and "dynamic". Simple traversal of DAGs can classify internal nodes and statements into three stages.

When the run-time code generator is generated, the stage information is used as follows: If the stages of a subgraph is "compile time", its value is calculated at compile time and the result is embedded into the run-time code generator. If its stage is "code generation time", a C++ expression that calculates the run-time

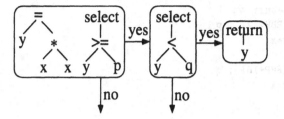

**Fig. 5.** Intermediate representation before run-time constant propagation

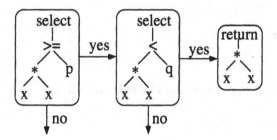

**Fig. 6.** Intermediate representation after run-time constant propagation

constant value is embedded into the code generator. If its stage is "dynamic", a code generation routine for it is embedded.

The system inlines functions during translation to intermediate representation. Functions that perform recursive calls are not inlined to prevent infinite loops of partial evaluation.

## 3.2 Global Run-Time Constant Propagation

This optimization is processed in the second phase (optimizer of intermediate representation). Like conventional compilers, this phase performs dataflow analysis on the flow graph, propagates compile-time constants, eliminates redundant code, etc. Simple extension of compile-time constant propagation allows run-time global constant propagation. In the normal constant propagation, only the values of compile time constant expressions are propagated to the places of their use. If the right operand of an assignment operator is an arithmetic expression consisting of run-time constants, this phase also propagates the expression. Thus, all the use of run-time constants are replaced with expressions that compute their values. In the third phase (generator of run-time code generator), the new expressions are classified as "compile time". The C++ expressions are reconstructed and embedded into the run-time code generator. This enables global run-time constant propagation.

For example, if x is a run-time constant in the block:

```
{ y=x*x; if(y>=p && y<q) return y; }
qqMOVdx(0,5,12); // MOV EAX,[EBP+12] ; p
qqCMP_I(0,x*x);  // CMP EAX,x*x
qqGenJccF(G,2);  // JG L2
qqMOVdx(1,5,16); // MOV ECX,[EBP+16] ; q
qqCMP_I(1,x*x);  // CMP ECX,x*x
qqGenJccF(G,5);  // JG L5
qqGenLbl(2);     //L2:
//
// code generator for other basic blocks
//
qqGenLbl(5);     //L5:
qqMOV_I(0,x*x);  // MOV EAX,x*x
QQEXIT           // exit code
```

**Fig. 7.** Run-time code generator (qqXX is a macro for code generation)

```
 MOV EAX,[EBP+12] ; p
 CMP EAX,9
 JG L2
 MOV ECX,[EBP+16] ; q
 CMP ECX,9
 JG L5
L2:
;
; code for other basic blocks
;
L5:
 MOV EAX,9
; exit code
```

**Fig. 8.** Generated machine code if x=3 (translated into Intel mnemonic)

(its intermediate representation is in Figure 5), uses of y are replaced with the run-time constant expression x*x (see Figure 6). In the next phase, a code generation routine shown in Figure 7 is generated. If run-time constant x=3 is supplied to the code generator at run time, machine code shown in Figure 8 will be generated.

Since this optimization technique is flow-sensitive, it successfully processes cases in which a variable is a run-time constant at one point in the program, but not at another point. For example, suppose p and q are not run-time constants and an assignment y=q-p; follows the code in Figure 5. In this case, the variable y does not always hold a run-time constant, but an assignment y=x*x; is successfully propagated using dataflow analysis. An assignment y=q-p; does not disturb the optimization in Figure 6.

Using the Static Single Assignment Form (SSA) and a flat intermediate representation format also allows flow-sensitive stage classification. This method

```
int C::g(int p,int q)
{
  int s=0;
  for(i=0;i<n;i++) {
    int y=a[i];
    if(y>=p && y<q) s++;
  }
  return s;
}
```

**Fig. 9.** Member function **g**

avoids duplicated run-time constant expressions (e.g. x*x in the previous example) but requires stage annotations for all of the temporary variables. The system does not adopt it and leaves the optimization to eliminate duplicated run-time constant expressions, if any, to the C++ compiler.

### 3.3 Complete Loop Unrolling

Unlike other run-time code generation systems (see Section 5), the author's system can unroll only simple loops. But it automatically decides whether each loop should be fully unrolled or not, depending on the upper limit of the number of iterations of the loop.

In the second phase (optimizer of intermediate representation), loops are detected during dataflow analysis. It checks to see if one of the exits of the loop is a simple comparison of the control variable and compile- or run-time constant, and if the initial value and the update step are compile- or run-time constants. The loop may have other exits. If a loop passes the check, its upper limit of the number of iterations are compile- or run-time constant.

The third phase (generator of run-time code generator) emits a code fragment to unroll the loop based on this information. If the upper limit of the number of iterations is a compile-time constant, either a normal code generation routine or a complete unrolling routine of the loop is generated, depending on the upper limit. If it is a run-time constant, code generators of both versions are generated, and the selection is performed at code generation time.

To support both versions, the run-time constant propagator is extended. If a run-time constant expression contains a loop control variable, the propagated expression (for calculating the value of the run-time constant) is represented as a special node that also holds the original variable. An example is a loop in function g in Figure 9. If a and n are run-time constant data members of class C, the use of y is replaced with a special node that holds both y and a[i]. If the loop is not unrolled, variable y is used in the if statement. If the loop is completely unrolled, run-time constant a[i] is used in the if statement.

If the loop is completely unrolled, the stage of the loop control structure is assumed to be "code generation time" in the output code generator. The loop

```
qq0i=0;                  // i=0
for(;;) {
  qqMOVdx(0,5,12);       // MOV EAX,[EBP+12] ; p
  qqCMP_I(0,a[qq0i]);    // CMP EAX,a[qq0i]  ; a[i]
  qqGenJccF(G,5);        // JG L5
  qqMOVdx(1,5,16);       // MOV ECX,[EBP+16] ; q
  qqCMP_I(1,a[qq0i]);    // CMP ECX,a[qq0i]  ; a[i]
  qqGenJccF(LE,5);       // JLE L5
  qqADD_I(6,1);          // INC ESI          ; s
  qqGenLbl(5);           //L5:
  qq0i=qq0i+1;           // i++
  if(!(qq0i<n)) break;
}
```

**Fig. 10.** Code generator for the loop in **g** (qqXX is a macro for code generation)

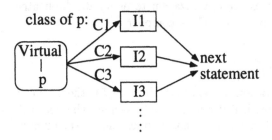

**Fig. 11.** Flow graph of virtual function invocation

control variable becomes a variable of the run-time code generator and is treated as a run-time constant in the body of the loop (see Figure 10).

### 3.4 Inlining Virtual Functions

Suppose a run-time constant is a pointer to a class object. If virtual function invocation is used with this pointer, the actual invoked function can be determined at code generation time. This is because of the following reason:

> Since the pointer value is constant, the object's address cannot be changed, and a legal way to change the class is to use union. A class with some virtual functions should have an implicit or an explicit constructor. If a class has any constructor, it cannot be a member of union. Thus the actual class of the object cannot be changed.

Furthermore, if the invoked function is declared as inline, it can be inlined[4].

---

[4] Virtual functions of C++ can be declared as inline. Normal compilers inline them only if the invoked functions can be determined at compile time.

```
class objectTableType {
  int count;                      // graphics object counter
  objectType *table[MAXOBJECT]; // pointers to graphics objects
 public:
  objectTableType(): count(0) {}
  int add(objectType *p);         // add graphics object
  runtime const objectType *intersect_all(rayType &, myfloat &);
};                                // return the first object the ray intersects
```

**Fig. 12.** Definition of class `objectTableType`

```
const objectType *
objectTableType::intersect_all(rayType &ray, myfloat &t)
{
  myfloat t1;
  const objectType *obj=0;
  for(int i=0;i<count;i++) {
    if(table[i]->intersect(ray,t1)) {
      if(t1>MIN_DISTANCE && (obj==0 || t1<t-MIN_DISTANCE)) {
        t=t1; obj=table[i];
      }
    }
  }
  return obj;
}
```

**Fig. 13.** Member function `intersect_all`

In the intermediate representation used in RPCC.EXE, virtual function invocation is represented as a special node "Virtual" (see Figure 11). Each I$k$ represents a call of a member function of derived class C$n$ or an inlined image of it. RPCC.EXE embeds code to test the actual class and to generate machine code for I$k$ if the class is C$k$. Operator `typeid`, which returns run-time type information, is used in the test.

Other run-time optimizations, such as constant propagation and complete loop unrolling, help this optimization. For example, Figure 12 shows a class that represents a set of graphics objects. Member function `intersect_all` has the keyword `runtime`, and its implementation is given in Figure 13. Each element of `table` can point to any graphics object (derived class of `objectType`: see Figure 14). If the loop is unrolled, the invocation of virtual function `intersect` is determined and inlined. If `table[0]` points to an object of class `Plane` and `table[1]` points to an object of class `discType`, then the unrolled loop looks like:

```
Inlined image of Plane::intersect
Rest of the loop body
```

```
class objectType {
protected:
  const surfaceType * surface;
  const pointType center;
 public:
  inline virtual int intersect(const rayType&,myfloat &t) const = 0;
  objectType(surfaceType * s, const pointType& c);
  virtual const SinfoType * getSinfo(const pointType & pos) const;
  virtual vectorType getNormal(const pointType &) const =0;
  virtual int flat() const = 0;
};

class Plane: public objectType {
  const vectorType N;
  const myfloat d;
 public:
  Plane(surfaceType *s,pointType &pos,vectorType &NN);
  inline int intersect(const rayType &,myfloat &) const;
  vectorType getNormal(const pointType &) const { return N; }
  int flat() const { return 1; }
};

int
Plane::intersect(const rayType &ray,myfloat &t) const
{
  myfloat t1=inner(N,ray.v);
  if(t1==0.0) return 0;
  t=(d-inner(N,ray.p))/t1;
  if(t<=MIN_DISTANCE) return 0;
  return 1;
}
```

**Fig. 14.** Class objectType, derived class Plane and virtual member function intersect

```
Inlined image of disc::intersect
Rest of the loop body
...
```

This is impossible for conventional techniques, such as type inference of variables or variable occurrences in call sites.

Inlined member functions are further optimized through run-time constant propagation/folding, algebraic simplification, etc. In the previous example, run-time constants table[0], table[1], ⋯ are propagated to the this pointers of inlined member functions Plane::intersect, discType::intersect, ⋯, and they are specialized with respect to const data members, if any, of graphics objects pointed to by table[0], table[1], ⋯.

| Program | execution time (sec) | speed ratio | |
|---------|:--------------------:|:-----------:|:----:|
| original (C) | 72.5 | 1.00 | 0.59 |
| new (C++) | 42.6 | 1.70 | 1.00 |
| optimized (C++) | 30.4 | 2.38 | 1.40 |

**Table 1.** Evaluation results (ray tracer)

| Program | execution time (sec) | speed ratio | |
|---------|:--------------------:|:-----------:|:----:|
| original (C) | 69.2 | 1.00 | 1.04 |
| original (C++) | 72.3 | 0.96 | 1.00 |
| optimized (C++) | 36.9 | 1.87 | 1.96 |

**Table 2.** Evaluation results (puzzle solver)

Figure 14 shows definitions of class Plane and member function intersect. If an instance of Plane represents a plane parallel to the x-y plane, the x and y components of its normal vector N are zeros. In this case, inlined image of function inner (inner product: three multiplications and two additions) is algebraically simplified into a single multiplication.

# 4  Evaluation

This section reports the evaluation results of the implementation. The evaluation environment is as follows:

**Machine:** NEC PC-9821St15/L16 (Pentium Pro 150MHz, RAM: 48MBytes)
**Operating System:** Microsoft Windows 95 Operating System
**Compiler:** Borland C++ Version 5.0J
**Compiler Options:** -6 -O2 -OS -vi (Pentium Pro, optimize for speed, instruction scheduling, enable inlining)

The first program is a ray tracer. Table 1 shows the results. The program reads a scene file at run time and displays the ray-traced image. It contains class objectTableType in Figures 12 and 13. The keyword "runtime" is inserted before the declaration of member function intersect_all. The ray-traced scene contains three transparent spheres, seventeen opaque spheres, two mirrors, one disc, one checked square, and one light source. The output is a 512 × 512 24-bit color image. The original program is in [6] and is written in C ("original" in Table 1). The author's part-time assistant rewrote it into C++ ("new" in Table 1). The new program runs about 1.7 times as fast as the original one[5] and the run-time-optimized one is 1.4 times as fast as the new one. Analyzing the generated code shows that the speedup is mostly due to determination of virtual member function invocation combined with inlining.

---

[5] The original program uses a switch statement to classify graphics objects. Using virtual member function optimized the classification.

```
class Piece {
 private:
  int index,dirs,num;
  int offset[MaxDir][MaxSize];
 public:
  Piece(int i);
  runtime void put(Box *b,int o,int i0,PieceList *l);
 private:
  void set(Box* b,int o,int j);
  void reset(Box* b,int o,int j);
};

void
Piece::put(Box *b,int o,int i0,PieceList *l)
{
  int j,k;
  for(j=0;j<dirs;j++) {
    for(k=0;k<num;k++) if((*b)[o+offset[j][k]]!=null) goto next;
    set(b,o,j);
    l->putok(b,o,index,i0);
    reset(b,o,j);
  next:;
  }
}
```

**Fig. 15.** Class Piece

The second program is a box-packing puzzle solver. Table 2 shows the results. It reads a puzzle definition file that describes the box and the pieces and prints the solutions. Run-time optimization is applied to member function put of class Piece (see Figure 15). Its instance variables represent the shapes of the pieces and are run-time constants. The goal here is to pack 11 pieces into a size 4 cubic box. There are three solutions. The optimized program runs about twice as fast as the normal one. Here the speedup is mostly due to loop unrolling and constant folding. The author wrote the puzzle solver in both C and C++. Notice that the program in C++ is a little bit slower than that in C.

In both cases, the optimized program runs faster than the original one and the one written in C. Optimized programs in C++ can run faster than their C counterparts.

The cost for code generation is 625 microseconds per 7638 bytes of generated instructions, or about 12 machine cycles per bytes in the case of the ray tracer. It is low enough compared with the code generation system that manipulates intermediate representations [7] but it is still higher than the result of [8], which emits run-time code generators in machine code. The cause of this const seems to be that the compiled code generator contains quite a few instructions operating on byte data. The Pentium Pro processor cannot execute such instructions efficiently. Rewriting the generator of code generator will make the cost even lower.

## 5 Related Work

There are a number of related research papers on optimization of object-oriented languages [9] [10] [11] [12] [13] [14] [15]. These papers focus on run-time type feedback or static type inference to optimize method dispatch, and the methods are partially evaluated with respect to the inferred type. Since the author focuses on values, more aggressive optimizations can be applied, and run-time value-specific optimizations help to determine dynamic method dispatches. However, the author's system cannot optimize cases where the pointer value is not constant but the type of the pointed object is fixed. Using the results of these research papers will enable optimization of both cases.

A framework named specialization classes [16] focuses on the instance variables of objects and can specialize methods with respect to their values at both compile time and run time. Its prototype was implemented for Java. Since it does not specialize methods with respect to run-time types or to constant objects[6], and since it cannot consider array variables as invariants, inlining methods combined with loop unrolling, run-time constant propagation, and algebraic simplification (see Subsection 3.4) is impossible.

There is another value-specific partial evaluator for an object-oriented language [17]; however, objects are not regarded as closures in it.

There are also various systems for run-time code generation. Fabius [18] [8] [19] is a compiler for a subset of ML with automatic run-time light-weight code generation. It requires the programmer to declare functions to take their arguments in curried form. The idea is very similar to that of using objects as closures. It is also very natural in functional programming languages. But in languages with assignments, it is not desirable because the actual values may be different from the values embedded in partially evaluated functions. The author's method is preferable in richer and efficient languages like C++, because the values of their instance variables can be changed after instantiation.

Tempo [20] [21] is an online and offline partial evaluator of system programs in C. It automatically generates quite efficient run-time code generators. But the programmer has to invoke the code generator explicitly and has to manage the generated code. It is the programmer's responsibility to maintain consistency between the actual value and the value embedded in the generated code.

DyC and its predecessor [22] [23] [24] implicitly generate machine code for program regions the programmer indicates. The indications include run-time constants for those regions. If the values of some run-time constants change, the corresponding machine code is automatically generated. The system uses a pair of dataflow analyses to identify which variables will be constant at run time. The

---

[6] If an instance variable is of object type, it can specialize methods with respect to the specialization state (declared by specialization class name) of the object.

system, however, is error prone because it requires the programmer to insert the keyword **dynamic** at every use of a C pointer that refers to dynamic values.

The system can manage multiple machine code routines for each region. The generated code is looked up using the values of run-time constants. The author's method uses a pointer in each object instance and is therefore more efficient. If a number of object instances share the same set of values of the instance variables, the author's method requires larger storage for generated code. Reusing code at code generation time reduces the storage requirement without a significant effect on speed.

'C [25] is a language for run-time code generation. The programmer can control run-time code generation explicitly. It may be efficient, but the programmer has to rewrite the source program using ' and $ operators.

## 6 Summary and Future Work

This paper showed that RTCG can be used to determine dynamic method dispatches. It can produce a better result than conventional method dispatch prediction mechanisms because other run-time optimizations, such as global run-time constant propagation and complete loop unrolling, help the determination. Further, the determined functions can be inlined. This may lead to other optimizations.

These optimizations are implemented in the author's RTCG system by simple extension of the intermediate representation optimizer and the generator of run-time code generator. The system is implemented as a preprocessor of a C++ compiler, and time-consuming operations are performed only at compile time. The evaluation results showed good performance improvement.

The author plans to extend the system to optimize groups of objects. Commonly used data structures, such as linked lists and hash tables, consist of groups of objects. Operations on these data structures can be represented as code fragments held in the objects. This is similar to *executable data structures* or *Quajects* by Massalin [26] [27], which were implemented using some handwritten templates in an assembly language. Object-oriented languages may permit automatic application of this optimization. The author has already proposed basic ideas to optimize groups of objects [28].

The author is also going to release the preprocessor RPCC.EXE as a free software (tentative name: C++ Doubler).

## Acknowledgments

I would like to express my gratitude to Dr. Mario Tokoro for supervising the research. I also appreciate the many suggestions offered by Dr. Satoshi Matsuoka and Dr. Calton Pu as well as the work of programming ray tracer in C++ by Ms. Kayoko Sakai. Finally, I would like to thank the members of Sony CSL for their valuable advice.

# References

1. Neil D. Jones. An Introduction to Partial Evaluation. *ACM Computing Surveys*, Vol. 28, No. 3, pp. 480–503, September 1996.
2. Nobuhisa Fujinami. Run-Time Optimization in Object-Oriented Languages. In *Proceedings of 12th Conference of Japan Society for Software Science and Technology*, September 1995. In Japanese. Received Takahashi Award.
3. Nobuhisa Fujinami. Automatic Run-Time Code Generation in C++. In Yutaka Ishikawa, Rodney R. Oldehoeft, John V.W. Reynders, and Marydell Tholburn, editors, *LNCS 1343: Scientific Computing in Object-Oriented Parallel Environments*. *Proceedings*, December 1997. Also appeared as Technical Report SCSL-TR-97-006 of Sony Computer Science Laboratory Inc.
4. Nobuhisa Fujinami. Automatic and Efficient Run-Time Code Generation Using Object-Oriented Languages. *To appear in Computer Software, Japan Society for Software Science and Technology*, 1998. Also appeared as Technical Report SCSL-TR-98-001 of Sony Computer Science Laboratory Inc. (In Japanese).
5. Uday S. Reddy. Objects As Closures: Abstract Semantics of Object Oriented Languages. In *Proceedings of the ACM Conference on Lisp and Functional Programming*. ACM Press, July 1988.
6. Peter Holst Andersen. Partial Evaluation Applied to Ray Tracing. Student Report, DIKU, University of Copenhagen, 1993.
7. Dawson R. Engler and Todd A. Proebsting. DCG: An Efficient, Retargetable Dynamic Code Generation System. In *Proceedings of the Sixth International Conference on Architectural Support for Programming Languages and Operating Systems*, pp. 263–272. ACM Press, October 1994. Also appeared in SIGPLAN NOTICES, Vol.29, No.10.
8. Peter Lee and Mark Leone. Optimizing ML with Run-Time Code Generation. In *Proceedings of the SIGPLAN '96 Conference on Programming Language Design and Implementation*, pp. 137–148, May 1996.
9. Jeffrey Dean, Craig Chambers, and David Grove. Identifying Profitable Specialization in Object-Oriented Languages. Technical Report 94-02-05, Department of Computer Science and Engineering, University of Washington, 1994.
10. Jeffrey Dean, David Grove, and Craig Chambers. Optimization of Object-Oriented Programs Using Static Class Hierarchy Analysis. In Walter Olthoff, editor, *LNCS 952, Object-Oriented Programming, Proceedings of ECOOP'95*, August 1995. Also appeared as Technical Report 94-12-01, Department of Computer Science and Engineering, University of Washington.
11. Jeffrey Dean, Greg DeFouw, David Grove, Vassily Litvinov, and Craig Chambers. Vortex: An Optimizing Compiler for Object-Oriented Languages. In *Proceedings of Object-Oriented Programming Systems, Languages and Applications in 1996*. ACM Press, October 1996.
12. David F. Bacon and Peter F. Sweeney. Fast Static Analysis of C++ Virtual Function Calls. In *Proceedings of Object-Oriented Programming Systems, Languages and Applications in 1996*. ACM Press, October 1996.
13. Urs Hölzle and David Ungar. Optimizing Dynamically-Dispatched Calls with Run-Time Type Feedback. In *Proceedings of the SIGPLAN '94 Conference on Programming Language Design and Implementation*, pp. 326–336, 1994.
14. Gerald Aigner and Urs Hölzle. Eliminating Virtual Function Calls in C++ Programs. In *Proceedings of ECOOP'96*, June 1996.

15. Jan Vitek, R. Nigel Horspool, and James S. Uhl. Compile-Time Analysis of Object-Oriented Programs. In U. Kastens and P. Pfahler, editors, *LNCS 641, Compiler Construction, 4th International Conference, CC '92*, pp. 236–250, October 1992.

16. Eugen N. Volanshi, Charles Consel, Gilles Muller, and Crispin Cowan. Declarative Specialization of Object-Oriented Programs. In *Proceedings of Object-Oriented Programming Systems, Languages and Applications in 1997*. ACM Press, October 1997.

17. Morten Marquard and Bjarne Steensgaard. Partial Evaluation of an Object-Oriented Imperative Language. Master's thesis, University of Copenhagen, April 1992.

18. Mark Leone and Peter Lee. Lightweight Run-Time Code Generation. In *Proceedings of the 1994 ACM SIGPLAN Workshop on Partial Evaluation and Semantics-Based Program Manipulation*, pp. 97–106. ACM Press, June 1994.

19. Mark Leone and Peter Lee. A Declarative Approach to Run-Time Code Generation. In *Workshop Record of WCSSS'96: The Inaugural Workshop on Compiler Support for System Software*, pp. 8–17, February 1996.

20. Charles Consel, Luke Hornof, François Nöel, and Nicolae Volanshi. A Uniform Approach for Compile-time and Run-time Specialization. Technical Report No. 2775, INRIA, January 1996.

21. Eugen-Nicolae Volanshi, Gilles Muller, Charles Consel, Luke Hornof, Jacques Noyé, and Calton Pu. A Uniform and Automatic Approach to Copy Elimination in System Extensions via Program Specialization. Technical Report No. 1021, IRISA, June 1996.

22. Joel Auslander, Matthai Philipose, Crig Chambers, Susan J. Eggers, and Brian N. Bershad. Fast, Effective Dynamic Compilation. In *Proceedings of the SIGPLAN '96 Conference on Programming Language Design and Implementation*, pp. 149–159, May 1996.

23. Brian Grant, Markus Mock, Matthai Philipose, Graig Chambers, and Susan J. Eggers. Annotation-Directed Run-Time Specialization in C. In *Proceedings of Workshop on Partial Evaluation and Semantics-Based Program Manipulation (PEPM'97)*, June 1997.

24. Brian Grant, Markus Mock, Matthai Philipose, Graig Chambers, and Susan J. Eggers. DyC: An Expressive Annotation-Directed Dynamic Compiler for C. Technical Report 97-03-03, Department of Computer Science and Engineering, University of Washington, 1997.

25. Dawson R. Engler, Wilson C. Hsieh, and M. Frans Kaashoek. 'C: A language For High-Level, Efficient, and Machine-independent Dynamic Code Generation. In *Conference Record of POPL '96: The 23rd ACM SIGPLAN-SIGACT Symposium on Principles of Programming Languages*, pp. 258–270, January 1996.

26. Calton Pu, Henry Massalin, and John Ioannidis. The Synthesis kernel. *Computing Systems*, Vol. 1, No. 1, pp. 11–32, Winter 1988.

27. Henry Massalin. *Synthesis: An Efficient Implementation of Fundamental Operating System Services*. PhD thesis, Graduate School of Arts and Sciences, Columbia University, April 1992.

28. Nobuhisa Fujinami. Run-Time Optimization of Groups of Objects. In *Proceedings of 14th Conference of Japan Society for Software Science and Technology*, September 1997. Also appeared as Technical Memo SCSL-TM-97-007 of Sony Computer Science Laboratory Inc. (In Japanese).

# Type-Based Analysis of Concurrent Programs

Naoki Kobayashi

Department of Information Science, University of Tokyo
7-3-1 Hongo, Bunkyo-ku, Tokyo 113-0033, Japan
koba@is.s.u-tokyo.ac.jp

Analysis and compilation of concurrent programs are challenging tasks: since concurrency primitives for thread creation and communication have a much more dynamic nature than sequential primitives like function creation and application, it is difficult to reason about program behavior for both programmers and compilers. For example, unlike in sequential programming languages, it is not easy to know which part of a program is executed first — consider scheduling of a process that tries to receive a value from a communication channel: if a value is available, the process is executed immediately, while, if not, the process is suspended and another process must be scheduled. This kind of dynamic program behavior complicates not just a programmer's debugging but also a compiler's efficient code generation.

In order to deal with the above problems, several type systems and program analyses have been studied through process calculi. In this talk, we focus on Kobayashi, Pierce, and Turner's type system for linear (use-once) channels [3] and its extensions [1, 2]. The main idea of those type systems is to augment ordinary types with information on how often and in which order each communication channel can be used. With such extra information, we can ensure that a certain part of a concurrent program is confluent and/or deadlock-free. After giving an overview of the type systems, we show how such type information can be used for reasoning about program behavior and program optimizations.[1]

## References

1. Atsushi Igarashi and Naoki Kobayashi. Type-based analysis of usage of communication channels for concurrent programming languages. In *Proceedings of International Static Analysis Symposium (SAS'97)*, Lecture Notes in Computer Science, Vol. 1302. Springer-Verlag, Berlin Heidelberg New York (1997) 187–201.
2. Naoki Kobayashi. A partially deadlock-free typed process calculus. To appear in *ACM Transactions on Programming Languages and Systems*, ACM, New York (1998). A preliminary summary appeared in Proceedings of LICS'97, (1997) 128–139.
3. Naoki Kobayashi, Benjamin C. Pierce, and David N. Turner. Linearity and the pi-calculus. In *Proceedings of ACM SIGPLAN/SIGACT Symposium on Principles of Programming Languages*, ACM, New York (1996) 358–371.

---

[1] An electronic copy of the slides is available through http://www.yl.is.s.u-tokyo.ac.jp/members/koba/publications.html.

# A Type-Based Semantics for User-Defined Marshalling in Polymorphic Languages

Dominic Duggan

Department of Computer Science,
Stevens Institute of Technology,
Castle Point on the Hudson,
Hoboken, New Jersey 07030.
dduggan@cs.stevens-tech.edu

**Abstract.** Marshalling is an important aspect of distributed programming, particularly in typed programming languages. A semantics is provided for user-defined marshalling operations in polymorphic languages such as ML. The semantics of this are expressed in an internal language with recursion and dynamic type dispatch at both the term and type levels. User-defined marshalling amounts to reifying dynamic type dispatch to the programmer level in an ML-like language. A "external" language $\mathrm{XML}_\Pi^{\mathrm{dyn}}$ is provided with explicit pickle types and operations for building and deconstructing pickles with user-defined marshalling.

## 1 Introduction

In distributed programming environments, where programs operate in separate address spaces, there must be some way of converting values from their internal format to an external "wire" format for communication to other programs. This conversion process is referred to as *marshalling*, and its converse as *unmarshalling*. *User-defined marshalling* is now widely recognized as essential for monomorphic distributed programming languages. For example Birrell et al. [5] report:

> It is difficult to provide fully general marshalling code in a satisfactory way. Existing systems fail in one or more of the following ways. Some apply restrictions to the types that can be marshalled, typically prohibiting linked, cyclic or graph-structured values. Some generate elaborate code for almost any data type, but the resulting stub modules are excessively large. Some handle a lot of data types, but the marshalling code is excessively inefficient.

The Modula-3 `Pickle` module allows user-defined type-specific pickling and unpickling routines (called "specials") to be registered with the pickler. Such a facility is also found in languages designed for distributed programming; for example the Argus distributed programming language [26], and Concurrent CLU, developed for use in the Cambridge Distributed Computer System [4], allow ADT implementations to export programmer-defined marshalling code, to support efficient remote procedure call. Allowing a user-defining pickling operation essentially provides a mechanism for reflection in distributed programming [18].

Our intent in this paper is to provide a semantics for user-defined marshalling in polymorphic language, based on the use of run-time type information to guide user-defined marshalling operations that recurse over type descriptions. Recent work has suggested type-based transformations as a general framework for program optimization for polymorphic languages [20, 30]. Our semantics is couched in terms of this framework. We extend this framework with *refinement kinds*, that allow the exhaustiveness of dynamic type dispatching to be checked statically. Refinement kinds play a crucial rôle in typing our semantics.

Although not essential to our work, we attach our semantics to explicit pickles in the language. Explicit pickle types are found in many distributed languages. For example the OMG CORBA provides for a type of ANY, the type of pickles that can be transmitted between address spaces. Abadi et al. [2] suggested a similar mechanism for adding dynamic typing to statically typed languages, the type dynamic. This mechanism incorporated an operation dynamic for bundling a value with its type, and a typecase construct for examining the value:

```
fun print (x:dynamic) = typecase x of
   int(xi) ⇒ output (toString xi)
 | string(xs) ⇒ output xs
print(if true then dynamic 3 else dynamic "hello")
```

We attach our semantics for user-defined marshalling to dynamics; however this semantics could just as well be attached to the message-passing operations themselves.

The usefulness of a facility such as dynamics for distributed programming has been echoed by practical experience. For example, Krumvieda reports from his implementation of a distributed dialect of Standard ML that:

> The lack of a dynamic type or some other method of implicitly attaching marshalling functions to SML types hampered much of DML's interface development and complicated its signature. Although DML was originally intended to support dynamic types, the necessary work never materialized and group type objects have proliferated and propogated through its implementation and coding examples [23].

We introduce a new construct for dynamics that allows user-definable marshalling routines to be attached to the dynamic construct. Our semantics for dynamics is particularly aimed at polymorphic languages, such as ML. We make use of a new approach to computing with dynamics, based on dynamic type dispatch, that fixes some problems with the use of dynamics in polymorphic languages. User-definable marshalling is based fundamentally on allowing user-specified type-based transformations to be reflected in a semantics based on dynamic type dispatch.

Languages such as Modula-3 allow many parts of the run-time to be implemented in the language itself. For example, most of the threads and garbage collection code, and all of the marshalling code, for Modula-3 is implemented in Modula-3 itself [28]. For a "high-level" language such as ML, it should be possible to define a "safe" subset of ML in which low-level operations such as marshalling can be implemented. As examples of this endeavour, the SML/NJ compiler generates ML code for polymorphic equality (including reference equality), while Cardelli considers a subset of Quest in which a garbage collector for Quest can be implemented [8]. If there is any intrinsic reason that a safe subset of ML cannot be defined in which marshalling can be implemented, then the semantics presented here should be considered as being for a hypothetical language that is not so deficient.

Sect. 2 reviews our approach to dynamic type dispatch with *refinement kinds*, reviewing the language XML$^{dyn}$ originally introduced by Duggan [12]. In this approach, dynamic type dispatch is refined so that the programmer can control where run-time failures happen due to the use of dynamic type dispatch. Sect. 3 introduces our operations for user-definable marshalling, including their static semantics. We call the language introduced in this section XML$_\Pi^{dyn}$, since it extends XML$^{dyn}$. Sect. 4 gives a translation semantics from XML$_\Pi^{dyn}$ into XML$_T^{dyn}$, an extension of XML$^{dyn}$ with iteration at the type level. In Sect. 5 we give an alternative semantics for user-definable marshalling. This uses a simpler version of the static semantics for XML$_\Pi^{dyn}$, but requires a somewhat more complicated "internal language" for its operational semantics.

## 2 Dynamic Type Dispatch With Refinement Kinds

In this section we describe XML$^{dyn}$, the kernel language that is at the heart of our approach. XML$^{dyn}$ combines dynamic type dispatch with "refinement kinds" that ensure the absence of run-time type failures. Type failure is isolated to a particular construct. XML$^{dyn}$ was originally introduced by Duggan [12].

Types in our approach are stratified into simple types $\tau$ and polymorphic types $\sigma$:

$$\tau ::= \alpha \mid t \mid (\tau_1 \ \tau_2)$$
$$\sigma ::= \tau \mid \sigma_1 \to \sigma_2 \mid \forall \alpha <: \tau.\sigma \mid \forall \alpha <: \chi.\sigma \mid \forall \kappa <: \chi.\sigma$$

Our type system is based on the two-level stratified type system used by Harper and Mitchell [19] to explain ML's polymorphic type discipline. In this approach we have the usual collection of monomorphic types or *monotypes* (closed under the $\to$ type constructor and any other type constructors), and a second level of polymorphic types or *polytypes*, based on the closure of the collection of monotypes under the universal type quantifier $\forall$. Type constructors $t$ denote both base types, such as int and real, as well as type constructors such as list and the product and function type constructors ($\tau * \tau'$ and $\tau \to \tau'$, respectively). Type variables range over both types and type constructors, so type expressions include both list(int) and $\alpha$(int) (the latter being the application of the type constructor variable $\alpha$ to int). We sometimes use the syntax $t(\tau_1,\ldots,\tau_n)$ to denote $(t \ \tau_1 \ \ldots \ \tau_n)$. Polymorphic types abstract over both type variables $\alpha$ and kind variables $\kappa$.

Kinds are regular tree expressions denoting (possibly infinite) sets of types. The syntax of kinds is given by:

$$\chi ::= \rho \mid \chi_1 \to \chi_2$$
$$\rho ::= \bot \mid \top \mid \kappa \mid \underline{t}(\overline{\rho_n}) \mid \rho_1 \cup \rho_2 \mid \mu\kappa.\rho$$

where $\rho$ denotes kinds, and $\kappa$ denotes kind variables. $\chi$ is used to denote *arities* for type variables ranging over type constructors. For example $\top$ denotes the arity of all types, while $\top \to \top$ denotes the arity of unary type constructors (for example, `list`).

Kinds $\rho$ denote *refinement kinds*, that refine the arity $\top$ denoting the set of all ground monotypes. The kind operator $\cup$ denotes union, and $\mu$ is the fixed point operator. Kinds intuitively form a lattice of sets of types, with $\bot$ and $\top$ as the bottom and top of the lattice, respectively. Each type constructor $t$ has an associated kind constructor $\underline{t}$ of the same arity; a kind expression $\underline{t}(\rho_1,\ldots,\rho_n)$ denotes the set of types with outermost type constructor $t$ applied to types $\tau_1 \in \rho_1,\ldots,\tau_n \in \rho_n$. Then for example the kind $\underline{\texttt{int}} \cup \underline{\texttt{real}}$ denotes the set of types $\{\texttt{int},\texttt{real}\}$, while the recursive kind $\mu\kappa.\underline{\texttt{int}} \cup (\kappa~\underline{\texttt{list}})$ denotes the infinite set of types $\{\texttt{int},\texttt{int list},\texttt{int list list},\ldots\}$.

We let $\tau <: \rho$ denote that $\tau$ is contained in the set of types denoted by $\rho$, and we refer to this as the *containment relation*. So for example $\texttt{int} <: (\underline{\texttt{int}} \cup \underline{\texttt{real}})$. The subset relation between the interpretation of kinds induces a *subkinding relationship* $\rho <: \rho'$ between kinds. For example we have

$$\underline{\texttt{list}}(\underline{\texttt{list}}(\underline{\texttt{int}})) <: \mu\kappa.\underline{\texttt{int}} \cup \underline{\texttt{list}}(\kappa)$$

Inclusion between kinds $\rho$ induces a subtype inclusion between the arities of type constructors. For example we have $(\chi_1 \to \chi_2) <: (\chi'_1 \to \chi'_2)$ if $\chi'_1 <: \chi_1$ and $\chi_2 <: \chi'_2$. The function arity constructor should not be confused with the kind constructor $\underline{\to}$, that describes the set of types with outermost type constructor $\to$, and where $\tau_1 \to \tau_2 <: \rho_1 \underline{\to} \rho_2$ if $\tau_1 <: \rho_1$ and $\tau_2 <: \rho_2$.

Our type system involves constraints of the form $\tau <: \chi$ (with in particular $\tau <: \rho$ denoting that $\tau$ is included in the kind $\rho$), $\chi_1 <: \chi_2$ (with in particular $\rho_1 <: \rho_2$ denoting that the set of types described by $\rho_1$ is included in the corresponding set for $\rho_2$), and $\sigma_1 <: \sigma_2$ (denoting that $\sigma_1$ is a subtype of $\sigma_2$). We use $\gamma,\delta$ to denote both type variables $\alpha,\beta$ and kind variables $\kappa$. Furthermore we use $\psi$ to denote both types $\sigma$ and kinds $\rho$. Then $\psi_1 <: \psi_2$ stands generically for any of the above three forms of constraints. We have the following judgement forms:

| Judgement | Meaning |
|---|---|
| $\Gamma \vdash \chi_1 = \chi_2$ | Kind equality |
| $\Gamma \vdash \chi_1 <: \chi_2$ | Kind containment |
| $\Gamma \vdash \tau <: \chi$ | Kind membership |
| $\Gamma \vdash \sigma_1 <: \sigma_2$ | Subtyping |

where $\Gamma$ is a context of constraints on type and kind variables:

$$\Gamma ::= \{\} \mid \{\kappa <: \rho\} \mid \{\alpha <: \chi\} \mid \{\alpha <: \tau\} \mid \Gamma_1 \cup \Gamma_2$$

We require that kinds are *contractive* [12]. This allows us to assume that kinds have the following form:

$$\rho ::= \kappa \mid \top \mid \mu\kappa.t_1(\overline{\rho_1}) \cup \cdots \cup t_n(\overline{\rho_n})$$

We furthermore require that kinds are *discriminative*: in a union kind, the outermost type constructors $t_1,\ldots,t_n$ are required to be distinct.

The abstract syntax for the core language of $\text{XML}^{\text{dyn}}$ is given by:

$$e ::= x \mid \lambda x : \sigma.e \mid (e_1\ e_2) \mid \text{let } x = e_1 \text{ in } e_2 \mid$$
$$\text{rec}_{\sigma_1 \to \sigma_2}\ e \mid \Lambda\gamma <: \psi.e \mid e[\psi]$$

The construct for dynamic type dispatch in $\text{XML}^{\text{dyn}}$ is provided by the typerec construct:

$$e ::= \ldots \mid \text{typerec } f : \sigma \text{ of } t_1(\overline{\alpha_1}) \Rightarrow e_1 \mid \ldots \mid t_k(\overline{\alpha_k}) \Rightarrow e_k$$

The novelty of this construct is that it defines a function that recurses over a type rather than over a value. The fixed point of this function is given by the variable $f$ that is introduced by the typerec. Such a function specifies a form of type-safe *dynamic type dispatch*, wherein a polymorphic function dispatches at run-time on the basis of type arguments.

The type rule for this construct is provided by the TYREC type rule:

$$\frac{\sigma = (\forall \alpha <: \rho.\sigma') \quad \rho = \mu\kappa.\bigcup \underline{t_k(\overline{\rho_k})} \quad t_i \neq t_j \text{ if } i \neq j \quad \Gamma,\overline{\alpha_i} <: \overline{\{\rho/\kappa\}\rho_i}; A, f : \sigma \vdash e_i : \{t_i(\overline{\alpha_i})/\alpha\}\sigma' \text{ for } i = 1,\ldots,k}{\Gamma; A \vdash (\text{typerec } f : \sigma \text{ of } t_1(\overline{\alpha_1}) \Rightarrow e_1 \mid \ldots \mid t_k(\overline{\alpha_k}) \Rightarrow e_k) : \sigma} \quad \text{(TYREC)}$$

The rule demonstrates that the typerec defines a polymorphic function of type $\forall \alpha <: \rho.\sigma$. The kind constraint on $\alpha$ restricts the domain of applicability of this function, to types for which the cases in dynamic type dispatch are defined. Since the typerec in general defines a recursive function, this domain kind constraint must also be recursive.

Besides the obvious computation rules for the other constructs, the typerec has this computation rule:

$$e[t_i(\overline{\tau})] \longrightarrow \{\overline{\tau}/\overline{\alpha_i}, e/f\}e_i$$

where:

$$e = (\text{typerec } f : \sigma \text{ of } t_1(\overline{\alpha_1}) \Rightarrow e_1 \mid \ldots \mid t_k(\overline{\alpha_k}) \Rightarrow e_k)$$

For example, the following defines a function that can be applied to integers, references (no matter their element type), lists of integers, lists of references, lists of lists of integers, and so on:

```
typerec f : (∀α <: (μκ.int ∪ ref(⊤) ∪ list(κ)).α → α) of
    int  ⇒ λx : int. intPlus(x,x)
  | ref(α) ⇒ λx : ref(α). x
  | list(α) ⇒ λxs : list(α). map (f [α]) xs
```

The first clause defines a function of type $\text{int} \to \text{int}$. The second clause defines a function of type $\forall \alpha <: \top.\text{ref}(\alpha) \to \text{ref}(\alpha)$, where the type variable $\alpha$ is unconstrained because no operations are defined on the element type of the reference cell. The third clause defines a function of type $\forall \alpha <: (\mu\kappa.\text{int} \cup \text{ref}(\top) \cup \text{list}(\kappa)).\text{list}(\alpha) \to \text{list}(\alpha)$. In this third clause, the fixed point $f$ of the typerec is applied to the list element type, and hence the element type $\alpha$ in this clause is constrained by the declared domain kind of f. The domain of the typerec is then $\underline{\texttt{int}} \cup \underline{\texttt{ref}}(\top) \cup \underline{\texttt{list}}(\mu\kappa.\underline{\texttt{int}} \cup \underline{\texttt{ref}}(\top) \cup \underline{\texttt{list}}(\kappa))$. By the fixed point unrolling rule for kinds ($\mu\kappa.\rho = \{(\mu\kappa.\rho)/\kappa\}\rho$), this is equal to $\mu\kappa.\underline{\texttt{int}} \cup \underline{\texttt{ref}}(\top) \cup \underline{\texttt{list}}(\kappa)$.

Harper and Morrisett [20] and Morrisett [27] present a calculus, $\lambda_i^{ML}$, that includes a typerec construct for dynamic type dispatch by recursing over type descriptions. The motivation for their framework is in using dynamic type dispatch for type-based compilation based on transformations of data representations. The most important difference in the approaches is our provision of "refinement kinds" that refine the structure of $\top$, the set of all simple monotypes. Harper and Morrisett assume that all uses of dynamic type dispatch are total (defined for all types). Morrisett [27] describes an approach where a "characteristic function" $F$ can be defined for the domain of an operation that uses dynamic type dispatch, using Typerec. $F(\tau) = \texttt{void}$, the empty type, if $\tau$ contains any type constructor outside the domain of the operation, and $F(\tau) = \tau$ otherwise. Beyond the fact that type inference is hard or impossible with the Typerec construct, there is also the problem that this approach does not prevent instantiation of an operator with a type outside its domain kind. For the example above, the function would be instantiated to type $\texttt{void} \to \texttt{void}$ when applied to the string type, under the approach described by Morrisett. This is not as precise as preventing the erroneous instantiation of the function in the first place.

Dubois et al. [11] have considered another approach to dynamic type dispatch, with different guarantees of type correctness relative to this and other work. Essentially they use dynamic type dispatch to provide unsafe operations such as a C-like printf function and variable-arity procedures in ML, as an alternative to Haskell-style parametric overloading. Their type system only distinguishes between "static" and "dynamic" type variables, the latter being variables which need to be instantiated with run-time type arguments. They also provide a static check for the exhaustiveness of the dynamic type dispatching code. However this check is not formalized in a type system. Furthermore it requires abstract interpretation of the entire program, and so is inapplicable for separate compilation of reusable software components; type checking of uses of overloaded operations is done at link-time.

Once we have bounded universal types $\forall \alpha <: \rho.\sigma$, an obvious next step is to consider bounded existential types $\exists \alpha <: \rho.\tau$. These are useful in the sequel, so we add them here:

$$e ::= ... \mid \texttt{pack}_{\exists\alpha<:\rho.\tau}(\tau',e) \mid \texttt{open } e_1 \texttt{ as pack}_{\exists\alpha<:\rho.\tau}(\alpha,x) \texttt{ in } e_2 \mid$$
$$\texttt{narrow}_{\exists\alpha<:\rho.\alpha,\exists\alpha<:\rho'.\alpha}(e)$$
$$\tau ::= ... \mid \exists\alpha <: \rho.\tau$$

Kind inclusion induces a type widening rule for existentials: $(\exists\alpha <: \rho.\tau) <: (\exists\alpha <: \rho'.\tau)$ if $\rho <: \rho'$. The narrow construct allows us to narrow a value of existential type to a more specific type. All type failure in our framework is isolated to the narrow construct.

# 3 Primitives for Marshalling

We now consider how to extend the language introduced in the previous section with primitives for marshalling and unmarshalling data. We name the language introduced in this section $XML_\Pi^{dyn}$. An obvious first choice for marshalling operations is:

```
extern :  ∀α.α * port → unit
intern :  ∀α.port → α
```

There are some problems with this approach. These operations are not total (for example, in general it is not possible to marshall native-code functions in a heterogeneous environment), but this partiality is not captured by the above types. Invoking marshalling may therefore lead to a run-time type failure that should have been caught at compiletime. One approach to this problem, in a language such as Haskell with parametric overloading, is to define a type class for marshalling:

```
class Extern(α) where
    extern :  α * port → unit
    intern :  port → α
```

This is similar to the approach taken with Java [17], where only objects that implement the Serializable interface can be marshalled. There are several advantages to this approach. Applications of extern to types for which no marshalling operation is available are detected statically in the Haskell type system. This framework allows the programmer to define her own marshalling operations for a type, as instances of this class. Finally the compiler can automatically generate specialized marshalling operations based on combining instances of these operations.

Rather than using type classes to restrict the domain of marshalling operations and dispatch the operations, we instead rely on the approach to dynamic type dispatch summarized in the previous section. The precise relationship between this approach and type classes is developed in another paper [14]. We choose this course because the framework of dynamic type dispatch is the basis for an approach to computing with dynamically typed values, that overcomes several problems with the traditional approach to computing with dynamically typed values in polymorphic languages. This is explained more fully by Duggan [12]. Nevertheless if the marshalling primitives are expressed using (an extended version of) type classes, it is possible to adapt our semantics based on dynamic type dispatch to this situation.

Our second reason for deviating from the type class approach is that the Extern class above does not ensure that an instance of the intern operation is in agreement with the corresponding extern operation on what should be the external representation "on the wire" of the type. This is also an issue with the Serializable interface in Java. Our approach is to define marshalling operations as pickling and extraction operations that map to and from an external representation type. Marshalling a data value consists of first transforming it to the corresponding external type, then using the built-in marshaller to pickle the value. Unmarshalling a data value consists of first unpickling a value from external storage, then using the extraction function to obtain a copy of the original pickled value. An attempt to express this in the parlance of type classes is given by:

```
class Pickle(α) where
  pickle : α → pickleType(α)
  extract : pickleType(α) → α
```

`extern` and `intern` can then be represented as ordinary (non-overloaded) functions, of type $\forall\alpha.\text{Pickle}(\alpha) \Rightarrow \alpha * \text{port} \to \text{unit}$ and $\forall\alpha.\text{Pickle}(\alpha) \Rightarrow \text{port} \to \alpha$.

The intention is that `pickleType` be a function that maps from a type to the corresponding representation type. Each instance for the `Pickle` class should then specify a case in this type function for transforming the instance type. In general this type function must be applied recursively to the element types for a collection type. Essentially we need a construct analogous to the `Typerec` construct introduced by Harper and Morrisett [20] and Morrisett [27]. In general implementing type inference in the presence of `Typerec` appears difficult or impossible. However for the special case of user-definable marshalling, we can make use of a construct similar to `Typerec` internally, while providing type inference in the external language.

In order to introduce our semantics independent of any particular message-passing operations, we make pickles explicit in the language as *dynamics* [2, 1, 25, 24, 7]. A dynamic is a bundling of a value and a type descriptor for that value, into a single value of type `dynamic`. A `typecase` construct allows the tag in a dynamic to be examined, and the bundled value to be extracted in a type-safe way.

$$\frac{\sigma = \forall\kappa <: DOMAIN(\Pi).\forall\alpha <: \kappa.\alpha \to \text{Dynamic}(\kappa)}{\Pi;\Gamma;A \vdash \text{dynamic} : \sigma} \quad (\text{DIntro})$$

$$\frac{\Gamma \vdash \rho <: \rho'}{\Gamma \vdash \text{Dynamic}(\rho) <: \text{Dynamic}(\rho')} \quad (\text{DWid})$$

$$\frac{\Pi;\Gamma;A \vdash e : \text{Dynamic}(\rho) \quad \Gamma \vdash \rho' <: \rho}{\Pi;\Gamma;A \vdash \text{narrow}_{\rho,\rho'}(e) : \text{Dynamic}(\rho')} \quad (\text{DNar})$$

$$\frac{\Pi;\Gamma;A \vdash e_1 : (\forall\alpha <: \rho.\alpha \to \tau) \quad (\alpha \notin FV(\tau)) \quad \Pi;\Gamma;A \vdash e_2 : \text{Dynamic}(\rho)}{\Pi;\Gamma;A \vdash \text{typecase}(e_1, e_2) : \tau} \quad (\text{DElim})$$

$$\frac{\begin{array}{c}\not\exists t_2.(t_1 \mapsto t_2) \in \Pi \\ \Pi;\Gamma,\kappa <: \top, \overline{\alpha_n} <: \kappa, \beta <: (\top \to \top);A,(f : \forall\alpha <: \kappa.\alpha \to \beta(\alpha)) \vdash e_1 : t_1(\overline{\alpha_n}) \to t_2(\overline{\beta(\alpha_n)}) \\ \Pi;\Gamma,\kappa <: \top, \overline{\alpha_n} <: \kappa, \beta <: (\top \to \top);A,(g : \forall\alpha <: \kappa.\beta(\alpha) \to \alpha) \vdash e_2 : t_2(\overline{\beta(\alpha_n)}) \to t_1(\overline{\alpha_n}) \\ \Pi \cup \{t_1 \mapsto t_2\};\Gamma;A \vdash e : \tau\end{array}}{\Pi;\Gamma;A \vdash (\text{defdynamic } t_1 \Rightarrow t_2 \text{ with } (f.e_1, g.e_2) \text{ in } e) : \tau} \quad (\text{DDef})$$

**Fig. 1.** Type Rules for Dynamics in XML$^{\text{dyn}}$

A dynamic is essentially a data algebra inhabiting an existential type $\exists\alpha <: \top.\alpha$. The refinement kinds introduced in the previous section motivate an obvious generalization of dynamics to *safe dynamics*, originally introduced by Duggan [12]. A safe dynamic type Dynamic($\rho$) exports a refinement kind revealing the structure of the encapsulated type; semantically it is a bounded existential type $\exists \alpha <: \rho.\alpha$. The constructs for safe dynamics are given by:

$$\tau ::= \dots \mid \text{Dynamic}(\rho)$$
$$e ::= \dots \mid \text{dynamic} \mid \text{narrow}_{\rho,\rho'}(e) \mid \text{typecase}(e_1, e_2)$$

narrow is the only operation where type failure can arise; it allows us to refine the kind of a safe dynamic (for example, from $\top$ to $\underline{\text{int}} \cup \underline{\text{real}}$). In the expression typecase($e_1, e_2$), $e_2$ is a safe dynamic of type Dynamic($\rho$), while $e_1$ is a polymorphic function with type $\forall \alpha <: \rho'.\sigma$. In the semantics of the typecase, the dynamic value $e_2$ is unbundled and the polymorphic function $e_1$ applied to both the type and value components of the dynamic. Provided $\rho <: \rho'$ (which can be checked statically), this application of dynamic type dispatch is guaranteed not to encounter run-time type failure. The type rules for safe dynamics are provided in Fig. 1.

The dynamic operation creates a dynamic value. There are several possible typings for this operation:

dynamic : $\forall \alpha.\alpha \rightarrow \text{Dynamic}(\top)$
dynamic : $\forall \alpha <: \rho.\alpha \rightarrow \text{Dynamic}(\top)$
dynamic : $\forall \alpha <: \rho.\alpha \rightarrow \text{Dynamic}(\rho)$
dynamic : $\forall \kappa <: \rho.\forall \alpha <: \kappa.\alpha \rightarrow \text{Dynamic}(\kappa)$

The latter three of these types define dynamic as a polymorphic operation whose argument type variable is constrained by a kind describing the set of types for which dynamic is defined. The second type is sufficient if we are not concerned with safe dynamics (only full dynamics). The fourth rule gives the most precise typing if we are interested in using safe dynamics. For example, suppose dynamic is only defined for integers and reals. Then the following type-checks:

(dynamic [$\underline{\text{int}}$] [int] 3) : Dynamic($\underline{\text{int}} \cup \text{string}$)

This following point is worth emphasizing: *Our semantics for user-definable marshalling can be adapted to work with any of the above possible typings for* dynamic, *and with or without safe dynamics.* Although we use safe dynamics and the fourth typing for dynamics, our semantics for user-definable marshalling can be adapted fairly easily to the following types for the dynamic operations:

dynamic$_\tau$ : $\tau \rightarrow$ dynamic
typecase$_\tau$ : dynamic $\rightarrow \tau$

Refinement kinds and safe dynamics ensure static checking of the uses of dynamic type dispatch. Using the latter form of dynamic operations amounts to foresaking this static checking in the programming language. However such static checking might still be used internally, in an analogous manner to the use of refinement types and soft types [16, 32].

The construct for attaching user-defined marshalling and unmarshalling operations to the operations for building pickles is given by:

$$e ::= \ldots \mid \texttt{defdynamic } t_1 \Rightarrow t_2 \texttt{ with } (f.e_1, g.e_2) \texttt{ in } e$$

The type rule for this construct is given by the DDEF rule in Fig. 1. This construct has all of the elements of user-defined marshalling operations that were discussed earlier in this section. $t_2$ denotes the external representation for the type $t_1$. A use of this construct must specify a clause in the definition of the external type representation function, `pickleType`. The following clause is added to the final definition of this function:

$$pickleType(t_1(\alpha_1, \ldots, \alpha_n)) = t_2(pickleType(\alpha_1), \ldots, pickleType(\alpha_n))$$

The static semantics of $XML^{dyn}$ uses type judgements of the form $\Pi; \Gamma; A \vdash e : \sigma$. The environment $\Pi$ carries information about clauses in the type pickle function that have been contributed by uses of the `defdynamic`. $\Pi$ contains pairs of the form $t_1 \mapsto t_2$, representing clauses in the type pickle function. $\Pi$ is used to define the domain of the `dynamic` operation, used in the DINTRO rule:

$$DOMAIN(\Pi) = \mu\kappa.t_1^1(\overline{\kappa}) \cup \cdots \cup t_1^1(\overline{\kappa}) \text{ where } \Pi = \{t_1^i \mapsto t_2^i \mid i = 1, \ldots, k\}$$

$e_1$ is the pickling operation for the $t_1$ type constructor; $e_1$ has type $\forall \overline{\alpha_n} <: \kappa.t_1(\overline{\alpha_n}) \to t_2(\overline{pickleType(\alpha_n)})$, where $\kappa$ is a local rigid "kind" variable in the scope of the definition of $e_1$ and $e_2$. $e_2$ is the corresponding extraction operation, of type $\forall \overline{\alpha_n} <: \kappa.t_2(\overline{pickleType(\alpha_n)}) \to t_1(\overline{\alpha_n})$.

In defining $e_1$, the programmer in general will need to transform values of type $\alpha_i$ to type $pickleType(\alpha_i)$. This is provided by the local variable $f$ introduced by the construct, bound to a function of type $\forall \alpha <: \kappa.\alpha \to pickleType(\alpha)$. Note that within the definition of $e_1$, each $\alpha_i$ is constrained from above by $\kappa$; this restricts the application of $f$ to values of type $\alpha_1, \ldots, \alpha_n$. A similar explanation is given for the definition of $e_2$. $f$ (in the definition of $e_1$) and $g$ (in the definition of $e_2$) represent the final fixed points of the pickling and extraction functions that are built up using the `defdynamic` construct.

In typing $e_1$ and $e_2$, reference must be made to the final fixed point of the type representation function $pickleType$. This reference is represented by the type constructor variable $\beta$ that is introduced locally by the `defdynamic` construct.

At the use site for the `dynamic` operation, the clauses contributed by the `defdynamic` construct are joined to form the type representation function $pickleType$. The pickle and extraction operations are also formed by joining the instances contributed by `defdynamic`, to define the operations of type:

$$\forall \alpha <: \rho.\alpha \to pickleType(\alpha)$$

$$\forall \alpha <: \rho.pickleType(\alpha) \to \alpha$$

where $\rho$ is the domain of `dynamic`. These operations are used to build a pickle, as described in the next section.

# 4  Semantics for User-Definable Marshalling

In this section we consider the operational semantics for user-definable marshalling. The language $\text{XML}_\Pi^{\text{dyn}}$ introduced in the previous section was an extension of $\text{XML}^{\text{dyn}}$. In this section we introduce another extension of $\text{XML}^{\text{dyn}}$, and then map the extensions of $\text{XML}_\Pi^{\text{dyn}}$ into this latter language. We name the new language $\text{XML}_T^{\text{dyn}}$. This language adds one new construct to $\text{XML}^{\text{dyn}}$, a type-level Typerec construct:

$$\tau ::= \ldots \mid \text{Typerec}_{\rho \to \chi} \ t_1(\overline{\alpha_1}) \Rightarrow \tau_1 \mid \cdots \mid t_k(\overline{\alpha_k}) \Rightarrow \tau_k$$

This is essentially the Typerec introduced by Harper and Morrisett [20]. We use a slightly simpler form of it, supporting iteration rather than recursion (this is sufficient for our purposes). We keep $\text{XML}^{\text{dyn}}$ and $\text{XML}_T^{\text{dyn}}$ separate because type inference is possible with an implicitly-typed version of $\text{XML}^{\text{dyn}}$, whereas type inference appears difficult or impossible with the Typerec. $\text{XML}_T^{\text{dyn}}$ is only intended to be used as an "internal" language, into which source programs (in $\text{XML}_\Pi^{\text{dyn}}$) are translated.

The type rule for the Typerec is given by:

$$\frac{\rho = \mu\kappa.t_1(\overline{\rho_1}) \cup \cdots \cup t_k(\overline{\rho_k}) \qquad \Gamma, \overline{\alpha_i} <: \overline{\{\rho/\kappa\}\rho_i} \vdash \tau_i <: \chi \text{ for } i = 1,\ldots,k}{\Gamma \vdash (\text{Typerec}_{\rho \to \chi} \ t_1(\overline{\alpha_1}) \Rightarrow \tau_1 \mid \cdots \mid t_k(\overline{\alpha_k}) \Rightarrow \tau_k) <: (\rho \to \chi)} \qquad \text{(TYREC)}$$

The type-level computation rule for the Typerec is given by:

$$\tau'(t_i(\tau'_1,\ldots,\tau'_{n_i})) \longrightarrow \{\tau'(\tau'_1)/\alpha^i_1,\ldots,\tau'(\tau'_{n_i})/\alpha^i_{n_i}\}\tau_i$$

where:

$$\tau' = (\text{Typerec}_{\rho \to \chi} \ t_1(\overline{\alpha_1^1}) \Rightarrow \tau_1 \mid \cdots \mid t_k(\overline{\alpha_{n_k}^k}) \Rightarrow \tau_k)$$

We can define the notions of *canonical forms* for terms and types ($v$ and $\upsilon$, respectively), and *evaluation contexts* for terms and types ($E[\ ]$ and $T[\ ]$, respectively), in a fairly standard manner. A term $e$ is *failed* if $e$ is not a (term) value, and $e \equiv E[e']$ where $e' \equiv \text{narrow}_{\rho,\rho'}(\text{pack}(\upsilon, v))$ for some $v$ and $\upsilon$, and $e'$ is not a redex. A term $e$ is *faulty* if $e$ is not a value, $e$ is not failed, and $e \equiv E[e']$ or $e \equiv E[\tau]$ where $e'$, $\tau$ are not redices. A type $\tau$ is *faulty* if $\tau$ is not a (type) value, and $\tau \equiv T[\tau']$ or $\tau \equiv T[e]$ where $e$, $\tau'$ are not redices. A term or type is closed if it has no free variables. $e \Uparrow$ denotes that the evaluation of $e$ loops infinitely i.e. there is an infinite sequence $e \longrightarrow \cdots \longrightarrow e_i \longrightarrow e_{i+1} \longrightarrow \cdots$.

**Theorem 1 (Semantic Soundness).**

1. *If $\Gamma; A \vdash e : \tau$, then $e \Uparrow$, or $e \longrightarrow e'$ where $e'$ is failed or $e'$ is some value $v$.*
2. *If $\Gamma \vdash \tau <: \chi$ then $\tau \Uparrow$, or $\tau \longrightarrow \upsilon$ for some value $\upsilon$.*

To define the translation from $\text{XML}_\Pi^{\text{dyn}}$ to $\text{XML}_T^{\text{dyn}}$, we start with the following translation of types in $\text{XML}_\Pi^{\text{dyn}}$:

$$[\![\alpha]\!] = \alpha$$

$$[\Gamma];[A]\cup ENV(\Pi)\vdash e:(\forall\kappa<:\rho.\forall\alpha<:\kappa.\alpha\rightarrow[\text{Dynamic}(\kappa)]) \qquad (\text{DINTRO})$$

where:

$\tau_{\text{pkl}}=PICKLE(\Pi)$ and $\rho=DOMAIN(\Pi)$

$\sigma_{\text{pkl}}=\forall\alpha<:\rho.\alpha\rightarrow\tau_{\text{pkl}}(\alpha)$ and $\sigma_{\text{ext}}=\forall\alpha<:\rho.\tau_{\text{pkl}}(\alpha)\rightarrow\alpha$

$e_{\text{pkl}}=\text{typerec }f:\sigma_{\text{pkl}}\text{ of }t_1^j(\overline{\alpha})\Rightarrow(f_{t_1^j}\ [\rho]\ \tau_{\text{pkl}}\ f\ [\overline{\alpha}])\ |\ \ldots\ |\ t_1^k(\overline{\alpha})\Rightarrow(f_{t_1^k}\ [\rho]\ \tau_{\text{pkl}}\ f\ [\overline{\alpha}])$

$e_{\text{ext}}=\text{typerec }f:\sigma_{\text{ext}}\text{ of }t_1^j(\overline{\alpha})\Rightarrow(g_{t_1^j}\ [\rho]\ \tau_{\text{pkl}}\ g\ [\overline{\alpha}])\ |\ \ldots\ |\ t_1^k(\overline{\alpha})\Rightarrow(g_{t_1^k}\ [\rho]\ \tau_{\text{pkl}}\ g\ [\overline{\alpha}])$

$e=\Lambda\kappa.\Lambda\alpha_{\text{wit}}.\lambda x.\text{pack}(\alpha_{\text{wit}},\text{pack}(\tau_{\text{pkl}}(\alpha_{\text{wit}}),(e_{\text{pkl}}\ [\alpha_{\text{wit}}]\ (x),e_{\text{ext}}\ [\alpha_{\text{wit}}])))$

$$\frac{[\Gamma];[A]\cup ENV(\Pi)\vdash e_1:\forall\alpha<:\rho.[\sigma'] \qquad [\Gamma];[A]\cup ENV(\Pi)\vdash e_2:[\text{Dynamic}(\rho)]}{[\Gamma];[A]\cup ENV(\Pi)\vdash e:[\tau]} \qquad (\text{DELIM})$$

where:

$e=(\text{open }e_2\text{ as pack}(\alpha_{\text{pkl}},\text{pack}(\beta,(x,extract))))\text{ in }e_1\ [\alpha]\ (extract\ x))$

$$\frac{\begin{array}{c}[\Gamma],\kappa<:\top,\overline{\alpha_n}<:\kappa,\beta<:\top\rightarrow\top\};[A,(f:\forall\alpha<:\kappa.\alpha\rightarrow\beta(\alpha))]\cup ENV(\Pi)\vdash\\ e_1:t_1(\overline{\alpha_n})\rightarrow t_2(\overline{\beta(\alpha)})\\[4pt] [\Gamma],\kappa<:\top,\overline{\alpha_n}<:\kappa,\beta<:\top\rightarrow\top\};[A,(g:\forall\alpha<:\kappa.\beta(\alpha)\rightarrow\alpha)]\cup ENV(\Pi)\vdash\\ e_2:t_2(\overline{\beta(\alpha)})\rightarrow t_1(\overline{\alpha_n})\\[4pt] [\Gamma];[A]\cup ENV(\Pi\cup\{t_1\mapsto t_2\})\vdash e:[\tau]\end{array}}{[\Gamma];[A]\vdash e':[\tau]}$$

$$\qquad (\text{DDEF})$$

where:

$e'=\text{let }f_{t_1}=\Lambda\kappa.\Lambda\beta.\lambda f.\Lambda\overline{\alpha_n}.e_1\text{ in let }g_{t_1}=\Lambda\kappa.\Lambda\beta.\lambda g.\Lambda\overline{\alpha_n}.e_2\text{ in }e$

**Fig. 2.** Translation of Dynamics in $XML_{<:}^{\text{dyn}}$

$$[t(\tau_1,\ldots,\tau_n)]=t([\tau_1],\ldots,[\tau_n])$$
$$[\sigma_1\rightarrow\sigma_2]=[\sigma_1]\rightarrow[\sigma_2]$$
$$[\forall\gamma<:\psi.\sigma]=\forall\gamma<:[\psi].[\sigma]$$
$$[\text{Dynamic}(\rho)]=\exists\alpha<:\rho.\exists\beta<:\top.\beta*(\beta\rightarrow\alpha)$$

The last case in this definition is the real point of this translation, i.e. dynamic types are translated as existential types. The data algebra for a dynamic now has two witness types: $\alpha$ is the external type of the value that has been bundled in a dynamic, with the external kind constraint $\rho$ which reveals some of the structure of the type. $\beta$ is the internal pickle type, encapsulated by the existential type quantifier, and with no structure revealed by the kind witness constraint. The dynamic contains two values: the pickled copy of the value that has been bundled in the dynamic, and an extraction operation for converting from the pickle value back to the original value. This extraction operation is bundled in the dynamic when it is created, and is invoked when the dynamic is unbundled. As such we refer to these as *self-extracting dynamics*. The translation of kinds is simply the identity: $[\rho] = \rho$. We also have:

$$[\Gamma] = \{\gamma <: [\psi] \mid (\gamma <: \psi) \in \Gamma\}$$
$$[A] = \{(x : [\sigma]) \mid (x : \sigma) \in A\}$$

The interpretation of $\text{XML}_{\Pi}^{\text{dyn}}$ is $\text{XML}_{T}^{\text{dyn}}$ is defined by induction on type environments in the former. A type derivation for the judgement $\Pi; \Gamma; A \vdash e : \sigma$ in $\text{XML}_{\Pi}^{\text{dyn}}$ is used to construct a program $e'$ in $\text{XML}_{T}^{\text{dyn}}$, with correctness given by the following:

**Theorem 2.** *If* $\Pi; \Gamma; A \vdash e : \sigma$ *in* $\text{XML}_{\Pi}^{\text{dyn}}$, *with* $e'$ *the program in* $\text{XML}_{T}^{\text{dyn}}$ *constructed based on this type derivation, then* $[\Gamma]; [A] \cup ENV(\Pi) \vdash e' : [\sigma]$.

$ENV(\Pi)$ denotes the types of the pickling and extraction function fragments defined by uses of `defdynamic`. This metafunction is defined by:

$PTYPE(t_1, t_2) =$
$$\forall \kappa <: T. \forall \beta <: T \to T.(\forall \alpha <: \kappa.\alpha \to \beta(\alpha)) \to (\forall \overline{\alpha_n} <: \overline{\kappa}.t_1(\overline{\alpha_n}) \to t_2(\overline{\beta(\alpha_n)}))$$
$ETYPE(t_1, t_2) =$
$$\forall \kappa <: T. \forall \beta <: T \to T.(\forall \alpha <: \kappa.\beta(\alpha) \to \alpha) \to (\forall \overline{\alpha_n} <: \overline{\kappa}.t_2(\overline{\beta(\alpha_n)}) \to t_1(\overline{\alpha_n}))$$
$ENV(\Pi) = \{f_{t_1} : PTYPE(t_1, t_2), g_{t_1} : ETYPE(t_1, t_2) \mid (t_1 \mapsto t_2) \in \Pi\}$

Each use of `defdynamic` defines two functions, $f_{t_1}$ and $g_{t_1}$, that represent clauses in the definition of the pickling and extraction functions. We maintain these functions in the environment, extracting them from the environment when they are needed. $PTYPE(t_1, t_2)$ denotes the type of a clause for the pickling function, for the case when values of type $t_1(\overline{\tau})$ are pickled to type $pickleType(t_1(\overline{\tau})) = t_2(\overline{pickleType(\tau)})$. The function $f_{t_1}$ abstracts over the domain kind $\kappa$ of the final pickling function, the final definition $\beta$ of the pickle type function, and the fixed point of the pickling function itself. A similar explanation can be given for $ETYPE(t_1, t_2)$. The metafunction $ENV(\Pi)$ generates a type environment for those instances of these functions that have been defined.

Fig. 2 gives the cases for the translation of the `dynamic` constructs. The case for the `defdynamic`, DDEF, is fairly uninteresting. This simply builds the functions $f_{t_1}$ and $g_{t_2}$. The main work is done by uses of `dynamic`, given by the DINTRO rule. At the use site for `dynamic`, the final definition of the pickle type function is constructed, defined by:

$$PICKLE(\Pi) = \texttt{Typerec } t_1^1(\overline{\alpha}) \Rightarrow t_2^1(\overline{\alpha}) \mid \cdots \mid t_1^k(\overline{\alpha}) \Rightarrow t_2^k(\overline{\alpha})$$
$$\text{where } \Pi = \{t_1^i \mapsto t_2^i \mid i = 1, \ldots, k\}$$

The pickling function is constructed by using the `typerec` construct to assemble the various clauses defined using `defdynamic`. Each such clause, say of type $PTYPE(t_1, t_2)$, is applied to $\rho = DOMAIN(\Pi)$ and $\tau_{\text{pkl}} = PICKLE(\Pi)$, giving a function of type

$$(f_{t_1} [\rho] \tau_{\text{pkl}}) \in (\forall \alpha <: \rho.\alpha \to \tau_{\text{pkl}}(\alpha)) \to (\forall \overline{\alpha_n} <: \overline{\rho_n}.t_1(\overline{\alpha_n}) \to t_2(\overline{\tau_{\text{pkl}}(\alpha_n)}))$$

Let $f$ be the fixed point of the function defined by the `typerec`, then we have:

$$(f_{t_1} [\rho] \tau_{pk1} f) \in (\forall \overline{\alpha_n} <: \overline{\rho_n}.t_1(\overline{\alpha_n}) \to t_2(\overline{\tau_{pk1}(\alpha_n)}))$$

This clause of the `typerec` is defined to be:

$$(t_1(\overline{\alpha_n}) \Rightarrow f_{t_1} [\rho] \tau_{pk1} f [\overline{\alpha_n}]) \in (t_1(\overline{\alpha_n}) \to t_2(\overline{\tau_{pk1}(\alpha_n)}))$$

By the definition of $\tau_{pk1}$, this latter type is equal to $(t_1(\overline{\alpha_n}) \to \tau_{pk1}(t_1(\overline{\alpha_n})))$. Therefore by the TYREC rule, the function $e_{pk1}$ has type $\forall \alpha <: \rho.\alpha \to \tau_{pk1}(\alpha)$.

The translation of `dynamic` is a function that takes a type $\alpha_{wit}$ and a value $x$ of type $\alpha_{wit}$. The pickling of this value consists of creating the pickled value $(e_{pk1} [\alpha_{wit}] x)$, of type $\tau_{pk1}(\alpha_{wit})$ (the external representation type). The extraction function $e_{ext}$, of type $\forall \alpha <: \rho.\tau_{pk1}(\alpha) \to \alpha$ is constructed in a manner similar to $e_{pk1}$. The expression $(e_{ext} [\alpha_{wit}])$ gives the extraction function specialized to the type of $x$. The resulting pair of type

$$\tau_{pk1}(\alpha_{wit}) * (\tau_{pk1}(\alpha_{wit}) \to \alpha_{wit})$$

denoting the pickled value, and an operation for extracting the original value from this pickle value, is then encapsulated in the data algebra for the dynamic that is constructed, with existential type $[\![ \text{Dynamic}(\rho) ]\!] = \exists \alpha <: \rho.\exists \beta <: \top.\beta * (\beta \to \alpha)$. We call this value a *self-extracting dynamic*.

The translation of the `typecase` is reasonably obvious: the data algebra for the dynamic is opened, the bundled extraction function is applied to the pickle value, and the typecase function is then applied to the resulting extracted value.

## 5 An Alternative Semantics for User-Definable Marshalling

$$\Gamma;\Lambda \vdash \text{dynamic} : A(\text{dynamic}) \qquad \text{(DINTRO)}$$

$$A(\text{dynamic}) = \forall \kappa <: (\mu\kappa.\rho).\forall \alpha <: \kappa.\alpha \to \text{Dynamic}(\kappa) \quad t_1 \notin tc(\rho)$$

$$\Gamma, \kappa <: \top, \overline{\alpha_n} <: \kappa, \beta <: (\top \to \top)\};\Lambda, (f : \forall \alpha <: \kappa.\alpha \to \beta(\alpha)) \vdash e_1 : t_1(\overline{\alpha_n}) \to t_2(\overline{\beta(\alpha_n)})$$

$$\Gamma', \kappa <: \top, \overline{\alpha_n} <: \kappa, \beta <: (\top \to \top);\Lambda, (g : \forall \alpha <: \kappa.\beta(\alpha) \to \alpha) \vdash e_2 : t_2(\overline{\beta(\alpha_n)}) \to t_1(\overline{\alpha_n})$$

$$\Gamma;\Lambda, (\text{dynamic} : (\forall \kappa <: (\mu\kappa.\rho \cup t_1(\overline{\kappa})).\forall \alpha <: \kappa.\alpha \to \text{Dynamic}(\kappa))) \vdash e : \tau$$

$$\overline{\Gamma;\Lambda \vdash (\text{defdynamic } t_1 \Rightarrow t_2 \text{ with } (f.e_1, g.e_2) \text{ in } e) : \tau}$$

$$\text{(DDEF)}$$

**Fig. 3.** Type Rules for Dynamics in $\text{XML}_{\Pi-}^{\text{dyn}}$

The approach to user-defined marshalling provided in the previous two sections was facilitated by the $\Pi$ environment in the static semantics for $\text{XML}_{\Pi}^{\text{dyn}}$. The disadvantage of this environment in the semantics is that the clauses of the external representation type (the `pickleType` function) are exposed in the environment. In this section we consider the repercussions of abstracting over this external representation type function.

In this section we demonstrate how this may be done. With this alternative approach, the semantics no longer requires the $\Pi$ environment recording external representations. Instead the type of `dynamic` is recorded as a type of the form $\forall \kappa <: \rho.\forall \alpha <: \kappa.\alpha \rightarrow$ `Dynamic(`$\kappa$`)` in the type environment, with the domain $\rho$ providing the only information about the abstract type representation function. This approach admittedly brings with it some complexity in the internal language. In particular our internal language requires both coproducts and general recursion *at the type level* in order to type our semantics. To ensure equational consistency, we require that type functions are strict [6].

Fig. 3 gives the type rules of $\text{XML}_{\Pi}^{\text{dyn}}$ that are modified with this alternative approach. We name this variation $\text{XML}_{\Pi-}^{\text{dyn}}$. tc denotes the outermost type constructors of a kind: $tc(\underline{t}_1(\overline{\rho_1}) \cup \cdots \cup \underline{t}_m(\overline{\rho_m})) = \{t_1, \ldots, t_m\}$. We concentrate in the sequel on the translation semantics for this language.

The basis for our semantics is a new language, $\text{XML}^\Delta$. $\text{XML}^\Delta$ is formed by taking $\text{XML}^{\text{dyn}}$ as defined in Sect. 2, omitting the `typerec` construct, and adding the following constructs:

$$e ::= \ldots \mid \text{abort}_\tau \mid t(\overline{\alpha_n : \rho_n}) \Longrightarrow e \mid e_1 \oplus e_2 \mid \text{cl}(e) \mid \text{tyrec}_{(\forall \alpha <: \rho.\sigma)} e$$
$$\sigma ::= \ldots \mid \Delta\alpha <: \rho.\tau$$

The type rules for these constructs are provided in Sect. 5. The construct $t(\alpha_1 : \rho_1, \ldots, \alpha_n : \rho_n) \Longrightarrow e$ is used to define the individual clauses in the definition of a typecase. The construct $e_1 \oplus e_2$ is used to combine these clauses. The resulting combination is a polymorphic function with non-$\top$ domain kind, that uses run-time type discrimination with respect to its single type argument. $\text{tyrec}_{(\forall \alpha <: \rho.\sigma)} e$ denotes the fixed point of a recursively defined polymorphic function. This fixed point operator is necessary because the typecase defines a function that computes by recursing over its type argument.

The special type $\Delta\alpha <: \rho.\tau$ is used to type the composition of a collection of clauses that make up a typecase. The operation $\text{cl}(e)$ closes up a typecase definition to an ordinary polymorphic function. The fixed point operator for kinds $\mu\kappa.\rho$ is used to define recursive domain kinds, while the fixed point operator for polymorphic functions $\text{tyrec}_\sigma e$ is used to define recursive dynamic type dispatch.

To see how the `typerec` can be translated into this language, consider that the `typerec` construct in $\text{XML}^{\text{dyn}}$ has the form:

$$\text{typerec } f : \sigma \text{ of } t_1(\overline{\alpha_1}) \Rightarrow e_1 \mid \ldots \mid t_k(\overline{\alpha_k}) \Rightarrow e_k$$

where $\sigma = \forall \alpha <: \rho.\sigma'$ and $\rho = \mu\kappa.\bigcup \overline{t_k(\overline{\rho_k})}$. Assuming $e_i'$ is the translation of $e_i$ from $\text{XML}_{\Pi-}^{\text{dyn}}$ into $\text{XML}^\Delta$, then the translation of the clauses of the `typerec` is given by:

$$\text{cl}((t_1(\overline{\alpha_1 : \{\rho/\kappa\}\rho_1}) \Longrightarrow e_1') \oplus \cdots \oplus (t_k(\overline{\alpha_k : \{\rho/\kappa\}\rho_k}) \Longrightarrow e_k'))$$
$$\in (\forall \alpha <: (\underline{t}_1(\{\rho/\kappa\}\rho_1) \cup \cdots \cup \underline{t}_k(\{\rho/\kappa\}\rho_k)).[\sigma']) = (\forall \alpha <: \rho.[\sigma'])$$

Abstracting over the fixed point, and then using the fixed point operator for polymorphic functions, gives the translation of the `typerec`:

$$\text{tyrec}(\lambda f. \text{cl}((t_1(\overline{\alpha_1 : \{\rho/\kappa\}\rho_1}) \Longrightarrow e_1') \oplus \cdots \oplus (t_k(\overline{\alpha_k : \{\rho/\kappa\}\rho_k}) \Longrightarrow e_n')))$$

XML$^{\text{dyn}}$ incorporates a monolithic typerec construct that is the basis for defining dynamic type dispatch. All clauses in a typerec are defined at once. In XML$^{\Delta}$, by contrast, the clauses in a function using dynamic type dispatch are defined as independent program fragments, of the form $t(\overline{\alpha} : \overline{\rho}) \Longrightarrow e$. The $\oplus$ operation combines these clauses, and the $\text{cl}(e)$ operation forms this collection of clauses into a polymorphic function.

The reason for taking this approach is that the clauses of the pickling and extraction operations in the implementation of the dynamic operation are contributed by independent uses of the defdynamic construct. There needs to be some way of combining these clauses at the use sites for the dynamic operation. The approach pursued in the previous section was to carry the individual clauses as polymorphic functions in the environment, and then use the typerec construct to combine them at the use site.

The problem with this approach, with the static semantics of XML$^{\text{dyn}}_{\Pi-}$, is that it does not help us with the combination of the clauses of the pickle type function, that are also contributed by uses of the defdynamic construct. The approach we adopt is to extend the approach for dynamic type dispatch in the term language of XML$^{\Delta}$, to the type level. In other words, we now allow type functions at the type level, which discriminate based on their type argument, giving a form of typecase for types. We also add a recursion operator at the type level to define the fixed points of such recursive type functions. We extend the syntax of types and kinds in XML$^{\Delta}$ with:

$$e ::= \ldots \mid (e_1, e_2) \mid \pi_1(e) \mid \pi_2(e)$$
$$\tau ::= \ldots \mid \lambda\alpha : \chi.\tau \mid (\tau_1 \, \tau_2) \mid (t(\overline{\alpha} : \overline{\rho}) \Longrightarrow \tau) \mid$$
$$\tau_1 \oplus \tau_2 \mid \text{abort} \mid \text{cl}(\tau) \mid \text{tyrec}_{\chi_1 \to \chi_2}(\tau)$$
$$\sigma ::= \ldots \mid \sigma * \sigma \mid \exists\alpha <: \rho.\sigma$$
$$\chi ::= \ldots \mid \Delta\alpha <: \rho.\chi$$

Figure 6 in App. A provides the kind rules for functions, recursion and dynamic type dispatch at the type level. These essentially repeat the corresponding type rules for programs. The TYABS and TYCASE rules include the proviso that the variables introduced by $\lambda$-abstraction and type-casing occur in the body of the type operator (so type operators are a variation of the $\lambda I$-calculus). We provide the kind rules as congruence rules for the equality relation on type operators, omitting the obvious reflexivity, symmetry and transitivity rules. Figure 6 in App. A provides the conversion rules for type operators. The TYCASECOP rule characterizes union kinds as coproducts, and allows reasoning-by-cases when verifying the equality of type operators defined over types of union kind. The TYFIXBETA rule allows folding and unfolding of fixed points at the type level. These rules are necessary in Theorem 3 when verifying that the translation of programs in XML$^{\text{dyn}}_{\Pi-}$ preserves well-typedness in XML$^{\Delta}$. The $\lambda I$-calculus restriction in the TYABS and TYCASE rules is necessary in order to preserve the equational consistency of the type system [6].

**Proposition 1.** *The equality theory for types in* XML$^{\Delta}$ *is consistent.*

PROOF SKETCH: We give an interpretation for types using Scott domains, where union kinds are interpreted as separated sums and type operators are interpreted as strict continuous maps [6]. □

The computation rules for terms include the computation rules:

$$\texttt{tyrec}_{(\forall \alpha <: \rho.\sigma)} \ e \longrightarrow e \ (\Lambda \alpha <: \rho.(\texttt{tyrec}_{(\forall \alpha <: \rho.\sigma)} \ e) \ [\alpha])$$

$$\texttt{cl}(\ldots \oplus (\texttt{t}(\alpha_1 : \rho_1, \ldots, \alpha_n : \rho_n) \Longrightarrow e_1) \oplus \ldots) \ [\texttt{t}(\tau_1, \ldots, \tau_n)] \longrightarrow \{\tau_1/\alpha_1, \ldots, \tau_n/\alpha_n\}e$$

The reduction rules for types are obtained by orienting the TYFUNBETA, TYCASEBETA and TYFIXBETA rules in Fig. 6 from left to right as rewrite rules. We do not include the extensionality rules TYFUNETA and TYCASECOP in this rewrite system. In recent work on rewrite systems, these extensionality rules are oriented from right to left, as expansion rules rather than as reduction rules [9, 10]. Expansion rules, and their complications, do not appear appropriate in a run-time evaluator for a programming language.

The translation of types $\sigma$, kinds $\rho$ and kind environments $\Gamma$ of $\text{XML}_{\Pi_-}^{\text{dyn}}$ into $\text{XML}^{\Delta}$ is similar to the translation of $\text{XML}_{\Pi}^{\text{dyn}}$ into $\text{XML}^{\text{dyn}}$. For type environments we have:

$$[A] = \{(x : [\sigma]) \mid (x : \sigma) \in A, \ x \neq \texttt{dynamic}\}$$
$$\cup \{(f_{\text{dyn}} : (\forall \kappa. \exists \alpha_{\text{pkl}} <: \rho_{\text{pkl}}.\tau_{\text{in}} * \tau_{\text{out}})) \mid (\texttt{dynamic} : \sigma_{\text{dyn}}) \in A\}$$

where $\sigma_{\text{dyn}} = \forall \kappa <: (\mu \kappa.\rho).\forall \alpha <: \kappa.\alpha \rightarrow \text{Dynamic}(\kappa)$, and

$$\rho_{\text{pkl}} = (\kappa \rightarrow \top) \rightarrow \Delta \alpha <: \rho.\top$$

$$\tau_{\text{in}} = \forall \beta <: \kappa \rightarrow \top.(\forall \alpha <: \kappa.\alpha \rightarrow \beta(\alpha)) \rightarrow$$
$$(\Delta \alpha <: \rho.\alpha \rightarrow \texttt{tycase}(\alpha_{\text{pkl}} \ \beta)(\alpha))$$

$$\tau_{\text{out}} = \forall \beta <: \kappa \rightarrow \top.(\forall \alpha <: \kappa.\beta(\alpha) \rightarrow \alpha) \rightarrow$$
$$(\Delta \alpha <: \rho.\texttt{tycase}(\alpha_{\text{pkl}} \ \beta)(\alpha) \rightarrow \alpha))$$

Essentially the dynamic operation consists of three parts: a type function $\alpha_{\text{pkl}}$ mapping from external types to internal pickle types, a pickling function *pickle* mapping from values of an external type to the corresponding internal pickle type, and an extraction function *extract* mapping from values of an internal pickle type to values of the corresponding external type. *pickle* constructs a pickled value, while *extract* recovers the original value from a pickled value. Therefore the dynamic operation is represented in the environment as a data algebra inhabiting an existential type. This existential type is parameterized by $\kappa$, the fixed point of the kind constraining the domain of the pickling operation. The pickle type function is parameterized by its fixed point (of kind $\kappa \rightarrow \top$). The pickling functions are parameterized by the fixed point of the pickle type function, and the fixed point of the pickling operation; similarly for the extraction operation. These fixed points are left open to further extension by the defdynamic construct.

**Theorem 3.** *If* $\Gamma; A \vdash e : \sigma$, *then* $\Gamma; [A] \vdash e' : [\sigma]$, *where* $e'$ *is the translated program extracted using the algorithm in Fig. 4.*

$$A(\text{dynamic}) = \forall \kappa <: \rho. \forall \alpha <: \kappa. \alpha \to \text{Dynamic}(\kappa)$$
$$\tau_{\text{pkl}} = TYCLOS(\alpha_{\text{pkl}})$$
$$e_{\text{pkl}} = CLOS(pickle\,[\tau_{\text{pkl}}])\,[\alpha_{\text{wit}}] \quad e_{\text{ext}} = CLOS(extract\,[\tau_{\text{pkl}}])\,[\alpha_{\text{wit}}]$$
$$e_{\text{dyn}} = \text{pack}(\alpha_{\text{wit}}, \text{pack}(\tau_{\text{pkl}}(\alpha_{\text{wit}}), (e_{\text{pkl}}(x), e_{\text{ext}})))$$
$$\overline{[\Gamma]; [A] \vdash e' : [A(\text{dynamic})]}$$

$\qquad\qquad\qquad\qquad\qquad\qquad\qquad\qquad\qquad\qquad\qquad$ (DINTRO)

where:

$$e' \equiv (\Lambda\kappa.\Lambda\alpha_{\text{wit}}.\lambda x.\text{open } f_{\text{dyn}}[\mu\kappa.\rho] \text{ as } \text{pack}(\alpha_{\text{pkl}}, (pickle, extract)) \text{ in } e_{\text{dyn}})$$

$$[\Gamma]; [A] \vdash e_1 : \forall \alpha <: \rho. [\sigma']$$
$$[\Gamma]; [A] \vdash e_2 : [\text{Dynamic}(\rho)]$$
$$\overline{[\Gamma]; [A] \vdash (\text{open } e_2 \text{ as } \text{pack}(\alpha_{\text{pkl}}, \text{pack}(\beta, (x, extract))) \text{ in } e_1 \, [\alpha] \, (extract\, x)) : [\tau]}$$

$\qquad\qquad\qquad\qquad\qquad\qquad\qquad\qquad\qquad\qquad\qquad$ (DELIM)

$$A(\text{dynamic}) = \forall \kappa <: (\mu\kappa.\rho). \forall \alpha <: \kappa. \alpha \to \text{Dynamic}(\kappa)$$
$$[\Gamma], \kappa <: \top, \overline{\alpha_n} <: \kappa, \beta <: \top \to \top]; [A, (f : \forall \alpha <: \kappa. \alpha \to \beta(\alpha))] \vdash e_1 : t_1(\overline{\alpha_n}) \to t_2(\overline{\beta(\alpha)})$$
$$[\Gamma], \kappa <: \top, \overline{\alpha_n} <: \kappa, \beta <: \top \to \top]; [A, (g : \forall \alpha <: \kappa. \beta(\alpha) \to \alpha)] \vdash e_2 : t_2(\overline{\beta(\alpha)}) \to t_1(\overline{\alpha_n})$$
$$e_{\text{pkl}} = \Lambda\beta.\lambda f.(pickle\,[\beta]\,f) \oplus (t_1(\overline{\alpha_n}) \Longrightarrow e_1)$$
$$e_{\text{ext}} = \Lambda\beta.\lambda g.(extract\,[\beta]\,g) \oplus (t_2(\overline{\alpha_n}) \Longrightarrow e_2)$$
$$\tau_{\text{pkl}} = \lambda\beta.(t(\overline{\alpha}) \Longrightarrow \text{cl}(\alpha_{\text{pkl}}\,\beta)(t(\overline{\alpha}))) \oplus (t_1(\overline{\alpha_n}) \Longrightarrow t_2(\overline{\beta(\alpha)}))$$
$$e_{\text{dyn}} = \text{pack}(\tau_{\text{pkl}}, (e_{\text{pkl}}, e_{\text{ext}}))$$
$$[\Gamma]; [A, (\text{dynamic} : (\forall \kappa <: (\mu\kappa.\rho \cup t_1(\overline{\kappa})). \forall \alpha <: \kappa. \alpha \to \text{Dynamic}(\kappa)))] \vdash e : [\tau]$$
$$\overline{[\Gamma]; [A] \vdash e' : [\tau]}$$

$\qquad\qquad\qquad\qquad\qquad\qquad\qquad\qquad\qquad\qquad\qquad$ (DDEF)

where:

$$e' \equiv (\text{let } f_{\text{dyn}} = (\Lambda\kappa.\text{open } f_{\text{dyn}}[\kappa] \text{ as } \text{pack}(\alpha_{\text{pkl}}, (pickle, extract)) \text{ in } e_{\text{dyn}}) \text{ in } e)$$

**Fig. 4.** Translation of Dynamics in $\text{XML}_{\Pi-}^{\text{dyn}}$

*Proof.* By induction on the translation of the program $e$, which in turn is defined by induction on type derivations in $\text{XML}_{\Pi-}^{\text{dyn}}$. The cases for DINTRO and DDEF are non-trivial, because the type pickle function is encapsulated in the existential type for the dynamic implementation. We therefore rely on certain equality rules, the TYCASECOP and TYFIXBETA rules, in order to reason about the encapsulated type transformation.

We consider the case for DINTRO first of all. The translation for the dynamic operation constructs a polymorphic function from the data algebra for dynamic in the environment. This function abstracts over $\kappa$ and $\alpha_{\text{wit}}$, the kind and type arguments in any application of dynamic. The following metafunctions are used to build the body of the polymorphic function:

$$TYCLOS(\tau) = \text{tyrec }(\lambda\alpha.\text{cl}(\tau\,\alpha))$$
$$CLOS(e) = \text{tyrec }(\lambda f.\text{cl}(e\,f))$$

The witness type $\alpha_{pkl}$ in the data algebra for the implementation of dynamics has kind $\rho_{pkl} = ((\kappa \to \mathsf{T}) \to \Delta\alpha <: \rho.\mathsf{T})$. Instantiating $\kappa$ with the domain kind $\mu\kappa.\rho$, and closing the (type-level) typecase in this type function, produces a functional $\lambda\alpha.cl(\alpha_{pkl}\ \alpha)$ of type

$$((\mu\kappa.\rho) \to \mathsf{T}) \to ((\mu\kappa.\rho) \to \mathsf{T})$$

and the fixed point operator for types, applied to this, gives the transformation function $\tau_{pkl}$ that maps external types (in the domain of the dynamic operation) to internal pickle types. $\alpha_{wit}$ is the type of the value being bundled (a use-site type argument to dynamic). Then $\tau_{pkl}(\alpha_{wit})$ denotes the type of the argument to dynamic once it is pickled.

The data algebra also contains a pickling operation *pickle* of type $\tau_{in}$. This polymorphic function is parameterized by the fixed point $\beta$ of the witness type function $\alpha_{pkl}$. Instantiating $\kappa$ with $\mu\kappa.\rho$, and instantiating $\beta$ with $\tau_{pkl}$, and closing up the type case for the body of the pickling function, produces a functional $\lambda f.cl(pickle\ [\tau_{pkl}]\ f)$ of type:

$$(\forall\alpha <: (\mu\kappa.\rho).\alpha \to \tau_{pkl}(\alpha)) \to (\forall\alpha <: (\mu\kappa.\rho).\alpha \to cl(\alpha_{pkl}\ \tau_{pkl})(\alpha))$$

Using the TYFIXBETA rule we have the equivalence:

$$(cl(\alpha_{pkl}\ (tyrec(\lambda\beta.cl(\alpha_{pkl}\ \beta))))) \longleftrightarrow (tyrec(\lambda\beta.cl(\alpha_{pkl}\ \beta)))$$

Then using the congruence rules in Fig. 6 in App. A, we have that $\lambda f.cl(pickle\ [\tau_{pkl}]\ f)$ has type:

$$(\forall\alpha <: (\mu\kappa.\rho).\alpha \to \tau_{pkl}(\alpha)) \to (\forall\alpha <: (\mu\kappa.\rho).\alpha \to \tau_{pkl}(\alpha))$$

Taking the fixed point of this functional gives a function $e_{pkl}$ with type:

$$\forall\alpha <: (\mu\kappa.\rho).\alpha \to \tau_{pkl}(\alpha)$$

which is the expected type of the pickling operation at the use sites for the dynamic operation.

The data algebra also contains an extraction operation *extract* of type $\tau_{out}$. Applying the same specializations as with the pickling operation, we obtain a function $e_{ext}$ of type:

$$\forall\alpha <: (\mu\kappa.\rho).\tau_{pkl}(\alpha) \to \alpha$$

which is the expected type of the extraction operation at the use sites for the dynamic operation.

We now consider the case for the DDEF rule. We need to verify that the extension of a dynamic implementation is well-typed. In the context of the definition of the extended type function, we have

$$\alpha_{pkl} <: ((\kappa \to \mathsf{T}) \to \Delta\alpha <: \rho.\mathsf{T}),\ \beta <: \kappa \to \mathsf{T}$$

Therefore we have:

$$\overline{(t(\overline{\alpha}) \Longrightarrow cl(\alpha_{pkl}\ \beta)(t(\overline{\alpha})))} <: (\Delta\alpha <: \rho.\mathsf{T})$$

$$(t_1(\overline{\alpha_n}) \Longrightarrow t_2(\overline{\beta(\alpha)})) <: (\Delta\alpha <: t_1(\overline{\kappa}).T)$$

Therefore using TYJOIN and TYABS we have:

$$\tau_{pkl} = \lambda\beta.(\overline{(t(\overline{\alpha}) \Longrightarrow cl(\alpha_{pkl}\,\beta)(t(\overline{\alpha})))} \oplus (t_1(\overline{\alpha_n}) \Longrightarrow t_2(\overline{\beta(\alpha)})))$$

$$\tau_{pkl} <: ((\kappa \to T) \to \Delta\alpha <: \rho \cup t(\overline{\kappa}).T)$$

Now consider the well-typedness of the definition of the extended pickling function. The environment contains the constraints and types:

$$\alpha_{pkl} <: ((\kappa \to T) \to \Delta\alpha <: \rho.T), \beta <: \kappa \to T$$

$$pickle : \tau_{in}, \ f : (\forall\alpha <: \kappa.\alpha \to \beta(\alpha)$$

Then we have

$$(pickle\ [\beta]\ f) \ : \ (\Delta\alpha <: \rho.\alpha \to cl(\alpha_{pkl}\,\beta)(\alpha))$$

We have $cl(\tau_{pkl}\,\beta) <: (\rho \to T)$ where $\rho = \bigcup t(\overline{\kappa})$. By the TYFUNBETA and TYCASEBETA rules, we have:

$$cl(\tau_{pkl}\,\beta)(t(\overline{\alpha})) \longleftrightarrow cl(\alpha_{pkl}\,\beta)(t(\overline{\alpha})) <: T$$

for all $t \in \{\overline{t}\}$. By congruence we have:

$$cl(\overline{t(\overline{\alpha}) \Longrightarrow cl(\tau_{pkl}\,\beta)(t(\overline{\alpha}))})(\alpha) \longleftrightarrow cl(\overline{t(\overline{\alpha}) \Longrightarrow cl(\alpha_{pkl}\,\beta)(t(\overline{\alpha}))})(\alpha)$$

for $\alpha <: \rho$. Therefore by TYCASECOP we have:

$$cl(\tau_{pkl}\,\beta)(\alpha) \longleftrightarrow cl(\alpha_{pkl}\,\beta)(\alpha)$$

Thus we have

$$(pickle\ [\beta]\ f) \ : \ \Delta\alpha <: \rho.\alpha \to cl(\tau_{pkl}\,\beta)(\alpha)$$

We also have the series of type judgements:

$$e_1 \ : \ t_1(\overline{\alpha_n}) \to t_2(\overline{\beta(\alpha_n)})$$

$$e_1 \ : \ t_1(\overline{\alpha_n}) \to cl(\tau_{pkl}\,\beta)(t_1(\overline{\alpha_n}))$$

$$(t_1(\overline{\alpha_n}) \Longrightarrow e_1) \ : \ \Delta\alpha <: t_1(\overline{\kappa}).\alpha \to cl(\tau_{pkl}\,\beta)(\alpha)$$

where the step from the first to the second judgement follows from the definition of $\tau_{pkl}$, and using TYCASEBETA. Then combining these with TMJOIN, we have:

$$((pickle\ [\beta]\ f) \oplus (t_1(\overline{\alpha_n}) \Longrightarrow e_1)) \ : \\ \Delta\alpha <: \rho \cup t_1(\overline{\kappa}).\alpha \to cl(\tau_{pkl}\,\beta)(\alpha)$$

The new pickling function is then formed by abstracting over $f$ and $\kappa$. The well-typedness of the extension of the extraction operation is similar.

The major point of difference between $XML^\Delta$ and the framework of Harper and Morrisett [20] is the formulation of the $\lambda$-calculus at the type level. The latter use a simple typed $\lambda$-calculus extended with bounded recursion over the free algebra generated by the type constructors. They are able to verify strong normalization and confluence for their calculus, and are then able to perform type-checking on the intermediate language of their compiler. Strong normalization also provides a definitional notion of equality for their calculus.

By contrast, and as already noted, the abstraction of the pickle type function in our semantics means that we require a stronger equality theory for types in order to type our semantics: specifically, the TYFIXBETA rule for the DINTRO rule, and the TYCASECOP rule for the DDEF rule. Because our type calculus combines fixed points and coproducts, we add the $\lambda I$-restriction (requiring that all type operators are strict) to ensure equational consistency.

Without the fixed point operator, Dougherty [10] has verified strong normalization for a $\lambda$-calculus similar to our calculus of types, with the TYCASECOP and TYFUNETA rules oriented as expansion rules. Dougherty also verifies confluence for base types, and these properties still hold with bounded recursion. These results suggest that, if desired, we can at least expect to have a type-checking algorithm for our internal language that is practically useful, even if theoretically incomplete. The main problem is with the unrolling rule for fixed points, TYFIXBETA. However there are two places in the translation of programs into $XML^{dyn}$ where we expect to use this unrolling rule: first, where a type transformation is applied to a type (but all type transformations are restricted by the defdynamic to be primitive recursive); and secondly in the typing of the translation of the dynamic construct (but in this case the recursion in the type is regular, and there are by now well-known algorithms for checking the equivalence of regular recursive types [3]).

## 6  Related Work

Dynamics have received some attention in the literature [2, 24, 25, 1]. More recently Duggan [12] has considered an approach to computing with dynamics, based on dynamic type dispatch, that overcomes some problems with the traditional typecase construct in polymorphic languages. Duggan [12] introduces safe dynamics, which are superficially related to partial dynamics [7], although in fact quite different. The difference is that safe dynamics incorporate recursion at the kind level, not the type level (as with some extensions of partial dynamics). As an example of the difference, the following can be type-checked with recursion at the type level:

```
fun Ap (f,x) = typecase (f, x) of
    ((α → β)(f),α(x)) ⇒ dynamic(f x)
```

However type-checking is undecidable with safe dynamics extended with this form of multi-parameter typecase patterns [15]. It remains to be seen if a restricted version of these patterns could be added to safe dynamics.

Herlihy and Liskov [21] propose an approach to adding user-definable marshalling code to a distributed programming language. In this case, the language is CLU, and the approach is based on defining overloaded *marshall* and *unmarshall* operations that are exported by a CLU cluster. For parameterized types, Herlihy and Liskov use Ada-style constrained genericity to parameterize the overloaded marshalling operations by marshalling operations for the element types. Herlihy and Liskov do not consider a formal semantics for their approach. They also do not consider type inference. Although we have omitted details from the current presentation for lack of space, our semantics can be used in an implicitly typed language with type inference [13].

There is a relationship between our type system and parametric overloading, explored in more detail in other papers [12, 14]. Essentially our approach is based on a "closed world assumption," as opposed to the "open world assumption" underlying parametric overloading. This allows us to make direct use of dynamic type dispatch for our semantics, whereas the semantics of parametric overloading is based on call-site closure construction [14].

Knabe [22] has considered the problem of preventing the marshalling of native-code-implemented functions, in the Facile distributed programming environment [31]. Knabe introduces `xfun` and `xfn` constructs, analogous to the `fun` and `fn` constructs in Standard ML, for building transmissible closures (referred to by him as "potentially transmissible functions"). Potentially transmissible functions require two representations, one as a transmissible representation, the other as machine code. When a transmissible function is received at a remote site, it is typed as an ordinary function, with the run-time system implicitly compiling it to native code as it is used. However Knabe does not formalize potential transmissibility in the type system. Instead the compiler attempts to marshall potentially transmissible functions at compile-time, with the marshaller raising an exception if there is an attempt to marshal a function without a transmissible representation [22, Page 62]. Our type system can be extended to distinguish transmissible closures from other forms of closures: `dynamic` can be given the domain kind $\mu\kappa.(\ldots \cup (\top \xrightarrow{t} \top) \cup \ldots)$ where values of type $\tau_1 \xrightarrow{t} \tau_2$ are transmissible closures.

Ohori and Kato [29] give a semantics for marshalling in polymorphic languages. In their approach functions are not transmitted, instead proxy functions are transmitted that invoke the function at the sender site when invoked on the receiver site. Ohori and Kato do not consider the issue of providing user-specified marshalling code in polymorphic languages.

# 7 Conclusions

We have considered a semantics for dynamic typing for distributed programming in polymorphic languages, that allows the addition of user-defined marshalling operations. The semantics of this are expressed in an internal language with recursion and dynamic type dispatch at both the term and type levels. User-defined marshalling amounts to reifying dynamic type dispatch to the programmer level in an ML-like language.

In practice there is an obvious inefficiency in having the marshaller make a copy of a data structure before transmitting it. This is somewhat orthogonal to the concern of the current paper. It should be possible to apply "deforestation" optimizations to build transformed data structures "on the wire." This remains an important topic for further work.

# Bibliography

[1] Martin Abadi, Luca Cardeli, Benjamin Pierce, and Didier Remy. Dynamic typing in polymorphic languages. In Peter Lee, editor, *Proceedings of the ACM SIGPLAN Workshop on ML and its Applications*, San Francisco, California, 1992. Carnegie-Mellon University Technical Report CMU-CS-93-105.

[2] Martin Abadi, Luca Cardelli, Benjamin Pierce, and Gordon Plotkin. Dynamic typing in a statically typed language. *ACM Transactions on Programming Languages and Systems*, 13(2):237–268, 1991.

[3] Roberto Amadio and Luca Cardelli. Subtyping recursive types. *ACM Transactions on Programming Languages and Systems*, 15(4):575–631, 1993.

[4] J. Bacon and K. G. Hamilton. Distributed computing with RPC: The Cambridge approach. In *Proceedings of IFIP Conference on Distributed Computing*, Amsterdam, 1987. North-Holland.

[5] A. Birrell, G. Nelson, S. Owicki, and E. Wobber. Network objects. Technical report, DEC Systems Research Center, Palo Alto, California, 1993.

[6] Val Breazu-Tannen, Thierry Coquand, Carl Gunter, and Andre Scedrov. Inheritance as implicit coercion. *Information and Computation*, 93(1):172–221, 1991.

[7] Peter Buneman and Atsushi Ohori. Polymorphism and type inference in database programming. *ACM Transactions on Database Systems*, 1996. To appear.

[8] Luca Cardelli. Typeful programming. Technical report, DEC Systems Research Center, 1989.

[9] Roberto Di Cosmo and Delia Kesner. A confluent reduction for the extensional typed λ-calculus with pairs, sums, recursion and terminal object. In *Proceedings of the International Conference on Automata, Languages and Programming*, volume 700 of *Lecture Notes in Computer Science*, pages 645–656. Springer-Verlag, 1993.

[10] Daniel Dougherty. Some lambda calculi with categorical sums and products. In *Rewriting Techniques and Applications*, Lecture Notes in Computer Science. Springer-Verlag, 1993.

[11] Catherine Dubois, Francois Rouaix, and Pierre Weis. Extensional polymorphism. In *Proceedings of ACM Symposium on Principles of Programming Languages*, San Francisco, California, 1995. ACM Press.

[12] Dominic Duggan. Dynamic typing for distributed programming in polymorphic languages. To appear in *Transactions on Programming Languages and Systems*, 1998.

[13] Dominic Duggan. Finite subtype inference with explicit polymorphism. Submitted for publication, 1998.

[14] Dominic Duggan and John Ophel. Scoped parametric overloading. Submitted for publication, 1997.

[15] Dominic Duggan and John Ophel. Type-checking multi-parameter type classes. Submitted for publication, 1997.

[16] Tim Freeman and Frank Pfenning. Refinement types for ML. In *Proceedings of ACM SIGPLAN Conference on Programming Language Design and Implementation*, pages 268–277. ACM Press, 1991.

[17] James Gosling, Bill Joy, and Guy Steele. *The Java Language Specification*. The Java Series. Addison-Wesley, 1997.

[18] Graham Hamilton, Michael L. Powell, and James J. Mitchell. Subcontract: A flexible base for distributed programming. In *Symposium on Operating Systems Principles*, pages 69–79. ACM Press, 1993.

[19] Robert Harper and John C. Mitchell. On the type structure of Standard ML. *ACM Transactions on Programming Languages and Systems*, 15(2):211–252, 1993.

[20] Robert Harper and Gregory Morrisett. Compiling polymorphism using intensional type analysis. In *Proceedings of ACM Symposium on Principles of Programming Languages*, San Francisco, California, 1995. ACM Press.

[21] Maurice Herlihy and Barbara Liskov. A value transmission method for abstract data types. *ACM Transactions on Programming Languages and Systems*, 4(4): 527–551, 1982.

[22] Frederick Knabe. *Language Support for Mobile Agents*. PhD thesis, Carnegie Mellon University, 1995.

[23] Clifford Krumvieda. *Distributed ML: Abstraction for Efficient and Fault-Tolerant Programming*. PhD thesis, Cornell University, Ithaca, New York, 1993.

[24] Xavier Leroy and Michel Mauny. Dynamics in ML. *Journal of Functional Programming*, 3(4):431–463, 1993.

[25] Xavier Leroy and Pierre Weiss. Dynamics in ML. In *Proceedings of ACM Symposium on Functional Programming and Computer Architecture*, 1991.

[26] Barbara Liskov. Distributed programming in Argus. *Communications of the ACM*, 31(3), 1988.

[27] J. Gregory Morrisett. *Compiling With Types*. PhD thesis, Carnegie-Mellon University, 1995.

[28] Greg Nelson. *Systems Programming in Modula-3*. Prentice-Hall Series in Innovative Technology. Prentice-Hall, 1991.

[29] Atsushi Ohori and Kazuhiko Kato. Semantics for communication primitives in a polymorphic language. In *Proceedings of ACM Symposium on Principles of Programming Languages*, pages 99–112. ACM Press, 1993.

[30] David Tarditi, Greg Morrisett, Perry Cheng, Christopher Stone, Robert Harper, and Peter Lee. TIL: A type-directed optimizing compiler for ML. In *Proceedings of ACM SIGPLAN Conference on Programming Language Design and Implementation*, Philadelphia, Pennsylvania, 1996. ACM Press.

[31] Bent Thomsen, Lone Leth, Sanjiva Prasad, Tsung-Min Kuo, Andre Kramer, Fritz Knabe, and Alessandro Giacalone. Facile Antigua release programming guide. Technical Report ECRC-93-20, European Computer-Industry Research Centre, Munich, Germany, 1993.

[32] Andrew Wright and Robert Cartwright. A practical soft type system for Scheme. In *Proceedings of ACM Symposium on Lisp and Functional Programming*, pages 250–262, Orland, Florida, 1994. ACM Press.

# A  Kind Rules for XML$^\Delta$

$$\frac{\Gamma, \overline{\alpha_n} <: \overline{\rho_n}\}; A \vdash e : \{t(\overline{\alpha_n})/\alpha\}\tau}{\Gamma; A \vdash (t(\alpha_1 : \rho_1, \ldots, \alpha_n : \rho_n) \Longrightarrow e) : (\Delta\alpha <: \underline{t}(\rho_1, \ldots, \rho_n).\tau)} \quad \text{(TMCASE)}$$

$$\frac{}{\Gamma; A \vdash \texttt{abort} : (\Delta\alpha <: \bot.\tau)} \quad \text{(TMABORT)}$$

$$\frac{\Gamma; A \vdash e_1 : (\Delta\alpha <: \rho_1.\tau) \quad \Gamma; A \vdash e_2 : (\Delta\alpha <: \rho_2.\tau) \quad tc(\rho_1) \cap tc(\rho_2) = \{\}}{\Gamma; A \vdash e_1 \oplus e_2 : (\Delta\alpha <: \rho_1 \cup \rho_2.\tau)}$$

$$\text{(TMJOIN)}$$

$$\frac{\Gamma; A \vdash e : (\Delta\alpha <: \rho.\tau)}{\Gamma; A \vdash \texttt{cl}(e) : (\forall\alpha <: \rho.\tau)} \quad \text{(TMCLOS)}$$

**Fig. 5.** Type Rules for Dynamic Type Dispatch with XML$^\Delta$

$$\frac{t \text{ has arity } \top^n \to \top}{\Gamma \vdash t \longleftrightarrow t <: \rho_1 \to \cdots \to \rho_n \to \underline{t}(\rho_1, \ldots, \rho_n)} \quad \text{(TYCON)}$$

$$\frac{\Gamma, \alpha <: \chi_1 \vdash \tau \longleftrightarrow \tau' <: \chi_2 \quad (\alpha \in FV(\tau) \cap FV(\tau'))}{\Gamma \vdash (\lambda\alpha.\tau) \longleftrightarrow (\lambda\alpha.\tau') <: \chi_1 \to \chi_2} \quad \text{(TYABS)}$$

$$\frac{\Gamma, \overline{\alpha_n} <: \overline{\rho_n}; \tau \vdash \tau' \longleftrightarrow \chi <: \quad \{\overline{\alpha_n}\} \subseteq FV(\tau) \cap FV(\tau')}{\Gamma \vdash (t(\alpha_1, \ldots, \alpha_n) \Longrightarrow \tau) \longleftrightarrow (t(\alpha_1, \ldots, \alpha_n) \Longrightarrow \tau') <: (\Delta\alpha <: \underline{t}(\rho_1, \ldots, \rho_n).\chi)}$$

$$\text{(TYCASE)}$$

$$\frac{\Gamma \vdash \tau_1 \longleftrightarrow \tau_1' <: (\Delta\alpha <: \rho_1.\chi) \quad \Gamma \vdash \tau_2 \longleftrightarrow \tau_2' <: (\Delta\alpha <: \rho_2.\chi) \quad tc(\rho_1) \cap tc(\rho_2) = \{\}}{\Gamma \vdash \tau_1 \oplus \tau_2 \longleftrightarrow \tau_1' \oplus \tau_2' <: (\Delta\alpha <: \rho_1 \cup \rho_2.\chi)}$$

$$\text{(TYJOIN)}$$

$$\frac{\Gamma \vdash \tau \longleftrightarrow \tau' <: (\Delta\alpha <: \rho.\chi)}{\Gamma \vdash \texttt{cl}(\tau) \longleftrightarrow \texttt{cl}(\tau') <: \rho \to \chi} \quad \text{(TYCLOS)}$$

$$\frac{\Gamma, \alpha <: \chi' \vdash \tau \longleftrightarrow \tau <: \chi \quad \Gamma \vdash \tau' <: \chi'}{\Gamma \vdash ((\lambda\alpha.\tau)\,\tau') \longleftrightarrow \{\tau'/\alpha\}\tau <: \chi} \quad \text{(TYFUNBETA)}$$

$$\frac{\Gamma \vdash \tau <: \chi \to \chi'}{\Gamma \vdash (\lambda\alpha.\tau\,\alpha) \longleftrightarrow \tau <: \chi \to \chi'} \quad \text{(TYFUNETA)}$$

$$\frac{\Gamma; \Gamma, \overline{\alpha_i} <: \overline{\rho_i} \vdash \tau_i <: \rho \text{ for } i = 1, \ldots, n \quad \Gamma; \Gamma \vdash \overline{\tau'} <: \overline{\rho_j}}{\Gamma; \Gamma \vdash (\texttt{cl}(\overline{t_n(\overline{\alpha_n})} \Longrightarrow \tau))(t_j(\overline{\tau'})) \longleftrightarrow \{\overline{\tau'}/\overline{\alpha_j}\}\tau_j <: \rho} \quad \text{(TYCASEBETA)}$$

$$\frac{\Gamma \vdash \tau <: \rho \to \chi \quad \Gamma \vdash \tau' <: \rho \quad \rho = \bigcup \underline{t}(\overline{\rho})}{\Gamma \vdash (\tau\,\tau') \longleftrightarrow \texttt{cl}(t(\overline{\alpha}) \Longrightarrow \tau(t(\overline{\alpha})))(\tau') <: \chi} \quad \text{(TYCASECOP)}$$

$$\frac{\Gamma \vdash \tau <: (\chi_1 \to \chi_2) \to (\chi_1 \to \chi_2)}{\Gamma \vdash \texttt{tyrec}(\tau) \longleftrightarrow (\tau\,(\lambda\alpha.\texttt{tyrec}(\tau)(\alpha))) <: (\chi_1 \to \chi_2)} \quad \text{(TYFIXBETA)}$$

**Fig. 6.** Kind and Conversion Rules for Type Operators in XML$^\Delta$

# Author Index

Alexander Aiken .................. 78
Vincent Balat ................... 240
Andrew Bernard ................. 53
Karl Crary ...................... 28
Olivier Danvy ................... 240
Dominic Duggan ................ 273
Martin Elsman .................. 136
Manuel Fähndrich ............... 78
Jeffrey S. Foster ................ 78
Nobuhisa Fujinami .............. 253
Daniela Genius ................. 194
Neal Glew ....................... 28
Robert Harper ................... 53
Aaron Hertzmann ................. 9
Haruo Hosoya ................... 215
Suresh Jagannathan .............. 9

Naoki Kobayashi ................ 272
Peter Lee ........................ 53
Xavier Leroy ..................... 1
Greg Morrisett .................. 28
Bratin Saha .................... 156
Zhong Shao ............... 116, 156
Zhendong Su .................... 78
Peter Thiemann ................ 178
Andrew Tolmach ................ 97
Martin Trapp ................... 194
Valery Trifonov ................ 116
Cristian Ungureanu .............. 9
David Walker .................... 28
Andrew Wright .................. 9
Akinori Yonezawa .............. 215
Wolf Zimmermann .............. 194

# Springer
# and the
# environment

At Springer we firmly believe that an
international science publisher has a
special obligation to the environment,
and our corporate policies consistently
reflect this conviction.
We also expect our business partners –
paper mills, printers, packaging
manufacturers, etc. – to commit
themselves to using materials and
production processes that do not harm
the environment. The paper in this
book is made from low- or no-chlorine
pulp and is acid free, in conformance
with international standards for paper
permanency.

# Lecture Notes in Computer Science

For information about Vols. 1–1386

please contact your bookseller or Springer-Verlag

Vol. 1387: C. Lee Giles, M. Gori (Eds.), Adaptive Processing of Sequences and Data Structures. Proceedings, 1997. XII, 434 pages. 1998. (Subseries LNAI).

Vol. 1388: J. Rolim (Ed.), Parallel and Distributed Processing. Proceedings, 1998. XVII, 1168 pages. 1998.

Vol. 1389: K. Tombre, A.K. Chhabra (Eds.), Graphics Recognition. Proceedings, 1997. XII, 421 pages. 1998.

Vol. 1390: C. Scheideler, Universal Routing Strategies for Interconnection Networks. XVII, 234 pages. 1998.

Vol. 1391: W. Banzhaf, R. Poli, M. Schoenauer, T.C. Fogarty (Eds.), Genetic Programming. Proceedings, 1998. X, 232 pages. 1998.

Vol. 1392: A. Barth, M. Breu, A. Endres, A. de Kemp (Eds.), Digital Libraries in Computer Science: The MeDoc Approach. VIII, 239 pages. 1998.

Vol. 1393: D. Bert (Ed.), B'98: Recent Advances in the Development and Use of the B Method. Proceedings, 1998. VIII, 313 pages. 1998.

Vol. 1394: X. Wu. R. Kotagiri, K.B. Korb (Eds.), Research and Development in Knowledge Discovery and Data Mining. Proceedings, 1998. XVI, 424 pages. 1998. (Subseries LNAI).

Vol. 1395: H. Kitano (Ed.), RoboCup-97: Robot Soccer World Cup I. XIV, 520 pages. 1998. (Subseries LNAI).

Vol. 1396: E. Okamoto, G. Davida, M. Mambo (Eds.), Information Security. Proceedings, 1997. XII, 357 pages. 1998.

Vol. 1397: H. de Swart (Ed.), Automated Reasoning with Analytic Tableaux and Related Methods. Proceedings, 1998. X, 325 pages. 1998. (Subseries LNAI).

Vol. 1398: C. Nédellec, C. Rouveirol (Eds.), Machine Learning: ECML-98. Proceedings, 1998. XII, 420 pages. 1998. (Subseries LNAI).

Vol. 1399: O. Etzion, S. Jajodia, S. Sripada (Eds.), Temporal Databases: Research and Practice. X, 429 pages. 1998.

Vol. 1400: M. Lenz, B. Bartsch-Spörl, H.-D. Burkhard, S. Wess (Eds.), Case-Based Reasoning Technology. XVIII, 405 pages. 1998. (Subseries LNAI).

Vol. 1401: P. Sloot, M. Bubak, B. Hertzberger (Eds.), High-Performance Computing and Networking. Proceedings, 1998. XX, 1309 pages. 1998.

Vol. 1402: W. Lamersdorf, M. Merz (Eds.), Trends in Distributed Systems for Electronic Commerce. Proceedings, 1998. XII, 255 pages. 1998.

Vol. 1403: K. Nyberg (Ed.), Advances in Cryptology – EUROCRYPT '98. Proceedings, 1998. X, 607 pages. 1998.

Vol. 1404: C. Freksa, C. Habel. K.F. Wender (Eds.), Spatial Cognition. VIII, 491 pages. 1998. (Subseries LNAI).

Vol. 1405: S.M. Embury, N.J. Fiddian, W.A. Gray, A.C. Jones (Eds.), Advances in Databases. Proceedings, 1998. XII, 183 pages. 1998.

Vol. 1406: H. Burkhardt, B. Neumann (Eds.), Computer Vision – ECCV'98. Vol. I. Proceedings, 1998. XVI, 927 pages. 1998.

Vol. 1407: H. Burkhardt, B. Neumann (Eds.), Computer Vision – ECCV'98. Vol. II. Proceedings, 1998. XVI, 881 pages. 1998.

Vol. 1409: T. Schaub, The Automation of Reasoning with Incomplete Information. XI, 159 pages. 1998. (Subseries LNAI).

Vol. 1411: L. Asplund (Ed.), Reliable Software Technologies – Ada-Europe. Proceedings, 1998. XI, 297 pages. 1998.

Vol. 1412: R.E. Bixby, E.A. Boyd, R.Z. Ríos-Mercado (Eds.), Integer Programming and Combinatorial Optimization. Proceedings, 1998. IX, 437 pages. 1998.

Vol. 1413: B. Pernici, C. Thanos (Eds.), Advanced Information Systems Engineering. Proceedings, 1998. X, 423 pages. 1998.

Vol. 1414: M. Nielsen, W. Thomas (Eds.), Computer Science Logic. Selected Papers, 1997. VIII, 511 pages. 1998.

Vol. 1415: J. Mira, A.P. del Pobil, M.Ali (Eds.), Methodology and Tools in Knowledge-Based Systems. Vol. I. Proceedings, 1998. XXIV, 887 pages. 1998. (Subseries LNAI).

Vol. 1416: A.P. del Pobil, J. Mira, M.Ali (Eds.), Tasks and Methods in Applied Artificial Intelligence. Vol.II. Proceedings, 1998. XXIII, 943 pages. 1998. (Subseries LNAI).

Vol. 1417: S. Yalamanchili, J. Duato (Eds.), Parallel Computer Routing and Communication. Proceedings, 1997. XII, 309 pages. 1998.

Vol. 1418: R. Mercer, E. Neufeld (Eds.), Advances in Artificial Intelligence. Proceedings, 1998. XII, 467 pages. 1998. (Subseries LNAI).

Vol. 1419: G. Vigna (Ed.), Mobile Agents and Security. XII, 257 pages. 1998.

Vol. 1420: J. Desel, M. Silva (Eds.), Application and Theory of Petri Nets 1998. Proceedings, 1998. VIII, 385 pages. 1998.

Vol. 1421: C. Kirchner, H. Kirchner (Eds.), Automated Deduction – CADE-15. Proceedings, 1998. XIV, 443 pages. 1998. (Subseries LNAI).

Vol. 1422: J. Jeuring (Ed.), Mathematics of Program Construction. Proceedings, 1998. X, 383 pages. 1998.

Vol. 1423: J.P. Buhler (Ed.), Algorithmic Number Theory. Proceedings, 1998. X, 640 pages. 1998.

Vol. 1424: L. Polkowski, A. Skowron (Eds.), Rough Sets and Current Trends in Computing. Proceedings, 1998. XIII, 626 pages. 1998. (Subseries LNAI).

Vol. 1425: D. Hutchison, R. Schäfer (Eds.), Multimedia Applications, Services and Techniques – ECMAST'98. Proceedings, 1998. XVI, 532 pages. 1998.

Vol. 1427: A.J. Hu, M.Y. Vardi (Eds.), Computer Aided Verification. Proceedings, 1998. IX, 552 pages. 1998.

Vol. 1429: F. van der Linden (Ed.), Development and Evolution of Software Architectures for Product Families. Proceedings, 1998. IX, 258 pages. 1998.

Vol. 1430: S. Trigila, A. Mullery, M. Campolargo, H. Vanderstraeten, M. Mampaey (Eds.), Intelligence in Services and Networks: Technology for Ubiquitous Telecom Services. Proceedings, 1998. XII, 550 pages. 1998.

Vol. 1431: H. Imai, Y. Zheng (Eds.), Public Key Cryptography. Proceedings, 1998. XI, 263 pages. 1998.

Vol. 1432: S. Arnborg, L. Ivansson (Eds.), Algorithm Theory – SWAT '98. Proceedings, 1998. IX, 347 pages. 1998.

Vol. 1433: V. Honavar, G. Slutzki (Eds.), Grammatical Inference. Proceedings, 1998. X, 271 pages. 1998. (Subseries LNAI).

Vol. 1434: J.-C. Heudin (Ed.), Virtual Worlds. Proceedings, 1998. XII, 412 pages. 1998. (Subseries LNAI).

Vol. 1435: M. Klusch, G. Weiß (Eds.), Cooperative Information Agents II. Proceedings, 1998. IX, 307 pages. 1998. (Subseries LNAI).

Vol. 1436: D. Wood, S. Yu (Eds.), Automata Implementation. Proceedings, 1997. VIII, 253 pages. 1998.

Vol. 1437: S. Albayrak, F.J. Garijo (Eds.), Intelligent Agents for Telecommunication Applications. Proceedings, 1998. XII, 251 pages. 1998. (Subseries LNAI).

Vol. 1438: C. Boyd, E. Dawson (Eds.), Information Security and Privacy. Proceedings, 1998. XI, 423 pages. 1998.

Vol. 1439: B. Magnusson (Ed.), System Configuration Management. Proceedings, 1998. X, 207 pages. 1998.

Vol. 1441: W. Wobcke, M. Pagnucco, C. Zhang (Eds.), Agents and Multi-Agent Systems. Proceedings, 1997. XII, 241 pages. 1998. (Subseries LNAI).

Vol. 1442: A. Fiat. G.J. Woeginger (Eds.), Online Algorithms. XVIII, 436 pages. 1998.

Vol. 1443: K.G. Larsen, S. Skyum, G. Winskel (Eds.), Automata, Languages and Programming. Proceedings, 1998. XVI, 932 pages. 1998.

Vol. 1444: K. Jansen, J. Rolim (Eds.), Approximation Algorithms for Combinatorial Optimization. Proceedings, 1998. VIII, 201 pages. 1998.

Vol. 1445: E. Jul (Ed.), ECOOP'98 – Object-Oriented Programming. Proceedings, 1998. XII, 635 pages. 1998.

Vol. 1446: D. Page (Ed.), Inductive Logic Programming. Proceedings, 1998. VIII, 301 pages. 1998. (Subseries LNAI).

Vol. 1447: V.W. Porto, N. Saravanan, D. Waagen, A.E. Eiben (Eds.), Evolutionary Programming VII. Proceedings, 1998. XVI, 840 pages. 1998.

Vol. 1448: M. Farach-Colton (Ed.), Combinatorial Pattern Matching. Proceedings, 1998. VIII, 251 pages. 1998.

Vol. 1449: W.-L. Hsu, M.-Y. Kao (Eds.), Computing and Combinatorics. Proceedings, 1998. XII, 372 pages. 1998.

Vol. 1450: L. Brim, F. Gruska, J. Zlatuška (Eds.), Mathematical Foundations of Computer Science 1998. Proceedings, 1998. XVII, 846 pages. 1998.

Vol. 1451: A. Amin, D. Dori, P. Pudil, H. Freeman (Eds.), Advances in Pattern Recognition. Proceedings, 1998. XXI, 1048 pages. 1998.

Vol. 1452: B.P. Goettl, H.M. Halff, C.L. Redfield, V.J. Shute (Eds.), Intelligent Tutoring Systems. Proceedings, 1998. XIX, 629 pages. 1998.

Vol. 1453: M.-L. Mugnier, M. Chein (Eds.), Conceptual Structures: Theory, Tools and Applications. Proceedings, 1998. XIII, 439 pages. 1998. (Subseries LNAI).

Vol. 1454: I. Smith (Ed.), Artificial Intelligence in Structural Engineering. XI, 497 pages. 1998. (Subseries LNAI).

Vol. 1456: A. Drogoul, M. Tambe, T. Fukuda (Eds.), Collective Robotics. Proceedings, 1998. VII, 161 pages. 1998. (Subseries LNAI).

Vol. 1457: A. Ferreira, J. Rolim, H. Simon, S.-H. Teng (Eds.), Solving Irregularly Structured Problems in Prallel. Proceedings, 1998. X, 408 pages. 1998.

Vol. 1458: V.O. Mittal, H.A. Yanco, J. Aronis, R-. Simpson (Eds.), Assistive Technology in Artificial Intelligence. X, 273 pages. 1998. (Subseries LNAI).

Vol. 1459: D.G. Feitelson, L. Rudolph (Eds.), Job Scheduling Strategies for Parallel Processing. Proceedings, 1998. VII, 257 pages. 1998.

Vol. 1460: G. Quirchmayr, E. Schweighofer, T.J.M. Bench-Capon (Eds.), Database and Expert Systems Applications. Proceedings, 1998. XVI, 905 pages. 1998.

Vol. 1461: G. Bilardi, G.F. Italiano, A. Pietracaprina, G. Pucci (Eds.), Algorithms – ESA'98. Proceedings, 1998. XII, 516 pages. 1998.

Vol. 1462: H. Krawczyk (Ed.), Advances in Cryptology - CRYPTO '98. Proceedings, 1998. XII, 519 pages. 1998.

Vol. 1464: H.H.S. Ip, A.W.M. Smeulders (Eds.), Multimedia Information Analysis and Retrieval. Proceedings, 1998. VIII, 264 pages. 1998.

Vol. 1465: R. Hirschfeld (Ed.), Financial Cryptography. Proceedings, 1998. VIII, 311 pages. 1998.

Vol. 1466: D. Sangiorgi, R. de Simone (Eds.), CONCUR'98: Concurrency Theory. Proceedings, 1998. XI, 657 pages. 1998.

Vol. 1467: C. Clack, K. Hammond, T. Davie (Eds.), Implementation of Functional Languages. Proceedings, 1997. X, 375 pages. 1998.

Vol. 1469: R. Puigjaner, N.N. Savino, B. Serra (Eds.), Computer Performance Evaluation. Proceedings, 1998. XIII, 376 pages. 1998.

Vol. 1473: X. Leroy, A. Ohori (Eds.), Types in Compilation. Proceedings, 1998. VIII, 299 pages. 1998.

Vol. 1475: W. Litwin, T. Morzy, G. Vossen (Eds.), Advances in Databases and Information Systems. Proceedings, 1998. XIV, 369 pages. 1998.

Vol. 1482: R.W. Hartenstein, A. Keevallik (Eds.), Field-Programmable Logic and Applications. Proceedings, 1998. XI, 533 pages. 1998.